CASTLEREA

by the same author
GEORGE CANNING

An engraving of the Lawrence portrait drawn by W. Evans, engraved by H. Meyer

CASTLEREAGH

Wendy Hinde

COLLINS
St James's Place, London
1981

William Collins Sons & Co Ltd
London · Glasgow · Sydney · Auckland
Toronto · Johannesburg

British Library CIP data
Hinde, Wendy
 Castlereagh.
 1. Castlereagh, Robert Stewart, *Viscount*
 941.07'30924 DA522.L8

First published 1981
© Wendy Hinde 1981
ISBN 0 00 216308-X
Set in Lasercomp Garamond
Made and Printed in Great Britain by
William Collins Sons & Co Ltd Glasgow

Contents

Part I THE IRISH DIMENSION (1769–1801)

I	Early life 1769–90	page 13
II	Irish or English? 1791–95	25
III	Ireland's slippery slope 1795–97	41
IV	'The sword is drawn' 1798	53
V	Union: the last resource 1798–99	70
VI	The union carried 1799–1801	83

Part II ENGLISH POLITICIAN (1801–12)

VII	Westminster and Whitehall 1801–06	103
VIII	Trials of a War Minister 1806–07	124
IX	'Preserve me from my friends and I shall not fear my enemies' 1808–09	144
X	'I am not playing a game for office' 1809–12	171

Part III EUROPEAN STATESMAN (1812–22)

XI	Closing the net round Napoleon 1812–13	187
XII	Mission to Allied headquarters 1813–14	201
XIII	The search for peace: Paris, London, Vienna 1814–15	213
XIV	Parliamentary battleground 1816–18	235
XV	Unrest at home and abroad 1819–21	250
XVI	The enemy within 1821–22	265

Abbreviations	283
References	284
Select Bibliography	303
Index	309

Acknowledgements

I would like to thank the following for their kind permission to quote from manuscript material in their possession or care, or of which they hold the copyright:– the Marquess of Londonderry (Castlereagh Mss); the Marquess Camden (Pratt Mss); the Hon. J.L. Hamilton (Goulburn Mss); the British Library; the Keeper of the Public Record Office; the Deputy Keeper, Public Record Office of Northern Ireland; the Keeper, State Paper Office, Dublin; the Librarian, Royal Irish Academy, Dublin; the County Archivist, Norfolk Record Office (Castlereagh Mss deposited by the National Trust); the County Archivist, Kent Archives Office; and the Controller of Her Majesty's Stationery Office (Crown-copyright material in the India Office Records). I would also like to thank the County Archivists at the Durham County Record Office and at the Surrey Record Office for their help in obtaining permission for me to quote from material in their care, and Mr Richard Walker of the National Portrait Gallery for his help in tracing portraits of Castlereagh and Lady Castlereagh. I am also very grateful to my editor, Richard Ollard; to Patricia Norton for painstakingly going through my manuscript; and to Alan Norton for his expert advice on Castlereagh's last illness. Finally, I would again like to pay tribute to the London Library, its helpful staff, its comprehensive resources and its generous lending policy.

In the interests of clarity I have modernised the punctuation and spelling in quotations.

Illustrations

Castlereagh
National Portrait Gallery   *Frontispiece*

Emma, Lady Castlereagh   Between pages 64 and 65
National Trust, Blickling Hall

Castlereagh's return from the Congress of Vienna
The debates on the Corn Law
British Museum

The two Emperors at Tilsit   Between pages 96 and 97
BBC Hulton Picture Library

North Cray Cottage
Directorate of Education, Bexley, London

Frederick William III of Prussia
By gracious permission of H.M. The Queen

Napoleon's farewell to his Guard   Between pages 176 and 177
BBC Hulton Picture Library

The British Army in the Bois de Boulogne
BBC Hulton Picture Library

Tsar Alexander I, painted in 1806
BBC Hulton Picture Library

Tsar Alexander I, painted in 1815
By gracious permission of H.M. The Queen

Peace celebrations in Hyde Park
BBC Hulton Picture Library

Metternich
By gracious permission of H.M. The Queen

Between pages 208 and 209

The Congress of Vienna
BBC Hulton Picture Library

Castlereagh
By gracious permission of H.M. The Queen

Map
France. Spring 1814   203

PART I

The Irish Dimension
(1769–1801)

CHAPTER I

Early life
1769–90

On June 18, 1769, in a house in Henry Street in the fashionable part of Dublin, a son was born to Robert Stewart of Newtownards, County Down, and Lady Sarah Stewart, the second daughter of Francis Seymour-Conway, Earl of Hertford. Within three weeks of his birth the baby was taken to the chapel of the Protestant Dissenting Congregation in Strand Street and baptised with his father's name.

The house in Henry Street belonged to young Robert's grandfather, Alexander Stewart, whose forebears had come over from Scotland early in the seventeenth century and settled at Ballylawn in Donegal. Alexander's father, Colonel William Stewart, had raised a troop of cavalry at his own expense and played a dashing part in the defence of Londonderry in 1689. He had two sons, the younger of whom, Alexander, set up in business in Belfast where he embraced Whig principles and became an elder of the Presbyterian Church. When his elder brother died without heirs, Alexander succeeded to the family estate in Donegal. He retired from business and in 1737 married an heiress, Mary Cowan, with whose fortune he bought two estates at Newtownards and Comber at the head of Strangford Lough in County Down. Although his political ambitions were thwarted, as a landlord he flourished, and his tenants as well as his growing family benefited from his prosperity.

Alexander Stewart's eldest son, Robert, was born in 1739 and brought up a staunch Presbyterian. In June 1766 he was married in the Chapel Royal of Dublin Castle to Lady Sarah Seymour-Conway whose father had been made Lord Lieutenant the previous year. Lady Sarah, who was only eighteen at the time of her marriage, was described by a contemporary as 'admired for her fine person and accomplishments, and beloved for the unaffected goodness of her mind and manners'.[1] But her life was tragically short. In July 1770, just before she was due to give birth to her third child, she was taken ill with some prenatal complication and died with the baby unborn.* She left to her only

---

*Her eldest son, Alexander, was born in 1768, and died just before Robert's birth.

surviving child a miniature of herself and a plait of her hair. They were later made into a large square gold brooch which Robert wore all his life.[2]

But although young Robert Stewart lost his mother so soon, he did not suffer from the further misfortune of a lonely and neglected childhood. He was taken back to Newtownards where his grandparents looked after him until, five years later, his father married Miss Frances Pratt, eldest daughter of Lord Camden, the former Lord Chancellor of England. By all accounts she was as amiable as she was beautiful. She gave her husband eleven children, only one of whom died in infancy, and she treated her step-son as if he were one of her own brood. He for his part treated her as if she were his mother. His siblings could hardly have been playmates for him since he was already eight when the eldest was born, but the scanty references to them in his early years suggest nothing but mutual affection, and for his eldest half-brother, Charles, nine years his junior, he felt an affection that survived all his shortcomings.

Two years after his father's second marriage Robert was sent as a boarder to the Royal School at Armagh, a well-known grammar school founded during the reign of Charles I. Since Dissenters were still barred from civil or military office, it was the prudent custom of many Ulster Presbyterians to have their sons educated under the auspices of the Established Church. The Royal School at Armagh had a high scholastic reputation under an excellent headmaster. It also enjoyed the patronage of the energetic and wealthy Primate Archbishop of Armagh, Richard Robinson, who in the course of converting Armagh – in Arthur Young's words – from 'a nest of mud cabbins' to 'a well-built city of stone and slate', had completely rebuilt the school.[3]

Very little is known of how the eight-year-old boy fared in the rough-and-tumble of an eighteenth-century school. But to judge from a letter he wrote to an uncle in October 1777, soon after his arrival at Armagh, he was fully determined to keep his end up. 'At present', he wrote, 'I am highest in my class – no boy shall get above me. I am resolved to study very close when at my book, and to play very briskly when disengaged.' He then redeemed this touch of smugness with a dash of homesickness – after referring to his sister Fanny, born earlier that year, who had had smallpox, he added: 'I wish she understood how much I love her and all my friends. Indeed I long to see Papa and Mamma soon, and my Newtown friends at vacation.' He ended with the ringing declaration, 'I am still a true American' – a reference to the popular enthusiasm in Ulster for the American colonists who had declared their independence the year before.[4]

EARLY LIFE 1769-90

After about four years at Armagh, Robert was moved to a small private school in the little fishing village of Portaferry at the seaward end of Strangford Lough. The school was run by the Chancellor of the diocese, the Reverend William Sturrock, who, according to a contemporary account, combined all the qualifications of an excellent schoolmaster with a singularly sweet and gentle disposition. At any rate neither Robert nor his parents seem to have had any reason to regret a move which was primarily made in order to bring the boy nearer to his new home at Mount Stewart.

Mount Stewart, originally named Mount Pleasant, was part of the Newtownards estate on the eastern shore of Strangford Lough, about four miles from the town. When Arthur Young passed that way in 1776 he saw 'a row of neat stone and slate cabbins, in the neighbourhood of some new plantations which surround an improved lawn, where Mr Stewart intends building'.[5] By 1781, when old Mr Alexander Stewart died, his intentions had not progressed very far. So his son moved his family from Newtownards into cabins along the lough while the big house was being built. The accommodation may have been cramped, but obviously had compensations, especially for a boy in his early teens who thoroughly enjoyed boating and fishing on the lough, roaming the estate and making friends with his father's tenants. The house itself was planned on a large and imposing scale in the Adam style, but after the completion of the west wing the building proceeded only spasmodically, and even stopped altogether, largely because Robert's father decided it was more important to buy his son's way into Parliament than to complete the family home.

The elder Stewart had turned to politics after the death of his first wife and in 1771 was returned for County Down in the 'independent' interest by the local Whigs and Dissenters. It was a notable victory because in the past both the County Down seats had been held in the 'official' interest by candidates put up by the Hill family whose head, Lord Hillsborough (later Marquess of Downshire), was one of the wealthiest landowners in Ireland.

The Dublin Parliament in which Stewart first took his seat had no real independence. Its legislation could be vetoed or amended in London, while laws passed at Westminster could be imposed on the Irish. Moreover the Opposition could make little headway against the government's majority of bribed placemen. Ten years later, the Lord Lieutenant, Lord Carlisle, was advising his colleagues in London that legislative independence had become the creed of the kingdom and they had better accept the Irish demands. The change was primarily due to the American revolt, which stimulated the irritation of the ruling Protestant minority at their galling dependence on England, even though in the last resort they depended on the English to maintain their ascendancy over the huge Roman Catholic majority – four-fifths of the whole – who were excluded from virtually all civil and political rights. In March 1778 France and Spain joined in on the American side, and that summer a French invasion of Ireland was believed to be imminent. The country had been dangerously denuded of troops for the war in America, and as the Irish Protestants, whatever their grievances against the English, had no desire to become a French dependency, they spontaneously sprang to arms. Within a year the Volunteers, with the Ulster Presbyterians in the van, were 30,000 strong. The Catholic gentry and merchants, unable themselves to bear arms, gave the movement generous financial support, and later were gradually admitted unofficially to its ranks. The authorities in Dublin Castle looked on helplessly, unable to condemn this rallying to the country's defence but deeply alarmed about where it might lead.

It led first to a vigorous agitation, both inside and outside the Dublin Parliament, for the removal of all restrictions on Irish trade. Shortly before Christmas 1779, Lord North agreed to abandon them all. But the Irish realised that what the English Parliament removed it might again impose. If their commercial freedom was to be really secure, they would have to throw off the authority of Westminster – the cause for which the Americans had gone to war.

During the next two years the efforts of Henry Grattan and Henry Flood to achieve this aim through the Dublin Parliament were frustrated by the government's built-in majority. But in February 1782 delegates of the Ulster Volunteers, meeting at Dungannon, unanimously approved a series of demands of which the first was an independent parliament. The Dungannon resolutions were adopted by grand juries throughout the country, while Grattan, Flood and others resumed their campaign inside Parliament. In London, the Whig ministry, headed by Lord Rockingham, which succeeded North's administration in March 1782, was basically sympathetic to the Irish cause. Before May was out, it had conceded all Grattan's demands, and the Irish Parliament which came to be known by his name was born. Its independence was always more theoretical than real, and the interests it claimed to defend were those of a tiny minority. But its birth was celebrated with bonfires, pealing bells and public rejoicing; and the part that Robert Stewart, Viscount Castlereagh, played in its destruction eighteen years later made his name, then and ever since, one of the most hated in Ireland.

EARLY LIFE 1769–90

In all these stirring events the elder Robert Stewart played an active part. He reflected the radical outlook of his Presbyterian Ulster background and in Parliament he usually voted with the Opposition. In April 1780 he seconded Grattan's famous motion that the people of Ireland 'ought only to be bound by laws made by the King, Lords and Commons of Ireland', although many of Grattan's closest associates thought he was trying to move too far too fast. Stewart was also prominent in the Volunteer movement, raising and commanding a regiment of County Down men called the Ards Independents, and acting as a trusted aide to the General of the Volunteers, the Earl of Charlemont.

It was at a Volunteer review at Belfast in 1782 that young Robert Stewart made his first recorded public appearance. During a sham fight staged after the review, Robert commanded a company of infantry, consisting mostly of boys little older than himself, which was ordered to overpower the enemy's rearguard. His dash, judgment and enthusiasm attracted widespread notice and applause; and when the rearguard at last abandoned their gun, 'young Stewart', in the words of Mr Dickson, a local Presbyterian minister, 'rushed forward in the ardour of his soul, grasped it with his arms, then mounted its carriage, and with tears of triumph huzzaed to the main body, and called them to come on'.[6]

During his father's election contest at Downpatrick in the following year, Robert again attracted favourable comment. Unfortunately, after a hard-fought contest, Colonel Stewart was defeated by Lord Kilwarlin, 'of whose political demerits', noted Charlemont acidly, 'it is enough to say that he was son to the Earl of Hillsborough'.[7] The electioneering methods of Kilwarlin's supporters were considered shady even by the standards of the time. But some thought that Colonel Stewart had lost support by behaving badly to a third candidate with whom he was supposed to have formed an alliance. In any case, he never sat in Parliament again. In Mr Dickson's view, Colonel Stewart's record as a patriotic Ulsterman had made him deservedly popular among his constituents, but 'a toadish coldness and haughty distance of deportment' disgusted and alienated many.[8] It is an interesting comment because when his eldest son grew up he too was widely criticised for his coldness and reserve in public.

Mr Dickson's account of the younger Robert Stewart as a boy is very different. Indeed, it is almost too good to be true. He was writing many years later, after he had become a prominent member of the United Irishmen in Ulster and had been imprisoned, on Castlereagh's orders, for several years after the rebellion of 1798. Perhaps his eulogistic account of the boy and of the expectations he had aroused was paradoxically coloured by his bitter disillusionment with the man.

Yet if Mr Dickson had not been genuinely impressed by young Stewart he would hardly have included in an appendix to his *Narrative of Confinement and Exile* a detailed account of a boating accident on Strangford Lough in which Robert, then just seventeen, saved the life of his companion, Henry Sturrock, who was only twelve. Their boat capsized in a sudden storm and Henry, who could not swim a stroke, was kept afloat by Robert for over an hour. By the time they were rescued the younger boy was completely unconscious, and Robert's limbs were paralysed by the coldness of the water. They told their story afterwards to Mr Dickson, who in his account did full justice to Robert's coolness, resourcefulness and courage.[9] The story also found its way into the *Belfast News-Letter*, whose editor congratulated Robert's friends on his escape, 'and the community of which he promises one day to be a valuable member'. How many, one wonders, of those who read this came to feel, like Mr Dickson, that Robert Stewart had grievously betrayed his early promise?

In October 1786 Robert Stewart went up to St John's College, Cambridge, as a fellow commoner. The university had barely begun to emerge from its eighteenth-century slumber, but St John's was one of the few colleges where academic studies were taken seriously. The undergraduates were examined every half year in classics, mathematics, logic and moral philosophy. Robert was apparently a quiet and polite young man, who applied himself to his studies a good deal more seriously than was usually expected of men of his rank. Although his step-grandfather, Lord Camden, urged him not to neglect the classics because of his 'strong propensity to the sciences', he came near the top in all his examinations, and his obligatory Latin declamation was described as being 'in a very superior style'.[10] How much his academic success was due to intellectual distinction, hard work or lack of competition is not clear.

Robert spent just over two years at Cambridge, returning to Mount Stewart for the long summer vacations. We know little about these years, but they were undoubtedly important for Robert because during this time in England he developed a profound admiration and love for his mother's country, which strongly influenced his political career in Ireland. He spent the Christmas and Easter vacations with his English relatives – the Hertfords and the Camdens – or with his closest Cambridge friend, Frederick Hervey.* In December 1787, after coming out first in the first class in his examinations, he fell ill and went to convalesce with the Camdens in London. On February 12 Lord Camden reported to his daughter at Mount Stewart that he was writing 'with Betty and Robert laughing and chattering about me'. Robert was improving daily 'and your husband may be assured that I shall not consent to his returning to Cambridge till his health is perfectly established'.[11] Two months later Robert was said to be 'perfectly well' and to be talking of returning to Cambridge 'next week'.[12] But it is not clear whether he did actually go up again before setting out for Mount Stewart early in June. Possibly, he could not tear himself away from London. Lord Camden was a member of Pitt's Cabinet, and there was presumably much interesting political talk in the house in Hill Street. Robert attended the trial of Warren Hastings 'constantly' and, according to his grandfather, commented 'as pertinently upon the evidence as if he had been bred a lawyer'. He was also indefatigably practising upon 'his instrument' (violoncello), and had become a 'staunch Handelian'.[13]

Robert went back to Cambridge in October 1788, but by the end of term he had decided not to complete his third year and take his degree. By New Year's Day 1789 he was back at Mount Stewart. He was not yet twenty, but he had already seen and heard enough of the world to grow impatient with the limitations of academic life, and to begin to look forward to taking his father's place on the political stage.

It was barely seven years since Grattan had triumphantly told the Dublin Parliament that Ireland was at last a nation. Little, in fact, had really changed. The Dublin Parliament might in theory pass what laws it liked. But in practice those laws were still dictated by an English Viceroy advised by a small group of English officials and Anglo-Irish grandees, who still had the means to procure a majority for laws based on the wishes of Downing Street. And, unlike the Westminster Parliament, it had no means of getting rid of an administration that it disliked. Yet the Dublin Parliament was not corrupt enough to ignore completely the

---

*Frederick William Hervey (1769–1859) was a younger son of the eccentric Earl of Bristol and Bishop of Derry. His political career got no further than an Under-Secretaryship at the Foreign Office in 1801, but he eventually became the first Marquess of Bristol. Castlereagh used to go regularly to his Suffolk home at Ickworth for the shooting.

increasingly lively and articulate public discontent. There were never quite enough pensions and places. Moreover, the members were Irishmen and, as Grattan once said, they 'did not like to meet every hour faces that looked shame upon them'.[14]

Robert Stewart had not been home for many weeks before the Dublin Parliament was reflecting the crisis over George III's grave illness with which Pitt was grappling in London. The Irish Opposition, seeing a chance to make a reality of their parliamentary independence, joined forces with a sizeable section of Dublin Castle's supporters who were anxious to desert Pitt's apparently sinking ship. Between them they forced through an invitation to the Prince of Wales to assume the Irish Regency. But the King's recovery dished the Opposition on both sides of the Irish Sea, and the government's erring supporters in Dublin were swiftly made to toe the line or lose their places.

'*What is it* that in truth will give satisfaction and restore permanent tranquillity to Ireland?', Pitt had asked soon after he came to power.[15] In 1789 he was perhaps further than ever from an answer. Grattan and his friends, the only Irish politicians who might have helped him, had damned themselves in his eyes by identifying themselves during the Regency crisis with Fox and the English Whigs. They did not retrieve their reputation when they founded the Whig Club in Dublin the following June; its aims were moderate, but its name was not. In normal times it might not have mattered. But the uncritical welcome that Charles James Fox gave to the storming of the Bastille in July 1789 harmed his Irish friends as well as himself. Nobody – except Edmund Burke – could foresee where it would all end in France. Pitt, indeed, prophesied peaceful constitutional change for the French. But he did not advocate similar experiments in Ireland, where the Declaration of the Rights of Man and other proceedings of the French Assembly were received with alarmingly lively interest, especially in the North. For a busy politician, with little time or inclination for studying Irish affairs, it seemed more sensible to support the Lord Lieutenant in maintaining control by the time-honoured methods.

In January 1790 a new Viceroy arrived at Dublin Castle. He was John Fane, tenth Earl of Westmorland, a Cambridge friend of Pitt's. A stranger to Ireland, reactionary by instinct and not very intelligent, Westmorland was no match for the small group of determined men who opposed any sort of change in the existing order. They included Sir John Parnell, Chancellor of the Irish Exchequer, John Foster, Speaker of the Commons (a much more political post in Dublin than at Westminster), John Beresford, known as the King of Ireland because he was the biggest borough-owner of them all, and above all, John Fitzgibbon, who for his loyalty during the Regency crisis had just been promoted from Attorney-General to Lord Chancellor and raised to the peerage. Nicknamed Fitzpetulant in the press because of his uncertain temper, Fitzgibbon was the first Irishman to be made Lord Chancellor. He was an uncompromising champion of the Protestant Ascendancy in Ireland. 'When we speak of the people of Ireland', he solemnly warned the Protestant country gentlemen in the Commons, 'it is a melancholy truth that we do not speak of the great body of the people.' And he went on to add the further home truth: 'that Act by which most of us hold our estates was an act of violence'.[16] To him the Protestants were a beleaguered garrison in a hostile country who could not hope to survive without repressing the Catholic majority and maintaining the connection with Britain.

Fitzgibbon also took it for granted that, since the administration was essentially a foreign one, men's loyalty would have to be bought. More than one-third of the 300 members of the Dublin House of Commons were in receipt of a place or a pension from the Crown. More than two-thirds were chosen by fewer than a hundred borough-owners. Many MPs regarded their seats as an investment and expected the government to pay them substantial interest. One-eighth of the public revenue was divided among them, and peerages were created and sold in order to raise more funds for vote-buying in the lower house.[17]

It was against this system that Grattan and the Opposition discharged all their oratorical guns when Parliament met on January 21, 1790. Their aim was to make Parliament a genuine mouthpiece for the Anglo-Irish Protestant minority. It was a limited aim, but they pursued it with vigour and passion, introducing a whole string of measures designed to check bribery and violently attacking those who profited from it – 'an impudent phalanx of political mercenaries [in Grattan's words] coming from their little respective offices to vote for their bribe and vapour for their character – who are governed not by deliberation but by discipline, and lick the hands that feed, and worship the patron who bribes them'.[18] But it all ended in sound and fury. On this issue, if not on any other, the Viceroy could count on his majority standing firm.

Outside Parliament, however, the Opposition's impassioned speeches made a considerable impression. Westmorland was indignant and alarmed and wrote to London for authority to dissolve Parliament early in order to prevent 'a ferment prejudicial to good order'. Parliament was duly dissolved on April 1, and political polemics were temporarily transferred to the comparatively few constituencies where there was a genuine contest.

The largest of these open two-member constituencies was County Down with 6000 voters, and one of the candidates there, in the Whig or 'independent' interest, was young Robert Stewart. He owed his chance to the fact that Lord Camden's persevering efforts to secure a peerage for his son-in-law had been crowned with success the previous August when the elder Robert Stewart became Baron of Londonderry. Since he would no longer be able to contest the next election, he suggested that his eldest son should take his place, and the fact that Robert would not be of age till the following June was considered no bar since the election was not expected before the autumn. Robert apparently had no qualms on the score of youth or inexperience, and cheerfully embarked, under his father's guidance, on nursing his constituency. He also confirmed his Opposition credentials by becoming one of the original members of the Northern Whig Club, which was established in Belfast in imitation of the Dublin Whig Club, but later became much more extreme. At the inaugural meeting, attended by some of the most solid and sober county gentlemen, it was decided to make all parliamentary candidates who wanted the club's support sign a 'test' pledging themselves to support measures to eliminate parliamentary bribery and reform the representation. The immensely long list of toasts at the celebratory banquet which followed the meeting illustrated the confusion of the members' political aims and beliefs; it began with 'The King' and ended with 'Our Sovereign Lord the People'.[19]

The news that the election was likely to be held before rather than after his twenty-first birthday did not deter Robert Stewart from standing. A second candidate, who was also a founder member of the Northern Whig Club, was Edward Ward, younger son of Lord Bangor, a local landowner and a distant relative of Robert's. They decided to join forces, choosing 'Honour and Honesty' as their motto and blue and buff as their colours. They were opposed by the Marquess of Downshire's son, Lord Hillsborough (formerly Lord Kilwarlin), who had defeated Robert's father six years previously. At the last minute, Hillsborough was joined by a friend, a Captain Matthews. Before the polling opened on May 1, the four candidates' nominations were received in the Sheriff's court before a large audience of freeholders. Robert's right to stand was challenged because of his age, but fortunately the Sheriff decided his court was not competent to decide the issue. After Hillsborough's speech of acceptance, several of his cheering supporters cried out: 'No Test, we know you well and can trust you.' But when Stewart and Ward were presented with the test by some members of the Northern Whig Club, they signed it at once. The *Belfast News-Letter*, which clearly disapproved of such goings-on, summed up the situation with the comment that 'a little time will decide whether the man who has devoted his life to the support of the manufacturers and agriculture of the county, and the protection of the navigation of the Channel – or the men who support *civil and religious liberty* by *once in seven years haranguing* in such pulpits as they can get possession of – are most deserving the *grateful return of a high-spirited people*'.[20]

The 'little time' foretold by the local paper was in fact dragged out to nearly three months. Stewart and Ward had to contend against all the various forms of pressure that the Establishment could exert. In addition, Robert was handicapped by his youth and by his Anglican education which alienated some of the more extreme nonconformists. But he had some enthusiastic supporters, among them the Presbyterian minister, Mr Dickson, who had exerted himself on Robert's father's behalf seven years earlier.

The contest was also followed with the closest interest by the Opposition leaders, who regarded the supplanting of the Marquess of Downshire's son as the most important victory they could have. 'If we can carry this election', wrote Charlemont to Burke, 'of which I have the most sanguine hope, we shall have been successful indeed.'[21] Charlemont's sanguine hopes were only partly fulfilled. After the poll was closed on July 21, the Earl of Hillsborough, with 3534 votes, and Robert Stewart, with 3114, were declared elected.

'Our election this day ended', wrote Robert to Lord Moira, 'not with that triumph we first expected, but still I trust with credit to the Independent interest. Many unforeseen accidents abridged our numbers, but nothing, not even Lord Hillsborough, could detach us from each other.' He went on to thank Moira warmly for his support. 'Your tenantry with some exceptions acted as you wished them. Perhaps it may be necessary to make those who from interested motives opposed your wishes feel your resentment. Such conduct when overlooked serves to increase that inattention to the landlord's recommendation.'[22] The old traditions of political management were not always easy to reconcile with the new democratic theories. Did this censorious young man know what Mr Dickson had been up to on his behalf? He had annoyed some of his best friends by persuading their tenants to vote for Stewart, contrary to their orders and in their presence.[23]

A few days later youthful idealism was again in the ascendant. Robert's letter to the independent electors of County Down, prominently displayed on the front page of the local paper, ended with the declaration: 'I *love* the cause of the people – I revere the constitution –

and I will maintain and defend both with that ardour and affection which a youthful heart dictates, and your generous confidence demands.'[24]

It is said that it cost Lord Londonderry £60,000 to get his son into Parliament. There is some doubt about this figure, but what is not in doubt is that money was no longer forthcoming for building the house at Mount Stewart, and that the family property in Dublin as well as the family collection of pictures and books were sold to help meet Robert's election expenses.[25] Presumably Londonderry thought it was worth it, especially if it helped his son to settle down in Ireland. Indeed, his father-in-law, old Lord Camden, suspected that, consciously or unconsciously, Londonderry's chief aim was to anchor Robert in Ireland. If so, the money was wasted.

By the time the exceptionally protracted County Down election was over, the new Parliament had already met briefly for a fortnight and adjourned until the following January. In the peaceful surroundings of Mount Stewart, Robert had plenty of time to think about his future, and apparently he was not entirely satisfied with it. Perhaps he could not forget his brief contacts with the great world while staying with his grandfather in London. Perhaps he had read the passionate attack of an independent member, Sir Lawrence Parsons, on the Dublin Castle system in the Irish Commons – 'Who out of Ireland ever hears of Ireland? ... A suburb to England, we are sunk in her shade.'[26] At any rate he had begun to wonder whether he would not prefer to sit at Westminster rather than Dublin. His grandfather's sensible advice and, no doubt, his own affection for his family and home settled him for the time being.[27] But for several years the problem of where he belonged – or rather where he wanted to belong – continued to trouble him.

CHAPTER II
Irish or English?
1791—95

When Robert Stewart first entered the Irish Parliament in January, 1791, Dublin was in its heyday as the flourishing and beautiful capital of the Protestant Ascendancy. Throughout the eighteenth century the ruling minority had celebrated their growing sense of security in bricks and mortar, and the city's social life matched the splendour of its setting. The life style of the privileged few was in startling contrast to the atrocious squalor in which the great majority of Dublin's citizens existed. Most visitors, accustomed though they must have been to the spectacle of urban poverty, commented on the degradation of the Dublin poor. For their part, the poor would relieve their feelings, especially in times of political tension or industrial depression, by violently rioting in the better parts of the town. From time to time they would disfigure with pitch or paint the statue of William III on College Green which their political masters venerated as the symbol of their ascendancy. Sometimes too they would burst noisily into the public gallery of the House of Commons, and sometimes even manhandle members trying to make their way into the building.

Robert Stewart's initiation into Dublin politics was a comparatively quiet even dull one, although Grattan still pressed on unavailingly with his campaign to introduce some genuine parliamentary control over the Castle. Robert's first task was to decide his own political line. He did not find this particularly easy since, in spite of all the fine Whig sentiments spoken on the hustings in County Down, he was greatly attracted by the Pitt administration in London of which his much-revered grandfather, Lord Camden, was a member. Camden's advice was to honour any election pledges and otherwise to 'be upon the reserve'. He also suggested that there would be no harm in Robert acknowledging that he was a friend of Pitt's government in London, although he was opposed to the administration in Dublin Castle[1] – advice which might procure him the worst as easily as the best of both worlds.

Robert dutifully tried to follow his grandfather's advice. On any of the reform issues on which he had pledged himself, he voted with the Opposition; and when after barely a month he could no longer refrain from attempting his maiden speech, it was upon an issue where he could to some extent distance himself between Castle and Opposition. Grattan moved for an inquiry into the legislation which forbade Ireland to trade directly with China and the Far East and forced it to obtain all its tea through the East India Company. There were respectable arguments on both sides and Robert could reasonably press for the inquiry while refusing to commit himself on the merits of the case. The motion was duly voted down, and when a similar one was introduced about a fortnight later Robert pressed for an inquiry with enough eloquence to be chosen to act as one of the tellers for the Opposition.

Young Stewart was sufficiently well connected, both in England and Ireland, for his parliamentary progress to be followed by the authorities in Dublin and London with close interest and increasingly mixed feelings. To the Viceroy it was simply a question of Lord Londonderry's son paying off a political debt run up by his father; and when the son showed small awareness of what was expected of him, Westmorland grew increasingly indignant. After Robert's first two votes for the Opposition he wrote to Lord Grenville, the Home Secretary in London, pointing out that Londonderry had done nothing to deserve his peerage and urging him to make a 'terrible grievance' of it to Lord Camden, who ought to be responsible for his son-in-law's conduct.[2] Three weeks later, the Viceroy was not in the least mollified by Robert's cautious maiden speech and compliments to Mr Pitt, although he grudgingly acknowledged that he seemed a promising young man.[3] Lord Grenville was inclined to take a more lenient view. He told Robert Hobart, the Viceroy's Chief Secretary and right-hand man, that Stewart's English friends were sure that 'you might contribute very much to fix him in the right way'.[4] Hobart replied that he would have been very happy to oblige 'a young man, certainly of talents, and of very pleasing manners'. But, he solemnly added, 'take my word for it he is a decided enemy of the King's Government in *Ireland*'.[5]

Early in June, 1791, as soon as the Dublin Parliament had risen, Robert set out on the Holyhead packet to widen his horizons by a visit to the continent. He may not have been sorry to get away from Ireland for he was already losing patience with the Whig politicians who had helped him get into Parliament. 'I see', he wrote to a friend from Lord Camden's house in London, 'the Irish Whigs are going to celebrate the French Revolution. They are as unreasonable in this as in offering the Regency to the Prince.'[6]

Next day he set out for Spa, in the Austrian Netherlands, where he believed he would get the earliest news of what was happening in France and meet the leaders of the 'aristocratic party'. Less than a week earlier the French royal family had made their ill-fated attempt to flee the country. But the disastrous flight to Varennes failed to inject any greater sense of realism into the émigrés' debates. 'It was impossible to convince them', wrote Robert, 'that matters never could be reinstated as they formerly were ... that to escape disappointment they must moderate their views.'[7] When he got to Paris and attended some of the debates of the new Legislative Assembly, he was astonished by the self-confidence of the deputies and their 'inconceivable fluency of language'. (He himself was to be mocked all his life for his incoherence.) Summing up his impressions for the benefit of his grandfather, he wrote that he could not be counted an enthusiastic and unqualified admirer of the French Revolution. He found much to approve and much to condemn. 'I feel as strongly as any man that an essential change was necessary for the happiness and dignity of a great people, long sunk in a state of degradation.' But he lamented that so much more had been attempted than could be achieved without throwing the country into confusion. He condemned the principles of France's present leaders as 'tumultuous pedantry'. 'I am convinced they are unsafe, and I trust that no country in which I have either stake or affection will follow their example.' As for Ireland, the country to which his thoughts naturally turned, he did not like its government, and he feared that reform would be postponed until too late. The moderates could not withstand popular violence unless the imperfections in the constitution were removed, 'and it is a bad reason to give for preserving them, that the people of Ireland are not fit to be entrusted with the freedom Great Britain enjoys, lest they might misuse it, that the connection between the countries must be preserved by abuse, and that they must be contented to live in subordination and corruption'.[8]

But in Belfast popular violence was in the ascendant. The Dissenters, always in the van of political agitation, celebrated France's new (and short-lived) political institutions with joyous abandon, marching through the streets and firing off their guns; and they studied Tom Paine's *The Rights of Man* as if, in Wolfe Tone's words, it was their Koran. The extreme ebullience of the northerners did not spread, but throughout the country the dramatic events unfolding in France acted as yeast upon a political ferment already seething below the surface. 'Paine's book', wrote Robert Stewart, 'has wonderfully altered the people of Ireland. It has done inconceivable mischief. It has made them infinitely more discontented with their Government, and by holding up to their imitation the example of France, led them to look forward to a similar regeneration.'⁹

The Catholic middle classes were benefiting from the slow increase in the country's prosperity, and as usual in a time of rising expectations their political disabilities seemed even more irksome. When their discreet appeals to the government were spurned or ignored, they inevitably began to turn to the rising political force in the North. In September 1791 Wolfe Tone, under the pseudonym A Northern Whig, published *An Argument on Behalf of the Catholics of Ireland*; and the first society of United Irishmen, founded by Tone in Belfast a month later, showed in its manifesto and resolutions the same concern for all Irishmen, whatever their religious faith.

Although the United Irishmen were at first neither illegal nor revolutionary, they were regarded with suspicion by Grattan and the parliamentary Opposition because of their obvious sympathy for the upheaval in France, and with downright hostility by the government in Dublin as dangerous underminers of the status quo. The clique of officials and powerful borough-owners surrounding the Viceroy advised total opposition to any concessions. But in London Pitt observed with disquiet the beginnings of a potentially dangerous combination between the Catholics and the northern Dissenters. The events in France had killed his earlier leanings towards parliamentary reform, but he had considerable sympathy for the Irish Catholics, and he strongly advised the Irish government to offer them substantial concessions. At first Lord Westmorland vehemently rejected the advice, but early in the 1792 session he was forced to back down to the extent of supporting a Catholic Relief bill introduced by a private member, Sir Hercules Langrishe. The bill removed various irksome restrictions on mixed marriages, on Catholics practising the law, on education and so on. It fell far short of the Catholics' hopes; but at least their political aspirations were exhaustively discussed, and the argument was heard that there could surely be no harm in granting them a limited franchise since their loyalty was no longer in doubt. No harm to the state, certainly; but what about the political monopoly enjoyed by the ruling Protestant minority?

Robert Stewart took it for granted that that must be the primary consideration. He supported Langrishe's bill although he feared it would only encourage the Catholics to ask for more. The Bar, he told his uncle, Lord Bayham, was the only important concession. 'The Bar alone weakens the system of self-defence which we the minority are obliged to adopt. It will educate their men of talents. When they arrive at the top of their profession their feelings will be exasperated by finding themselves shut out of the House of Commons and incapable of rising to the Bench. They will naturally compose a very formidable body to direct the future operations of the Catholic body in their struggles for power...'[10] That Robert was here reflecting the deepest fears of the Protestant minority was demonstrated later that session when two petitions for the complete repeal of all Catholic disabilities were rejected by a crushing majority of 208 to 23 votes after a debate of extreme violence and virulence.

Offensive language and political extremism were never to Robert Stewart's taste, and throughout the 1792 session he was seeking the independent middle way to which he instinctively inclined. He accepted his commitments to his constituents, but the French Revolution, which stimulated the radicals, steadied those, like Robert, whose deepest instincts were conservative. Moreover, although he cannot yet have had many first-hand contacts with English political leaders, the pull exerted by Pitt's personality was already strong. 'You know my attachment to him', he wrote to Lord Bayham (Camden's son), 'I often lament that I am thrown into a situation where I am precluded from affording him that support which my feelings incline me to give.'[11] In this frame of mind he was not likely to satisfy his constituents in County Down. One of them, who had been showing concern at Robert's political development, was Alexander Haliday, a local physician who had founded the Northern Whig Club, was a great friend of Charlemont's and a regular visitor to Mount Stewart. To his warning that he should not lightly risk his popularity, Robert replied that the effort and fatigue it had cost him to win his seat in Parliament was no reason for sacrificing his private judgment. He certainly felt bound by his pledges to his constituents, 'but I am not bound to argue in favour of opinions which I do not hold; neither am I bound to suppress my individual sentiments in an assembly where it is the privilege of a Member of Parliament to deliver his ideas'.[12] He did not intend to be frightened by unpopularity. 'I know too well', he wrote to Lord Bayham about this time, 'what popularity in itself is, and the grounds upon which it can alone be either obtained or retained in this country, to be much flattered by the possession of it, or much mortified when it is withdrawn.'[13] Unfortunately for his reputation in later years, he never lost this deep disdain of personal popularity, although as a practical politician he learned to appreciate the importance of public opinion.

At this stage only a tiny minority of Irishmen were contemplating separation, but many, especially in the North, felt that the relationship needed a radical overhaul, and they saw the problem entirely through

Irish eyes. Robert Stewart, half English by birth, and brought up among strong English influences, saw Ireland's problems in a wider context. To the criticism that he was too English, he replied that it was with the feelings of 'a member of the Empire' that he tried to discuss every question. 'I trust', he wrote to Haliday, 'I never shall be an Irishman in contradistinction to the justice due to Britain, nor an Englishman as opposing and betraying the interests of this country ...' He was convinced that 'if we wish to preserve internal harmony and external respectability, above all it is our object to remain connected with Great Britain'. It was absurd to suppose that Ireland could remain for long an independent state, and who would want France – 'that melancholy example of misapplied philosophy, of political experiment and popular delirium' – as Britain's successor?[14]

To his critics Robert Stewart presented a bold front, but privately he was dubious about the ambiguities of his situation. 'In politics, as in life', he wrote to a friend, 'it is an uninteresting effort to advance without a party on whose success you place your hopes ... In opposing both parties you alienate both, you have nothing but your own solidity to support you ... Thus am I circumstanced in this country – and thus am I likely to remain ...' So, he concluded, if he grew sick of his present state of inactivity he would return to philosophy – 'a pursuit, I am convinced, infinitely more productive of happiness to the person engaged in it'.[15]

Despite his strictures on the state of France, Robert was anxious to discover for himself how its political experiments were faring. But Paris in the summer of 1792 was no place for an English tourist. So Robert eventually went to Brussels where he stayed until November, distressed by the predicament of the refugees amongst whom he was living and observing from afar the raw French levies pushing back the trained troops of the German powers. He left for home just before the victorious French general Dumouriez took over the Belgian capital.

One letter has survived from this visit to Brussels which shows Robert Stewart in a very different light from the serious-minded young man who sent his elders long and earnest analyses of the political situation. The letter, written early in October, is to Lady Elizabeth Pratt, Lord Camden's unmarried daughter, who lived with her father. Robert, it is clear, was more than a little in love with her, if only platonically. Addressing his step-aunt with unusual familiarity as 'Dearest Elizabeth', he revealed himself as an uninhibitedly warm-hearted young man, who delighted both to give and receive affection, was devoted to his family and was not above a little good-humoured gossiping about his friends. 'I have', he wrote, 'a thousand things to ask your advice about, and some difficulties which always diminish when I have a friend so Dr to me as you to whom I can communicate them.' Meanwhile he is glad that 'Our Dearest Fanny', his eldest sister who is staying with the Camdens, is quite recovered, and delighted that his next sister, Bess, then about thirteen, is also staying in Hill Street, adding with brotherly condescension that 'she is a charming girl, and in good hands will prove a treasure'. He had had a letter from Frederick Hervey, which indicated that he had abandoned his pursuit of the law and was suffering from a return 'of the old complaint with additional symptoms'. Hervey's heart, wrote Robert, 'is most combustible', and having thrown over someone called Pamela, he is now more than ever in love with 'Ly C'. Robert's attitude to such flightiness is mildly censorious. 'I can understand a young man's falling in love (at least what is called falling in love) repeatedly, yet I confess I have no idea of a sentiment which sinks deep enough to cost a single sigh, being so soon not merely forgotten, but transferred. I really believe it is from an excessive warmth of heart, perhaps in the present instance mixed with compassion.'[16]

Towards the end of 1792 Robert Stewart returned from his foreign travels to find an alarmingly troubled political scene at home. A new breed of Volunteers, with extreme democratic and republican ideas, were being recruited; in Dublin they called themselves National Guards, in imitation of the French. Anxious to head off the extremists, a group of moderate Whigs, including Grattan, formed an association called the 'Friends of the Constitution, Liberty and Peace'; its manifesto, advocating parliamentary reform, Catholic emancipation and opposition to all republican innovation, attracted considerable support. Meanwhile a Catholic convention, meeting in Dublin, decided to send a delegation to London to petition the King directly for equality of rights with the Protestants.

Pitt, faced with the imminent prospect of war with France, was determined not to drive the Irish Catholics to revolt. He insisted that they must be granted substantial concessions at once. Not surprisingly, Westmorland reported from Dublin on January 11, 1793, that his colleagues were 'all in so unpleasing a temper that I can hardly persuade them to consult upon anything'.[17]

But in the end they had to swallow the bitter pill of a complete reversal of policy. The Catholic Relief bill introduced by Hobart swept away most of the remaining restrictions on the Catholics and, by giving them the vote on the same terms as Protestants, enfranchised the great mass of Catholic peasants who qualified as forty-shilling freeholders. But the educated Catholics were still excluded from a seat in Parliament or from holding virtually any government or judicial position. The bill was a compromise designed to prop up the Protestant establishment in Ireland by allaying Catholic discontent with a limited (and therefore safe) measure of political equality. But it gave equality to the ignorant and turbulent Catholic peasants, most of whom were not interested anyway, and withheld it from the Catholic gentry, who did want it and who were loyal and law-abiding.

Grattan, who had tried in vain to persuade Pitt to introduce a more limited franchise, urged that it would now be better to give the Catholics complete political equality at once. Those, on the other hand, who were not convinced that the Catholic peasants would vote as their Protestant landlords told them maintained that it was too risky to grant the Catholics any political concessions at all. Robert Stewart belonged to this second school of thought. He warmly supported removing all civil disabilities from the Catholics, but any political concession was incompatible with his chief preoccupation, the mounting Protestant discontent, which he believed could only be allayed by giving them a more adequate system of representation in Parliament. In a letter to Lord Camden on January 26, 1793, he strongly criticised the way the country was being governed. Ireland, he wrote, must either be governed by reason or united to Britain by force. 'A government of gross corruption – for it is not a government of influence – extinguishing every possibility of parliamentary authority, will no longer be quietly endured.' The demands of the Protestants must be met, so that they would lose the incentive to push the Catholics' claims along with their own. If, he pointed out, the Catholics had the vote under a reformed system of representation, they would become an overwhelming majority – three-quarters – of those represented in the Irish Parliament. 'Can a Protestant superstructure long continue supported on such a base?' Let the Catholics have anything rather than the franchise 'for it forces everything else'.[18]

But as usual the Opposition had no success with parliamentary reform, and the fact that the 'public voice' was in the process of being swelled by some 30,000 Catholic votes cannot have helped them. In other respects, however, the reformers did better. At the beginning of

February 1793 France declared war, and in the more co-operative atmosphere this created the Irish Parliament carried several important administrative reforms, including measures to reduce the Castle's control over the Commons through pensions and places. The Volunteers and National Guards were dissolved by proclamation, and in their place Parliament authorised an increase in the regular army of 5000 (to 20,000) and the raising by ballot (or conscription) of a militia force of 16,000 men to serve for four years.

Robert Stewart joined the militia at the end of April. He was gazetted Lieutenant-Colonel of the Londonderry militia, his commanding officer being a wealthy landowner and MP, Thomas Conolly, whom Charlemont described as 'a man of excellent heart, and a good share of whimsical parts'.[19] As soon as the parliamentary session was over, Robert was off to the North to begin his military career. Although his own military training was virtually non-existent, he found himself, in the absence of Colonel Conolly, organising from a camp at Newtown Limavady the enrolment and training of recruits in County Derry. He seems to have taken to his new life without enthusiasm. He would have much preferred to pay his annual visit to his English relations. But he was consoled by his leaves at Mount Stewart, where his sisters Fanny and Bess, aged sixteen and fourteen, were 'now grown to be a real resource', where he could entertain Frederick Hervey and other friends, and where he could practise his music – not always, it seems, with great success. He had been trying, he told Lady Elizabeth Pratt, to play some of the slow movements in Corelli on the violoncello, 'but I find myself totally incapable of striking one note in tune'. However, he looked forward to singing Italian arias with her by moonlight, sitting by the lough or perhaps in Camden Wood 'which grows more beautiful every day – every visit to this place rivets my affections more closely to it. I foresee endless improvements to effect, which will lead me with interesting occupation to my grave; and the woods which I shall cultivate with care may happily keep my children, if they should be extravagant, from a prison.'[20]

The woods at Mount Stewart were Robert's special pride and joy. 'I assure you', he told his grandfather that spring, 'the plantations become very respectable, they fully deserve to be styled groves, and will in ten years take the rank of woods.'[21] During his Christmas holiday he enlisted the help of four 'old men armed with hatchets' and embarked on a major pruning of the Scotch firs in Camden Wood. 'The side of the wood', he reported to Lady Elizabeth, 'removed from the sea and southwest wind is stripped pretty nearly of fir and makes a magnificent appearance in beech and oak. Before we have done with it, I should imagine the number of scotchmen removed will amount to *500* (five) and yet I am persuaded even Lord Camden, who is not sanguinary in his principles of pruning, would admit we had done essential service.'[22]

Towards the beginning of October Robert and his regiment moved into winter quarters at Ballyshannon, a remote spot in the west of Ireland, not far from Donegal Bay. Here, with letters from Mount Stewart taking twelve days, he felt sadly isolated, but not too out-of-touch to forget about the matrimonial projects of Frederick Hervey which were again in disarray. With Robert's enthusiastic assistance, Hervey had apparently been pressing his suit on a girl whom none of his female relations wanted him to marry because – according to Robert – they wanted to keep him 'totally' in England. And now Hervey's 'conduct to the individual, who seems the best girl in the world and well looking, has been such, and his declarations through me so strong, that a retreat is certainly difficult'. Not surprisingly, especially in view of his own rash part in the affair, he was 'a good deal perplexed about our friend Hervey'.[23]

It was perhaps as well that the local society at Ballyshannon did not tempt Robert to get into a similar scrape. Instead, with the ability cheerfully to make the best of things which rarely deserted him throughout his life, he settled down to being a good regimental officer. 'It is', he wrote to Lady Elizabeth Pratt, 'a little community to manage, the progress of which in discipline it is interesting to observe.' He was in fact very satisfied with the regiment's progress, especially as it had been achieved without any resort to flogging. He also took the opportunity to train his men in the use of musical instruments as well as firearms – 'I have now the little boys making the most horrible noises possible on the different instruments.' But in a year or two he hoped to have a very good band, and as they were local lads from County Down, he looked forward to musical breakfasts in the grounds of Mount Stewart with the band installed on the banks of the lough.[24]

In spite of occasional daydreaming, however, Robert continued to follow the progress of the war on the continent with lively interest. He was astonished by the efficiency with which the French organised, provisioned and armed their soldiers. In Ireland it was very different, although the numbers involved were so much smaller. 'We were obliged', he told his grandfather, 'to leave our cartridges at home, or carry them in our pockets, for want of belts.' Although the famous *levée en masse* had been proclaimed in Paris only a month earlier, he had already grasped the significance of what was happening in France. 'The tranquillity of Europe', he wrote, 'is at stake, and we contend with an opponent whose strength we have no means of measuring. *It is the first time* that *all* the population and *all* the wealth of a great kingdom have been concentrated in the field: *what may be the result is beyond my perception* ...'[25]

In the spring of 1794 Robert Stewart made up for the uneventful months he had spent soldiering in County Donegal: he got married and he took his seat in the Westminster Parliament. How premeditated either of these developments were, if premeditated at all, is not clear. Early in March, he was summoned urgently to London because his grandfather was gravely ill; and before Lord Camden's death at the end of April Robert Stewart had wooed and won Lady Amelia (Emily) Hobart. She was a lively, pretty, good-humoured girl of twenty-two, the youngest daughter of the second Earl of Buckinghamshire, who had died the previous year. His second wife, Emily's mother, was Catherine Conolly, sister of Thomas Conolly, Robert's commanding officer. Emily and Robert may possibly have met before at the Conollys' house in Ireland, but there is no evidence that they had. It was apparently love at first sight followed by an astonishingly swift courtship. He was swept completely off his feet. During a brief separation very shortly after their engagement, he wrote passionately begging two lines from her. 'Tell me that you feel a regard for Ly Elizth, for Fanny, give me a hope that you will derive from my friends the happiness they have conferred on me, but above all tell me *you love me*, on that my existence depends, and I never can grow tired of hearing it.'[26]

He need not have worried. Throughout their twenty-eight years together, she seems to have felt for him a devotion every bit as great as his for her. Posterity has not treated her with much enthusiasm. She is remembered, if she is remembered at all, for the kind of things that were likely to embarrass her husband after he had become a famous European statesman – wearing his Garter cross in her hair at a Viennese reception, or obstinately refusing to make up her quarrel with the King's favourite, Lady Conyngham. She probably was sometimes indiscreet and rather wayward. She certainly did not reach her husband's intellectual level, and she may not even have been particularly interested in politics, although she went electioneering on his behalf in County Down and never shirked her duties as political or diplomatic hostess. On the whole, she was a sensible, cheerful and kind person, who never left her husband's side if she could help it, and gave him the stable domestic companionship he needed. She never had a child although there are hints during their early married life that they were anxiously hoping for one.

Robert Stewart and Emily Hobart were married at St George's, Hanover Square, on June 9, 1794, and on the same day moved into No.3 Cleveland Square. By this time he was MP for the Cornish borough of Tregony, which belonged to an Indian 'nabob' called Barwell who was happy to instruct the burgesses to vote for whomever Pitt chose to nominate. Robert Stewart's record in the Dublin Parliament did not suggest that he was likely to make reliable voting fodder. But Pitt must have heard his praises sung by Lord Camden, and he was shown one of Robert's letters to his uncle, Lord Bayham, which vigorously criticised the Dublin government and lamented that 'the openness of conduct which Mr Pitt invariably adopts in the British Parliament is not yet a part of the Irish system'.[27] Pitt was sufficiently impressed (or flattered) to write and thank Robert for the letter's 'obliging' tone.[28] He liked to encourage promising young politicians and it is not surprising that he should have offered Lord Camden's grandson a safe seat. It cost Robert £200 and a brief visit to Cornwall, which he made out of courtesy, not because he had to.

Robert arrived at Westminster too late to listen to the maiden speech of his future rival George Canning, who first took his seat at the beginning of the session, but he may have heard Fox's passionate opposition to the suspension of habeas corpus which the government pushed through the Commons in eleven divisions early on the morning of May 17. England was being buffeted by the first of the waves of alarm at enemies both internal and external, which were to continue throughout most of Robert Stewart's career at Westminster.

Robert and Emily arrived at Mount Stewart in the middle of July after a delayed honeymoon in the Lake District. Robert was soon reporting to Lady Elizabeth Pratt that his wife 'seems as happy here as if she had been born [in] a shack', and he was delighted to observe 'that she recommends herself to both my Father and my Mother'.[29] After only a few days at Mount Stewart, they had to go on to Drogheda where the militia regiments were assembling for a review at the beginning of August. Robert found his regiment full of new recruits and had plenty to do. But after a month or so of soldiering, he began to yearn for Mount Stewart, all the more so since Lady Elizabeth had arrived on a visit to her sister. His marriage had made no difference to Robert's friendship for his aunt. 'I cannot tell you how I languish for Mount Stewart again', he told her. 'It is sometimes right to leave places where we are very happy, absence soon teaches their value. Music is an unadulterated sweet, and your friendship one of the *few human joys* I can look to as imperishable.' Lady Emily, he added, 'sent her best love – she was grievously fatigued by the two balls, however she has suffered no sort of inconvenience from giving way to her spirits.'[30]

Robert's hopes of getting back quickly to Mount Stewart for some more 'musical studies and confidential intercourse' with his aunt, were dashed by a summons from Pitt to attend the Westminster Parliament which was to assemble on November 25. He set off in the middle of November, leaving Emily behind at Mount Stewart. Throughout the long, cold, uncomfortable journey, the wife he had left behind was never far from his thoughts. He worried about how she was getting on with her in-laws. 'You are surrounded by those who sincerely love you and are anxious to make your time pass pleasantly. Cultivate my mother and Lady Elizth, they are friends invaluable to those they love ...' He thought up ways for her to fill her time, and asked her to pay calls on two neighbours – it would not be at all disagreeable if she made up a party with Fanny and Charles. ('I leave my electioneering interests in your hands.') He worried about her health and instructed her not to neglect the bad effects of the piercing easterly winds. 'Remember the charge you are entrusted with – the *happiness of the man* you love – that reflection says more than a folio of prudential maxims ...'[31]

In the event, this journey, which Robert philosophically described as 'a necessary piece of self-denial', turned out not to be necessary at all. Pitt, contending with recalcitrant Cabinet colleagues and a sharp attack of gout, decided to prorogue Parliament to a more auspicious time. Robert Stewart was told to retrace his steps and to be ready to take his place in the Dublin Parliament in the new year.

Pitt had put off the opening of the Westminster Parliament mainly because he was at odds over Irish policy with the group of Whigs who had joined his government the previous July. Their leader, the Duke of Portland, was made Home Secretary and thus put in charge of Ireland, and it was understood that another Whig, Earl Fitzwilliam, would shortly replace Westmorland as Lord Lieutenant. Fitzwilliam spent the autumn preparing the 'new system' which would rescue Ireland from anarchy and make it a support instead of a burden to England in the struggle against revolutionary France. Grattan and other members of the Irish Opposition came over to London to advise him and Portland on a package of reforms which included further measures to make the Commons less of a rubber stamp, and the admission of Catholics to Parliament.

Pitt did not openly discourage this new Irish policy, but he was uneasy about it and procrastinated over the recall of Westmorland. In October there was a blazing row over Ireland which nearly shattered Pitt's frail alliance with the Portland Whigs. The quarrel was patched up, Westmorland was at last recalled and the new Viceroy was given vague (and unwritten) instructions on how far he might go. The opportunities for misunderstanding were obvious.

Fitzwilliam arrived in Dublin on January 4, 1795, and was received with enthusiasm and hope. There was need for optimism since the comparative peace which had prevailed through most of the previous year was rapidly crumbling. Throughout the country the Catholics, excited by reports that the new Viceroy was sympathetic to their cause, were preparing to inundate Parliament with petitions. The Protestant gentry, anxious to enlist the educated Catholics on the side of law and order, were supporting their demands. In the countryside the Catholic peasants enrolled in the 'Defender' movement were stepping up their attacks on their Protestant neighbours. The peasants' violence was rooted in poverty, ignorance and religious fanaticism, but the political confrontation between the educated Catholics and the government sharpened the impact of the agrarian disturbances. Finally, the United Irishmen were taking on a new lease of life as underground societies, bound by secret oaths and subscribing to treasonable aims. They collected arms, drilled by night and disseminated seditious literature. The appeal of their revolutionary doctrines was strengthened by the comparative failure of the parliamentary Opposition to effect reforms, while the successes of French arms in the Low Countries made foreign aid seem a real possibility. The United Irishmen were not interested in conciliating the educated Catholics, since their aim was to break the system, not mend it. But they were beginning to realise that the Catholic peasants, whom they used to scorn as ignorant fanatics, were ideal material for political exploitation.

Fitzwilliam, convinced that sweeping concessions were urgently necessary, at once began to make changes among the Castle officials, who were equally convinced that any concessions would inevitably destroy the British connection. He also sent repeated warnings to Portland that unless he received peremptory orders to the contrary, he did not intend to oppose Catholic emancipation. For a month no comment, let alone peremptory orders, came from London.

The Dublin Parliament met on January 22, 1795, and so close was the accord between the new Viceroy and the parliamentary Opposition that Grattan himself rose to propose the Address of Thanks for the

Speech from the Throne. Robert Stewart was chosen to second the Address. It was the last time he found himself speaking on the same side as Henry Grattan. Immediately afterwards Catholic petitions began to flood in from all over the country, and Fitzwilliam made up his mind to support the Catholic Relief bill which Grattan introduced on February 12. But the ministers in London did not approve and at last began to say so. They were not impressed by Fitzwilliam's desperate appeals. Even Portland, who should have been his stoutest ally, deserted him, and on February 19 he was recalled.

Fitzwilliam may have been inexperienced, unrealistic and politically hamfisted, but it is difficult not to feel that he was much more sinned against than sinning. The Cabinet in London were preoccupied with their own political future, with domestic unrest and with the threat of foreign invasion. As always, Ireland did not get the attention it deserved. It had to make do with expedients based on ignorance and designed to serve other ends than the welfare of the Irish people. Fitzwilliam may not have known, as Pitt did, of the King's hostility to Catholic relief, but he should have realised that any British government would have felt extreme reluctance to abandon the traditional policy of controlling Ireland through the political monopoly of the Protestant minority. Yet he kept the Cabinet, through Portland, fully informed of his intentions, and he can hardly be blamed for taking silence for consent.

Most ordinary Irishmen had no doubt that the new Viceroy had been recalled so abruptly because he was too sympathetic to the Catholics. So the tragic outcome of Fitzwilliam's mission was the exact opposite of what he had intended: not pacification and reconciliation, but a sickening lurch down the slope towards revolt, bloodshed and repression. And when Fitzwilliam left Dublin, the citizens, as if they foresaw what lay ahead, closed their shops, dragged his coach to the waterfront and saw him off with every sign of grief and mourning.

As Fitzwilliam's successor, Pitt chose John Pratt, the second Earl Camden, a close friend from Cambridge days, and the son of Robert Stewart's beloved step-grandfather. Charlemont described Camden as 'a plain, unaffected, good-humoured man, of pleasing conversation and conciliatory address', but not of the same calibre as his father.[32] He had the right qualities to bring Ireland through its immediate crisis, but in the long run was too easy-going to resist a fatal acquiescence in the outlook of the Castle junta.

Camden seems to have taken it for granted that he could count on his nephew's support and immediately summoned Robert to London to brief him on the Irish situation. On their return to Ireland at the end of March, Robert must have witnessed the serious rioting with which the Dublin mob welcomed the new Viceroy's arrival. Prominent members of the administration had the windows of their houses smashed, while the hated Fitzgibbon nearly had his head broken by a piece of paving-stone. (He was consoled for this indignity by being made Earl of Clare.)

So far as we know, Robert did not question his uncle's assumption that he was ready to assume his place as a defender of the Protestant Ascendancy. The triumphs and excesses of the French revolutionaries, the unrest in Ireland, the spell cast by Pitt, and his own essentially conservative temperament, must all have combined to line him up with the forces of law and order – or, from another point of view, of repression. When the Dublin Parliament met for a brief session in mid-April, Robert stoutly defended the recall of Fitzwilliam, and opposed granting any more political concessions to the Catholics. 'I cannot help but love him', wrote Charlemont, 'yet, why so be-Pitted?'[33]

One reason was that Pitt took trouble with his young disciples. That autumn he asked Robert Stewart, who had not yet even made his maiden speech at Westminster, to second the Address. It was in fact a compliment which a more experienced politician might have preferred to do without. The war was going badly and was intensely unpopular; food was dear and jobs were scarce; political discontent throve on economic distress: and on his way to open Parliament on October 29, 1795 the King had to pass through a violently hostile crowd. Ignoring the tumult outside, Robert Stewart made the kind of platitudinous speech customary on such occasions. He claimed that France's finances and energy were largely exhausted, and his only reference to the unrest at home was the surprising assertion that 'Nowhere were the people deprived of the comforts of life by the effects of the war'. His complacency could hardly have been less justified. Nearly twenty years of almost uninterrupted war against France lay ahead; and he himself was to become the popular scapegoat for the government's methods of coping with the economic and social consequences of the war.

CHAPTER III

Ireland's slippery slope
1795-97

If England was disturbed and restless during the winter of 1795-96, the state of Ireland was infinitely worse. The shock of Fitzwilliam's sudden recall had destroyed the Catholics' hopes of a new deal and left instead a mood of sullen disloyalty. In the countryside the Catholic peasants intensified their endemic warfare against their Protestant neighbours, and in retaliation the Orange Society was formed. Its professed aims were to keep the peace and defend the Protestant constitution, but its members immediately embarked on a vicious persecution of the Catholics which rapidly spread throughout the northern counties.

Thousands of Catholic peasants, forced to flee from their burning cabins, were dispersed throughout the country, leaving behind them a trail of fear, bitterness and horrifying rumours. The failure, or refusal, of some of the magistrates to punish the Orangemen's excesses added to the anger and despair of the persecuted Catholics. Convinced – wrongly – that the authorities in Dublin had condoned, if not actively promoted, their dispossession, they willingly listened to the United Irishmen, who not only taught them revolutionary doctrines but also gave them shelter and tried to prosecute their persecutors. The Catholic peasants cared not a jot for parliamentary reform or Catholic emancipation. But they knew that one of the first consequences of the French Revolution had been the abolition of tithes, and for years they had been seething at the injustice and hardship of being forced to pay tithes to the clergy of an alien creed. Grattan had made repeated efforts to get the tithes abolished, but a Protestant Parliament and a Protestant administration were unwilling to undermine the privileges of the established Protestant Church. Thus active political disaffection was added to the agrarian and sectarian grievances of the Catholic peasants, while the United Irishmen, although they tried to preserve the non-sectarian image which Wolfe Tone had originally given them, became irretrievably identified with the Catholics. At the same time the Orange societies spread rapidly, attracting Dissenters as well as Church of Ireland Protestants. It was the end of Grattan's hopes that Protestants and Catholics might learn to live together as Irishmen, putting the needs of their country before their sectarian prejudices.

It was also the end of any attempt to settle Ireland by conciliation rather than confrontation. When the Dublin Parliament met in January 1796 the government introduced first an Indemnity bill, to protect magistrates who had exceeded their legal powers in putting down disorder, and then an Insurrection bill which allowed the Lord Lieutenant, by proclamation, to place any district under a control little short of martial law. Few votes were cast against either measure.

Robert Stewart was back in Dublin in time to defend Pitt's policies towards Ireland and the war in the opening debate in the Irish Parliament. But before the short session ended in mid-April he had yet again crossed the Irish Sea to take his place at Westminster. Since his election to the English Parliament in May 1794, he had made the tedious journey between London and Dublin eight times. Not surprisingly, he was beginning to wonder which country he really belonged to. Would he not do better to try to make a useful career for himself in one of them, instead of constantly shuttling between them? It was a very difficult choice, since few responsible posts were open to an Irishman in his own country, but Robert Stewart's home and family and everything he loved best were in Ireland.

Before he set off for England towards the end of March, Robert had made up his mind. He would settle for a career in Ireland; he was too uncertain of himself and too attached to his home to make the more ambitious choice. 'Two reasons alone', he explained to his uncle, 'can induce an Irishman to pursue the politics of the other country, rather than those of his own, the one is the superior interest of a more extended field of public affairs, the other a feeling of confidence in his own powers, which may encourage him to risk his natural advantages in hopes of commanding by the weight of his talents, superior objects in another kingdom. The former temptation I feel most strongly, and I shall always regret that my lot has placed me in the narrower sphere – the latter inducement weighs not at all with me. I feel no confidence in myself, beyond a general disposition for business, which perseverance and experience might ripen so as to qualify me to discharge the duties of an active situation, but none of those talents do I feel fitted with, which could enable me to force my way in a country not my own, or entitle me to any reward, which could at all compensate for the sacrifices I should be [forced] to make even at the outset *of my probation*, namely the surrender of my situation in this country, and a separation from my own family.'[1] It was an astonishing confession of diffidence from someone whose name, twenty years later, was to be one of the best known in Europe.

IRELAND'S SLIPPERY SLOPE 1795-97

He was also more firmly attached by his Irish roots than most of his compatriots seem to have been. Unlike Lord Mornington, Arthur Wellesley's eldest brother, who was systematically disposing of his Irish assets – they were all he had – Robert Stewart felt himself to be under an obligation not to desert his native country while all Europe was undergoing such upheavals. So for these and many other reasons 'too tedious to enumerate', he decided 'to make Ireland, as Nature has already decided it for me, my country, and to consider England, though superior in every point of view, as secondary to me, at least in this'. As for a seat at Westminster, if Pitt offered one, he would certainly accept it. But if he could not acquire a seat without a great deal of expense, he would go without and concentrate on Ireland – 'though nothing shall ever prevent me from passing a good deal of my time in England'.[2]

That summer there was a general election in England. The owner of Robert's seat at Tregony decided to put it up for sale again, but the pocket borough of Orford, belonging to his uncle Lord Hertford, fell comfortably into his lap. In the end, however, he never took his seat in what turned out to be the last Parliament of Great Britain.

By the middle of August 1796 Robert Stewart was back in Ireland. He found that his father, who had been made Viscount Castlereagh the previous year on his brother-in-law's recommendation, had just climbed another step in the peerage and become Earl of Londonderry. Robert thus acquired the courtesy title of Viscount Castlereagh by which he has gone down in history. Camden had recommended the further advancement of his sister's husband's family more as a 'particular compliment' to himself than as a recognition of anything that Londonderry had done to deserve it. Inevitably, it strengthened the links between the Stewarts and Dublin Castle, and was consequently deplored by Robert's old friends in the Opposition. They did not, however, let it affect their own friendly relations with the family. When Charlemont, through Dr Haliday, sent his kind remembrances to the new Earl and Countess, he also included 'the new lord, who notwithstanding his title and his *Pitticism*, I must still style my dear Robert'.[3] Ten days later, on August 23, he reported that he had just been visited by 'our dear friend Robert, who, with wonder I speak it, is not the worse for being a lord ...'[4]

Castlereagh had been investigating the situation in the North and had come down to Dublin to add his warning to all the other warnings that were flowing into the Castle. All the intelligence received by the government agreed that an insurrection was planned for after the harvest and would be aided by a French invasion. The persecution of the

Catholics was being used very successfully to undermine the loyalty of the militia, most of whom, especially the rank and file, were themselves Catholics. The Protestant gentry were clamouring to be allowed to raise a force of volunteer yeomanry, a demand with which Castlereagh thoroughly sympathised, in spite of the danger that armed volunteers might get out of hand – as Grattan's Volunteers had done a few years earlier. It would also be unwise to seem to be arming the Protestants against the Catholics, but Camden reluctantly came to the conclusion that it was impossible to refuse to allow the loyalists to arm in their own defence, and the British Cabinet even more reluctantly endorsed his conclusion.

As for the United Irishmen, the authorities would have had no hesitation in arresting their leaders, if they had had enough information to bring them to trial. But although informers revealed a great deal of what was going on, most were too frightened of assassination to confirm their evidence in a court of law. Early in August, however, Castlereagh obtained detailed information about United Irishmen activities in the Belfast area, including a sworn deposition which he thought was sufficient to convict six men, two of them leaders of the organisation. He took his information to Dublin and was asked to help round up the conspirators.

Emily had been left behind at Mount Stewart and while waiting in Dublin for the operation to begin, Castlereagh kept her posted of his doings. He had been told he was 'verging towards corpulence' and so rode every day to keep himself in bounds, 'for you know my present life requires some regulating principle. Great dinners and eternal sleep are too much for my habit.' He went to a grand review of the local garrison in Phoenix Park, but wished 'my favourite aide de camp was of the party'. He went to stay with Emily's uncle Thomas Conolly at his superb house at Castletown in County Kildare, but without his wife it was so unlike all former visits that he could not enjoy it. He was pleased when she made herself agreeable to his constituents, but worried greatly when she would ride a horse called Prince and begged her not to unless his father was with her. 'Horses of that class are never to be depended on – they are asleep one minute and frantic the next . . .' On one occasion he had kept his own horses waiting for six hours in the hope of getting away to visit her, but was detained too long at a meeting at the Castle.[5]

The rounding-up of the northern conspirators eventually took place on September 16. Castlereagh began the day by making some arrests in Lisburn, including a young man of eighteen called Charles Teeling, whose father he had known for years. He then rode off to Belfast where a large force of cavalry, supported by the local garrison, searched the town for conspirators and made a number of arrests. At the end of the day, Castlereagh returned to Lisburn, and before supervising the transfer of his prisoners to Dublin, he invited Charles Teeling to share some food and wine with him. Teeling has left an account of their meal together. He noted Castlereagh's 'most fascinating manners and engaging address heightened by a personal appearance peculiarly attractive'. He also noticed that he was tired and seemed greatly dispirited. Castlereagh admitted his fatigue, but added that they had made some important arrests. He asked Teeling if he knew two of those arrested, Samuel Neilson and Thomas Russell. Teeling replied emphatically that he did, warmly praising the first as a 'man of talent and devoted patriotism', and the second as 'the soul of honour'. Castlereagh made no reply but merely filled his own glass, and passed the wine across the table. By mutual consent they turned to less embarrassing topics.[6]

Fewer than a dozen were arrested in this round-up, and in the end it was not found possible to bring them to trial. But the authorities were highly satisfied, their opponents were extremely indignant, and those actually planning revolt were dismayed at the disruption to their organisation. Castlereagh was the object of particularly bitter recrimination because of the hopes he had once aroused as a champion of reform. He himself was unmoved by the reproaches, although he admitted it had been a painful experience. With somewhat confused vehemence he justified himself to Lady Elizabeth Pratt. 'I am sure you will not regret that I am an apostate with Lord Charlemont and many others from a set of them, who compose a French party in this country, and are endeavouring to lead us through the same succession of horrors, that have been produced in France by similar men and similar principles.'[7]

Early in October, Castlereagh was summoned to Dublin for a special session of Parliament, called principally to authorise the suspension of habeas corpus and the recruiting of the yeomanry. Grattan warmly supported the latter, but he attacked the suspension of habeas corpus with passion and despair. He warned the Commons that they were giving the Lord Lieutenant's Secretary – an Englishman (Thomas Pelham) with no stake in the country – the power to send anyone he chose to prison on any pretext whatever. The people of Ireland were to lose their civil liberty lest they should use it to recover the political liberty they had already lost. But only six voted with him in opposition to the suspension. Nor did he do much better when he raised the issue of Catholic emancipation. Many who in principle were in favour of full political equality for the Catholics felt the present crisis was the wrong time to raise the issue. But it was precisely because the crisis was so grave that Grattan besought the government to make sure of the loyalty of the great majority of the people of Ireland by giving them full political equality with the minority. His pleas fell on deaf ears.

There was no question that autumn of Castlereagh taking his seat in the new Westminster Parliament which met early in October 1796. He did not even sit right through the brief session of the Irish Parliament. Before the end of the month he was again on his way north, sent by Lord Camden to help stop the rot in his own part of Ireland.

One morning soon after his return, when he was riding along the road to Comber, he came across 'a pretty sight: a great number of young men marching along with smart girls leaning on their arms'. They were, he discovered, on their way to dig the potatoes of a local man who was on the run from the authorities. Marching through the countryside in large, well-organised bands, with spades held as muskets, had become a recognised way for the rebels to demonstrate their strength and practise their discipline. It was perfectly legal, and Castlereagh had no choice but to make the best of the encounter. 'I rode some distance with them', he told Emily afterwards, 'and had a good deal of funny conversation; you may easily conceive I neither scolded nor attempted to argue them out of their intentions. We had a great number of jokes and nothing could be more good-humoured than they were to me.'[8] He was not merely making light to his wife of what might have been a dangerous encounter. 'I never saw', he also told Pelham, 'a finer race of young men, full of zeal in a cause they are made to feel a good one.'[9]

In a story of such unrelieved sombreness, when the failure of communication was almost total, this brief encounter is worth recording. But it was not typical. The reality of the situation which Castlereagh found in Down was even worse than he had supposed. Large areas of the North were living under a reign of terror. Throughout the county arms were being distributed, and there seemed no reasonable doubt that active preparations for revolt were under way. Yet with the coolness that was to become one of his most notable characteristics, Castlereagh did not automatically endorse Lord Downshire's wish to 'proclaim' the county or parts of it under the Insurrection Act. 'I have always entertained', he wrote to Pelham, 'very great doubts on the applicability of that law to the spirit against which we are contending.' To confine people to their houses, carry out searches for arms, and take weapons away from those legally entitled to hold them would, he felt, be too severe, and therefore — although he himself did not use the word — counterproductive. He also doubted whether the local magistrates were capable of enforcing tough measures.[10] However, at a meeting under Lord Downshire's chairmanship, they were almost unanimously in favour of proclaiming five particularly disturbed parishes. Castlereagh agreed because these districts were suffering from the kind of disturbances the Insurrection Act was aimed at: large bands of men roaming the countryside, breaking into houses, robbing and murdering. But he argued so strongly against proclaiming other districts where the trouble was not open disorder but the proliferation of secret societies that this was dropped.[11]

The most effective way of undermining the clandestine activities of the United Irishmen, as had been shown two months earlier, was to strike at their leaders — if one knew where to find them. When Castlereagh heard that the provincial directory of the United Irishmen were meeting in Portaferry on November 9, he rode over with an escort and within an hour had taken six men, together with the important papers they were carrying to their meeting. He went on to Belfast where he met Lord Carhampton, the new commander-in-chief, and next day helped to arrest seven 'principal rebels' in Belfast and four in the neighbourhood of Lisburn.

But, to Castlereagh, the 'hearts and minds' aspect of the fight against insurrection was almost as important as making arrests. He found his father's tenants wavering, not, he believed, deeply committed to the United Irishmen, but too frightened of the assassin's bullet to declare their loyalty. He was convinced that if only enough of them could be persuaded to stand up and be counted, they would not be afraid to come forward together and take the oath of allegiance. Neither Mr Conolly's requests to rejoin his regiment at Limerick, nor Emily's increasingly plaintive requests to rejoin her in Dublin, shook his determination 'to make something of my Father's people before I go'. He rode indefatigably around the estate, arguing and persuading. He really felt, he told Emily, that he could do more good where he was than on parade in Limerick. Eventually, after much effort and even more uncertainty, between three and four hundred tenants assembled in Newtownards and took the oath of allegiance. 'They did it with every mark of sincerity', Castlereagh reported, 'after the ice had been broken and their panic a little removed. They had been much deceived and much threatened.' Afterwards Londonderry and his son entertained the tenants to dinner in the Market House. 'We had a very jolly dinner. Cleland

[Londonderry's agent] quite drunk, Sinclair [the local Presbyterian minister] considerably so, my father not a little, others lying heads and points, the whole very happy, and God Save the King and Rule Britannia declared permanent.' For Castlereagh the only sting in this gratifying change of attitude was that it kept him 'a little longer separate from my *only happiness*'.[12]

By the time he left Mount Stewart, some 1700 of Lord Londonderry's tenants had taken the oath of allegiance and a troop of cavalry was being formed. There could also have been a large force of yeoman infantry, but Castlereagh decided not to encourage this 'since it is better, not to presume too much on so new a spirit'.[13]

Could the new spirit be presumed on at all? Even Lord Londonderry had doubts about the permanence of so many sudden conversions. But in those days men demonstrated their political allegiance not by the votes they cast but by the oaths they took. The members of all the secret societies the Irish formed in frustrated revolt against economic, religious or political repression were always bound by an oath. It was accepted that the loyal should pledge their allegiance to the King. In such troubled times the oaths might not stick, but Castlereagh and his father had nothing to lose, and perhaps much to gain, from trying persuasion before repression.

By the beginning of December, accompanied this time by Emily, Castlereagh had joined his regiment at Limerick. A few weeks later a French fleet appeared off Bantry Bay. The French invasion, so long expected, was at last upon them. All the available troops – there were lamentably few – were ordered to concentrate on the south-west coast, and on Christmas Eve Castlereagh marched out of Limerick at the head of 500 men, while Emily prepared to return to Dublin. Next day he sent her a cheerful letter from Charleville where the local people were being extremely kind, and the Mayor was going to provide them all with a Christmas dinner. Both he and his men were in great spirits. 'We reached Bruff last night about six o'clock. The weather was charming, a little cold, but marching on foot I did not feel it. Mr Whiskey had done a little mischief in our ranks, but upon the whole for a first day's march (taking leave of sweethearts, and parting with the inhabitants, who brought spirits in quantities to them when they were chilled on the street waiting for stores which they never received) we did fairly well. I have, however, this day declared war against Whiskey and it will not retard us again.'[14]

For the next week they marched and countermarched between Mallow and Cork. The French ships, prevented from landing by violent storms, had disappeared from Bantry Bay by the 29th, but it was feared they might try to land further west, perhaps at the mouth of the Shannon. Eventually the reappearance of some half dozen French ships at the entrance to Bantry Bay caused Castlereagh and his men to come to rest at Bandon, some 20 miles from Cork on the road to Bantry. By then most of them were very lame and, in Castlereagh's opinion, if the marching and countermarching had continued for a few days longer, his men would have been beaten by fatigue.[15]

General Dalrymple, the commander at Cork, complained that his officers were not accustomed to look after their men. This was certainly not true of Castlereagh. It was an especially cold winter and when Emily rather rashly offered to provide them with flannel waistcoats, her offer was taken up with the greatest enthusiasm. 'I am rejoiced to hear of the flannel waistcoats', Castlereagh wrote, 'they will be of great use whether the French come or not – pray take care of our Regt.' The flannel waistcoats became a constant refrain in his letters, and when 280 at last arrived, he was all the more anxious for the rest, 'to prevent jealousy'.[16]

The French ships which had reappeared off Bantry Bay sailed away again during the night of January 3/4. Foul weather, bad luck, poor seamanship and divided counsels had combined to disperse the force which was to have helped Ireland to throw off the English yoke. The Irish, to the surprise and gratification of the authorities, stayed quiet and in many cases generously helped the troops that were rushed to the area. But they might have behaved differently if the French invasion had been successful. As it was, all Castlereagh saw of the invading Frenchmen were those on the French frigate *Tartare*, the only warship captured by the British. He rode over to Cove, where the captured ship had been taken, and spent most of the day with the prisoners. He was impressed by the warmly clothed and hardy-looking troops, and as a memento he sent Emily two *assignats* from the store of French currency which had presumably been intended for circulation among the Irish.

When Castlereagh took his place in the Dublin Parliament in mid-January 1797, he found the Commons much preoccupied with their recent narrow escape from a French invasion. But some of the new taxes which the government proposed to raise to improve the country's defences were sharply criticised by the Opposition, especially the tax on salt, which would press most heavily on those least able to bear it. But the alternative of a tax on the rent rolls of the great Irish landowners who lived in England was defeated by 122 votes to 49. Castlereagh opposed the motion in a speech that did him little credit. Among other arguments he asserted that an absentee tax would lead to a separation of the two countries (which Grattan said was absurd) and would make an issue of the connection between them which in his opinion should never be made a matter of public debate. In his reply, Mr Vandeleur, who had proposed an absentee tax, sarcastically commented that the Castle was a hot-bed which ripened the understanding and matured the judgment. 'It had', he added, 'so completely eradicated all prejudices from the mind of the noble lord, that he was unable to perceive, whether he spoke the language of the minister, or deputy minister of the English cabinet, or that of the representative of a great, populous and independent county ... which ushered him into this House on the shoulders of popularity.'[17]

It was also a very disturbed country, especially in the North, where early in March 1797 the commanding officer, General Lake, was instructed to disarm the province by proclamation. Lake, a tough soldier who believed that nothing but terror would keep the people of Ulster in order, regretted that the country had not been put under martial law. He did well enough without it. Large quantities of arms were either surrendered voluntarily or seized in house-to-house searches. Most of the searches and disarming had to be carried out by locally-recruited yeomanry, ill-disciplined and violently partisan Orangemen, who had themselves been subjected to every species of intimidation by United Irishmen before they joined up, and now had no scruples about paying off old scores against their Catholic neighbours. The operation was officially accounted a success, but the resentment it created was immense.

The authorities' fears that the country was on the verge of revolt were confirmed in April when two United Irishmen committees, forty men in all, were rounded up in Belfast, together with a haul of documents that threw an alarming light on the aims and extent of the organisation. They revealed that more than 72,000 men had been enrolled in Ulster alone, that the aim of the conspiracy was a separate republic and that the insurgents were negotiating for aid from France. Outside Ulster, only Dublin and some central districts were fully organised, but the conspiracy seemed to be spreading throughout the country.

In the middle of May, Camden tried to combine firmness with leniency by offering an amnesty to those (with certain exceptions) who took the oath of allegiance before June 25. But by now the only oaths that counted were those that each side was rumoured (and believed) to have sworn to exterminate the other. To the Catholic peasants, only the United Irishmen seemed to offer hope that their ancient grievances would be remedied and protection against the excesses of the ill-disciplined Orange yeomanry searching for arms.

While the extremists gained strength, the moderates were becoming increasingly alienated from the government. The parliamentary Opposition abandoned their efforts to save the regime through moderate reforms and Grattan announced that he would withdraw from Parliament. Liberal peers, like the Duke of Leinster and Lord Bellamont, resigned their militia commands in protest at the severity of the military repression. Merchants in Belfast, barristers in Dublin, freeholders everywhere drew up addresses or passed resolutions, condemning the corrupt system of government, the treatment of the Catholics, the excesses of the military, while claiming that most of the evils under which they suffered would have been prevented if the 'people' had been fairly and adequately represented in Parliament. Those who were less starry-eyed about the effects of reform, still thought it essential because it would, as one of Lord Charlemont's correspondents put it, 'tranquillise the public mind', while withholding it 'weakens the attachment of the wise and the moderate'.[18]

Early in July Parliament was dissolved and elections to what was to be the last Irish Parliament took place shortly afterwards. Dr Haliday forecast that they would be 'the most peaceful and drowsy election' he had ever witnessed,[19] and he was right. To people living under what was little short of martial law, Parliament had lost whatever relevance it might once have had to their problems. The new Catholic voters, enfranchised in 1793, made virtually no impact because there were hardly any contested county elections. If there had been one in County Down, Castlereagh might well have had a rough passage. But Lord Downshire, unwilling to face the expense of another election like that of 1790, agreed not to force a contest. A brief courtesy visit to his constituents was all that was demanded of the sitting member seeking a new mandate.

By the autumn Ulster had been reduced to a state of sullen calm. The assizes were held as usual, and the congested gaols relieved of some of their inmates. Castlereagh attended the sessions at Downpatrick, providing the Attorney-General with evidence for the prosecution in some of the treasonable conspiracy cases. Haliday described these assizes as 'a tedious and sanguinary north-west circuit'.[20] Tedious they may have been, and sanguinary too, although by no means all the forty to fifty capital sentences were carried out, and some cases were dismissed for lack of evidence. On the whole the trials seem to have been carried out with a fairness and humanity that might easily have been lacking against such a disturbed and violent background.

By the end of 1797 Castlereagh had graduated from supporter to member of the Irish administration. In July he was appointed Keeper of His Majesty's Signet. It was only a sinecure post, worth £1500 a year, but he was obliged to surrender his Westminster seat and concentrate his energies and aspirations on Ireland. That had been precisely Camden's aim in offering his nephew the appointment. 'His ability and assiduity in Parliament', he explained to Portland, 'and his application to business out of it, render it very desirable for His Majesty's service in Ireland to attach a man of that description to this country, and to induce him to attend to its interests and to the business of the different departments of it.'[21]

In the autumn Camden found another way of initiating his nephew into the mysteries of government departments by making him a Lord of the Treasury without salary. Castlereagh took his new duties seriously, drawing up a statement of the country's income and expenditure for the next quarter for the benefit of Thomas Pelham, who had succeeded Hobart as Chief Secretary in 1795. He did not venture an opinion on the disagreement between the Viceroy and the Chancellor of the Exchequer on how best to raise money, but contented himself with the not very profound or helpful comment that 'The great object seems to be to get as much money as possible in a short time'.[22]

Finally, in October, Castlereagh was sworn in as a member of the Irish Privy Council. Before the end of the year he and Emily were established in her uncle, Thomas Conolly's, house in Merrion Street (now 5 Upper Merrion Street). They had usually stayed there in the past when Parliament was sitting, but the time had clearly come when they would need a more settled and independent establishment in Dublin. In fact, although Castlereagh could not have yet quite realised it, his comparatively carefree days with his militiamen were virtually over. For the rest of his career in Ireland he was to be at the centre of the storm, with all that implied in terms of worry, responsibility – and obloquy.

CHAPTER IV

'The sword is drawn'
1798

By early December 1797 General Bonaparte had finished dictating peace terms to the Austrians and was back in Paris ready to turn his attention to France's only remaining foe. He was made commander of the 'Army of England' and Wolfe Tone gave him several briefings on the possibility of invading Ireland. Bonaparte himself was non-committal, but promises of armed help were sent to Ireland by the French authorities, and were firmly believed by loyal and disloyal alike. Just before Christmas, a report reached Dublin Castle that Lord Edward Fitzgerald, a younger brother of the Duke of Leinster and the leading spirit among the extremists, had received orders from Paris to start a revolt as soon as possible. Neither the Castle authorities nor the Irish rebels were aware that by February 1798 Bonaparte had decided not to risk an invasion of the British Isles. Instead, he would strike at England through its Indian possessions.

It was against this background that Sir Ralph Abercromby, who had taken over as commander-in-chief in Ireland early in December, struggled to carry out what he conceived to be his duty. Abercromby was a distinguished and humane soldier, of independent character and liberal views. Earlier in his career he had served in Ireland for more than twenty years and the opinion he had then formed of the way Ireland was governed made him extremely reluctant to serve there again. Neither the system nor the people who ran it had, he found, improved during his absence. He was also appalled by the ruthless and indiscriminate way in which the delicate task of imposing law and order on a largely hostile population was being carried out. Camden in principle agreed with him. So did Pelham, who had travelled through the countryside and seen for himself what was going on. But Camden was weak and Pelham was ill, and the opposition to Abercromby's ideas was both vocal and powerful. The magistrates were clamouring for more military protection; most of the ruling clique – Clare, Foster, Beresford – were quite prepared to subdue the law-breakers by illegal means; and influential generals like Lake and Knox believed that only toughness amounting to terror could subdue the Irish.

At the end of February Abercromby's difficult situation got the better of him and he vented his frustration in his famous General Order which declared the army to be 'in a state of licentiousness which must render it formidable to everyone but the enemy', and demanded that the strictest discipline should be enforced.[1] To Sir Ralph, the Order was simply a matter of military discipline on which he was not obliged to consult the Castle. But when Camden and Pelham read it they immediately realised that if it became public it could have very unpleasant repercussions. They decided to do their best to hush it up.

Abercromby's time bomb ticked away quietly for about a fortnight and then suddenly blew up. Someone had sent a copy of his Order to London, it was published in the press and a shower of angry missives – from Pitt, from Portland, from various candid friends – descended on the unfortunate Camden. Pitt commented that such an indiscriminate censure of the whole Irish army was 'almost an invitation to a foreign enemy',[2] while Portland reported that the Irish gentry in London were convinced they could never set foot in Ireland again.[3] To make matters worse, the Order then appeared in a Dublin paper, reprinted from the London press. Outraged at the scathing references to their army, the ruling Protestant minority clamoured for Abercromby's dismissal. (He had already offered his resignation.) In the House of Commons there was talk of impeaching him, while in the Castle those who had always privately disapproved of Abercromby, began to intrigue openly against him. With extreme reluctance Camden eventually forwarded Abercromby's resignation to London, together with an urgent plea for a very good replacement. His plea was not heeded. The next commander-in-chief was General Lake, the exponent of terror, who had openly criticised his superior's orders and commented pityingly that he was 'quite in his dotage'.[4]

Abercromby had made his mistakes. He had concentrated too much on building up the country's defences against invasion and underestimated the danger from internal enemies. But he had not exaggerated the misbehaviour of the troops. He had, so it seemed, been blamed for trying to carry out the pacification of Ireland with humanity. His resignation was a victory for the hard-liners in the Castle, and an invitation to extremism for both sides.

By now Castlereagh had been brought by Camden into the inner circle at the Castle, and regimental duties at Dundalk were playing an ever smaller part in his life. He must have listened to Camden's agonisings over whether or not to arrest the rebel leaders even though the government lacked the sworn evidence to bring them to trial. The

'THE SWORD IS DRAWN' 1798

English Cabinet, remote from the fears and pressures of Ireland, had strongly discouraged such an unorthodox step. But towards the end of February, the Castle was put in touch with a new informer, a young Catholic silk merchant called Reynolds who had been taken up by Lord Edward Fitzgerald. He had risen to become a member of the Leinster Directory of the United Irishmen but, recoiling from the lengths to which his associates wanted to go, he decided to thwart their plans without, he hoped, endangering their lives. Through an intermediary he told the authorities the names of the Leinster Directory and revealed the existence (on paper, at least) of a vast secret army of nearly 280,000 men, which outnumbered the government forces by more than five to one and was spread fairly evenly throughout Leinster, Ulster and Munster.

At last it was possible to arrest and bring to trial all the principal leaders in the movement – and, it seemed, not a moment too soon. On March 12 the authorities struck. Acting on information provided by Reynolds, they raided the house of Oliver Bond, a woollen merchant, in Bridge Street, where the Leinster Directory was meeting. Twelve delegates were seized, together with their papers, and four other leaders were rounded up elsewhere in Dublin. But Lord Edward Fitzgerald, acting apparently on a tip-off from Reynolds, went into hiding instead of attending the meeting.*

At this time of acute crisis, Thomas Pelham, Camden's Chief Secretary, fell seriously ill. He was always in poor health in Dublin, and for nearly a year had been thinking of retiring altogether. Camden would have liked to replace him with Castlereagh, but he knew that in London his Irish birth would be considered an insuperable obstacle. On March 16, however, he wrote urgently to London for permission to appoint Castlereagh as temporary Chief Secretary. He knew, he wrote, that his nephew was an Irishman, 'but his other qualifications at this moment so completely counterbalance that objection that I trust I shall receive an immediate assent to this measure, as one indispensable to the present existence of my Administration'.[5] Neither Pitt nor the King (who had strong views on the matter) was prepared to ignore such a plea, and

---

*Lord Edward Fitzgerald, a warm-hearted, hot-headed, romantic revolutionary, was a great embarrassment to the government, because of his name, his popularity and his influential connections, who included Emily Castlereagh's uncle and aunt, Thomas and Lady Louisa Conolly. Two days after the arrests, Lady Louisa saw Castlereagh, who assured her that the government wished 'to do all they can for Lord Edward, who is so much loved, and as he can't be found, no harm can happen to him'. If Fitzgerald had chosen to flee abroad, the authorities would most probably have been relieved to see him go. (Hyde (1933), 206)

Camden was immediately told that Castlereagh 'though an Irishman' could be appointed as temporary Chief Secretary.[6]

That, however, was not the end of the opposition to the appointment. Castlereagh himself, as Camden had admitted to Portland, was very unwilling to undertake such a difficult office. His first reaction was to point out his inexperience and to suggest that the Under-Secretary in the military department, William Elliot, would be a better choice. But Elliot, who was nicknamed the Castle Spectre because he always looked so ill, protested that his health would not stand up to the work involved. So since there seemed to be no one else suitable, Castlereagh felt obliged to accept. 'I have ...', Camden assured Portland, 'a perfect confidence that his being a native of Ireland will neither sway his judgment nor his conduct.'[7]

Next day, March 30, 1798 the Lord Lieutenant at last nerved himself to take decisive action to deal with the crisis. Backed by a large gathering of the Irish Privy Council, he issued a Proclamation declaring Ireland to be in a state of rebellion and ordering the armed forces to suppress the revolt and disarm the rebels 'by the most summary and effectual measures'. It was the Castle's last desperate throw to prevent the rising, which was certainly being planned and would probably be backed by a French invasion. The papers seized at Bond's house had been disappointingly vague and unincriminating, but the reports flowing into the Castle from all over the south and centre of the country were increasingly alarming. Villages and houses were being raided for arms in broad daylight, magistrates assassinated and sentries attacked. Reports that the French were about to set out were being passed from cabin to cabin and it was widely believed that the hated tithes would never be paid again. The North seemed to be tranquil, but this, it was reported, was only because it was ready and waiting for the signal to rise.

Abercromby had not yet been replaced, and before he left Ireland on April 23 he set in train measures which he hoped would effectively but humanely snuff out the rebellion. He instructed each of his commanding officers to announce that if all the hidden arms in his district were not surrendered within ten days, he would billet his troops upon the local people and order them to live well at their hosts' expense. The aim of this collective threat was to frighten people into surrendering their arms with the minimum damage to the persons and property of individuals. It was, it might be thought, a surprising plan to emanate from Abercromby, since it depended so much on efficient and humane officers and well-disciplined troops. There were indeed some of these. Wellington's brother, Wellesley-Pole, for example, reported from Queen's County:

'THE SWORD IS DRAWN' 1798

'We reasoned, threatened, tried to bribe, beseeched, but all to no purpose', but a week of free quarters, during which the greatest care was taken to prevent indiscriminate plundering, produced amazing results as the peasants unearthed the muskets, pikes and pistols buried in their gardens, and good order was 'miraculously' restored.[8]

But officers like Wellesley-Pole, or General Sir John Moore in the South, seem to have been heavily outnumbered by ruthless men who let their troops loose as if they were a plague of locusts, turned a blind eye to murder and rape and burned houses indiscriminately. The more well-to-do, who had most to offer the marauding troops, tended to suffer more than the desperately poor peasants; they were also more likely to be loyal. The gentry, who suffered either directly or through the ruin of their tenants, complained bitterly to the government; and it was presumably primarily their complaints which made Castlereagh countermand the policy of free quarters, as indiscriminate and bad for military discipline, and tell General Lake to find other ways of enforcing the speedy surrender of arms.[9]

Lake did not find this difficult. He believed in getting results and did not bother too much how his troops got them. Half-hanging and burning 'pitch caps' were among the methods they used to extract information about hidden weapons, but their favourite method was merciless and indiscriminate flogging. 'Triangles' – wooden contraptions to which the victims were tied – were set up in the village streets and struck terror into innocent and guilty alike. Many did indeed have something to confess, but many others who were flogged into insensibility were innocent, the victims perhaps of private spite or revenge.

The methods used to disarm the countryside must have been known inside the Castle, but no instructions were sent to restrain, let alone stop, their use, as the policy of free quarters had been stopped. Property must be preserved at all costs, but the infliction of physical suffering could be tolerated in a good cause. Camden indeed was under continuous pressure to be more, not less, severe. If only, lamented a Castle official, John Lees, the Lord Lieutenant 'had a little of the devil in his disposition and that he would, as occasions arise, forget that law, or the semblance of law, exists among us'.[10] In the long run the brutalities of Lake's soldiers enormously increased the inherent instability of the regime because of the fund of implacable hatred they created. But at the time these dangerous consequences, if they were perceived at all, were brushed aside.

The rebellion had been checked, but it was not scotched. A new

Directory, in which two young barristers, John and Henry Sheares, were prominent, had been appointed, and early in May the authorities learned that Lord Edward Fitzgerald was still busy organising a huge rebel army from his various hiding places in Dublin. A few days later they had an extraordinary stroke of luck: a militia officer called Captain Armstrong was mistaken for a sympathiser and introduced to the Sheares brothers, who trustingly informed him of their plan to set off a general rising by a coup in Dublin itself without waiting for the French.

Armstrong's revelations were not quite so alarming as they sounded, since the rebel leaders were in fact divided and hesitant. But at last, on May 18, they decided to order an attack on the capital by the rebel armies in the four neighbouring counties – Dublin, Kildare, Meath and Wicklow. It was a desperate gamble and some of the Directory, including the Sheares brothers, refused to have anything to do with it. The rest agreed that the signal to rise should be on May 23, and Lord Edward arranged to leave the city and put himself at the head of the rebel forces.

But he never got away. The following day he was surprised and seized in the house of a leather merchant in the Liberties of Dublin. His capture deprived the rebels of his military talents, such as they were, but, what was much more important, of a charismatic leader with a great name, an aristocrat and a Protestant.* The Castle was jubilant, and all the more so when, on May 21, John and Henry Sheares were also rounded up. They had unsuspectingly kept in touch with Captain Armstrong and he – according to his own account – had reluctantly allowed himself to be persuaded by Lord Castlereagh that it was his duty to betray them in order to prevent widespread bloodshed. A draft proclamation in John Sheares's handwriting, found when the brothers were arrested and written, according to Lord Clare, 'in the genuine style of Marat and Robespierre',[11] left no doubt that the rebels' aim was to overthrow the government and kill or seize its members.

Camden, whose 'backwardness and timidity' continued to exasperate even the comparatively moderate John Beresford,[12] had been reluctant to let the Dublin yeomanry loose on the city. But now he could no longer resist the pressure not only of most of his own advisers but also of the city authorities. Extra troops were brought in to patrol the streets while the magistrates and yeomanry set out to search for arms.

*Lord Edward was wounded while resisting arrest. He was lodged in the best room in Newgate prison and attended by three of Dublin's most distinguished doctors. He died on June 4.

'THE SWORD IS DRAWN' 1798

Buildings were ransacked and burned, suspects were flogged, some of them on triangles in the Castle yard, and by these methods large quantities of arms were surrendered. Convinced that the Dublin plot had now been foiled as successfully as Lake had disarmed the countryside, Camden cheerfully reported to London that neither insurrection nor even tumult was now to be feared.[13]

The conspiracy inside Dublin had indeed been effectively broken up. But in the counties of Dublin, Meath and especially Kildare, bands of rebels, goaded to desperation by the successes, and brutalities, of Lake's soldiers, rose all the same. Within twenty-four hours they had fought fourteen engagements with loyalist troops, but in only two had they been victorious. It was not an auspicious beginning; but it was enough to set the whole south-east ablaze. On May 24 Camden reported to London: 'The sword is drawn. I have kept it within the scabbard as long as possible. It must not now be returned until this most alarming conspiracy is put down.'[14] That day the horribly mutilated bodies of three rebels, cut down by the Fifth Dragoons, were displayed on the pavement outside Castlereagh's office in Lower Castle Yard.

The events of the following month made an ineradicable impression on the history of Ireland. But at the time neither side had more than sporadic control over what happened. No co-ordinated strategic plan to overthrow the existing order materialised, because almost all those competent to attempt it were already behind bars. But once it had started, the revolt spread by a kind of spontaneous combustion, aided by a scattering of determined local leaders, and fanned by grossly inflated rumours of rebel successes or reports (not so inflated) of reprisals by loyalist troops. The authorities in Dublin Castle seldom had much idea of what was going on and consequently could do little to influence the course of events. Camden, preoccupied by the importance of not letting Dublin fall into rebel hands, refused to allow General Lake to leave the city until the arrival of reinforcements from England. In the meantime the local commanders were left to act, or fail to act, as the spirit moved them. Very few of them proved equal to their responsibilities.

At first Camden and his advisers were not unduly alarmed. The revolt on their own doorstep had ignominiously fizzled out, and they believed that further afield huge quantities of arms had been surrendered. Martial law was immediately proclaimed and was unanimously approved by the Irish House of Commons. Edward Cooke, the Civil

Under-Secretary, was not the only person to feel a sense of relief that the conspiracy had at last come into the open; if 200,000 men were sworn in a conspiracy, he asked, 'how could that conspiracy be cleared without a burst?'[15]

The difficulty was to control the forces released by the 'burst', and this was as true of the loyalist as of the insurgent forces. Most of the Protestant minority saw the rebellion not as an opportunity to give Ireland as a whole a better deal, but as a chance to screw the lid down more firmly on the Catholic majority. The MP who wanted martial law to be made retrospective, so that the rebels already in gaol could be tried and executed at once, might well have had his way if Castlereagh had not intervened with a plea to temper severity with mercy. And when, on May 28, General Sir Ralph Dundas let 3000 Kildare rebels, leaders and all, surrender on generous terms, his wise and humane attempt to restore popular confidence in the government was received with rage and ridicule in Dublin. Camden, as so often, seems to have wavered. He tried, unsuccessfully, to countermand Dundas's offer, but three days later Castlereagh reported to London that directions had been sent to the generals to avail themselves of the Kildare rebels' inclination to submit, provided they surrendered both their arms and their leaders.[16]

By that time, however, General Sir James Duff had effectively stifled the Kildare rebels' inclination to submit. Duff, who commanded at Limerick, had taken it upon himself to make a cross-country dash, with about 400 men, to County Kildare. Unfortunately he arrived on the Curragh just when another large body of rebels were negotiating their surrender with Dundas; through misunderstanding and mischance his ill-disciplined troops fell upon the rebels, many of them unarmed, and massacred between three and four hundred. For this involuntary exploit Duff received a vote of thanks from the House of Commons in Dublin where he was as widely praised as Dundas was reviled. It seemed, commented Camden sadly, that the loyal minority would scarcely be satisfied with anything short of the extirpation of the other three-quarters of the population.[17]

The failure of any reinforcements to arrive from England increased the loyalists' alarm and sense of isolation; they began to feel like a beleaguered garrison. And when the rebellion not only spread to the south-east, but seemed to be taking root there, even those least prone to panic, like Castlereagh and Cooke, began to be seriously alarmed. On May 26 Father John Murphy had raised the standard of revolt in County Wicklow, where reports from further north of loyalist atrocities and rebel successes had combined to goad the people into an uncontrollable

'THE SWORD IS DRAWN' 1798

state of fear and exhilaration. On the 28th Murphy captured Enniscorthy, and two days later Wexford town fell to the insurgents. Amidst wild and drunken rejoicing, the first Irish Republic was established, complete with a committee of public safety. On June 4 a column of troops under General Loftus, marching to the relief of Wexford, was ambushed near Ballymore; it was so badly mauled that Loftus had to withdraw northwards with the rest of his relief force. On June 13 Castlereagh confessed to Pelham that 'the rebellion in Wexford has disappointed all my speculations. I had not a conception that insurgents could remain together and act in such numbers.'[18]

By this time Camden was sending almost daily appeals to London for help. He and his advisers assumed – and they had good if mistaken grounds for their assumption – that a French invasion was imminent, and they believed it only needed the arrival of the French for the whole country to rise. Moreover, the Wexford rebels, reacting to the real and imagined outrages committed by equally fanatical Orangemen, fought not only with reckless determination but with a degree of religious fanaticism that had been absent further north. As Camden and his advisers were only too well aware, nothing could be more disastrous than a religious war, not least because it would put the loyalty of the government's largely Catholic troops and militia gravely at risk.

The rebels' drive to the west was blocked on June 5 when their attempt to capture the strategic town of New Ross, on the road to Waterford and the south-west, was defeated after a day-long battle of extreme ferocity. But apart from this hard-won victory the outlook was grim. Some of the Wexford rebels were reported to be marching northwards with the intention of seizing Arklow and then pressing on to the capital. Dublin itself had remained quiet but only, it was firmly believed, because it was 'kept in check and terror' (as Cooke put it) by a formidable force of 4000 very active yeomanry as well as its regular garrison.[19] A report had just been forwarded from London that Bonaparte and a large fleet had left Toulon on May 19 and their destination was believed (wrongly) to be Ireland. There was still no sign of the promised reinforcements from England, which had been delayed by a combination of mismanagement, inefficiency and a flat calm. Finally, on June 6 Castlereagh learnt that a rising in Ulster was imminent. Next day Antrim was attacked. Two days later Down rose, and according to Castlereagh's information the other northern counties were about to follow suit.

By this time his Majesty's ministers had decided to send another 5000 troops in addition to those already on their way. But when the first of the redcoats at last sailed into Dublin Bay on the evening of June 16, the crisis, which had seemed so ubiquitously threatening only a week before, had unexpectedly assumed more manageable proportions. The risings in Antrim and Down (where for a few days the rebels overran Mount Stewart) were swiftly, and humanely, dealt with by General Nugent, the northern commander, and the spark of revolt failed to ignite elsewhere in Ulster – perhaps because reports of the savagery and 'religious phrensy' of the Catholic rebels in Wexford had severely damped the revolutionary ardour of the Ulster Presbyterians. In the south-east the rebels' attempt to capture Arklow, the key town on the road to Dublin, was repulsed, and after this setback, the stuffing seemed to go out of the Wexford rebels; their leaders were divided about what to do next and demoralised by the unexpected silence from the rebel forces supposed to be operating further north. On June 21 General Lake defeated the main body of rebels at Vinegar Hill outside Enniscorthy. On the same day General Sir John Moore recaptured Wexford, too late to stop the massacre of nearly a hundred loyalist prisoners, but in time to prevent a general slaughter of the remaining prisoners. The insurgents never recovered from the disasters of that day, although it was many months before the country was restored to anything like tranquillity. After Vinegar Hill, even Lake was appalled by his troops' behaviour. Yet it was largely owing to the brutal methods of 'pacification' employed by his men that the surrender of the rest of the rebel armies was postponed until the end of July, and long after that bands of rebels, who had taken refuge in the Wicklow mountains, continued to terrorise the surrounding countryside.

Even the tardy arrival of the French failed to rekindle the embers of revolt. On August 22 General Humbert landed at Killala Bay on the Connaught coast with a thousand French troops, and announced that he had come to help the Irish to liberate themselves from English rule. He proclaimed an Irish Republic at Killala, routed the government forces at what came to be derisively nicknamed the 'races of Castlebar', gained control of most of County Mayo, and stung the British government into hastily dispatching large reinforcements to Ireland. Except, however, for two isolated outbreaks in Leinster, the country-wide insurrection, which the Irish exiles in Paris had led Humbert to expect, failed to materialise. So did the substantial reinforcements which should have followed him from France. Less than three weeks after setting foot in Ireland, Humbert was forced to surrender to the overwhelmingly superior forces mobilised to block his path to Dublin.

Comfortably established in the capital's best hotel, Humbert and his staff officers considered themselves well rid of a thoroughly unsatisfactory expedition. They had no use for a country where there was 'neither wine nor discipline', nor for allies who were 'only ragamuffins', living on 'roots, whiskey and lying'.[20] Meanwhile, in County Mayo those deluded 'ragamuffins' had met their reward at the hands of the forces of law and order. Their brief bout of insurrection had been marked by a restraint virtually unknown elsewhere, but that did not save their homes from burning, nor themselves and their families from sword and bullet. Rebels and loyalists alike fell victim to the uncontrollable, trigger-happy, marauding military, who, commented the local Protestant bishop bitterly, 'were incomparably superior to the Irish traitors in dexterity of stealing'.[21] The recapture of Killala turned out to be the last military engagement of the rebellion. As a punitive exercise by loyalist soldiers it was not untypical of what had gone before.

The day before the battle of Vinegar Hill Lord Cornwallis arrived in Dublin to take over from Camden and Lake as both commander-in-chief and Lord Lieutenant. Among the senior British generals, Cornwallis was considered second to none; his reputation had survived his surrender to the American colonists at Yorktown, and had since been greatly enhanced by his distinguished service as Governor-General in India. He was intelligent and humane, a skilful administrator as well as a brave soldier. Like Abercromby, he was totally out of sympathy with those on whom the Viceroy customarily leant for advice and support. Warned by Castlereagh that Camden had found the Irish 'cabinet' 'very inconvenient and embarrassing',[22] he ignored its members as much as he could. They had, he decided, demonstrated their total ignorance of the country. It was not, he firmly believed, the Catholics who were at the root of the rebellion, but the Jacobins with their 'deep-laid conspiracy to revolutionise Ireland on the principles of France'.[23] Before Cornwallis had been a fortnight in Dublin, the vindictive violence of the loyalists and the wanton ferocity of the militia and yeomanry – 'murder', he wrote, 'appears to be their favourite pastime'[24] – had driven him to confide to a friend that 'the life of a Lord Lieutenant of Ireland comes up to my idea of perfect misery'.[25]

The new Viceroy's disapproval of the Protestant notables who were supposed to be his closest advisers was thoroughly reciprocated. They had regarded his arrival with misgiving, and when they found he kept them at a distance, the men who had got rid of Fitzwilliam and dominated Camden felt that their worst forebodings were fulfilled. The rebellion, they believed, had conclusively demonstrated that the policy of gradual concessions to the Catholics followed in recent years was a recipe for disaster. They regarded the 'lower orders' of poor Catholic peasants almost as another (inferior) species – 'barbarous, ignorant and ferocious' was John Beresford's description[26] – and accepted their undying hostility to the English government as a fact of life. 'Fear alone', wrote Beresford, 'operates on my countrymen. The last ten days of Lord Camden laid them on their backs.'[27] And now Camden's successor, with his ill-judged policy of conciliation, seemed determined to set them on their feet again.

But Cornwallis at any rate had the strong support of his right-hand man, through whom all his political and administrative power was exercised. Castlereagh also felt that the rebellion was 'a Jacobinical conspiracy ... pursuing its object chiefly with Popish instruments', making use of the 'heated bigotry' of the ignorant Catholic peasants.[28] Once the revolt was militarily crushed, he believed, like Cornwallis, that what Ireland needed most was an end to violence and the creation of confidence between government and people. Although he should not have been surprised by it, he was dismayed by the blind fanaticism, exacerbated by fear, that he saw in many of those around him. He anxiously awaited the arrival of reinforcements not only for obvious military reasons; they would also, he felt, strengthen British influence and – as he cautiously explained to Mr Wickham of the Home Office – 'make it unnecessary for the Government to lend itself too much to a party in this country, highly exasperated by the religious persecution to which the Protestants in Wexford have been exposed'.[29] He was equally horrified by the behaviour of the loyalist troops (all the more so no doubt when he remembered that he himself had once been proud to be a militia officer), deploring their indiscipline, their thieving and their brutality.[30]

Cornwallis at once took steps to halt the sickening cycle of cruelty and counter-cruelty by troops and rebels alike. He put a stop to the practice of flogging and hanging suspected rebels without even the slightest pretence of a court martial or even a preliminary examination. He also decided to grant a general pardon. 'I propose', he told Portland on July 8, 'to exclude from security of life only those who have been guilty of cool and deliberate murder, and to leave the leaders liable to banishment...'[31]

It was a courageous proposal because so many rebels were still under arms. Castlereagh felt it was 'an absolute necessity' for precisely that reason. 'Although it may be necessary', he told Camden, 'to leave the principals in the Rebellion still liable to punishment, yet we must be cautious not to make them too desperate else we shall fail in

Emma, Lady Castlereagh
by Lawrence

Top Castlereagh's return from the Congress of Vienna
by C. Williams

Bottom The debates on the Corn Law in March 1815
by G. Cruikshank (*see* p. 229)

withdrawing the people from their influence – if they cannot hope to escape without being apprehended, and when taken if death is inevitable, there is no alternative but a desperate resistance ... it is therefore an obvious policy to tempt by as slight a punishment as the public safety will warrant the leaders to submit.' He added that 'banishment is as full a security to the state as a capital punishment, and it always has been the policy of the Crown to extend mercy in a certain degree to criminals pleading guilty and submitting to justice'.[32]

In Whitehall the proposed amnesty was greeted, if not with hostility at any rate with reserve, and the measure which Castlereagh finally submitted to the Irish House of Commons on July 17 was considerably less generous than Cornwallis had originally intended.* The most important group excluded from the amnesty were the eighty-two state prisoners arrested at Bond's house in March and in the subsequent round-up. For the authorities they posed an intractable problem since most informers refused to testify in open court and the sources of the intelligence about French support for the rebels could not be revealed. As defence counsel frequently complained, under Irish treason law the evidence of only one witness was sufficient to convict, but in most cases even that was not available.

There was, however, no lack of evidence to bring to trial the Sheares brothers and three other members of the Leinster Directory – John McCann, William Byrne and Oliver Bond. By July 24 all five had been convicted, three – John and Henry Sheares and McCann – had been executed, and the executions of Byrne and Bond were fixed for the two subsequent days. At this point, most of the remaining prisoners, uncertain how much was known of their activities and unnerved by the fate of their three companions, offered to reveal all they knew in return for the lives of all of them, including Byrne and Bond. At a meeting in the Castle early next morning to consider this offer, 'the leaning of Lord Castlereagh's mind', reported Elliot, 'was strongly for respiting Byrne, in order that the subject might be more fully considered ...'[33] But the two Chief Justices, although moderate men, emphatically disagreed, and in the end Byrne's execution was allowed to go ahead. Dismayed by this ruthlessness, the remaining prisoners hurriedly made their offer more specific, added the signatures of those who had previously refused, and

---

*So many difficulties were raised in England that the bill did not receive the royal assent until October 6, and the exceptions were so numerous that few who had played an active part in the rebellion benefited. They could, however, apply individually for a conditional pardon which was seldom refused. All the same, most of the 'inferior' rebels were covered by the bill. (Cornwallis, 11, p.359/60)

sent it back to the Castle. This time, after much discussion, the authorities decided to investigate the offer further and in the meantime to grant Bond a temporary reprieve.

Eventually, after several days of negotiations, the prisoners offered, in return for their lives, to reveal all they knew of the conspiracy, on condition that they were not asked to implicate anyone by name and were not banished to Botany Bay or any other penal settlement. Castlereagh accepted this proposal, retaining for the government discretion to keep any or all the prisoners in custody for the duration of the war.

This bargain created an uproar in the Irish Parliament and throughout Dublin. It was also thoroughly disliked by many of the prisoners who had accepted it. But to Castlereagh it was a most satisfactory outcome. It was the rebels' hostility to Britain and their plotting with the French which damned them most completely in his eyes, and he had been searching for some way of making this aspect of the revolt public without betraying the government's secret sources. The evidence of the leading prisoners – O'Connor, Emmet and McNevin – provided a solution, and the most incriminating parts were promptly published in the press. Unashamed of what they had done, and with nothing now to gain by denying it, they freely admitted that the United Irishmen had sought French military aid to carry out a revolution in Ireland, establish a republic and split away from England. All the prisoners' factual testimony about their activities and their dealings with the French could be corroborated by the secret intelligence already in the government's possession, and Castlereagh saw no reason to doubt it. What further justification did the government need for its efforts to stamp out disaffection and restore law and order?

Other parts of the prisoners' testimony were less acceptable. They insisted – and it would be hard to deny – that the unrest had been greatly increased, and the people finally goaded into premature revolt, by the deliberate terrorism practised by the army and many magistrates. More controversial was their claim that the United Irishmen had originally sought reform by peaceful means, and only when they had come to despair of this had they turned to revolution and a republic.* They exploded the theory, fashionable in Protestant circles in Dublin (but

---

*Wolfe Tone declared from the dock the following November that from his earliest youth he had always regarded the connection between Ireland and Great Britain as 'the curse of the Irish nation, and felt convinced that while it lasted, this country could never be free nor happy'. (Lecky.*Ireland*,V,76)

'THE SWORD IS DRAWN' 1798

denied by Cornwallis and Castlereagh), that the rebellion was a 'Popish plot'. What they were aiming at was the redress of the people's grievances – in particular, the abolition of tithes and a reduction in the rent of land. By comparison with these, Catholic emancipation was an irrelevance – in Emmet's phrase, it did not matter a feather.[34]

The state prisoners continued to plague the authorities for many months to come. When the Americans refused to let any of them set foot in the United States, Cornwallis decided to let most of them go to any neutral country in Europe on condition that they undertook not to move on to an enemy country. In March 1799 the fifteen, including O'Connor, Emmet and McNevin, who were excluded from this arrangement, were (to their great indignation) shipped off to Fort George in Scotland for the duration.

By the middle of 1802, shortly after the signing of the Treaty of Amiens, all the political prisoners had left Fort George and many were soon carving out satisfactory new careers for themselves in New York or France. On the whole they were a great deal more fortunate than hundreds of lesser men, who may well have been much less guilty, but ended up at Botany Bay, if they survived the voyage, or serving in the British army in the West Indies, where they probably died of yellow fever.*

Castlereagh's attitude towards the rank and file of United Irishmen prisoners was remarkably tolerant. 'Were it not', he told Wickham, 'that the loyal would be disgusted and indignant at their being at large in this kingdom, the greater part of them might be discharged on bail without much danger to the State.' As it was, however, it would be very desirable 'to get rid of them as speedily as possible, as it is difficult to confine them with the necessary precaution; and the expense of this regiment of

---

*It is very difficult to estimate the numbers of political prisoners. Replying to criticism that they had been too lenient, Castlereagh told Wickham in March 1799 that Cornwallis had dealt with nearly 400 courts martial sentences; of these 131 were death sentences and 81 were carried out. In addition 'numbers' had been tried by courts martial and their cases had never come before the Lord Lieutenant. According to a return of the Clerk of the Crown, 418 persons had been banished or transported by courts martial sentences. 'Great numbers' had also been convicted at the autumn assizes. Newenham, a contemporary writer on population, whom Lecky considers moderate and careful, reckoned that about 11,000 rebels and 1600 loyalist troops fell in the field; about 400 loyalists were massacred or murdered; and 2000 rebels exiled or hanged. Alexander Marsden reckoned in August 1798 that at least 20,000 had fallen. Other estimates were much higher. More than 300 prisoners were sent to serve in the Prussian king's army; according to one report they were sent to work in the mines for years. (see Pakenham, p.349, Lecky,V,103,105/6)

traitors exceeds fivefold that of the best regiment in the King's service'.³⁵

To Castlereagh and Cornwallis the political prisoners were only part of the greater problem of restoring peace and security to Ireland. And throughout the autumn of 1798 the twin dangers of foreign invasion and internal rebellion continued to threaten the country. At the end of September Napper Tandy, one of the Irish exiles living in France, put in a fleeting and inebriated appearance on the coast of Donegal. Next month another more formidable French invasion fleet, with Wolfe Tone and 3000 soldiers on board, appeared off Lough Swilly. It was intercepted by the Royal Navy and defeated after a hard-fought engagement. A month later Wolfe Tone cheated the hangman by taking his own life in a prison cell in Dublin.

After the failure of Tone's expedition (and Nelson's victory in the Battle of the Nile) the threat of foreign intervention in Ireland temporarily receded. So did the threat of an internal insurrection, although months later Castlereagh was still getting private intelligence that a revolutionary organisation remained in existence and had some control over the disaffected.³⁶ But large areas of the country remained in the grip of what Castlereagh described as 'a petty warfare, not less afflicting to the loyal inhabitants, though less formidable to the State' than open insurrection.³⁷ For this unsatisfactory state of affairs the loyalists blamed Cornwallis, who could not even try to see justice done without raising a furious hornets' nest of protest. In October he publicly rebuked the members of a court martial, headed by Lord Enniskillen, for having acquitted a yeoman named Wollaghan, who had deliberately killed a pardoned rebel. His rebuke caused a most tremendous outcry among the loyalists and their indignation spread to the English press. Even Camden, moderate but easily agitated, protested vigorously to Castlereagh at the Viceroy's action which, he claimed, would infinitely hurt the English interest in Ireland. It apparently did not occur to him to ask what kind of an English interest it was that would be so injured by the condemnation of a gross miscarriage of justice.

Castlereagh did not respond to Camden's complaint. There is indeed no doubt that he wholeheartedly supported Cornwallis's policy of conciliation. When he defended him in the Dublin Parliament against accusations of excessive leniency, mischief-making Irish Protestants in London put it about that he was really censuring his uncle Camden, who, because the end of his viceroyalty coincided with the success of Lake's ruthless measures to break the back of the revolt, had suddenly acquired a quite spurious reputation for toughness. Castlereagh wrote to Camden's sister, Lady Elizabeth Pratt, to explain that in fact he had argued that Cornwallis had been acting on his predecessor's principles but under different circumstances. 'The newspapers', he added, 'put such stuff and nonsense into our mouths that it is as easy to prove me an idiot as a false friend, but I know there is no man who heard me will impute to me the latter.'[38]

It was to be a characteristic of Castlereagh's political career that he frequently failed to make himself understood, even without the interposition of inaccurate press reports. In the case of the Irish rebellion, religious, political and nationalist passions were the real barriers. The Protestant loyalists deplored his refusal to share their fears or espouse their prejudices. The Irish nationalists, on the other hand, despised him for his devotion to the English connection, and hated him as the representative of Dublin Castle. That he himself deplored the excesses of the troops, which he was powerless to prevent, and always used his influence – in so far as he had any – in favour of moderation in the treatment of prisoners was usually unknown to them, and even when it was known, it made no difference. (Alexander Knox, for a time his private secretary, wrote of him when the rebellion was scarcely over. 'There is no bloodshed for which he does not grieve; and yet he has no tendency to injudicious mercy.'[39]) He was a symbol of all that the Irish nationalists were fighting against, and the fact that he was an Irishman made him a traitor as well as an oppressor. And as if that were not enough, he immediately went on to become organiser-in-chief of the self-destruction of the Irish Parliament. Small wonder that his name became one of the most hated in Irish history.

CHAPTER V

Union: the last resource
1798–99

Throughout the troubled summer and autumn of 1798 Castlereagh grappled with all the responsibilities of the Viceroy's right-hand man while remaining only a stop-gap occupant of the Chief Secretary's office. His future depended entirely on the health of Thomas Pelham. By the end of September Pelham had made up his mind to return to Dublin if he possibly could in time for the next session of Parliament, and he suggested that Castlereagh should be consoled by being made Chancellor of the Exchequer instead of Sir John Parnell who in his turn would be consoled with Castlereagh's sinecure of Keeper of the Signet and a peerage.

What Parnell, who although notoriously lazy had been Chancellor of the Exchequer for many years, thought of this proposal was never known because Castlereagh immediately turned it down. If the office had been vacant, he told Pelham, he would not have hesitated to accept it, but he would not turn Parnell out.[1] He took his own position so little for granted that he advised Cornwallis to be ready with his own arrangements for the Chief Secretaryship, since Pelham's return was still not quite certain, and requested 'that his having found me in the situation might not interfere in any degree with his decision'. Cornwallis replied 'with great kindness' that if it depended on him he would like Castlereagh to remain.[2]

As Castlereagh seems to have half-expected, Pelham's ill-health did again get the better of him and by the end of October he was doing his best to persuade the Home Secretary to replace him by Castlereagh. But Portland and King doubted the wisdom of putting an Irishman in charge of the office which supervised the Irish administration and controlled the viceregal patronage. It would, moreover, be a break with constitutional precedent, and this alone was enough to damn it in the King's eyes.

On the other hand, Castlereagh had acquitted himself well over the past six months, and there were obvious dangers in replacing him by someone new and inexperienced at such an unsettled time. Moreover, competition for the post was virtually nil. The only other candidate seriously mentioned that summer was Thomas Grenville, who dithered helplessly between his sense of duty and his 'utter aversion' to the post until his brothers, Lords Grenville and Buckingham, made up his mind for him by agreeing that it was 'in rank and estimation much below Tom's calibre'.[3]*

So the opposition to replacing Pelham by Castlereagh gradually crumbled; Pitt came out strongly in his favour while the Lord Lieutenant sang his praises in every letter home. Cornwallis agreed that the Chief Secretary should not usually be an Irishman, but as Lord Castlereagh 'is so very unlike an Irishman, I think he has a clear claim to an exception in his favour'.[4] On November 9 the new Chief Secretary went up to Mount Stewart to break the news of his appointment to his father.

The speed with which this young man had made his way to the top in Dublin Castle was bound to arouse jealousy; and inevitably (and to some extent correctly) some attributed his success more to his influential connections than to his own merits. To the remnants of Grattan's Opposition he was a renegade whose political ambitions had led him to jettison his liberal principles. On the other hand, he was suspect to the extreme Protestant politicians because he had identified himself so unequivocally with Cornwallis's 'system' of conciliation. Moreover, he conspicuously lacked the oratorical skills which Irish parliamentarians particularly esteemed, and he was too shy and reserved to shine at the long convivial dinner parties that were such an important feature of Dublin political life. Henry Alexander, MP for Londonderry, writing to Pelham at the end of September, commented that although 'every day and every way proves Lord Castlereagh a wiser man and even a more able man, there is a coldness of manner to the public, a limited intercourse ...' and, he added, if he himself felt like this, others felt it more strongly.[5] In short, Castlereagh lacked some of the basic skills of a political manager.

He never did acquire the easy bonhomie of the professional politician. Throughout his career, the reserve, the icy good manners, with which he confronted the world were held against him. But he got on very well with his colleagues, the men who worked closely and intimately with or for him, often under conditions of considerable pressure and strain. Alexander Knox described him as humane and

*But Lord Grenville, making a distinction more important to eighteenth- than twentieth-century minds, did concede that 'In point of real utility and scope for displaying the powers of his mind, God knows it [the post of Chief Secretary] is difficult, extensive and important enough for the talents of the greatest man this country ever saw'.

'good-natured beyond the usual standard of men'.[6] William Elliot, who seems to have been an exceptionally nice person, and was three years older than Castlereagh, became one of his closest friends. Edward Cooke was a very different proposition, and at the outset the chances of a harmonious relationship between him and his new chief could not be rated very high. Cooke was fifteen years older than Castlereagh, an Englishman who had spent twenty years working in the Castle in one capacity or another. He had entered Parliament in 1790 and was reckoned a hard-line Protestant. He was one of those whose dismissal Lord Fitzwilliam had considered an essential preliminary to reform in 1795. In character he was prickly and difficult. Cornwallis found him hard to get on with, but described him as a very clever fellow.[7]

'I am happy', wrote Cooke to the new Chief Secretary on November 9, 'your official notification arrived last night. Under all circumstances, I think your Lordship a bold man, and I hope you will be a successful one.' Then after some critical comments on Cornwallis, he added: 'You will, therefore, have much difficulty to encounter, and you have but little time.'[8] It was not a hostile letter – indeed, Cooke offered his services – but it was not very welcoming either. It did not suggest the beginning of a long and close working relationship. Cooke, in fact, became considerably more liberal under Castlereagh's influence. He also became devoted to him, and followed his fortunes until ill-health forced him to retire from the Foreign Office nearly twenty years later.

Castlereagh had no illusions about the difficulties that lay ahead. On October 4, he confessed to Camden: 'However I might prefer from feelings of ambition remaining in office, yet looking to the enterprise in which we are about to embark, it is a much less anxious task to assist than to lead.'[9] The enterprise he referred to was the British government's determination to try to settle the Irish problem, once and for all, by a legislative union between the two countries.

Over the past thirty years the idea of a union of the British and Irish Parliaments had become increasingly familiar to English politicians and Viceroys. From an English point of view the legislative independence won in principle by the Protestant minority in Ireland in 1782 was not a satisfactory settlement of Irish grievances for a number of reasons, and in particular because of the danger of a clash between the two Parliaments; it nearly happened in 1788 over the Regency question. On the other hand, having achieved Grattan's Parliament, Irish politicians were, naturally enough, vehemently opposed to being ruled from Westminster. In 1785, the Duke of Rutland, who was then Viceroy and himself favoured a union, declared that anyone who suggested it in

Ireland would be tarred and feathered.[10]

But the rebellion of 1798, the culmination of years of endemic unrest, convinced Pitt and his colleagues that something drastic had to be done about Ireland. So long as it remained so unsettled it would be wide open both to French revolutionary ideas and to French military attack – and the weather had seemed more of an obstacle to enemy invasion than the Royal Navy. Pitt was by now convinced that the group of bigoted, grasping Irish politicians who had forced the humane and moderate General Abercromby to resign were quite incapable of pacifying Ireland, and the old Opposition, led by Grattan, had placed itself beyond the pale by its association with the Whig Opposition in England. The only alternative seemed to be to make Westminster directly and openly responsible for Ireland. This, it was argued, would give the whole country better government, and if, as was planned, it included a commercial union, it would make Ireland more prosperous as well. It would also make it easier for the Protestant minority and the Catholic majority to live together on equal terms and without fear. The Protestants would acquire a solid buttress against the Catholic majority, while the Catholics, becoming only a small minority in the Imperial Parliament, could safely be given full political equality. To a well-meaning English statesman, who knew little and understood less about the Irish, it was a neat, logical solution. To most of the Irish who supported it, it was essentially a *pis aller*, a counsel of despair.

Cornwallis was in favour of a union but doubted whether it could be introduced in the immediate future. At present, he told Pitt, the country was too disturbed, but if they waited till it was pacified, the borough-owners would not want to sacrifice their property nor the politicians their lucrative jobs. What was needed, he added, was a time of neither too much danger nor too much security.[11] Castlereagh's attitude was equally realistic. He was convinced that the present system was irrational in principle and unworkable in practice and he could see no satisfactory alternative except in a union. To him, Ireland's dependence on England was a fact of life and he saw nothing in it either to be ashamed of or to resent. But many members of the Protestant Ascendancy had developed an exclusive national pride for the country they had taken over, and Castlereagh did not underestimate the obstacle this presented to a union. 'Whether', he wrote to Pelham, 'the pride or good sense of the country will triumph it is a little difficult to calculate...'[12]

Throughout the autumn of 1798 a draft for a union was being prepared in London in consultation with Lord Clare and other prominent members of the Irish administration. The position of the

Catholics had been the chief bone of contention, with Clare vehemently opposed to Pitt's wish to grant them political concessions. Cornwallis was dismayed when he heard that Pitt was giving way to Clare. 'I certainly wish', he wrote to Pitt, 'that England could now make a union with the Irish nation, instead of making it with a party in Ireland.'[13] A week later he sent William Elliot, who was strongly pro-Catholic, over to London to try to counter Clare's ultra-Protestant arguments. Elliot's efforts were only partly successful: no immediate concessions for the Catholics, but at least the Act of Union would not contain any clause permanently excluding them from full political equality.

In public, Castlereagh loyally supported the Viceroy's arguments for immediate emancipation, although privately he took a cooler view. 'The principle of incorporation is everything in my mind', he told Camden, 'and makes it more a matter of feeling than of substance, what decision is taken on the other.'[14] He meant, presumably, that once union was achieved, emancipation would inevitably follow. Some influential Catholics in Dublin were inclined to agree with him, especially as they were given to understand that something was soon going to be done to lift the burden of tithes and provide stipends for Catholic priests.

The English Cabinet's draft plan for a union reached Dublin Castle on November 16, 1798. That a union was being planned had become public knowledge weeks, even months, earlier in the worst possible way – through rumour and hearsay and without any official backing or explanation. 'The question', wrote Castlereagh, 'is very little understood; of course, much feared.'[15] He set to work to remedy this ignorance in personal interviews, letters, pamphlets and through the press. The government's chief literary advocate was Edward Cooke, whose 56-page, ostensibly anonymous, pamphlet was being distributed by the end of November.

The Castle's general impression was that the initial reception of the union might have been worse. Most of the big borough-owners seemed to be in favour, or at least prepared to consider the plan on its merits, while the Catholic leaders, although disappointed that they were not to get full equality at once, seemed ready to accept union as a step towards their own emancipation. The Dublin Bar was violently hostile; '... yet the ground is so strong', wrote Castlereagh, 'that it is impossible we should not succeed, if the bar is not lost to every principle of decorum as well as good sense'.[16] His own conviction was so strong that he could not realise that to Dublin's lawyers there could be neither good sense nor decorum in a measure which, by demoting Dublin to the status of a provincial capital, not only affronted their patriotic feelings, but

UNION: THE LAST RESOURCE 1798 – 99

drastically reduced their opportunities for professional and political advancement.

But perhaps the chief stumbling block was the opposition inside the Irish administration. The Speaker, John Foster, and the Chancellor of the Exchequer, Sir John Parnell, had stayed behind in London and stubbornly resisted all Pitt's arguments and blandishments. Discouraged by this opposition, the English ministers hesitated, and sent an urgent appeal to Castlereagh to come over for consultations. He arrived in London in the middle of December and for the next week was busy discussing the details of the union plan with the Cabinet. It was the English ministers' first opportunity to take the measure of the new Chief Secretary, and they liked what they saw. Portland praised his 'perspicacity' over the details of the union,[17] while Grenville, who had previously thought him too much of a lightweight for the job, told his critical brother Buckingham that he was better satisfied than he had expected to be with Castlereagh's manner of doing business which he found both 'ready and clear'; and, he added, 'he seems to me to have the success of this measure most thoroughly at heart'.[18]

At last, on December 21, the Cabinet decided to ignore the opposition to the union and press ahead with it as soon as possible. How much influence, if any, Castlereagh had on this decision it is impossible to say. He did not hide the fact that he was strongly in favour of the measure, but then so were Pitt and most of his colleagues. He did not, however, try to persuade Pitt that the union could be carried on what they both believed to be its merits. With a realism that would appal an Irish nationalist, he gave it as his opinion that the measure could be safely and successfully carried out provided the British government showed itself to be sufficiently determined, and provided an adequate force of English troops was kept in the island.[19]

Before he returned to Dublin, Castlereagh joined the handful of Irishmen who were members of the English Privy Council. It was an unusual distinction for a young man – and an Irishman – not yet thirty. But it was probably not so much a tribute to Castlereagh personally as an acknowledgment that in the task ahead he would need all the prestige and backing the English government could give him.

The prospects for union had not improved during Castlereagh's absence in London. The propaganda battle was going badly for the government. Cooke's pamphlet was considered to be full of inconsistencies and more likely to displease all parties than satisfy any. It provoked a furious flood of anti-union pamphlets which appeared to have nearly swamped those in favour. Castlereagh sent off an urgent request to London for £5000 in bank-notes to persuade impecunious young barristers to write pro-union articles for the newspapers.[20] The money was sent by return, but whether it was laid out to much advantage may be doubted. In Dublin, meetings of barristers, merchants and bankers all passed anti-union resolutions, and the leading Catholics retreated from their initially favourable attitude into a suspicious neutrality. On January 2, 1799, Castlereagh described the 'inflammation' in Dublin as extreme, but as yet confined to 'the middling and higher classes'. The 'lower orders', he added, were naturally indifferent to the question, but could be easily set in motion by the anti-unionists.[21]

In parts of the countryside outside Dublin the lower orders already seemed disturbed, with nocturnal meetings and more than the usual crop of robberies and murders. But it was not clear whether this was due to the union (Cornwallis thought not), or renewed expectations of a foreign invasion. The government in fact had only the haziest idea of the state of public opinion outside the capital. It was believed that the Catholic south and west would support the union, for both religious and commercial reasons, and the pro-union resolutions passed by the common council of Cork early in January gave encouraging backing to this view. Belfast and Londonderry, like Cork, reckoned they would prosper if Ireland was given commercial equality with Britain; so did the increasingly important linen manufacturers of Ulster. The Presbyterian republicans had been shocked out of much of their revolutionary ardour by the excesses of the Wexford rebels, and they were not likely to shed many tears over the Dublin Parliament which they had always condemned as incurably corrupt. In mid-January 1799 Castlereagh reckoned that opinion in the North was divided 'and acquiescence is perhaps as much as we can expect'.[22]

But for a step so momentous as a union something more positive than public acquiescence was desirable, even though the government had a built-in majority in the Irish Parliament and plenty of English troops to overawe the 'lower orders'. 'If it should unfortunately appear', wrote Sir George Shee, a pro-unionist, 'that the enemy has gained possession of all the vantage ground in the cities and counties in general, I fear a vote of the House of Commons passed by a small majority (which I hear is all that can be expected) will not be considered as expressing the sense of the people, and that instead of proving the symbol of concord it may prove to be the signal of battle.'[23]

Even a small majority could not be guaranteed. The members of the Irish House of Commons had always been capable of throwing over the traces if persuaded by a Grattan or a sufficiently emotive issue – and it is hard to imagine a more emotive issue than self-extinction. 'Your Grace will easily understand', wrote Castlereagh to Portland, 'that the measure cannot be expected to be *peculiarly grateful* to the members of either House of Parliament.'²⁴* Two-thirds of the Commons would lose their seat, with all the political, social and pecuniary advantages that went with it, while the borough-owners would lose a valuable piece of property and a source of political prestige and influence. Small wonder that MPs made use of the public outcry against the union as an excuse for opposing it themselves, or dropped heavy hints about some little favour they would like from government.

Neither the Lord Lieutenant nor his Chief Secretary were – to use Beresford's phrase – 'well-adapted for the purpose' of collecting parliamentary majorities.²⁵ Lord Cornwallis 'is rather inattentive to parliamentary management', lamented Castlereagh in a letter to Elliot in November, 'and ... he is disposed to underrate the embarrassment which may arise in a popular assembly'.²⁶ In the new year, however, urged on by his Chief Secretary and his own conviction of the importance of the measure, Cornwallis began to step up his efforts to collect support. But he detested his task, he loathed the way in which even government supporters tried to strike a bargain for their vote, and he often found it difficult to keep his temper.²⁷ One suspects that sometimes he did not completely succeed. Castlereagh, on the other hand, might have done better if he had not kept his temper so well. His cool reserve, his lack of bonhomie, alienated even those who agreed with him. One of Pelham's correspondents in Dublin, who feared that not enough was being done to make the union popular, wrote: 'If I had any acquaintance with Lord Castlereagh, I should certainly suggest some hints to him on the present occasion – but I am told he is cold and distant and might possibly think me officious and obtrusive.'²⁸

A fortnight before Parliament was due to meet, Castlereagh sent a circular letter to all MPs informing them that business of the greatest importance was to be submitted to Parliament on the opening day and politely hoping that he would have an opportunity to explain it to them beforehand.²⁹ This was an innovation and may well have been counter-productive. No one was fooled by the tactful omission of the name of the measure. Sir John Blackwood told Castlereagh he would not make up his mind until he had heard the debates and consulted the constitutional authorities, and in the meantime he strongly resented the Lord

*In fact the House of Lords, which was completely dominated by Lord Clare, gave no serious difficulty apart from a determined protest against allowing the King to retain the right to create Irish peers.

Lieutenant's attempt to summon him 'in the style as to one of the vassals of Administration'.[30] The Duke of Leinster roundly declared that as he had already made up his mind to oppose the union, he could see no necessity to attend Parliament until the measure was laid before it.[31] Many county members, who did not have the pronounced opposition leanings of Leinster or Blackwood, still cherished their independence and were bound to resent this transparent attempt to commit them in advance.

Those who had in theory surrendered their independence for a government place also showed much repugnance to the union. Castlereagh complained that the government 'was rather thwarted than supported by some of its leading departments', in particular the Treasury and the Revenue Board.[32] The recognised punishment for such insubordination was dismissal, and on January 15 Cornwallis deprived Sir John Parnell of the Chancellorship of the Exchequer after Parnell had refused to abandon his opposition to union. Cornwallis told Portland that he would mete out the same treatment 'without favour or partiality' whenever he thought it would promote the success of the measure.[33] But in spite of these brave words he wielded the axe with extreme caution, even timidity. Only one other senior member of the government, the Prime Serjeant, James Fitzgerald, was dismissed at this time.

Over George Knox, a Commissioner of Revenue who opposed the union, the Castle was in a dilemma because he was connected with Lord Abercorn, who controlled seven seats in the Commons and had declared that he would withdraw his own support for union if Knox was dismissed. But just before Parliament met Castlereagh reported with relief that 'George Knox has released us from all embarrassment by resigning his office'.[34] The Inspector-General of Imports and Exports, John Claudius Beresford (the son of John Beresford), was another source of embarrassment. He had shown great public hostility to the measure, and his dismissal would be a desirable sign of the government's determination; 'on the other hand', as Cornwallis explained to Portland, 'as we profess to encourage discussion, and neither to precipitate Parliament or the country on the decision, much less to force it against the public sentiment, there seemed an objection to a very early exercise of ministerial authority on the inferior servants of the Crown'.[35] Fortunately, Beresford, like Knox, tactfully decided to resign.

The most important opponent of the union, John Foster, could not be dismissed from the Speakership. His return from London had been – 'very fortunately', in Castlereagh's opinion[36] – delayed at Holyhead, but when he did get back to Dublin he left no one in any doubt that his opposition to the union was quite unchanged by the arguments of the English ministers.

Even more worrying was the wavering, or downright hostility, of some of the important borough-owners on whose support the government relied to swing the Commons in favour of union. Chief among the waverers were the second Marquess of Downshire, Castlereagh's rival on the hustings in 1790, and Lord Ely, a notoriously shifty nobleman who, like Downshire, was given the full treatment by Pitt when in London but still refused to commit himself. When it was rumoured in Dublin that Ely had made up his mind to oppose, Cornwallis gloomily pointed out to Portland the consequences of 'this important defection'. 'It not only transfers 18 votes in the Commons to the Opposition, but strikes a damp among the supporters of the measure, which may operate in a fatal extent against us.'[37] The 'domino theory' operated powerfully among Irish politicians.

When the union was first seriously mooted it appears that Ely had supported it in the hope of thereby securing a step in the peerage. Other borough-owners had similar hopes. But the Viceroy and his Chief Secretary were even more reluctant to resort to bribery through the distribution of honours or places than they were to dismissal. Cornwallis detested the whole business of patronage, and Castlereagh also found it distasteful. In November he told Elliot that he hoped to avoid 'the politics of John Lees's shop' by inducing the Viceroy to use his personal powers of persuasion on recalcitrant politicians. (John Lees was an official in the Post Office who had advised previous Viceroys on patronage matters.[38]) It was in fact impossible in that political milieu to spurn the use of patronage altogether. But Plunket's accusation of a 'system of black corruption', and Barrington's allegation that Castlereagh had used 'corrupt and unconstitutional means' to obtain votes, have not been sustained by historical research. Nationalist historians have always made much of Barrington's accusation that peerages were sold for votes, but the modern historian of the union could find, during the winter of 1798-99, 'definite evidence for the promise of two peerages, and circumstantial details suggesting the offer of two others; and this is all'.[39]* In any case, since Castlereagh felt confident of victory,

*Barrington, the nationalist historian, claims that one MP, Frederick Trench, changed sides during the debate of January 22/23, after Cooke had bribed him with the offer of a peerage. But Bolton points out that the *Anti-Union* attributes Trench's conversion to another MP, Richard Archdall, and does not mention any peerage, that Cornwallis called Trench 'honourable and disinterested', and that Trench was not among the main body of union peers, but was promoted later. (Bolton, p.169) in spite of so many signs to the contrary, there was no need to buy votes on a large scale.

When the Irish Parliament met on January 22, 1799, the Opposition immediately moved an amendment to the Address maintaining 'the undoubted birthright of the people of Ireland to have a resident and independent legislature'. This precipitated a sixteen-hour debate which was carried on with a turbulence and clamour that surprised and shocked those who witnessed it. Castlereagh afterwards compared the scene to a fox hunt,[40] and John Beresford to a Polish diet. 'I never was witness to such a scene', wrote Beresford indignantly. '... Direct treason spoken, resistance to the law declared, encouraged, and recommended.'[41] The Opposition speakers included all the oratorical talent in a Chamber famous for the brilliance of its oratory, and the case they had to present lent itself to the emotional rhetoric in which they excelled. Men who were accustomed to boast of their loyalty to the British Crown, and who six months earlier had been enthusiastically hunting down fellow countrymen fighting for independence from British rule, now posed as Irish patriots ready to protect the constitution and liberties of their native land with the last drop of their blood.

Against the fervent diatribes of a Plunket, Barrington or Ponsonby the government had only the most inadequate defences. Moreover, few of its troops had any stomach for the fight. Only two speakers gave Castlereagh really effective support. He himself, rising to his feet well after midnight, made a good speech, but his cool, realistic assessment of Ireland's military, economic and financial dependence on England was not likely to win support or sympathy from an audience indulging in an orgy of patriotic fervour. He was followed by William Plunket, then a rising young barrister, who for two hours held the House spellbound with a display of verbal fireworks in which a bitter condemnation of the measure was combined with a scathing personal attack on the minister. Not content with several contemptuous references to Castlereagh's youth, Plunket went on to describe him as 'a green and sapless twig' – which, as everyone, including Emily sitting in the gallery, must have realised, was a reference to the Castlereaghs' childlessness.[42]

Castlereagh's self-control was equal to the trials and taunts of that night. So, more surprisingly, was his optimism. As he walked into the division lobby at 1.30 on the afternoon of the 23rd, he was observed to clap a friend on the shoulder and tell him the division would be carried by 45 votes.[43] When the votes were counted, it was found that 105 members had voted for Ponsonby's amendment, and 106 against. A second division, on a motion for agreeing to the original Address, was carried by 107 votes to 105. In that Parliament, to carry the Address by such a tiny majority was tantamount to a thumping defeat.

Ponsonby immediately asked the Chief Secretary whether he intended to bring the measure forward again during that session. Castlereagh, after a slight hesitation, agreed that he would not press it while the House was so hostile, but he added that he was so convinced of the wisdom of the measure that 'whenever the House and the nation appeared to understand its merits, he should think it his duty to bring it forward'.[44]

That night Dublin was illuminated in honour of the Opposition's victory and the Dublin mob took to the streets. They applauded the Speaker, who had carried out his duties with gross partiality, by dragging him home in his coach, and they stoned all windows that were not lit up, among them those of the Lord Chancellor, Lord Clare, who ordered his servants to fire on his attackers, and hoped afterwards that some had been winged. A menacing crowd assembled near Castlereagh's house, but were dispersed by troops and heavy rain.

The following day, the 24th, battle was again joined in the Commons. Sir Lawrence Parsons moved to delete the paragraph in the Address which in effect pledged Parliament to consider a proposal for a union. The debate which followed was described as 'acrimonious and violent'.[45] For once Castlereagh's customary composure deserted him and he vehemently attacked the Opposition as 'a desperate faction composed of men who agree in no one measure of public good'. Castlereagh's furious denunciation of the Opposition's tactics and language was said to have raised the spirits of government supporters, but it did not save the day. The rowdy debate continued all night, and when at last, at 6.30 the following morning, the House divided on Parsons's motion, the government found itself defeated by five votes. It was more than ten years since it had suffered such a humiliation. That night Dublin was again illuminated and the mob again roamed the streets.

The outcome of the two debates was a sobering revelation to Castlereagh of how much he still had to learn about the ways of politicians. Yet the much more experienced Cooke was equally wrong. So was Lord Clare, who had believed the government would have a majority of at least thirty. The Castle had had some bad luck; on the second night, four of its supporters were too ill to attend and one changed sides, while three Opposition supporters arrived in town just in time to vote. The government was also let down by a number of borough-owners. But the chief cause of the disaster, as Castlereagh admitted, was the opposition of the independent country gentlemen.[46] The warmth and energy with which they opposed a union took him by surprise. It also encouraged waverers to join what seemed the winning side. One member commented afterwards that he had never seen a debate in which so many votes were decided by the eloquence of the speakers.[47]

But in neither Dublin nor London was there any question of giving up the struggle. The British government, Portland privately assured Cornwallis, would *never* abandon union and he must make sure this was clearly understood in Ireland.[48] Cornwallis promised to do his best, but took his usual gloomy view of the outcome. Castlereagh, on the other hand, believed that most of the opponents of the union would be willing to change their minds if they understood the measure better, and if they felt it could be reconciled with their personal interests.[49]

CHAPTER VI

The union carried
1799–1801

'I am *truly sorry*', wrote Castlereagh to Portland after the first union debate.[1] To his chagrin, he had found himself unable to manage the uncharacteristically turbulent Commons and he was suitably apologetic. But he was gaining experience all the time and, according to Cooke, had made great progress as a speaker. 'He does not show quite that attention to everyone, which the vanity and folly of the Irish world expects, and as the Lord Lieutenant shows no attention at all, the consequence is unfavourable. I should not hint this but for my attachment to him, for he is a very honourable and very able man; and the circumstance of his being an Irishman of noble family and great property is of the utmost consequence.'[2] In other words, he was better fitted than an Englishman to persuade a majority of the Irish Parliament to vote themselves out of existence.

To this task – the most controversial of his career – Castlereagh devoted himself for the rest of 1799. He worked against a continuously threatening background of domestic unrest and fears of foreign invasion. How much of the unrest was due to the remaining United Irishmen was of course unclear, but the authorities received enough secret information (true or false) to convince them that although the rebels' organisation had been greatly damaged, they would still be able to mount a formidable insurrection if the French should succeed in landing in Ireland. Some of the critics of the union argued that the various dangers threatening the country were additional reasons for not embarking on such a far-reaching constitutional experiment. But to Castlereagh they only made the union seem more necessary, since he could see no other way out of Ireland's troubles.

The main practical difficulty of a legislative union was that there were 300 members of the Irish House of Commons and the English Cabinet adamantly refused to accept more than a hundred Irish members at Westminster. How were 300 seats, each one a source of wealth, influence and prestige, to be reduced by two-thirds? In January 1799 the original proposals for Irish representation at Westminster never got as far as being presented to the Dublin Parliament. But they were of course no secret, and the fact that both the county members and the borough-owners had reason to feel aggrieved by them presumably influenced the voting.* Castlereagh was firmly convinced that if the 'private interests' of members and their patrons were treated more tenderly, the opposition would largely disappear. Within a week of the government's defeat, he had sent Portland revised proposals designed to conciliate the two most important groups opposing the union. He suggested that the thirty-two counties should be given back their second seats, and that the owners of the eighty-six 'close' boroughs – 'which are strictly speaking property' – should be given pecuniary compensation for the value that their boroughs would lose by being grouped in twos, or perhaps in threes.[3]

On the whole, these proposals were well received in London. But if sixty-four seats were allotted to the counties, how were the remaining thirty-six seats to be divided among 108 boroughs? Castlereagh's first solution was to give one seat to each of the thirty-two 'open' boroughs and disfranchise completely the eighty-six 'close' boroughs, paying compensation to their proprietors. Fifteen years earlier, before the French Revolution had created an almost hysterical fear of tampering with the constitution, Pitt had proposed a similar plan to get rid of the English rotten boroughs. But by now Pitt had turned his back on any constitutional change, and Castlereagh's plan was rejected because of the handle it would give to parliamentary reformers.

A solution seems to have been reached during Castlereagh's lengthy visit to London that autumn. The English government agreed that the thirty-one largest boroughs (in addition to Dublin, Cork and Dublin University) should return one member and the remainder be disfranchised completely, in return for monetary compensation set at £15,000 per borough. This arrangement made no invidious distinctions between the electoral practices of the boroughs and took advantage of the accepted political convention that a borough seat was a marketable commodity. It was also practicable. But Castlereagh admitted that there was 'much and deep objection' to buying out borough-owners.[4] Most politicians, whether or not they were in favour of parliamentary reform, felt it was distasteful to recognise too blatantly that a man's influence over other men – or the right to represent other people – could be

*These proposals gave one member, instead of two, to each of the thirty-two counties; two each to Dublin and Cork; one each to eight other large towns; and one to each of the remaining 108 boroughs, which were to send their members to alternate parliaments through a system of pairing. The value of a seat would of course be lessened if it no longer sent a member to every parliament.

bought and sold for hard cash. Yet after the union had been passed, every one of the anti-union borough-owners swallowed his objections sufficiently to apply for the compensation to which he was entitled. The most influential opponent, Lord Downshire, received the most compensation – £52,000.

To get the union through Parliament, however, Castlereagh could not avoid 'the politics of John Lees's shop'. 'Those', he wrote, 'who thrive by the game of Parliament are in general in their hearts against it, and unless connected with their own aggrandisement in some shape, will either oppose it, or give it but a languid support which encourages opposition in others.'[5] For many the most desirable form of aggrandisement was an honour, either a peerage or a step in the peerage. It was the traditional reward for political services, its use checked only by the King's reluctance to let his ministers debase the honours currency too far. To carry the union, however, Portland gave Cornwallis virtually a free hand to grant whatever honours were necessary. Sixteen new baronies and fifteen promotions in the peerage were a fairly lavish use of this authority, but not excessive by contemporary standards.[6] The most important beneficiary was the slippery Earl of Ely, who in return for ensuring that all the ten seats he controlled were occupied by unionists repeatedly demanded a marquessate. His persistence was eventually rewarded.*

Other more concrete ways of building up a unionist majority were provided by the judicious disposal of government patronage, ranging from a commission, curacy, pension or minor office for a member's relative or protégé, to a lucrative sinecure, an important legal appointment or an influential administrative appointment in Dublin Castle for the member himself. Office-holders who had opposed the union were dismissed and their places used to gain support. Some members who were neutral or hostile agreed to vacate their seats in favour of unionists in return for monetary compensation, which was sometimes provided by the government out of public funds and sometimes by a borough-owner who had some reason for ingratiating himself with the authorities.

*Most honours were given to borough-owners for filling the seats they controlled with unionists. A member who owed his seat to a borough-owner felt an obligation to vote as his patron wished, and was therefore amenable to pressure to resign if he did not. The Irish equivalent of the Chiltern Hundreds were the escheatorships of the four provinces. In May 1799 Castlereagh was strongly attacked in the Commons for refusing an escheatorship to two anti-unionists. He did not give way, but after Portland had privately advised Cornwallis that there seemed no constitutional precedent for refusing escheatorships, they were always granted.

'The political jobbing of this country gets the better of me', complained Cornwallis. '... How I long to kick those whom my public duty obliges me to court.'[7] The Viceroy's private lamentations were matched in public by the anti-unionists' denunciations of corruption, and these have been echoed by nationalist historians ever since, although modern research tends to the view that the amount of corruption used to carry the union has been exaggerated.[8] Most Irish politicians who supported the administration expected as a matter of course that their loyalty would be rewarded. It may not have been quite so well established that an office-holder who went into opposition automatically forfeited his place, but it was a logical development of an established practice. It certainly did smack of bribery to pay a member to vacate his seat; on the other hand, borough seats had a recognised market value and Opposition members, even Grattan, were prepared if necessary to buy their seats.

Whether votes were ever actually bought for cash is uncertain.* Castlereagh certainly sent several urgent, even agonised, appeals for money to the Home Office in London. But this would have been needed to pay the members who had agreed to vacate their seats, to finance the government's considerable propaganda campaign, and probably to compensate cotton and wool manufacturers likely to suffer from the reduction in duties. Cornwallis would certainly not have approved of any direct bribery. But the Castle undoubtedly exploited up to the hilt the traditional methods by which Ireland was governed. Most Irish politicians had supported the system because it was in their interest to do so. They denounced it when it was made use of to destroy their independent political life. And even then a good many still could not resist the opportunity to feather their own nests while the going was still good. Of course not all the unionist votes were cast from selfish motives; there were patriots on both sides. Some unionists were impressed by the economic arguments – the hope of increased trade and an inflow of English capital – while others were reluctantly convinced that Ireland was ungovernable in any other way. Castlereagh was forced to involve himself so deeply in exploiting the corrupt and selfish motives of some that he may have tended to overlook the completely respectable motives of others. At any rate, if he is to be believed, the part played by political jobbery and the distribution of honours was crucial. 'You can easily imagine', he wrote to Lord Camden in the middle of July, 'the

---

*There appears to be no contemporary evidence for O'Connell's claim, made in 1834, that Castlereagh paid £8000 for a vote.

complicated negotiations of private objects we are at present incessantly engaged in – every individual is now playing his game as if it was his last stake, and it is most difficult to meet their expectations in any degree, keeping within the possibility of accomplishment – you must be prepared for having the favours and patronage of the Crown most deeply engaged to the actors in this contest. I wish much to see Mr Pitt on this subject and to know distinctly what his ideas are – what lengths he is prepared to go to carry this measure.' Although he was sure that the measure would eventually be carried 'by its own intrinsic merits', he assured his uncle that it would be delayed by 'an endeavour to economize the favours of the Crown', and he again warned that 'Mr Pitt, if he feels the union indispensable to the Empire and his Government, must be prepared to make great sacrifices ...'[9]

By now Castlereagh was deeply committed to using the system to destroy the system. 'Nothing', he wrote, 'but the utmost effort to meet private interest can enable us to buy up the fee simple of Irish corruption which is considered by so many as their means of getting forward and which they all look to as materially terminated by a Union.'[10] In fact the lengths to which Castlereagh pushed accepted political practices was bribery in all but name, and when in May 1802 John Foster directly accused him of buying votes to pass the union, Castlereagh did not reply. Nor did he on subsequent occasions when the charge was repeated, and for many years the methods he had used were a millstone round his neck.

One of the arguments most frequently used by Opposition speakers in January 1799 had been the public hostility or indifference to the union, and this argument was by no means merely a specious excuse for opposition. Most county members, and a few borough ones as well, did feel obliged to pay attention to the wishes of their constituents, by which was usually meant the local gentry, who in most cases could control the votes of their tenants. In the union contest both sides realised the crucial importance of winning over local opinion and getting it openly expressed – by petition, county meeting or grand jury – in the way most likely to impress MPs. 'I assure you', wrote Castlereagh to Camden, 'we have paid so dear for our converts hitherto that unless our public opinion will exert itself more strongly in our favour than it has yet done, the means of Government will not enable us to meet the difficulties we have to overcome.'[11]

In each constituency attitudes to the union were influenced by local political interests and animosities and swayed by calculations of the likely economic advantages – or disadvantages – of a union to the locality. The authorities in Dublin Castle could seldom offer much more than advice and encouragement to their supporters, but these were liberally forthcoming. So were supplies of pamphlets, speeches and other unionist literature. County meetings were regarded with some suspicion since they provided a platform for opponents as well as supporters and were liable to get out of hand. But they did provide anti-unionist county members with an excuse to change their minds. At a county meeting at Loughrea in Galway, for example, the question was argued for six hours to the accompaniment of a noisy mob and some window-breaking, but eventually, reported Castlereagh, the meeting 'terminated perfectly to our satisfaction' with a pro-unionist Address and instructions to the county members being carried by considerable majorities. 'This success', wrote Castlereagh triumphantly, 'was the result of much exertion amongst our friends, and being always looked upon as an attempt exposed to much risk, we consider it as a material victory.'[12] A county meeting that went the wrong way was a sad blow to government prestige. It was also likely to encourage others to follow suit.

At the Galway county meeting the Catholics played a major part in securing the unionist victory. But in the country as a whole their attitudes varied greatly. It was the first time since they got the vote six years earlier that they found themselves being wooed by both sides in a major political controversy. The great majority of the educated among them, as well as the Catholic hierarchy and most of the parish priests, were in favour of the union, because they realised they were very unlikely to get full political equality or a reform of the tithe system from the existing Irish Parliament. But there was also plenty of indifference and even downright hostility, especially in and around Dublin; and those Catholics who were in favour were often reluctant to say so openly, either for fear of stimulating Protestant hostility towards the measure, or because of local pressures and attitudes.

When Castlereagh went over to London at the end of September to settle the final details of a new union bill, the future of the Irish Catholics was at the front of his mind. After the defeat of the union the previous January Cornwallis had failed to get the English Cabinet's permission to hold out 'general expectations' to the Catholics that they would be allowed to sit in the Imperial Parliament. He could only make it crystal clear to them that they must expect no further concessions from the Irish Parliament. The Opposition, however, had not scrupled to hint the contrary – once the threat of a union was lifted. Uncertain where their interests really lay, the leading Catholics had several times tried to find

THE UNION CARRIED 1799–1801

out from Cornwallis what positive benefits they could expect from a union. The Viceroy had evaded their approaches because he was almost as uncertain as they were. He had always been friendly to the Catholics and he was desperately anxious not to make them promises which the British government might later disown.

By now Castlereagh had come round to the view that the Catholics could not be denied full political equality, and he gave Pitt no excuse to procrastinate. He told him bluntly that the union could not be carried without the active support of the Irish Catholics and this they certainly would not give unless convinced that they would be allowed to sit in the Westminster Parliament. At a Cabinet meeting called to consider Castlereagh's ultimatum, at which he was present, no one opposed the principle of full political equality for the Catholics. Direct assurances to them were considered inexpedient because they might increase Protestant hostility to the union, but short of these, the Viceroy was assured that he could give the Catholics every encouragement to support the union. The ministers were even prepared to allow direct assurances if Cornwallis could convince them that these were imperative.[13]

At the time both Castlereagh and Cornwallis were well satisfied with the outcome of this meeting. In a letter to Portland, written during the journey back to Dublin, Castlereagh confessed that he very much doubted 'whether any more distinct explanation than has already been given [to the Catholics] would at present be politically advantageous – it is enough to feel assured that we are not suffering them to form expectations which must afterwards be disappointed...'[14] It is clear that Castlereagh went back to Dublin believing that the union would in due course be followed by full emancipation for the Irish Catholics.

When the Dublin Parliament reassembled on January 15, 1800, more than thirty seats in the Commons were vacant, most of them because their occupants had either been persuaded to resign them in favour of a unionist, or had to seek re-election after accepting a place. The Castle's tactics were to make no mention of the union in the Speech from the Throne and to adjourn Parliament for three weeks immediately after the debate on the Address, so as to give time for the vacant seats to be filled – most of them with unionists. Not surprisingly, the Opposition saw through this stratagem and Sir Lawrence Parsons promptly moved an amendment to the Address, pledging the House to maintain an independent Irish Parliament. The amendment was debated for eighteen hours with warmth and passion. Assailed by the fierce, and often personal, invective of the greatest Irish orators of the day, Castlereagh lost neither his composure nor his courage. He frankly admitted that a union was to be the chief business of the session. Last year the measure had been withdrawn because it was not fully understood, but he was satisfied that it was now approved by the great majority of the people; nineteen counties, representing more than five-sevenths of the kingdom, had, he said, declared in favour of a union. With what seems astonishing naivety, he asked whether it was decent or constitutional to determine such an important issue when so many (in fact thirty-nine) members were having to seek re-election. As he might have foreseen, the Opposition greeted this appeal with scornful laughter.

As dawn was breaking on the morning of the 16th, the debate was dramatically interrupted by the sudden appearance of Grattan, dressed in his Volunteers uniform and supported by two friends. Although a very sick man, he had been persuaded to allow the seat of a recently deceased member to be bought for him so that he could join in the anti-union struggle. There is a tradition that when he entered the Chamber Castlereagh at once got up and remained standing while Grattan slowly made his way towards the Speaker and took the oaths. If Castlereagh did in fact make this instinctive gesture of respect towards the patriot leader whom he had once revered – and it would not have been out of character – it did not soften Grattan's invective. Too weak to stand and almost inaudible to begin with, he gathered strength as he went along, and for some two hours gave the House a dazzling display of his old eloquence. He ended by pointing his finger at Castlereagh and declaring: 'The thing which he proposes to buy is what cannot be sold – liberty ...'.[15]

But on this occasion the Parliament that has come to be known as Grattan's Parliament, was deaf to his oratory; it rejected Parsons's amendment by 138 votes to 96. The news of Grattan's dramatic intervention spread rapidly through Dublin and helped to make Castlereagh the best-hated man in the city. As he drove home, the mob surged menacingly round his carriage, and only fell back when he leaned out of the window and presented a pistol at them. Outside his house in Merrion Street the mob burnt him in effigy.

During the three-week adjournment the Opposition threw themselves energetically into a campaign to disprove Castlereagh's claim that a majority of the country now favoured a union. A circular letter, signed by Downshire, Charlemont and William Ponsonby, was sent to influential local dignitaries, urging them to organise anti-union petitions 'without delay'. Several county meetings repudiated the favourable petitions which they had produced the previous year, and eventually all but six counties decided against the union. In Dublin public meetings and inflammatory handbills kept the city in a continual ferment. The Dublin yeomanry, mostly shopkeepers and tradesmen, were particularly vociferous opponents of the union. Cornwallis brought some British troops into the capital, and redoubled his entreaties to London not to delay the reinforcements he had been promised.

The extra troops were wanted as much to reassure loyalists as to deter potential rebels. To Cornwallis and his Chief Secretary, with their eyes apprehensively fixed on the parliamentary battle ahead, 'our timid and lukewarm friends' – as Castlereagh called them[16] – were a source of growing concern. Several members who had voted for the union without any real conviction showed signs of using the clamour in Dublin or the pressure of county opinion as an excuse to defect. Taking a leaf from the government's book, the Opposition set up a fund to help finance those willing to change sides; £100,000 was subscribed or promised. Two seats which the Castle thought it could count on were unexpectedly filled by able anti-unionist lawyers, while Downshire provided a seat for William Saurin, who had been the moving spirit behind the protests of the Dublin Bar. Yet in spite of all these discouraging signs, Castlereagh with his usual optimism was still predicting a majority of more than sixty.[17] Cornwallis, on the other hand, had gloomily decided that 'God only knows how the business will terminate'.[18]

On February 5, Castlereagh gave a crowded House of Commons a very long and able account of the terms of the proposed union, explaining in detail the complicated financial and commercial provisions, as well as the system by which Ireland was to be represented at Westminster. He again insisted that the union was now supported by a majority of 'those whose stake in the property and interests of the country gave them a fair claim to due consideration'; and he blamed the recent hostility to the measure in some counties on the 'new political phenomenon' of a parliamentary minority trying to influence Parliament by whipping up the support of the 'mass of the people'.[19] What then, the Opposition replied, had the Lord Lieutenant been doing the previous summer and autumn during his tours through Ulster and the South, if not whipping up the support of the mass of the people?

It was five o'clock the following morning before the debate ended and, in what is believed to have been the largest division ever held in the Irish House of Commons, Castlereagh's motion was carried by 158 votes to 115. As the members made their way home, the Dublin mob showed what it felt about their night's labours by trying to tip the carriages of some of the more unpopular unionists into the Liffey. After that cavalry detachments were ordered to patrol the streets.

'I am sorry', wrote Castlereagh to Portland the following day, 'that the division on our part was so short of what we had every reason to expect.'[20] The majority of 43 was only one more than the government majority on January 16 when so many seats had been empty; it was much less than the 60 to 70 Castlereagh had been predicting. Seven unionists had changed sides; five who had abstained on January 16 voted with the Opposition; and eight new members voted against the union. Further defections could not be ruled out. The government had 'undoubted proofs' that the Opposition were offering as much as £5000 for a vote, and Castlereagh feared that the temptation might be too great for some, especially as the Opposition seemed determined to stir up disaffection and 'to hunt the people at the Government'.[21]

On February 17 the struggle recommenced in earnest when the Commons, in committee, began to consider the long string of resolutions embodying the union proposals. The preliminary resolution – that a legislative union was desirable – was carried by a majority of forty-six after a debate of nearly twenty hours, during which Grattan and the Chancellor of the Exchequer, Isaac Corry, carried their slanging match to such extreme lengths that while the House was still sitting they repaired with their seconds to a corner of Phoenix Park. Grattan escaped unhurt, but Corry was wounded in the arm. Cornwallis considered it an unlucky outcome since it tended to raise Grattan in popular estimation. But the luck was probably really on Corry's side, since the huge crowd of onlookers would hardly have let him escape unscathed if he had been the victor.

For nearly six weeks Castlereagh laboured to get the union resolutions through all their stages in the Commons. The debates seldom ended before midnight and often went on to twelve the next day. Contrary to Castlereagh's expectations the rather ill-assorted elements which made up the anti-union opposition showed no signs of disintegrating. By the end of February he had abandoned hope of winning any new converts and was concentrating on keeping the unionists loyal. On the other hand, the anti-unionists, realising that they could hardly now hope to destroy the government's majority, concentrated on trying to delay the measure in the hope that outside pressure would force a change of heart on the Castle. After Castlereagh had turned down with 'the utmost civility' a proposal to postpone all discussion on the union until the next session, George Ponsonby moved that the anti-union petitions recently presented by 26 counties and several important towns should be laid before the King. After the vexed issue of what constituted the 'sense of the people' had once again been threshed out, the motion was rejected by a majority of forty-eight.

Nine days later Sir John Parnell tried again with a motion that the King should be asked to dissolve Parliament before a union was concluded. William Saurin supported him with great vehemence, insisting that the people would have a moral right to resist a measure passed against their known wishes. Most of the Opposition were as hostile to such 'Jacobin' sentiments as anyone in the Castle. In a sensible and reasonable speech Grattan insisted that Saurin was not appealing to the 'mere multitude'; he was not referring to 'primary opinion, but to that of the constituent body, to the people legally and constitutionally described, to that mixture of strength and property, which forms the order of the country'.[22] Castlereagh, however, more impressed by Saurin's extremism than by Grattan's moderation, roundly denounced Saurin for misleading the people with his unconstitutional Jacobin principles and goading them into fresh rebellion. At three in the morning Parnell's motion was rejected by forty-six votes.

Three days later Castlereagh warned Portland that the Opposition's efforts to whip up the 'lower orders', who had previously been completely indifferent, were likely to have considerable success. 'I trust your Grace will preserve to us a strong British force during the remainder of the struggle – it is the only thing that will effectually discourage any attempt at resistance and in doing so prevent the effusion of much blood.'[23] The Opposition had some excuse for complaining that the government intended to push the union through by force.

But on the details of the measure Castlereagh was ready to modify the draft provisions to meet reasonable objections. The expected criticism of the compensation for borough-owners – which Cornwallis described as 'the most exceptionable in the present arrangement'[24] – failed to materialise. But the commercial provisions were stoutly contested by Foster and his friends in the Commons. They were energetically supported outside Parliament by merchants and manufacturers, who feared that they would be ruined by the drastic reductions in tariffs proposed by the government. Some petitioned Parliament, some stated their case in person at the bar of the House, and some wrote to Castlereagh. The cotton industry was particularly agitated, and after its representatives had had a meeting with Castlereagh at John Beresford's house, he wrote to London suggesting that reductions in the tariff on cotton yarn, calico and muslins should be postponed and then carried out gradually over a period of years. Pitt gave him a free hand, within limits, to settle the matter as he thought best. Believing that the Opposition intended to use the cotton duties to inflame the country, Castlereagh decided to cut the ground from under their feet, and eventually made concessions to the maximum extent authorised by Pitt.[25]

Mollifying the protectionist susceptibilities of Irish manufacturers took up a great deal of parliamentary time. But Castlereagh insisted that it was 'impossible upon any principle of common propriety and decency, to prevent those persons from being heard at the bar whose private situation and interests are really to be affected by the measure, and that the Government would lose all character for consistency and justice were they to refuse admitting their cases to be heard'. He did not believe that the Opposition were merely indulging in delaying tactics and he added the revealing comment that the commercial discussions had made government supporters more interested 'in the success of a measure which they found could be supported by argument and debate, and which improved in public estimation by discussion'.[26]

Once the commercial provisions were out of the way, there was in fact little further debate or discussion. By the end of March the union resolutions had passed through both Houses, and Parliament adjourned while the resolutions were being approved at Westminster. No serious difficulties were expected there, apart from angry lobbying by the English woollen manufacturers. But Castlereagh had no illusions about the final tricky stage of getting the actual union legislation through the Dublin Parliament.* Much had been accomplished, he wrote to Portland on March 29, but 'the discussion which leads to absolute extinction must be critical in a parliament constituted as ours is ...'[27]

But when the Dublin Parliament reassembled on May 8, the fight seemed to have gone out of the Opposition, and those like Parsons, Ponsonby, Grattan and Foster, who continued the struggle, did so as a matter of principle rather than with any hope of altering the outcome. Outside Parliament too the agitation seemed to have died away. 'The town seems indifferent', reported Cooke, 'and the fellows whom I

---

*This consisted of:– (a) a bill embodying the Articles of Union which had already been agreed to by resolution; (b) a bill to settle Irish representation in the Westminster Parliament by thirty-two peers (twenty-eight lords temporal elected for life and four lords spiritual chosen by rotation), and a hundred commoners (two for each county, two each for Dublin and Cork, one for Dublin University and one 'for each of the thirty-one most considerable cities, towns and boroughs'); (c) a bill authorising compensation for owners of disfranchised boroughs.

employ to bring me intelligence say that the lower classes are all come round for a union.'²⁸

Castlereagh, however, refused to rejoice until he was sure of the bill for the new representation of Ireland in the Imperial Parliament. It had eventually been decided that the least contentious and fairest way to choose the surviving thirty-one boroughs would be on the basis of the returns of the hearth and window taxes. The plan was accepted with much greater readiness than he had dared to hope; 'and', he told Mr King in the Home Office, 'as I always considered this question the hinge upon which the whole measure turned, I feel myself enabled for the first time (I trust without being imprudently sanguine) to offer my humble congratulations to his Grace [of Portland] upon the approaching accomplishment of this great measure'.²⁹

But for Castlereagh there was a further trial. The bill embodying the union resolutions roused Grattan to a final despairing outburst. He refused to accept the union as permanent and prophesied that Ireland's liberty would be restored. When Castlereagh rebuked him for inflaming the country by prophesying treason, Grattan rounded on him with a violent personal attack, accusing him of puerility, arrogance, presumption and downright lying. Castlereagh kept his temper and his brief dignified reply greatly impressed the House; according to one impartial observer, it fairly threw Grattan on his back. But afterwards Castlereagh was only with the greatest difficulty restrained from sending Grattan a challenge.³⁰

The sound and fury was not quite over, although members were already drifting quietly away from Dublin. On June 6 the anti-unionists recorded their case in a lengthy Address to the King. It was duly defeated by a large majority, and next day Castlereagh moved the third reading of the union bill. There was, he reported, 'much warmth and ill-temper', but perhaps not more than might rationally be expected.³¹ At the end of the debate, about two-thirds of the Opposition walked out in a body, and the bill was then passed. 'It is a great day over', wrote Cooke that evening, 'and, all things considered, over well.'³²

A week later the union bill passed its third reading in the Lords, and to celebrate the occasion Lady Castlereagh gave a masked fancy-dress ball in the grounds of Phoenix Park. The guests were asked to come in costumes of Irish manufacture, and Hibernia and Britannia, who were much applauded, were frequently seen shaking hands. Altogether it was, as the *Belfast News-Letter* reported, 'a scene of taste, elegance and magnificence that could not possibly be exceeded'.³³

For the Viceroy and his Chief Secretary, however, the successful outcome of the union struggle was marred by a blazing row with the Duke of Portland, who, under heavy pressure from the King, tried to wriggle out of the generous promises of honours that Cornwallis had made in the belief that he had been given a free hand. Both he and Castlereagh felt their personal honour was involved and threatened to resign. Chagrin stung Castlereagh into sending Camden at least two lengthy apologias for transactions which he admitted had perhaps been carried further than was strictly necessary. 'The Irish Government', he wrote, 'is certainly now liable to the charge of having gone too far in complying with the demands of individuals; but, had the Union miscarried, and the failure been traceable to a reluctance on the part of Government to interest a sufficient number of supporters in its success, I am inclined to think we should have met with and, in fact, deserved less mercy.'[34]

In the end the English Cabinet backed down, the King was somehow pacified, and the Viceroy was mollified by a 'very proper' letter from Portland. The satisfaction of those with lesser claims than peerages proved an equally vexatious and much more protracted business. In the heat of the moment, more patronage had been promised than there was to give, and the following February Cornwallis sent Portland a list of more than fifty promises of pensions, places and legal appointments which were still not redeemed.[35] 'The number of applications to which you have been exposed', wrote Castlereagh to his successor in October 1801, 'as the result of that measure [the union], have enabled you to judge of the embarrassments under which we acted.'[36]*

For fear of provoking a popular tumult, no guns were fired in Dublin on August 1 when Grattan's Parliament met for the last time to hear the Lord Lieutenant give the royal assent to the union bill. But the authorities need not have worried; the large crowds round the Parliament buildings remained entirely passive. Nor does there seem to have been any particular sense of occasion inside the House of Lords. De Quincey, then a youth of sixteen on a visit to Dublin, watched the

*Some of these commitments were still outstanding in 1806 when Pitt died, and were then repudiated by the new government. Of the 23 practising barristers who voted for the union in 1800, six had been appointed to the bench by 1803 and eight others had received high honours under the Crown. On the other hand, most of the prominent anti-union lawyers – Plunket, Curran, Saurin, Bushe – had accepted high legal preferment within a few years. A large number of pensions were also granted to holders of offices or sinecures abolished by the union. The Speaker was especially generously treated, being awarded an annual pension of £2500 for life. Castlereagh hoped that this liberality would 'tend much to soften the asperity of our opponents'. (HO. 100/93, June 11, 1800)

The meeting of the two Emperors at Tilsit, 25 June 1807

North Cray Cottage, the Castlereaghs' country home from 1810

Frederick William III of Prussia
by Lawrence

proceedings, and listened to the long and tedious recitation of legislation passed that session. The union bill received the royal assent 'without a muttering, or a whispering, or the protesting echo of a sigh ... All was or looked courtly, and free from vulgar emotion.' Only Castlereagh, usually so impassive, suddenly smiled and darted a penetrating glance at the group of ladies, amongst whom was his wife.[37]

Next day, in a mood of euphoria, Castlereagh described to Mr King the final completion of a measure which he hoped would 'give us advantages, either in the event of peace or war, which the Battle of Marengo cannot deprive us of'. And he added: 'I sincerely wish you joy and feel very proud myself of being less an Irishman and more an Englishman than hitherto.'[38]

Castlereagh's admiration for England lay at the root of his determination to force the union through. What to the Irish was a subordination was to him an enlargement. Many years later, when he was dying, Grattan told his son not to be hard on Castlereagh, 'for he loves Ireland'.[39] Indeed, Castlereagh never belittled his native country, describing it many years later at Westminster as 'that most valuable and interesting portion of the empire',[40] and on another occasion stoutly denying that the native Irish were as ignorant as they were often represented.[41] But he had never believed that Ireland could exist for long as a separate and independent state, and the English connection seemed both the most natural and the most beneficial for Ireland. Union was not for Castlereagh simply a last resource for ruling an apparently ungovernable country. It was a way of guaranteeing Ireland's prosperity and tranquillity by 'blending and uniting for ever with the great and powerful Empire of Great Britain'.[42]

The best men on both sides of the union debate believed that they were striving for the greater welfare and prosperity of Ireland, from which all – Catholics and Protestants – would eventually benefit. Castlereagh made the mistake of underestimating the strength of national feeling in Ireland, and refused to recognise that union could be opposed on perfectly respectable public grounds, just as the Irish nationalists refused to recognise that it could be supported from anything but sordid and corrupt motives. He also failed to recognise that unworthy means can fatally tarnish a worthy end. The methods used to carry the union were not the reason why it failed, but they did not help it to survive either. 'Lord Castlereagh's ideas of making men "amiable" must be forgotten', wrote Lord Redesdale, who became Irish Chancellor in 1802. 'If this country is to be kept, it is to be by other politics.'[43]

'The Union', wrote Castlereagh, 'has removed a great impediment to a better system; but the Union will do little in itself unless it be followed up.'[44] He meant in particular three measures designed to remove the worst grievances of the Catholic majority: full political equality; the commutation of tithes to a fixed monetary charge; and state endowment for the Catholic and Dissenting clergy.* Tithes, it had long been recognised, were the greatest single cause of rural unrest in Ireland. The Catholic and Dissenting clergy, Castlereagh argued, between them guided the conduct of seven-eighths of the population; their loyalty might be assured by giving them financial security instead of dependence on what most of their parishioners could ill afford. Catholic emancipation was of less practical importance, but it seemed the most urgent because, as Cornwallis told Portland, in the struggle over union the Catholics 'certainly had it in their power to have frustrated the views of Government, and throw the country into the utmost confusion ...'[45] They had not done so and they were now confidently expecting their reward.†

Cornwallis was determined they should get it, and he sent Castlereagh over to London to keep the English government up to the mark. But when the Cabinet met to discuss Irish affairs, the Lord Chancellor, Lord Loughborough, launched a violent attack on Pitt's proposals for giving the Irish Catholics political equality. Pitt, taken aback by this unexpected opposition and too unwell to resist it firmly, decided to postpone the whole issue until the new year. What he did not know was that Loughborough was also implanting suspicions in the King's mind about the government's intentions towards the Irish Catholics. Castlereagh does not seem to have taken Loughborough's outburst very seriously. But on yet another visit to London at the end of the year, he was dismayed to learn that the Home Secretary was developing conscientious scruples about Catholic emancipation, and to be shown by Portland an anti-emancipation memorandum which Loughborough was circulating amongst the Cabinet.

By now thoroughly alarmed, Castlereagh sat down on New Year's Day, 1801, to compose a letter to Pitt recalling in detail his own consultations with the Cabinet in the autumn of 1799 as a result of which

---

*The Presbyterian Church already received a state grant which gave each minister about £30. Castlereagh proposed that this should be at least doubled and distributed on the basis of a fixed scale according to the needs of each congregation.

†Roman Catholics could not sit in Parliament or hold offices of state because of their religious scruples against taking the oaths prescribed in the Test Act. It was proposed to amend these oaths so that Catholics could conscientiously take them.

the Irish government had encouraged the Catholics to believe that it would be in their interests to support the union. He reminded him too of the 'highly useful' results of that encouragement.[46] On the same day the Act of Union came into force. In Dublin the guns were fired and the new Union Jack, with the cross of St Patrick added to those of St George and St Andrew, was hoisted above the Castle. The mob seemed delighted with the new flag, and the new era was greeted with no open signs of disapproval. 'This calm, however', wrote Cornwallis, 'cannot be expected to last, if the evil genius of Britain should induce the Cabinet to continue the proscription of the Catholics.'[47]

The Cabinet had in fact already lost their apparent unanimity on this issue. But Pitt, prodded by his conscience or Castlereagh's letter, had not yet lost his determination to carry a measure to which he felt deeply committed. The King was equally committed to his conscientious scruples that he would break his coronation oath to defend the Established Church if he allowed the Catholics to have political equality. Increasingly agitated by his suspicions of Pitt's intentions, he finally burst out at his levée on January 28, and pointing at Castlereagh, demanded of Dundas: 'What is this that this young lord has brought over that they are going to throw at my head? . . . I shall reckon any man my personal enemy who proposes any such measure – the most Jacobinical thing I ever heard of.'[48] Less than a week after this royal veto Pitt resigned, and the King appointed Henry Addington, who had just been chosen as Speaker, to replace him.

Cornwallis's feelings when he heard the news from London – the 'unexpected blast from St James's' – can be imagined.[49] He resigned at once, and his Chief Secretary went with him. Both, indeed, were even more committed to Catholic emancipation than Pitt, although there is no reason to doubt Castlereagh's positive assurance to Thomas Conolly 'that no promise of any kind was given to the Catholics'.[50]

From London, Castlereagh forwarded to Cornwallis Pitt's advice on how best to explain the new situation to the Catholics. It was a case of hope deferred, not lost for ever. But he admitted that the prospect was not encouraging. And having exhorted Cornwallis to persuade the Catholics that loyal and moderate conduct was better than giving way to disappointment and despair, he gloomily added: 'Such are the principles which we must preach; I wish it were reasonable to expect that they would be implicitly acted upon.'[51]

On the whole, however, the Catholics did follow Castlereagh's advice, and it was through no fault of his that they had to wait many years before they were rewarded for their forbearance. Catholic emancipation did not come until 1829, seven years after Castlereagh's death. The commutation of tithes was not carried through Parliament until 1838, and state provision for the Catholic clergy was never carried at all under the union. Of all the reforms which Castlereagh had been planning in 1800, only his proposal to increase the financial provision for the Presbyterian clergy was accepted, and introduced three years later.

PART II
English Politician
(1801-12)

CHAPTER VII
Westminster and Whitehall
1801–06

Unlike Canning, who stormed and raged at Pitt's resignation, Castlereagh loyally accepted it. 'Pitt', he told Lady Elizabeth Pratt, 'has closed an unexampled career in a manner which places him in point of character above the world'. If Castlereagh's loyalty was not unquestioning, his admiration remained unbounded. 'Whether the part he has taken is not too refined for the world, some people may doubt, but that it is great beyond example I am persuaded no man can deny.' The setback to his own career he treated philosophically, and with a modest recognition that it was of small account compared to Pitt's. 'What may be my destiny hereafter', he told his aunt, 'it is not worth enquiring – I shall feel happy myself in having been connected with him in what has occurred and shall return to my private situation without having any particular reproach to make to myself for what has happened whilst I have been engaged in the public service.'[1]

He might have added, if he had been less modest, that the vigour and ability he had shown as the Viceroy's right-hand man in Dublin also left him nothing to reproach himself with. It was acknowledged by the English ministers that the credit (as they saw it) for getting the union through the Dublin Parliament belonged almost entirely to Castlereagh. Although handicapped by his manner, his control of the Commons had improved steadily. He was no orator, and he was opposed by the Dublin Parliament's greatest orators, but the imperturbable spirit and dogged courage with which he invariably stood up to them gained him the respect of most of his listeners and the admiration of many. He was a ready and resourceful debater, and his mastery of complicated commercial and financial details allowed him to hold his own even with that acknowledged expert, John Foster, the Speaker.

It was generally assumed that Castlereagh had a great future in front of him, and, wrote Cornwallis, 'the gratification of national pride, which the Irish feel at the prospect of his making a figure in the great political world, has much diminished the unpopularity which his cold and distant manners in private society had produced'.[2] Before his resignation Pitt had counted on having Castlereagh to reinforce the government's distinctly mediocre front bench in the Commons. So he was unenthusiastic about Cornwallis's suggestion that Lord Londonderry should be given a British peerage in recognition of his son's services, since this might at any time cause Castlereagh to be translated to another place. Portland diplomatically informed Castlereagh that the King felt it would be much better for him, his family and the Empire at large if he did not enter the Lords 'until age, infirmity, or the desire of repose, should make you wish to retire from the more busy and active scene of the House of Commons ...', but his Majesty wanted him to know that a British peerage would be given to him or his father whenever they asked for it.[3] Both father and son waived the honour, and neither ever asked for it afterwards. 'No man', wrote Cooke to Castlereagh, 'ever was so flatteringly pressed to decline honours. The real fact is, that they hope you will make the same figure, and take the same lead which you have done in Ireland ...'[4]

Pitt's resignation seemed to change all that, and when Castlereagh wrote to Lady Elizabeth Pratt in the middle of March, he was 'about to resume my private habits and I hope many of my private comforts'. Unfortunately very little is known of Castlereagh's private habits and comforts – or indeed of his personal character. He was essentially a private person who kept his feelings to himself and did not feel the need to indulge in long epistolary outpourings to his friends. He often gave outsiders an impression of cold and haughty aloofness. But since those who worked under him, like Cooke, Elliot and Alexander Knox, were unreservedly devoted to him, it is fair to assume that his apparent coldness sprang largely from shyness and a certain lack of self-confidence.

He did not seem to feel the need for close personal friends. His wife, from whom he hated to be parted, and his family were sufficient. When he came to England in the late summer of 1800 to consult Pitt about the union, he was able to show in a practical way the warmth of his affection for his family. His younger half-brother Alexander (Alec), a boy of seventeen who had just joined the Navy, was very seriously ill with consumption in London. Both his parents had come over from Ireland to be with him, and Castlereagh warned Emily that he could not possibly leave them until he had done all he could for them and his brother. 'I flatter myself', he told her, 'that I have had it in my power to render a scene, the most afflicting ever witnessed, more endurable to all parties, and this affords my own feelings very great satisfaction.'[5] By the time Castlereagh had finished his business with the Cabinet, it was painfully clear that Alec had not long to live, and the strain of watching him slowly die was beginning to prove too much for his mother. With great difficulty Castlereagh persuaded her to return to Ireland with him, leaving his father to watch by Alec's bedside. 'We have travelled slowly', he told Emily from Chester, 'as my mother required some care: she is better on the whole than I could have hoped for.'[6] Impatient though he was to see Emily, his first care was for his step-mother. He abandoned their first attempt to cross from Holyhead, after twenty hours at sea battling against a contrary wind, largely because Lady Londonderry was so ill; and he then hung about for eight days, letting several packets sail without him, until the weather improved sufficiently to satisfy him that his step-mother could stand the crossing. The delay was 'no small penance' but at least, unlike most delays, it was in a good cause.

Castlereagh's kindness was not confined to his own family. He gave generously both of his time and money to help those who had got into difficulties, often through no fault of their own – the poor Belfast widow with a large family who had been refused a pension because her husband, a boatswain on a revenue cutter, had been drunk when he fell overboard and was drowned; or the Dublin umbrella-maker, who had neglected his business and fallen into debt because he had devoted too much time to his duties as a yeomanry officer.[7]* When he found that Charles Abbot, his successor as Chief Secretary, had no independent means, he insisted on surrendering to him his sinecure office of Keeper of the Privy Seal, although pressed by Addington to keep it for life.[8] No doubt he could well afford this piece of generosity, but in his day such sinecures were eagerly sought after and seldom voluntarily relinquished.

On the small estate near Mount Stewart which he bought in 1795, Castlereagh seems to have been a model landlord, building houses for his tenants, endowing schools, establishing an annual horse and cattle fair, and building a proper chapel for the Catholics of Strangford when he heard that they were making do with an old house. At his suggestion, his father built a stone pier in the lough in front of Mount Stewart to shelter the local fishing boats; and when he heard that the local kelp (seaweed) industry was in difficulties, he persuaded his father to forgo for a year the dues levied on the collection of seaweed on the foreshore

---

*The umbrella-maker, a neighbour of Castlereagh's, went to him to resign his commission because an execution of £900 had just been put on his house. Castlereagh persuaded him to stay to dinner, sent Emily to pay off the requisition, presented the man with a post in the excise, gave him £100 for his present needs, and told him he had three years to repay the £1000 – 'for I know you to be a good man'. The debt was repaid within a year.

belonging to the Londonderry estate.⁹*

He loved Mount Stewart and the country pursuits connected with it – sailing, walking, tree-planting – although he got increasingly fewer opportunities to enjoy them. In England he enjoyed shooting over the estates of his relatives and friends. From Sudbourne Hall, on the Hertfords' Suffolk estate, he wrote to Cooke, 'I send you a brace of pheasants and a brace of partridges per coach, you shall not want game whilst you wield the *quil*[l] and I the *gun*.'[10]

He tried to keep abreast of current political writing, but he was not an intellectual. Nor does he seem to have been much interested in literature; for recreation on his tedious journeys between Dublin and London he usually contented himself with *The Fair Penitent*, *The Conscious Lovers*, or whatever else a circulating library might produce.* His great passion was music, and the making of music his never-failing indoor resource. As we have seen, however, he was dissatisfied with his progress – at any rate in playing Corelli – and only a few weeks after his resignation in 1801 he began to take music lessons.[11]

Early in April 1801 Castlereagh was taken ill with a severe fever. Perhaps the unremitting toil, strain and responsibility of the past three years had at last caught up with him. At any rate for a time he was very seriously ill, and it was well past the middle of June before he was well enough to travel by easy stages up to Harrogate with Emily.

The Harrogate waters – or the rest – did him good. 'I have', he told Cooke after a month's treatment, 'been very idle since I came, have forgot politics, and am grown very fat.' But there was another invasion scare that summer and he felt he should be with his militia regiment. 'Amidst the sound of invasion on all sides', he confessed, 'I have some difficulty in avoiding the fidgets so far as to remain here.'[12] But he managed to stick it out until his course of treatment was finished, reckoning that if necessary he could get to Belfast in three days. By early August he was back in Ireland with his regiment.

---

*The dues were in fact never revived, each ship merely paying one shilling to preserve the Londonderry family's rights to the beach. In gratitude, the kelp trade later presented Castlereagh with a brace of pistols mounted in Wicklow gold.

*On August 17, 1800, Castlereagh wrote to Emily from Barnaby Moor on his way to London: 'I have been miserably off for a library – only the first vol. of an absurd novel in which the hero gets to an unknown country; and as the others vols. are missing I must leave him there ...' (Hyde (1933) p.373)

Two months later he was summoned back to London for the debate on the peace terms that Addington had been negotiating with the French. Henceforward Castlereagh's English interests and responsibilities took up more and more of his time and his visits to Ireland became increasingly brief and rare. In July 1802 he joined Addington's government as President of the Board of Control (India Board). Henry Addington, whose father had been friend and doctor to Pitt's father, was an amiable lightweight with no outstanding attributes which might have silenced the sneers and mockery of those (like Canning) who bitterly deplored Pitt's resignation. His strongest card was Pitt's firm backing, and Pitt as well as Addington warmly pressed Castlereagh to help strengthen the government's weak front bench in the Commons. Addington considered him a readier debater than the Foreign Secretary, Lord Hawkesbury, and wanted him as his right-hand man in the Commons. There was no reason why Castlereagh should not join the government, since he had consistently supported it, even defending the controversial peace treaty signed at Amiens in May. The Catholic issue was not an obstacle since, according to the conventions of the day, only Cabinet ministers had to resign when the King rejected their advice. In any case, after the King's temporary relapse into mental illness, Pitt undertook to shelve the Catholic issue for the rest of his reign.

Castlereagh hoped, however, that he would still be able to do something for Ireland if he joined Addington's government. He secured an assurance from the Cabinet that they would accept his long-cherished plan to provide the Catholic clergy in Ireland with salaries provided by the state. But the clergy themselves turned down this offer on the grounds that they could not accept anything for themselves while lay Catholics were still denied equality.* In spite of this disappointment, Castlereagh could not easily push Ireland to the back of his mind. Its internal stability, its food shortages, its defence against foreign enemies, and of course the wretched 'union engagements', continued to take up a good deal of his thought and epistolary energy. Although, he told his successor as Chief Secretary, the East Indies had now become his 'proper

---

*Castlereagh told the Commons in 1813 that he had joined Addington's government in July 1802 on the understanding that state payment for the Irish clergy, both Catholic and Dissenting, would be introduced; and that the Catholic clergy themselves refused this concession so long as the Catholic laity were refused full emancipation (May 13, 1813. Hansard, 26, 154/5). By July 1802 Castlereagh had hoped that 'the insuperable obstacle to any constitutional favour' (i.e. the King's attitude) was so well understood by the lay Catholics that the clergy would feel able to accept something for themselves. (Dublin SPO. 620/18/7/22, July 5, 1802)

province', he would always feel the strongest desire to give what help he could to the Irish government.¹³

But before settling down to brief himself on his 'proper province' – about which his ignorance was almost total – Castlereagh had to go over to County Down to make sure of his seat in the general election due that summer. 'I am so far on my way to the north', he wrote from Harrogate on July 5, 'where I hope those who don't like me will at least let me alone. As I am again to be a *man of business*, I shall remain but a short time in Ireland...'¹⁴ For once they did let him alone, and on July 24 he was re-elected without opposition. A week later he was on his way to Henry Dundas's remote rural retreat at Dunira in Perthshire to begin his initiation into Indian affairs.

Henry Dundas, an amiable, downright lawyer from Edinburgh, had fallen under the young Pitt's spell eighteen years earlier and become his friend and right-hand man. A skilful politician and an extremely able administrator, he had, among all his other interests, become an expert on India, although he had never been there. He had helped Pitt to draw up the India Act of 1784 which, with some modifications, was to regulate the government of India until 1858.* He completely dominated the Board of Control, set up under the Act to oversee, and increasingly control, the activities of the East India Company. On the whole, he managed to establish a satisfactory working relationship with the Company's Directors, although differences over policy subjected it to increasingly severe strain.†

Castlereagh's immediate predecessor was Lord Lewisham, who was appointed when Dundas resigned (with Pitt) in March 1801. He lasted barely a year. Inexperienced and not very clever, he crossed swords with the Directors, was abandoned by Addington, and forced to resign. At the same time the Company's relations with its principal 'servant' in India, Lord Wellesley, the Governor-General of Bengal, reached a state of acrimony and mutual incomprehension that even Dundas might have been unable to resolve.

*Under the 1784 Act, the Board of Control consisted of six commissioners, all privy councillors, including one of the Secretaries of State and the Chancellor of the Exchequer. As Dundas was the only one really interested in India, he quickly established his ascendancy. This was recognised in 1793 when he was made President of the Board of Control. The other commissioners played a purely nominal role.

†The East India Company was run from its office in Leadenhall Street by the Court of (24) Directors, and in particular by the Chairman and his Deputy (known as the 'Chairs'). The Court's official dispatches to the Governor-General in Calcutta had to be agreed by the Board of Control.

WESTMINSTER AND WHITEHALL 1801–06

Richard, Lord Wellesley, the eldest of the Wellesley brothers, was known to his personal staff as 'the glorious little man'. He was immensely able, a brilliant and meticulous administrator, whose ideas were often startlingly grandiose and his methods bold and sometimes unscrupulous. He was also insufferably vain, arrogant, egocentric and temperamental. He sent home dispatches of stupefying length, complexity and detail, but took full advantage of what he once called 'all this dreadful space of half the convex world' to pay attention to no one but himself. Since the round trip by sea between London and Calcutta took at least a year, there was little, apart from sacking him, that the authorities in London could do to control a Governor-General determined to go his own way.

It could be argued that Wellesley was the right man for the job. His masters in Leadenhall Street may have understood in theory that successful commerce required a measure of political stability, but they failed – or refused – to grasp that in practice this meant fighting expansionist native princes and marauding tribesmen, ruling conquered territory and providing protection for friendly but weak native rulers. The 1784 Act forbade the Company to fight aggressive wars, and Wellesley did not deliberately set out to do so. He made a distinction between extending 'British territories in India by just and legitimate means' and 'schemes of conquest and irregular ambition'; but from Leadenhall Street it was difficult to see where one ended and the other began.

On the whole Pitt and Dundas sympathised with Wellesley's policies in India, although they had misgivings about the ruthlessness with which he pursued them. Britain's Indian possessions may have been acquired more by chance than by deliberate design, but ministers fully accepted that they must now be preserved, from native rulers and European rivals alike. The outbreak of war with France in 1793, followed by Bonaparte's expedition to Egypt five years later, stimulated fears in London that the French meant to try to recover the position in India which Clive had seized from them. Wellesley not only shared these fears but largely removed them by the vigour with which he subdued native princes friendly to the French and the French soldiers who trained and led native armies.

But the Directors in London felt differently. They were at this time an especially able and independent group. The most influential was the Deputy Chairman, Jacob Bosanquet, an industrious and ambitious man described by Castlereagh as 'a great coxcomb', who probably meant well, but 'in point of manners he is among the least pleasant men to act with that have fallen in my way'.[15] Bosanquet was the champion of the dominant 'shipping interest' whom Wellesley had particularly infuriated by his plans for developing private trade, which threatened their shipping monopoly as well as the trade monopoly of the Company as a whole. The Directors were also appalled by the cavalier way in which Wellesley financed his military campaigns with money earmarked for promoting the Company's commercial activities. And they were dismayed by the reckless way in which he had extended the Company's responsibilities, both direct and indirect, in Mysore, Oudh, Hyderabad, the Carnatic and elsewhere.

All these issues, and more, were simmering or boiling over in the late summer of 1802 when Castlereagh visited Dundas in Scotland. When he departed at the end of a week, he left his host with golden opinions of his ability and intentions. 'I am perfectly at my ease', wrote Dundas afterwards, 'as to his [Castlereagh's] administration and I have not the smallest apprehension that in his hands any one of the leading points I had in my mind will be neglected or not enforced with vigour and firmness.'[16]

Before he left Dunira Castlereagh composed a friendly and flattering letter to Wellesley, mentioning their 'former intercourse' and 'common connections' and hoping that Wellesley would not leave his work in India half-finished.[17] It was the first of a steady stream of missives, always tactful, often flattering, but concealing behind the urbane, convoluted sentences a patient determination to bring Wellesley down to earth, to make him realise and accept the constraints under which he had to operate.

'Nothing', wrote Castlereagh to Pitt shortly after he had begun to read himself in at the Board of Control, 'can have been more unpleasant than the tone in which the dispatches have been written during the last year on both sides.'[18] Wellesley had threatened to come home unless he received an immediate vote of confidence from both Company and government, and Castlereagh's most urgent task was to prevent his return, at least until all the new territory he had brought under the Company's sway had been satisfactorily assimilated. Wellesley was always ready to believe himself indispensable, but the Directors, who had been trying to provoke his resignation, were naturally reluctant to change tack and beg him to stay. It required, Castlereagh found, 'a little time to manage both their feelings and their dignity'.[19] By the end of September, however, his patient diplomacy was rewarded, and, he hoped, 'in a way that will secure Lord Wellesley's continuance without indulging him unreasonably'.[20]

Towards the end of October, Castlereagh was invited to join the Cabinet. The post of President of the Board of Control, created only in 1793, did not automatically carry Cabinet rank. Dundas had enjoyed it by virtue of his other responsibilities. Castlereagh, having demonstrated his competence at the Board of Control, was probably brought in primarily because Addington wanted to give his front bench in the Commons the added authority of a third member of the Cabinet.

In spite of his initial success over Wellesley's recall, the authority and prestige conferred by a seat in the Cabinet were virtually indispensable if Castlereagh was to hold his own with the Directors of the Company. Even with this backing he did not always succeed. His attempts to manage elections to the Court of Directors, as Dundas had once successfully done, were a failure. He was worsted in an attempt to stop the Directors from interfering with local appointments which were customarily left to the Governor-General (or the Governors in Bombay and Madras). He did succeed in persuading the Directors to accept a plan, thought up by Dundas, for reducing the huge Indian debt by the regular export of bullion to India. But the plan was a failure; Wellesley diverted the bullion to finance new wars and the Indian debt rose sharply.* He also failed, after a most tremendous battle, to stop the Directors from abolishing the college which Wellesley had set up at Fort William for the training of recruits to the Company. The college was obviously needed, but characteristically Wellesley planned it on too grandiose a scale and tactlessly embarked on it before getting the Company's approval.

When Henry Wellesley, who had been with his brother in Calcutta, returned to London in June 1803, Castlereagh confessed to him that nothing could be more disagreeable to him than his present situation.[21] It would have been more agreeable if he had not been seriously handicapped by the sheer complexity and strangeness of the issues with which he had to deal. He was soon sufficiently familiar with the Board of Control itself to introduce several important changes which greatly increased its administrative efficiency. But the Indian end of his assignment was a different matter. Although he conscientiously consulted the experts and studied the reading list supplied by Dundas, he tended to get behind with his homework on current problems. This did not prevent him from having a view, but it made it more difficult for him to stick to it when battered by the opposing opinions of the experts either in Calcutta or Leadenhall Street.

*A modern historian of the East India Company doubts whether the plan could have worked even if India had been at peace. (Philips, p.124)

When Castlereagh took over at the Board of Control, Wellesley's annexation of the Carnatic and his treaty with Oudh were waiting to be approved. In both cases the argument for a takeover had seemed to Wellesley unanswerable, since the Company was already pledged, in return for annual subsidies, to defend administrations that were hopelessly corrupt and incompetent. But his high-handed and totally unscrupulous methods aroused considerable disquiet in England, particularly in the case of the Nawab Vizier of Oudh, a loyal ally of the British, who had paid his subsidy regularly. After several years of ruthless pressure, Wellesley had coerced the Nawab into ceding a substantial slice of his richest territory, in lieu of any further subsidy, and to accept the position of British puppet in the territory remaining to him. It was the least defensible of all Wellesley's transactions with native rulers, however desirable it may have been to end the appalling misgovernment of the Nawab's subjects.

Both treaties were eventually approved, although in the case of Oudh the Chairman of the Court only signed the dispatch under protest, and Castlereagh privately warned Wellesley that many people had serious doubts about both treaties. At least, it was hopefully assumed in London, the Carnatic and Oudh settlements marked the end of Wellesley's expansionist phase in India. But Wellesley had still not dealt with the Mahrathas, whose confederacy spread across central India from coast to coast. They were a warlike race, constantly plundering and exacting tribute from their neighbours. Since Warren Hastings had made peace with them twenty years earlier, they had remained on friendly terms with the British while ignoring Wellesley's invitations to join his system of defensive alliances. But in 1802 the internal feuding of the Mahratha rulers gave him, he believed, an opportunity to establish British influence in that part of India on a secure foundation – and, he believed, without war.

At first his calculations seemed correct. The Peishwa of Poona appealed to Wellesley for help after being driven from his throne during a struggle for supremacy between two other Mahratha rulers, Holkar and Sindhia. Wellesley agreed to help, but first made the Peishwa agree, in the Treaty of Bassein, to allow a British force to be stationed permanently within his state and to surrender territories yielding sufficient revenues for the force's support. He also agreed to let the Company control his relations with other states and to dismiss all Frenchmen from his service. On May 13, 1803, General Arthur Wellesley peacefully placed the Peishwa back on his throne.

Castlereagh's first reaction to the news of these events was to send the Governor-General his warm approval. But the more he studied the Treaty of Bassein the stronger his doubts grew. Lord Wellesley regarded the treaty as an essential preliminary to extending British control throughout the Mahratha confederacy. But Castlereagh was not convinced that it was necessary to extend British power any further in the subcontinent; and he feared that the other Mahratha powers would not permanently tolerate the presence of British troops in Poona. Jacob Bosanquet, now Chairman of the Court of Directors, was quite certain they would not, and he pressed Castlereagh to disown the treaty and recall the Governor-General.

Castlereagh did neither. Instead he spelled out his doubts in an immensely long dispatch which by the time it was completed, in March 1804, was already hopelessly out-of-date.[22] As Castlereagh had foreseen, the Treaty of Bassein did unsettle the other Mahratha rulers, and in August 1803 war had broken out between two of them – Sindhia and the Raja of Berar – and the British. During the brief, brilliant campaign which followed, Arthur Wellesley won one of his most famous and closest-run victories at Assaye. By the end of the year it was all over. Sindhia and the Raja were forced to cede some of their possessions and both were brought firmly within the British orbit. A clutch of minor Rajput princes, and the old, blind Mughal emperor in Delhi, were also brought under British protection.

The first reports of these latest triumphs arrived in England early in April 1804 and aroused more apprehension than satisfaction. In the Commons Castlereagh introduced a vote of thanks to Lord Wellesley and the army for their victories in a speech which carefully ignored the policy behind the war. Wellesley's friends and relations thought he had handled the vote very badly. Wellesley-Pole reported to his brother in India that the discussion was 'by no means a pleasant one', and that public doubt about the justice and necessity of the Mahratha wars was being encouraged by the Directors and 'by the faint praise of the cautious Lord Castlereagh, who, professing the greatest esteem for you, always lamented the difficulty he found in making Leadenhall Street do you justice, and generally whispered that "in strict confidence he would acknowledge that his mind was not made up upon the policy of the war"...'[23]

Wellesley-Pole might sneer in fraternal indignation, but Castlereagh's professions, lamentations and whispers were perfectly sincere. He esteemed Lord Wellesley, and was perhaps even a little in awe of him, being always painfully aware that the Governor-General was the man on the spot and he was only an armchair critic. He made heroic and unremitting efforts to mediate between the Directors and the Governor-General, persuading the Directors to tone down the more abrasive passages in their dispatches and urging Wellesley to be more respectful and conciliatory in his. It was not really his fault that his efforts were almost totally unsuccessful. 'Your Lordship is aware', he laboriously explained, 'how difficult and delicate a task it is for the person who fills my situation (particularly when strong feelings have once been excited) to manage such a body as the Court of Directors, so as to shield the person in yours, from any unpleasant interference on their part.'[24]

But it was difficult to stifle doubts about the wisdom of a war fought six-months' sailing time away when just across the English Channel Napoleon's invasion army was waiting its opportunity, and sober Englishmen believed that only the winds and tides could save them from a life-or-death struggle on English soil. Towards the end of May 1804, Castlereagh suggested to Wellesley, in the politest possible way, that he might have badly overstepped his brief. Had not our dominions in India been pushed further than was either necessary or authorised by Parliament? And would not the administration of these acquisitions make the government of India so 'complicated and unwieldy' as to risk its becoming 'enfeebled and embarrassed in ordinary hands'? The implied compliment to Wellesley's extraordinary powers did not hide the disapproval. And when it came to the military establishment which Wellesley claimed he would need to defend his new responsibilities, Castlereagh told him quite explicitly that it was out of the question.[25]

By this time Addington's increasingly inept handling of Britain's defence effort had forced him to resign and Pitt was back in office.* He shared Castlereagh's misgivings about Wellesley's policy, but feared that to try to reverse it might only make matters worse. In September, however, news arrived that Wellesley had opened hostilities against Holkar, the Mahratha chieftain who had remained aloof from the previous fighting but refused to accept the new order imposed on India by the British. To Wellesley, the new campaign was simply a necessary mopping-up operation, but to his colleagues in London – and even more to the Directors of the Company – it was the last straw.

For once, government and Company were of one mind on the question of Wellesley's successor. Cornwallis, the soldier-statesman, was usually the government's first choice for any specially unattractive mission, and for this one his previous experience in India made him particularly suitable. At 67, he was of an age when, in those days, most

*War with France was resumed in May 1803.

men were reckoned to be firmly on the shelf. But he claimed to be in good health and accepted the post at once.

Cornwallis arrived in Calcutta on July 30, 1805, and as soon as his predecessor had sailed away down the Hooghly he began to carry out his instructions to turn the clock back as far as was possible without endangering the Company's position in India. He made conciliatory settlements with Holkar and Sindhia (which must have greatly surprised those robber barons), handed back much of Wellesley's most recent acquisitions and – to General Lake's intense shame – withdrew British protection from the Rajput princes. 'I find by my letters from India', wrote Lord Wellesley on January 30, 1806, 'that Lord [Cornwallis] had commenced a systematic demolition of all my plans of policy . . .'[26] Cornwallis had in fact died in October 1805, worn out by the Indian climate and his various infirmities. It was a sad end to a worthy and selfless career. His demolition work was completed by his successor, Sir George Barlow, and it led to ten years of lawless chaos in central India from which the chief sufferers were millions of helpless peasants.

For this policy of withdrawal Castlereagh, under Pitt, was responsible. Their first and overriding priority was the struggle against Napoleon in Europe. From this perspective it seemed culpable folly to go on pouring men and money into an operation which – as Cornwallis had put it – yielded 'little other profit than brilliant Gazettes'.[27] The itch to paint the maps of Asia and Africa red had not yet seized the British or their rulers, and it was difficult for them to grasp that commercial expansion, which was respectable, might involve territorial expansion, which as yet was not.

When Pitt at last decided to go into open opposition to Addington, he had hoped to form a government of national unity, containing the best men from all parties who would pool their efforts to overthrow Napoleon. This hope foundered, first, on the King's stubborn refusal to accept Fox, and then on Grenville's refusal to join a government from which his new ally, Fox, was excluded.* Apart from Pitt himself and Lord Melville (Henry Dundas), who was made First Lord of the Admiralty, the new ministry was little better than the old one. And the following spring it lost Melville after he had been involved in a scandal over abuses at the Navy Board. The Opposition seized with alacrity this opportunity to attack Pitt through one of his closest friends and

*Early in 1804 Grenville had joined forces with Fox to get rid of Addington, after failing to persuade Pitt to go into opposition.

colleagues. By the end of June 1805, after some very heated debates, the Commons had voted to impeach Lord Melville.

Throughout the debates Castlereagh had done his best to demonstrate his loyalty to Melville and Pitt, but not – it must be admitted – to any great effect. During one crucial debate the House refused to listen to him at all. And when, in another debate, he warmly defended the conduct and 'individual purity' of Pitt, which he thought Fox had aspersed, he got into a wrangle with Charles Grey about his own alleged use of corruption at the time of the union. A further wrangle with Grey on the same subject broke out next day after Samuel Whitbread had argued, in a cruelly mocking speech, that Castlereagh's record in Ireland made him unfit to sit on the Select Committee. On any issue involving the misuse of public funds Castlereagh was vulnerable, and his vulnerability did not help his standing in the Commons.

He was also a prominent target. Pitt, the only other Cabinet minister to sit in the Commons, was already a sick man, and to spare him Castlereagh took upon himself a great deal of government business. He got his reward at the end of 'a very laborious and painful session'[28] by being promoted to one of the most important posts in the Cabinet – Secretary of State for War and the Colonies. Pitt intended to relieve him of India after enlarging his ministry with some members of the Fox-Grenville alliance. But the King again refused to accept this arrangement; Pitt was too exhausted and overworked to press him; and Castlereagh was left to make what he could of two full-time Cabinet posts.

He had scarcely begun to read himself into his new responsibilities before he suffered another buffet from his Irish past. His new post obliged him to seek re-election as member for County Down, and Lady Downshire, widow of his old rival, the second Marquess, insisted on putting up and supporting a rival candidate, Colonel John Meade. Castlereagh hurried over to Ireland to defend his seat, but on the thirteenth day of polling he had to concede victory to his opponent. His defeat was received with acclamation in Dublin, where only the Mayor's veto prevented the city from being illuminated. In Belfast the shops were full of anti-Castlereagh prints and songs, and when Lady Downshire visited the theatre, the audience greeted her with wild applause followed by denunciations of Castlereagh.

Fortunately there was plenty of time to find a safe seat in England before Parliament reassembled in the new year. But it was a humiliating experience to be rejected with such opprobrium on his home ground and, moreover, just after he had become a senior member of the Cabinet.

As Secretary for War, Castlereagh worked in the shadow of Pitt, who in spite of his growing weariness and chronic ill-health still provided the main inspiration and motive force in every aspect of the struggle against Napoleon. Castlereagh's responsibility, briefly, was to find the troops and then to use them to the best advantage. He brought to his task immense industry, an ability to absorb detail without getting lost in it, and a drive and enthusiasm which had somehow been lacking in the frustrating atmosphere of the India Board. He was fortunate in having, as commander-in-chief, the King's much-maligned second son, the Duke of York, who for the past ten years had laboured strenuously to pull the army out of the slough of neglect into which it had been allowed to fall. But Castlereagh was gravely handicapped by having no authority over those on whom he had to depend for putting his plans into effect. In addition to the Duke of York, there was the Master-General of Ordnance, the intelligent but incurably idle Earl of Chatham (Pitt's elder brother); the Secretary-at-War, concerned primarily with financial and legal matters but also responsible for authorising all troop movements inside the country; the Transport Board; the Commissary-General; and the Board of Ordnance, which, although nominally subordinate to the Master-General, could and did function independently. All these were responsible to someone other than the Secretary for War, who had to depend on his own powers of persuasion when any member of the team was not so co-operative, active or efficient as he ought to be – and that was quite often.

Moreover, in his inadequately staffed office Castlereagh found no military experts to give him professional advice. Nor was there any regular and efficient method of gathering reasonably accurate intelligence about the enemy's intentions and dispositions. Agents, smugglers, intercepted letters and the foreign press were the main source of information, and if the significance of what these sources reported was wrongly assessed, they could be more of a danger than a help. There were also the inevitable gaps in intelligence created by distance and the slowness of communications. If ministers decided to send an expedition to the Caribbean or reinforcements to Wellesley in India, they had to take their decision on the basis of information that was hopelessly out-of-date, and it was months before they had any news of the outcome of their decision. One of Castlereagh's first tasks when he took over as Secretary for War in July 1805 was to authorise the departure of an expedition under Sir David Baird to recapture the Cape.

It was the following January before it reached its objective and many weeks after that before news of the Dutch capitulation got back to London.

But in the summer of 1805 the attention of Pitt and his ministers was concentrated nearer home: on Napoleon's invasion preparations just across the Channel – 93,000 men waiting an opportunity to cross and a huge flotilla of flat-bottomed invasion craft capable of carrying twice as many; on the movements of the French and Spanish fleets, commanded by Admiral Villeneuve, whose ability to seize temporary control of the Channel would make or mar the whole invasion project; and – looking further into Europe – on Pitt's desperate, and so far unsuccessful, efforts to construct a third coalition of European powers prepared to take the field against Napoleon.

During a long pursuit backwards and forwards across the Atlantic, Villeneuve managed to give Nelson the slip and by early August had taken refuge in Ferrol harbour in northern Spain. He emerged to make a very tentative attempt to penetrate the powerful concentration of the Royal Navy at the entrance to the English Channel, then turned south and made for Cadiz. By the end of August the whole of the Combined Fleet was safely corralled inside Cadiz harbour, with Admiral Collingwood on guard outside. Early in September, Nelson was once more on his way south, with orders to force the enemy fleet to give battle and then destroy it.

As soon as he heard that Villeneuve had turned south, Napoleon realised that his cherished plans for invading England were in ruins. About the same time he also learned that Russia and Austria had after much hesitation opted for war, and that their armies were concentrating in southern Germany, threatening his communications with Italy. He at once gave orders for the great camp at Boulogne to be broken up and for the bulk of the army to make for the upper Rhine. On August 26 the first contingent marched out of Boulogne. By the 1st of September they had all departed.

For the combination of his enemies which set Napoleon racing across Europe in the early days of September, he had himself largely to blame. His brazen over-confidence had made more impact than Pitt's quiet diplomacy. At the end of May the French emperor crowned himself King of Italy in Milan cathedral and shortly afterwards, with cavalier disregard of his treaty obligations to Austria, he annexed the Ligurian republic, including Genoa. Russia and Austria were outraged. By the beginning of August they had pledged themselves to put nearly half a million men into the field against France, and Britain was pledged to subsidise their war effort to the tune of more than £6 million a year.

'The subsidies we shall be called on to furnish', wrote Castlereagh, 'are large beyond example. It is not a contest which can be rationally undertaken upon the principle of half measures.'[29] Neither was it a contest in which the British wished to play only the inglorious role of paymaster. Most of the French troops occupying Hanover were believed to have been withdrawn to meet the threat from Austria, and to Pitt and Castlereagh the moment seemed ripe for a major thrust through northern Germany, liberating Hanover, and perhaps even driving the French out of Holland. They could count on 20,000 Russian troops who were on their way to Stralsund in Swedish Pomerania, and they were confidently hoping for a contingent of at least 10,000 from Gustavus Adolphus, the eccentric King of Sweden.

The unknown, but crucial, factor was Prussia. Weak and indecisive, the Prussian king was being wooed by both sides – by Napoleon with offers of Hanover and by Pitt with promises of generous subsidies in return for 100,000 troops. Frederick William III wanted more than anything to add Hanover to his dominions. On the other hand, Hanover was not really Napoleon's to give, and the young Tsar, Alexander I, whom the king greatly respected, was urgently pressing him to accept the British offer.

In mid-October, when Castlereagh joined Pitt at Walmer to take a final decision on the north German expedition, Frederick William was still clinging to his neutrality. They decided to go ahead all the same. The expeditionary force was to be commanded by General Don and would consist of 6000 men of the King's German (Hanoverian) Legion, who were almost ready to embark, and 5000 British troops.

One member of the Cabinet not present at the Cabinet meeting which endorsed this decision was the Master-General of Ordnance. Chatham preferred to remain in the country potting pheasants. He did, however, send a message offering to come up the following week if there was anything of importance. 'Things are grown so interesting', replied Castlereagh apologetically, 'that I trust you will forgive me for availing myself of your proposal; and if you could appropriate Sunday for the journey, you would, without wasting a sporting day, catch your brother before his return to Walmer on Monday.'[30] Chatham's irresponsibility is scarcely more surprising than Castlereagh's polite – or philosophical – acceptance of it.

The difficulties of waging war were not confined to idle colleagues who owed their positions to their influential connections. There appears to have been not a single map of Hanover in the Secretary for War's office. But there was one in the King's library. Castlereagh had it copied and sent it to General Don with instructions to 'preserve it with great care and return it to this office after the service is over'.[31]

There was also so little accurate information about the situation on the continent that Don was at first instructed to keep his men afloat until he himself had been to Berlin to make sure that it would be prudent for them to disembark. But on October 18 news arrived that Frederick William had swung over towards the Allies after learning that French troops had marched through his territory without permission. The Russians and Swedes had also – it was learned – begun their march from Stralsund across the north German plain towards Hanover. From London the outlook suddenly looked brighter, in spite of the astonishing and alarming news that Napoleon was already on the Danube, harrying the Austrians.

Since Hanover seemed on the way to being freed, the possibility of making straight for the Scheldt and liberating Holland was briefly discussed, and then rejected on military advice. Instead, General Don was ordered to sail for the Elbe and disembark his troops straight away, while Lord Harrowby was dispatched to Berlin to dangle a subsidy agreement before a much more receptive – so it was believed – Prussian monarch. On November 5, the first contingent of the expeditionary force sailed from the Downs.

In the early days of November, successive waves of alarm, grief and euphoria swept the country as news of great events belatedly arrived. On November 3 it was learned from a Dutch newspaper that the rumours of an Austrian capitulation at Ulm were true. 'One's mind is lost in astonishment and apprehension . . .', wrote Lord Grenville. 'An army of 100,000 men, reckoned the best troops in Europe, totally destroyed in three weeks, without (as far as yet appears) sustaining any one considerable action.'[32] Three days later arrived the news of Trafalgar, and elation at Nelson's victory mingled with grief at his death to produce a heady mixture of patriotic fervour. The London mob gave vent to its feelings by dragging the prime minister's coach through the streets to the Mansion House, where Pitt expressed the national mood in his famous declaration that 'England has saved herself by her exertions and will, as I trust, save Europe by her example'.

In this atmosphere of crisis and tension it was inconceivable that everything possible should not be thrown into General Don's expedition, which in the middle of November had arrived at Cuxhaven, at the mouth of the Elbe, and linked up with the Russo-Swedish force. On November 26 the Cabinet decided not to wait till Prussia joined the coalition but to reinforce the expeditionary force immediately with 10,000 men and place it under the command of one of the most senior generals, Lord Cathcart. Castlereagh must have had misgivings because only a week earlier he had told Harrowby that they must be sure of Prussia's intentions before embarking more troops for the continent.[33] Once the decision was taken, however, he threw himself with enthusiasm into the preparations, urging Chatham to produce ammunition, artillery and entrenching tools, and briefing Admiral Keith so as 'to guard against either delay or embarrassment in the execution of orders which may be sent from the respective departments'.[34] 'I am excessively anxious', wrote Castlereagh to Keith on December 6, 'not to lose this favourable weather.'[35] Four days later sixty-seven transports set out from the Downs, but by then the weather was no longer favourable, the transports were dispersed by a severe gale and four were lost.

By this time Pitt, utterly worn out by strain and ill-health, had gone down to Bath in the hope that rest and medicinal waters would give him a new lease of life, while Castlereagh held the fort in London. The reports filtering through from the continent suggested that there had been a major engagement (but not an Allied disaster), and on December 19 Castlereagh told Pitt that, the wind being fair, they had decided to order the transports to sail again at once. As always, they hoped to prod the Prussians into active intervention. 'We have acted for the best', wrote Castlereagh, 'and I hope you and your companions will approve.'[36] On the 23rd, still without any definite news from the continent but still eager to get at Napoleon, he sent Pitt 'a rough sketch of the state of our equipment and what is wanting'.[37]

Six days later he learned the painful truth. On December 2, Napoleon had fallen upon the Allied armies at Austerlitz and overwhelmingly defeated them. Russia and Austria, knocked out of the contest, were seeking an armistice. Castlereagh immediately gave orders that transports should be sent to the Elbe and the Weser to evacuate the British troops if necessary. It was, he reported mournfully to Cathcart, 'the only practical step it has occurred to me to take ...'[38]*

The next step was much more difficult, and there was much agonising and some disagreement over it in the Cabinet. If the rivers froze, the troops might be trapped in the ice – 'for Bonaparte's Christmas dinner', as Thomas Grenville graphically put it[39] – and some ministers thought they ought to be recalled without delay. But

*Cathcart had in fact heard about Austerlitz a fortnight earlier when he arrived at Cuxhaven, and he had taken the precaution of refusing to allow any transports to return to England.

Castlereagh, and apparently Pitt, wanted them to stay as long as it was reasonably safe and there was a prospect of them being 'usefully employed'.[40] Moreover, a British withdrawal might have a disastrous effect on Prussian morale. From London everything still seemed to depend on the Prussians. The ministers did not know that before the end of the year Russia and Austria had both accepted humiliating peace terms and that, to keep Frederick William sweet, Napoleon had thrown him Hanover.

This particular bad news travelled slowly. Even Harrowby in Berlin, still desperately trying to bribe Prussia into the coalition, was given only mysterious hints. It was not until January 11 that Castlereagh received 'convincing proof that Prussia is determined to make the best terms she can with France'.[41] He immediately ordered Cathcart to hasten his preparations for departure. Just over a week later, after more depressing reports from Berlin, Castlereagh sent Cathcart definite orders to return at once with all his troops.[42] By February 15 the whole expeditionary force had begun the voyage back to England.

Castlereagh spared no effort to prepare the expedition, but little more than three months in office was too short a time to repair the omissions of his predecessors or to get the better of the army's creaking administrative machine. Perhaps it was just as well that he was not more successful. According to the Duke of York, who knew what he was talking about, inadequate or non-existent equipment was only one of the factors which would most probably have doomed the expedition to disaster. There were immense practical difficulties in campaigning on the north German plain in the depths of winter, and heavy losses from sickness and prolonged exposure to cold and damp – let alone the enemy – were inevitable. The duke had set out his misgivings with sober frankness in a letter to Pitt on November 27.[43] But the expert's advice was brushed aside. For political reasons the ministers were determined to show the flag on the continent. They knew that little if anything could be achieved against Napoleon without active Prussian co-operation, and they hoped that a British advance into Hanover would encourage the Prussians to take the plunge. They took both a political and a military gamble. They lost the first, and were fortunate enough to be able to back out of the second.

Would it have been better to send an expedition – if there had to be one that winter – to the Mediterranean? The Cabinet thought not. The hazards of the long sea voyage and the difficulties of supply over such a distance seemed to rule out a major effort in the Mediterranean. Sir James Craig had been sent off there the previous April with a small force of about 4000 men and instructions to co-operate with the Russian force based on Corfu in preventing Sicily from falling into the hands of the French troops occupying Apulia. They arrived safely at Malta in July and an Anglo-Russian force duly landed at Naples in November. But the repercussions of Napoleon's sweeping victories in central Europe completely changed the assumptions on which Craig's instructions had been drawn up, and he got little help from London in adjusting to the new situation. 'I would give £5000 for reliable information', he wrote in January 1806. 'My dispatches from Lord Castlereagh come no lower than the 16th October, and for anything I can extract from them either useful or agreeable, they might just as well have remained in his lordship's secretaire to this moment.'[44] Castlereagh's attention and interest had never been very firmly focused on southern Italy, and after the middle of October his dispatches to Craig dried up altogether. That autumn and winter there was too much else to worry about – the north German expedition, Napoleon's lightning manoeuvres, the East India Directors' running battle with Wellesley, and, above all, the increasing deterioration in Pitt's health.

At the end of December Castlereagh went down to Bath to break the news of Austerlitz to Pitt. A fortnight later, when Pitt had returned to his home at Putney, Castlereagh and Hawkesbury had the even more painful task of persuading him that the British expedition would have to be withdrawn from Germany. It was the collapse of Pitt's greatly cherished plan to drive the French out of north Germany and Holland, and nothing that Castlereagh and Hawkesbury could say could soften the blow. Later that day, Pitt told his doctor that when discussing important business that morning, 'I felt suddenly as if I had been cut in two'[45]. Ten days later he was dead.

CHAPTER VIII

Trials of a War Minister
1806–07

Dismayed and disoriented by their leader's death, Pitt's colleagues were sure only about one thing – they could not carry on without him. The King would have dearly liked them to do so under Hawkesbury or Lord Sidmouth (Henry Addington), but both refused.* The only real alternative was Lord Grenville and the Whigs, and George III took it with surprisingly little fuss, accepting Fox as his Foreign Secretary with a good grace which Fox reciprocated. The King was reassured about his new ministry by the inclusion of Sidmouth, who overcame his reluctance to join such uncongenial colleagues largely out of a sense of duty to his monarch. He himself was equally uncongenial to Grenville and Fox, but he had the irresistible attraction of possessing a very useful block of supporters in the Commons.

To their astonishment and mortification the Pittites were excluded from this so-called Ministry of all the Talents. To make matters worse, they had no obvious leader to take Pitt's place. Instead, there were several candidates – Hawkesbury, Canning, Castlereagh, Spencer Perceval (Pitt's Attorney-General) – all about the same age, all with comparable qualifications and none anxious to defer to any of the others. Moreover, there was little to keep them together. Most would have agreed with Castlereagh that regular opposition would be 'impolitic and unbecoming'. Most, like him, would really have liked the new prime minister as their leader.[1] They seem to have regarded Grenville as a temporarily lapsed Pittite, who would eventually become disillusioned with his present associates. In the meantime, it was not too difficult for them to agree on parliamentary tactics: defend Mr Pitt's memory and measures and try to divide Grenville from the Whigs. But without leadership or organisation, it was difficult for them to translate their undoubted debating talents into votes, and by the end of the session they were uneasily debating (at a dinner at Castlereagh's house in St James's Square) how to stop Grenville from sowing divisions in their own ranks. It was a delicate but not academic question since Grenville was on

*Robert Jenkinson, Lord Hawkesbury, was the son of the first Earl of Liverpool. He was Home Secretary in Pitt's last ministry.

the look-out for recruits, being nervous about his government's prospects. Its supporters in the Commons were too often 'out-debated'. The acquittal of Lord Melville, whose impeachment had been dragging on all this time, was an unpleasant and humiliating surprise. Fox's efforts to come to terms with Napoleon had failed, and Fox himself was gravely ill.

On September 15 Fox died, and Grenville's need to strengthen his team in the Commons became pressing. He had already had tentative and abortive exchanges with Canning. Now he made an equally unsuccessful approach to Perceval. Neither would come in by himself. So Grenville put Grey (now Viscount Howick) in Fox's place, and brought his brother, Thomas, and Fox's nephew, Lord Holland, into the Cabinet. To the Pittites it was incredible that Grenville should prefer to stick to Whigs and Addingtonians (followers of Sidmouth) when he might have them. Lord Mulgrave could only attribute it 'to one of those strange inconsistencies in human nature which no sagacity could foretell and no reason can explain'.[2] In fact the explanation was quite simple. Grenville could not satisfy all the pretensions of the Pittites without sacking several of his present team, and that, he thought, would be 'most dishonourable conduct'.[3]

Castlereagh seems to have played little part in the summer's political manoeuvres. Lord Carysfort, passing on a report to Grenville that Castlereagh, Canning and George Rose were 'to be had, if you think it worth while to buy them', commented that 'Lord Castlereagh appeared to me in Ireland a man of application, and showed a good deal of firmness and discretion in his management of the union, but I never could consider him as a great statesman, or a powerful speaker'.[4] But Grenville would not agree even with such modified praise. He was willing to take in Perceval, Canning or Hawkesbury, but not Castlereagh whom he did not like and who he said was not fit for Cabinet office.[5] Perhaps it was a case of two shy and reserved men failing to hit it off, for no one accused Castlereagh of incompetence, however much they might deplore his incoherence. Grenville's attitude was not justified by Castlereagh's standing among the Pittites, where Canning considered him more of a rival than Perceval, even if his name was not among those bandied about as possible leaders. But the fact that he had already held two posts in the Cabinet, and would presumably refuse to be demoted by serving outside it, was a practical disadvantage for Grenville, although he was willing enough to find a seat in the Cabinet for Canning who had never yet had one.

How far Castlereagh was aware of Grenville's attitude to him is not clear, but the total lack of any friendly signals from the direction of the prime minister must have helped to harden his heart against the government. By the end of October he was reckoned among those – including Lord Eldon (Pitt's Lord Chancellor), Hawkesbury and Perceval – who had come round to the view that Grenville's ministry would have to be turned out, as opposed to those like Canning, Camden and Lord Bathurst who were still hoping for a compromise which would allow them to join it. A general election in October left the Pittites no better off, but when the new Parliament met in December, Perceval and Castlereagh still pegged away gamely. Castlereagh repeatedly attacked the Secretary for War, William Windham's military policies, and even had the temerity to wade into the treacherous and (for him) uncharted waters of high finance. Lord Henry Petty, the Chancellor of the Exchequer, proposed to pay for the war with a 'new plan of finance' which, although largely beyond the comprehension of most MPs, had the immense popular attraction of dispensing with any new taxes for three years. Making a great show of being merely helpful, Castlereagh tried to show that the foundations on which Lord Henry wished to rear his splendid edifice were unsound and ought to be modified.[6] The effect of his extremely long, elaborate and abstruse calculations was to bemuse rather than enlighten his audience. In any case, it turned out to be wasted effort because early in March 1807 the Talents were unexpectedly dismissed from office and all their unfinished projects went with them.

But before they fell, the Talents carried the measure which is their greatest claim to fame – the abolition of the slave trade. Grenville succeeded because, unlike Pitt, he made abolition a government measure, and because he first overpowered the strongest pocket of resistance – the House of Lords. After that blow to their cause, most of the anti-abolitionists gave up the struggle and on February 24 the bill passed its second reading in the Commons by the astonishing majority of 283 to 16.

On that memorable occasion Castlereagh neither spoke nor voted. Abolition was the only important issue on which he had not seen eye to eye with Pitt. In principle he was just as much against the slave trade as anyone, but he had opposed Wilberforce's abolition bills on the grounds that they were impracticable and would merely allow other countries to increase their trade. He argued that the slave trade could not be abolished by Britain alone, but only through international co-operation. It was not an unreasonable argument, but it put Castlereagh among the anti-abolitionists – rather unfairly since when he saw a chance to strike a practical blow against the trade he seized it firmly. After only two months as Secretary for War and the Colonies in 1805, he issued an Order-in-Council which had been buried in ministerial in-trays for a year; it prohibited the import of new slaves into Guiana, which had been captured from the Dutch. Wilberforce ascribed Castlereagh's prompt action to his businesslike methods. But there must have been plenty of goodwill as well.

After the overwhelming vote of February 24, Castlereagh still did not believe that the bill would accomplish what 'the liberal mind' of Wilberforce hoped from it. But he accepted the verdict of Parliament, and after Napoleon's defeat worked wholeheartedly and strenuously to force the other colonial powers to accept and enforce abolition. In April 1817 he told Wilberforce that he had written more on this subject than any other.[7] It was not his fault that his efforts were only moderately successful.

By the time the Abolition bill had received the royal assent, the prime minister had – in Wilberforce's words – run his ship aground 'on a rock above the water'.[8] The rock was the King's well-known and ineradicable suspicion of the Catholics. In an attempt to ward off the growing pressure from the Irish Roman Catholics for complete emancipation, the Cabinet decided to allow them to hold commissions in the armed forces. A month later the bill was withdrawn after the King had plainly indicated his hostility. But when the ministers refused to give him a pledge that they would never raise the subject again, he promptly decided to dismiss them.

On the advice of Eldon and Hawkesbury, the King sent for their nominal leader, the Duke of Portland, who more than a dozen years before had brought a group of Whigs into Pitt's government. By now he was an elderly and sick man, who had to fortify himself with regular doses of laudanum. But he was an ideal figurehead, greatly respected by all his younger colleagues, even if they sometimes failed to notify him of Cabinet meetings. He accepted the post entirely out of loyalty to the King, realising that it might shorten his life, as indeed it probably did.

Portland's Cabinet were entirely Pittite, Canning having virtually vetoed any offer to Sidmouth or his followers. Eight of the eleven ministers had served in Pitt's last Cabinet. Among them, Castlereagh returned to the War Office, Hawkesbury to the Home Office, Eldon to the Woolsack and Chatham again became Master-General of Ordnance. The three newcomers were Lord Bathurst, who entered the Cabinet as President of the Board of Trade, Canning and Perceval. Canning went to the Foreign Office, while Lord Mulgrave, who had been Pitt's last Foreign Secretary, took over the Admiralty. Perceval, after holding out for his old post of Attorney-General for several days, very reluctantly agreed to be Chancellor of the Exchequer. He also became leader of the House of Commons – an acceptable compromise between the two other Cabinet ministers in the Commons, Castlereagh and Canning. These three, together with Eldon and Hawkesbury in the Lords, were the real driving force of the ministry.

It was not in fact a very impressive team, and Perceval feared that with the present Parliament the battle might be 'quite desperate'.[9] But in the country as a whole the new government had a better reception. To many people it looked as if the 'good old King' had been sturdily resisting the Whigs' attempt to introduce popery and the Pittites had come to his rescue. It did not take the new ministers long to realise that they might take a leaf out of the Whigs' book and improve their situation by asking the King for a dissolution. The King, who much preferred his new ministers to his old ones, willingly agreed.

On April 30, Parliament was dissolved and the country had the unusual experience of a second general election in eight months. The outcome was even more satisfactory than the government had anticipated. At the first trial of strength in the new Parliament – the vote on the Address on June 26, 1807 – it had a remarkable majority of 195. The Opposition mustered only 155 votes, and in all but two of the subsequent divisions that session failed to scrape together even a hundred votes – which perhaps was just as well for ministers striving to grope their way through some of the blackest and most disheartening days of the war.

The armed forces were divided into three categories; the regular army, including the ordnance, primarily for service overseas; the militia; and the volunteers for home defence. The same pool of national manpower had to serve all three, and the problem was to keep each of them up to strength, without denuding either of the other two in the process. The militia and the volunteers came under the Home Office, but since all three forces were different facets of one problem, it was natural for an energetic Secretary for War to concern himself with raising all of them.

Service in the regular army was understandably unpopular. The pay was miserable – one shilling a day; until 1806 enlistment had to be for life; marriage was heavily discouraged; and the chances of dying of yellow fever in some remote colonial garrison were high. Wellington may have exaggerated when he called his soldiers the scum of the earth, but it was certainly true that the army was a refuge for fugitives from the law, fathers of illegitimate children and drunkards. Except when the country was being swept by one of its periodic waves of patriotic fervour, decent working-class parents did not want their sons to join the colours.

The traditional method of filling the ranks was to send out small regimental recruiting parties offering a bounty to those who would take the King's shilling. But this was quite inadequate in time of war, even when reinforced by offers of promotion to recruiting officers who collected a certain quota of recruits. In 1799 Pitt had introduced legislation authorising the transfer of 10,000 militiamen to the regular army; they were offered a generous bounty to encourage them to volunteer and the measure proved surprisingly successful; many militiamen were apparently not unwilling to opt permanently for a soldier's life. But of course the ranks of the militia were depleted, and the commanding officers of militia regiments bitterly resented losing their best men in this way.

The militia themselves were chosen for a five-year period of service by ballot from lists of able-bodied men in each county. Those picked could, and often did, pay a substitute to serve in their place. The snag about this concession was that the men willing to act as substitutes tended to be those who might otherwise have volunteered for the regular army.* It also forced up the bounty paid to regular recruits. But no government had felt able to forbid the practice of paying substitutes. The volunteers were exempt from the ballot, and this made them popular and the ranks of the militia harder to fill. The volunteers were part-time soldiers, not subject to strict discipline and their value had been questioned, although by the time of Pitt's death the long invasion scare and the tactful efforts of the Duke of York had achieved a marked improvement.

Pitt and Addington had experimented in various – and sometimes contradictory – ways to find the right mixture of carrot and stick to fill the ranks of Britain's armed forces. They both made mistakes, but on the whole their efforts were reasonably successful. William Windham, Castlereagh's immediate predecessor, was a well-meaning intellectual, full of ideas but rather short on common sense. The main effect of his exertions was to run down the internal defences of the country, thereby tying down regular troops who ought to have been free for garrison duty or offensive operations abroad. Castlereagh immediately set about

---

*Men liable to be balloted would join insurance clubs so as to be sure of having money quickly available to pay a substitute.

applying some first aid. His first priority was to stop the rot in the volunteers, by reintroducing the inspecting field officers – the invaluable link between professional and amateur soldier whom Windham had scrapped – and in various ways trying to restore the volunteers' zeal, morale and efficiency. But this was a temporary expedient. Like Windham, Castlereagh had serious doubts about the volunteers whom he unflatteringly described as 'a fleeting and inapplicable mass'.[10] On the other hand, he realised that they could not be dispensed with entirely until there was something better to put in their place.

In the summer of 1807 Castlereagh decided to restore balloting for the militia which Windham had also abolished. It was a reluctant decision imposed by another almost equally reluctant decision to draw on the militia to bring the regular army up to strength. There was no way of replenishing the army, Castlereagh warned his colleagues, that was not 'liable to considerable objections' and would not excite 'the opposition of some considerable class of interests, both in and out of Parliament'.[11] But he finally decided that the least undesirable way was to call on the militia to provide a total of 28,000 men – 21,000 from Britain and 7000 from Ireland. He offered generous bounties and gave recruits the choice of enlisting for life or for seven years. The response from the men was good, the officers were reasonably co-operative, and in the end Castlereagh got all but some 500 of the total he had asked for.

At the end of his first year in office, the balance sheet of Castlereagh's emergency measures was mixed. He could be reasonably satisfied with the regular army, which had received altogether 40,000 recruits by ordinary recruiting and transfer from the militia. But the replenishment of the depleted ranks of the militia had been less successful, and although the collapse of the volunteers had been halted, the reports from inspecting field officers had confirmed Castlereagh's feeling that it would be better to replace rather than reform them. His long-term aims therefore were to make sure that the army continued to receive a steady supply of recruits to replace its losses, and to establish the country's internal defences on a surer foundation than the volunteers.

As a former militia officer, Castlereagh sympathised with Windham's wish to introduce some form of conscription, and he drew up an elaborate, imaginative and carefully thought-out plan for regular compulsory military training for all able-bodied men between 18 and 30. But since, unlike Windham, he had a well-developed sense of the possible, the plan he actually introduced in April 1808 was much more modest. He proposed to raise a new 'local militia', of nearly 309,000 men, either by voluntary enlistment or by the ballot. But it was the ballot with a difference, for substitutes were forbidden, and those chosen were compelled to serve by heavy fines or imprisonment. The period of service was four years, but a man was free to volunteer for general service at any time. The force was to be formed into battalions with full complements of officers and permanent regimental staffs.

The volunteers were to be encouraged, with the help of modest bounties, to transfer into the new militia, preferably in entire units. As Castlereagh explained to Sir Arthur Wellesley, he intended 'not only to make a considerable addition to the general defensive force of the country, but to lay the foundation of a military establishment into which the volunteers may be gradually melted down ...'[12] Not all the volunteers relished being 'melted down', and later it was found necessary to disband compulsorily the really inefficient units, and use pressure rather than a bribe to get the better ones to transfer. The plan had other disadvantages which were not altogether removed by amending legislation. But by the end of a year more than 195,000 men had enlisted in the local militia, of whom 125,000 were volunteers, and it was clear that the plan's advantages outweighed its drawbacks. It provided a basic military training for a large number of men and – unlike Windham's measure – ensured that the training was efficient and the discipline strict. It firmly abolished the practice of substitution which had siphoned off some of the best potential recruits from the regulars. It provided a continuing source of basically-trained men for general service. And it was an effective way of turning the volunteers into an efficient, disciplined force so that the regular army could be released for service abroad.

Castlereagh's success in building up the country's armed forces was not due to any far-reaching innovations, although he planned them on paper. But he absorbed the advice of the Duke of York and other experts, and he studied his predecessors' experience, learning from their mistakes and adopting what had proved successful. Without Castlereagh's laborious efforts the army might not have been able to take advantage of the Spanish revolt in the spring of 1808 to launch its first really damaging blow at Napoleon. After Castlereagh resigned in September 1809, his successors carried on along the same lines, refilling the ranks of Wellington's armies from the militia, both local and regular, supplemented by traditional regimental recruiting.

It has been argued that if the war had gone on much longer, the system would almost certainly have broken down, and Castlereagh himself admitted that by 1815 the militia were beginning to fail under the strain. But what might have been is not the business of either the historian or the politician. What matters is that Wellington did have enough troops to drive the French out of Spain and a year later defeat them at Waterloo – and for that he had Castlereagh more than anyone else to thank.

In the spring of 1807, Waterloo would have seemed an improbable end to the career of the man who was by then well on the way to making himself master of Europe. Napoleon had cowed Austria with a humiliating peace, placed Italy under his control and made Spain his subservient ally. He had allotted the throne of Naples to one brother and the throne of Holland to another. A cluster of German states, including Bavaria, had formed themselves into the Confederation of the Rhine and made him their Protector. Then in the autumn of 1806 Frederick William of Prussia tried to turn back the rapidly advancing tide of French domination. Napoleon immediately swept through Germany and inflicted two defeats on the Prussian armies, at Jena and Auerstadt, on the same day. While Frederick William took refuge in East Prussia with what was left of his armies, Napoleon took possession of Berlin. From there on November 21 he declared economic war on his elusive island enemy and issued his famous Berlin decree prohibiting all commerce with the British Isles. He then marched eastwards to deal with Russia, the only major continental power still defying him. On February 8, 1807, the French emperor was checked at Eylau, near Koenigsberg, by Russian and Prussian forces. But his enemies were too demoralised and disunited to pursue their advantage, and after a few months in winter quarters, resting, regrouping and waiting for reinforcements, the French were again ready for the offensive.

No attempt was made by the Ministry of all the Talents to intervene in the struggle in north-east Europe. Discouraged by his failure to make peace with Napoleon, Grenville regarded the continental conflict with gloomy foreboding. He sent his Russian allies some arms and money, but to the Tsar's extreme disgust British offensive operations were confined to parts of the globe – the eastern Mediterranean and South America – where they could have little or no effect on the war in northern Europe.

The British public, on the other hand, was extremely enthusiastic about military expeditions to Spain's fabulous empire in South America, especially the commercial classes who were excluded by Spain from all legitimate trade with the continent. The Spanish colonists were simmering with revolt, and the commercial prizes to be won from a liberated continent seemed glittering. Grenville's government was reluctant to involve British troops in the impending struggle in South America, but when Sir Bruce Popham made an unauthorised dash across the Atlantic, captured Buenos Aires and sent home half a million gold dollars, public pressure forced the government to reinforce the small force of British troops, under General Beresford, which Popham left behind. (This did not save him from a court martial when he got home.) In the new year of 1807 it was learned in London that the colonists in Buenos Aires province had overthrown the Spanish Viceroy, ejected the British from the city and made General Beresford prisoner. More troops had to be sent to rescue him, under a new commanding officer, General Whitelocke, outstanding only for his bad manners and obscene language.

By the time Castlereagh took over at the war ministry, some 10,000 British troops had been committed to the South American adventure. He felt obliged to earmark a further 5 to 6000 as possible reinforcements, and when on April 12 the news of the capture of Monte Video arrived, he duly ordered the victory to be celebrated by the Tower and Park guns. 'But it is plain', he told Arthur Wellesley, 'we cannot get on upon the mere principle of conquest and military occupancy.'[13] And he somehow found time to write a long memorandum, explaining the background to the operations in South America and asking his colleagues urgently to decide whether or not they were worth the effort. It was not at all wonderful, he wrote, that the Spanish colonists should be so unfriendly, since the British force was not strong enough to protect them from their former masters and could make no promise not to hand them back after a peace. He ruled out any attempt by Britain either to establish itself permanently in South America or to help throw over the existing regime without having any idea what might succeed it. Since, however, Napoleon dominated Spain, he must somehow be denied the use of its colonial wealth. Castlereagh admitted he had very little idea how this could be done – perhaps, he vaguely wondered, by setting up a monarchy under the Duke of Orleans – but he did entertain 'a very *strong persuasion*' that the present policy was of little political or economic benefit and a great waste of military resources.[14]

Military resources were very much on Castlereagh's mind in the spring of 1807 as Napoleon prepared to resume hostilities against his enemies – Russians, Prussians and Swedes – in northern Europe. More than 15,000

British troops had been assembled in Sicily as a strategic reserve. There was the new commitment in South America, and because of a serious mutiny at Vellore, near Madras, 4000 reinforcements had been rushed off to India with perhaps more to follow. Altogether, Castlereagh reckoned it would not be prudent to commit more than 11,000 men to the European struggle.[15] But at least they would be mobile. One of his first actions on returning to the war ministry was to reassemble the military transports which he had kept on permanent standby but which Windham had dispersed on grounds of economy.

But where exactly should this 'disposable force' go? Lord Hutchinson, the British representative at the Tsar's headquarters, was urging the dispatch of a British expedition to the Baltic, and from Stralsund King Gustavus of Sweden was insisting that he could not begin to drive the French out of his Pomeranian territories without some British troops as well as a great deal of British cash. On the other hand, the Russian and Prussian envoys in London were pressing for a landing between the Elbe and the Weser, which they claimed would spark off risings all over Germany.

Gustavus, although difficult and eccentric to the point of derangement, had always been a loyal ally, and Stralsund was one of the few remaining European ports open to British trade. But there were great risks and formidable supply and transport problems for an expeditionary force operating so far from base. A landing on the Elbe or Weser, or somewhere on the Dutch, Flemish or French coasts, would be much easier to carry out, but the strength of the opposing French forces in those areas might well make the operation too hazardous. Lord Cathcart, when asked for his expert opinion, objected to every alternative, and advised Castlereagh to do nothing, except, in effect, keep his options open.[16]

Such negative advice was unacceptable, and by the end of June the Cabinet had made up their minds to send more than 10,000 men of the King's German (Hanoverian) Legion to the Baltic at once. They were to be commanded by Cathcart, who was instructed to co-operate with the King of Sweden. A force of British troops was to remain in readiness, either to land at a vulnerable point on the enemy's coast, or on the Elbe or Weser, or to proceed to the Baltic to reinforce Cathcart. The instructions were vague and the commander presumably was not enthusiastic. King George, who was shrewd where military matters were concerned, was also unenthusiastic, trusting that 'it will not be hastily determined' to subject the British force to the risks of a landing on the Elbe or the Weser.[17]

TRIALS OF A WAR MINISTER 1806−07

No risks were taken with the British force because Napoleon was far too swift for his hesitant opponents. On June 14, five days before the first contingent of the German Legion sailed for Stralsund, he decisively crushed the Russian armies at Friedland. Alexander immediately asked for an armistice, and a few days later met the French emperor on a raft in the river Niemen, near the town of Tilsit. Overwhelmed, apparently, by Napoleon's personality, he meekly agreed to underwrite his arrangements for the future of Europe. And in secret clauses to the Treaty of Tilsit he agreed to declare war on England, to withdraw from his bases in the Adriatic and the Ionian Islands and to allow the French a free hand in the Mediterranean.

The Royal Navy in fact controlled the Mediterranean. But in spite of Britain's naval superiority, Castlereagh did not manage to achieve a successful military diversion in the Mediterranean region that would have relieved some of the pressure on the Tsar's armies in the north. The British force based on Sicily was under the command of General Henry Fox, the brother of Charles James Fox, who found himself, much to his disgust, engaged in a running battle with Maria Carolina, the wife of the exiled King Ferdinand IV of Naples, over her harebrained schemes for the recovery of Naples. In February 1807, Fox learned that a British naval demonstration before Constantinople had failed, and Admiral Duckworth had been forced to retire ignominiously through the Dardanelles, taking the British minister to the Porte with him. Duckworth's object had been to support the envoy's efforts to eliminate French influence at the Porte and mediate between the Turks and the Russians who were at war over the Ottoman principalities on the Danube. Peace on his southern frontiers would have allowed the Tsar to strengthen the forces opposing Napoleon in the north. If Duckworth should fail, Windham had instructed Fox to make a landing in Egypt. This was an entirely pointless enterprise, and when Castlereagh eventually learned, on April 18, of Duckworth's retreat, he immediately assured Fox that he was free to move the troops he had just sent to Egypt − in accordance with Windham's orders − to the Dardanelles if he thought they could be usefully employed there. Although Castlereagh realised that the Turks would by now probably have strengthened the defences of Constantinople, he still hoped that by 'a coup de main or other efforts' the Turks might be compelled to shake off French influence. It was his first dispatch to Fox and he seems to have felt a need to excuse the vagueness of his instructions. The government, he added, has too little information to suggest any specific operation – 'the prudence and practicability of any attempt can be best judged of by those who, being on the spot, where full information can be alone obtained, have all the materials for forming a correct judgment'.[18] Presumably from London, Sicily and Constantinople did not seem far apart, although in fact there was about two weeks' sailing time between them.

But even from London it was soon apparent that the army could attempt nothing more in the eastern Mediterranean. Castlereagh lamented that so many troops were tied up uselessly in Egypt and urged Fox to make it clear to his commander there, General Mackenzie Fraser, that he could expect no reinforcements, must keep out of local politics and must make no commitment that might hamper his withdrawal.[19] Fox, who had always disapproved of the Egyptian expedition, found nothing to dislike in these instructions. Nor did his deputy, General Sir John Moore, who, although particularly hard to please, described Castlereagh's objections to hanging on to Alexandria as 'explicit and sensible'.[20]

But the generals gave a very different reception to further instructions from London, written on May 21 and received at the end of June. Desperately anxious to strike a blow at the French while Napoleon was heavily engaged in northern Europe, Castlereagh ordered Fox to prepare a force of 8000 British and 12,000 Sicilian troops for an attempt to recover Naples. Although the local troops were inferior, wrote Castlereagh, they were to be 'encouraged and improved' so that they could play a major part in the operation, leaving enough British troops behind to defend the island.[21] But Fox knew, and had reported, that instead of being merely inferior, the local troops were so ill-equipped, ill-disciplined and ill-led that they would be useless against the French troops in southern Italy whom he believed to be 20,000 strong. 'The whole of the dispatch', wrote Moore indignantly, 'is founded upon ... a state of things which does not exist in this island.' It was, he added, difficult to believe that Lord Castlereagh could have read General Fox's correspondence.[22] The King, who certainly had read Fox's dispatches, warned Castlereagh that the British troops in Sicily were 'inadequate to any extensive purposes', and the Neapolitan troops could not be relied upon.[23] But Castlereagh apparently preferred to take a chance on the more optimistic reports of William Drummond, the British envoy at Palermo, which were largely based on misinformation supplied by the queen. Fortunately, after receiving bad news from Egypt, Fox decided to ignore his instructions to recapture Naples. As he grimly pointed out to Drummond, Castlereagh's dispatch had been written under a misconception of the true position.[24]

It was nearly the middle of June before the government learned that General Mackenzie Fraser had lost two engagements with considerable casualties while trying to establish himself on the Nile delta at Rosetta. The King advised an immediate withdrawal from Egypt, pointing out that 'from the very first moment H.M. was inclined to doubt the use or expediency' of the expedition.[25] The ministers accepted his advice, but continued, hopefully, to plan operations on the mainland of Italy. With these in view, it was decided to replace General Fox by his younger and much more active deputy. Moore learnt of his promotion on July 9. He did not know that two days earlier the Treaty of Tilsit had completely destroyed the whole basis of the British war effort against Napoleon.

In spite of all the reports, rumours and speculation reaching London, it was hard for the British ministers to grasp the fact that Alexander had deserted them. It was not until the end of July that Canning learned that a Franco-Russian treaty had definitely been signed, and it was more than a week later before he read the published text of the treaty in a French newspaper. He suspected that there were also some secret clauses, but could only guess what were in them. Where would Napoleon strike next? Would he seize Sicily and Sardinia and try to turn the Mediterranean into a French lake? Would he begin to dismember the decrepit Ottoman Empire either through Egypt or more directly? Did he intend Turkey to be a stepping stone to India? Or would he concentrate first on the British, organising a maritime league to cripple their commerce, or even mounting a new invasion of the British Isles?

In the circumstances it is hardly surprising that over the next six to eight months Britain's military planning often appeared confused, fumbling and misdirected. Uncertainty about the enemy's intentions added immeasurably to the difficulties created by slow and uncertain communications and the strictly limited supply of soldiers available for active operations abroad. More surprising perhaps is the complete absence of defeatism. Far from allowing their difficulties to reduce them to a state of indecisive paralysis, the ministers responded boldly to every threat. In fact their shortcomings were both exacerbated and redeemed by their enthusiastic and dogged determination not to give up the struggle or settle for a compromise peace. Deeply divided though they were soon to become, in the dark months after the Treaty of Tilsit the Portland Cabinet pulled stoutly together.

From one direction, there were clear signs of impending danger even before the text of the Treaty of Tilsit arrived in London. The neutral Danes had suffered severely from Britain's countermeasures to the continental embargo on British goods instituted by Napoleon in his Berlin decree.* They scarcely bothered to hide their hostility to Britain and it was believed that not much pressure would be needed to force them into the French camp. For the British this would be a disaster; they would be excluded from the Baltic, and Napoleon, whose navy had not yet recovered from Trafalgar, would have the use of the large Danish navy. Moreover, the King's German Legion was still at Stralsund with its commander trying not to get involved in the increasingly hopeless defence of the city and wondering what he was supposed to do now that the Tsar had thrown in the sponge. If the Danes declared war, Cathcart and his troops would be trapped in the Baltic.

On July 14 the Cabinet decided to send a strong naval force to the Kattegat to watch the Danish navy and take whatever 'prompt and vigorous' action seemed called for.[26] Four days later Castlereagh told Cathcart that his new objective was to force the Danes to state their intentions; he was therefore to leave Stralsund and rendezvous in the Sound with the strong naval and military reinforcements that were, or shortly would be, on their way from England.[27] The King advised caution,[28] but the accumulation of evidence – including some mysterious intelligence straight from Tilsit – that Napoleon meant to force the Danes into war against England seemed overwhelming. The ministers were convinced that they had no choice but to act and to act fast. Helped for once by the unusually prompt co-operation of his colleagues, Castlereagh got the British troops away by the end of the month.

Among Cathcart's senior officers was Sir Arthur Wellesley, hoping to add some European laurels to those he had earned in India. There were not in fact many laurels to be won (although Sir Arthur got most of those that were going) because it was the three-day naval bombardment of Copenhagen, not Cathcart's investment of the city, that forced the Danes to capitulate and allow their fleet to be taken into British custody for the duration.

In an age when war was conducted by fairly well defined and observed rules, the decision to authorise the bombardment of Copenhagen was, if necessary, bound to be controversial. Some people were

*A British Order-in-Council, issued in January 1807, forbade all trade between French or French-controlled ports, but did not interfere with direct colonial or American trade with France. In practice, this annoyed the neutrals much more than it troubled the French.

genuinely shocked, and the Opposition professed to be outraged, its press bewailing the stain on the national character. But even Wilberforce conceded that the expedition was justified on grounds of self-defence and the ministers remained firmly convinced that they had done the right thing.

But their jubilation was quickly transformed into acute anxiety when they belatedly realised that together with the Danish fleet they had also acquired the Danes' violent hostility. Denmark had in fact declared war on England. This obviously meant that as soon as Cathcart evacuated Zealand, as he had undertaken to do within six weeks, the French would be hard on his heels. The British would still be excluded from the Baltic and the French would be well placed to menace Sweden and even Russia's northern frontier. Castlereagh had realised the importance of Zealand since the beginning of the operation, and he hardly needed Canning's eager prodding to decide to tell Cathcart that now the Danes were at war, 'as far as it can be done consistently with the engagements entered into, we are desirous of converting our present position in Zealand into an instrument for keeping the French out of it'.[29]

It could not be done. The Danes were scrupulously correct in fulfilling their side of the bargain and left no excuse for any British backsliding. Moreover, both Cathcart and Wellesley assured the ministers that it would be military madness to shut up 30,000 troops on Zealand. Very reluctantly Castlereagh and Canning accepted their advice. Instead, they proposed – rather wildly – to leave Cathcart and a 'respectable' force behind to defend Sweden.[30] But Gustavus Adolphus did not want them, and Cathcart, believing his mission accomplished and not wishing to be caught by the northern winter, made up his own mind to come home. By the end of October he and all his force were back in England.

By this time, the situation in southern Europe, whether seen from London or by the unfortunate generals on the spot, had become hopelessly confused. After seeing the published text of the Treaty of Tilsit Castlereagh decided that any offensive operations in the Mediterranean were no longer either useful or practicable. When the British expedition to Egypt arrived back in Sicily there would be some 16,000 British troops in the island. Reckoning that this was too many to lock up on garrison duty, he ordered Moore to bring 8000 to Gibraltar as soon as all the troops had returned from Egypt. 'The movement of this corps to Gibraltar', he explained to the King, 'will bring it more within your

Majesty's immediate reach, to be applied according to circumstances either to purposes of home defence, to the protection of your Majesty's colonies or to the annoyance of the enemy.'[31] Castlereagh was determined to be prepared, although he had very little idea what for.

Early in October, however, he wrote to Moore in Sicily instructing him to stay where he was. But in case the general had already left the island, Castlereagh sent a second letter to Gibraltar ordering him to come home. To some extent these confused orders were due to Castlereagh's characteristic reluctance to be ruthless when by a little management the same result could be achieved without 'awkwardness'. He was in fact anxious to find some tactful and uncensorious way of removing Moore from Sicily, because he had by now read enough of the general's scathing criticism of the island's Bourbon rulers to feel sure that he would never be able to win their co-operation, and he had no intention of taking up Moore's suggestion that it would be better to annex the island outright.[32] It was, all the same, a curious decision to recall Moore to England without knowing for certain whether Fraser had returned to supplement the defences of Sicily, especially now that Alexander's defection had made the island much more vulnerable.

At this point Castlereagh fell seriously ill and was not seen again at the war ministry until a few days before Christmas. His absence, Hawkesbury told Arthur Wellesley, 'has unavoidably thrown a very heavy burden upon me'.[33] To make matters worse, 'secret information' had reached the Cabinet that the Tsar had agreed to hand over the Ionian Islands to Napoleon; this made the threat to Sicily much more concrete. The news from Portugal was also bad. A French army under General Junot was on its way to Lisbon, and the Prince Regent of Portugal was showing ominous signs of truckling under to Napoleon, although Sir Sidney Smith with a British squadron was waiting in the Tagus to spirit him and his family away to Brazil.

Hoping to catch Moore at Gibraltar, Hawkesbury wrote to him on November 6, instructing him not to return to England, but to go to the Tagus where he was to co-operate with Sir Sidney Smith and also be prepared to send a force to occupy Madeira (a Portuguese possession). At the same time the Cabinet provided for Sicily's defence by ordering 7000 troops to proceed from England to Sicily under the command of General Brent Spencer. While these measures were being set in train, Moore, who had left Sicily in the middle of October, was battling with contrary winds in the Mediterranean. It was not until December 1 that he reached Gibraltar where he found both Castlereagh's dispatch ordering him to return to England and Hawkesbury's instructions telling him to go to the Tagus. He learnt from the captain of a passing British warship that on November 29 the Portuguese Regent had eventually decided to flee, taking the Portuguese fleet with him. Hearing nothing at all from Smith, Moore eventually decided to come home. He was back in England before the end of the year. Towards the end of his voyage, he must have passed General Spencer sailing in the opposite direction. Held up by delays in assembling and embarking his troops, it was December 20 before Spencer got away.

It may perhaps be supposed that the delays in assembling Spencer's expedition were not unconnected with Castlereagh's absence from the war ministry. How much his illness was due to the physical and mental strain of his job, it is impossible to say. He had been showing signs of fatigue during the summer, on one occasion in July being too exhausted by 8 o'clock in the evening to introduce in the Commons his proposals for increasing the army. The session did not end until early September and by then he was reported to seem 'very ill'.[34] For the next two months he carried on, as usual taking more than his full share of the anxiety and labour of the war. But sometime towards the end of October he collapsed and for a short time was so ill that the choice of his successor was being widely discussed. The Whig politician, George Tierney, reported on November 12 that he had met Hawkesbury – presumably a reliable informant – who told him that Castlereagh 'had the week before last been in great danger from a fever he had caught, but that it was not only gone off but had produced a change in his system from which, and with care, much advantage was expected to his general health'.[35]

Whatever, if anything, that might mean, Castlereagh did gradually recover. He convalesced at Brighton where he could follow the current medical fashion and get 'as many tepid [sic] sea baths as I can well manage'.[36] By the middle of December he felt ready to return to his departmental duties. 'I gain strength every day', he wrote, 'which in truth is all that is wanting to render me completely equal to the fatigue of the winter.'[37] Less than a week later he was back at his desk.

The outlook was distinctly unpromising. The Portuguese navy, as well as the Danish, had been snatched away from Napoleon. But French troops were occupying Portugal, Spain was Napoleon's totally subservient ally, and a peace mission to the Porte by a British diplomat, Sir Arthur Paget, had been a complete failure. Only Sweden and Sicily were left to Britain as launching pads for attacks on Napoleon in Europe, and the rulers of both were thoroughly unreliable. In South America Britain no longer had even the smallest toehold. General Whitelocke's expedition to Buenos Aires had been a dismal failure and he himself was on his way home to face a court martial. Moreover, relations with the United States were deteriorating sharply as the Americans saw their commerce being crippled by the increasingly fierce Anglo-French economic warfare. An invasion of Canada by the exasperated Americans could not be ruled out.

When Castlereagh surveyed this unpropitious scene just before Christmas, he had no idea where Moore was, but feared he might still be in the Mediterranean, where there was now no obvious opening for offensive operations. Castlereagh believed that for the present Britain should concentrate on safeguarding its own commerce and colonies and denying Napoleon the resources of Spain's colonial empire. The British might even perhaps lend a hand in establishing regimes in South America that would be independent of both Spain and France. It was, he suggested to his colleagues, a 'peculiarly favourable' moment for another attempt to seize Monte Video, and if Spencer were not, after all, needed in the Mediterranean he might be usefully employed on this mission instead.[38]

Although the prime minister was impressed by Castlereagh's glowing picture of what might be achieved by a strong British military post at the mouth of the River Plate, other members of the Cabinet, worried about a possible threat to India, wanted to consolidate Britain's position in the Mediterranean. Canning proposed an attempt to seize Corfu, but that, argued Castlereagh, would only mean adding a third naval base to our existing defence commitments – Sicily and Malta – in the Mediterranean.[39] Eventually both Corfu and Monte Video were dropped, and the Cabinet decided to send instructions to overtake Spencer at Gibraltar, ordering him to send two regiments on to Sicily, leave two at Gibraltar and himself proceed with the remainder to Nova Scotia by way of Bermuda where he was to reinforce the garrison with one regiment.[40]

A few days later the situation was transformed by the news of Moore's return. 'Knowing at last where Moore is', wrote a relieved Castlereagh to Chatham on December 28, 'our arrangements will become more simple.'[41] The whole of Spencer's force, apart from the two regiments to be left at Gibraltar, could now go on to Sicily, while a new force of 4000 men could be sent from England to reinforce the garrisons in North America and the West Indies.

Unfortunately, Spencer's expedition, having escaped being dispersed by the Cabinet in London, was shortly afterwards scattered by the elements. Early in January 1808, Spencer himself with half his transports was back in Falmouth and it was February 21 before he was ready to set out again. By that time Castlereagh had had time to change his orders once again: Spencer was to remain at Gibraltar and hold himself in readiness to help the Governor of Gibraltar, General Dalrymple, to seize the North African port of Ceuta, just across the straits, which the French were reported to be planning to occupy.[42] It seemed essential to stop the French from establishing themselves in North Africa, and when the half of Spencer's force that had not been dispersed by the storm reached Sicily, the island's British garrison would be raised to 16,000 men. To Castlereagh, who had been told by one general that Sicily should have 26,000 British troops and by another 10,000, this seemed about right. He did not know that Napoleon had ordered his brother Joseph in Naples to invade Sicily, and that British troops were being ejected from Sicily's first line of defence, the forts of Scilla and Reggio on the Calabrian shore of the Straits of Messina. With too few troops to plug too many gaps, he had made a misjudgment based on inadequate information. Fortunately, Sicily was saved by a change in Napoleon's plans and by the vigilance of the Royal Navy. As for Ceuta, when Spencer surveyed the town from the sea, he discovered that its fortifications had been recently renewed, and promptly decided that to capture the town would be quite impracticable.[43] Yet again, faulty intelligence had foiled the strategist in London.

CHAPTER IX

'Preserve me from my friends and I shall not fear my enemies'
1808–09

For a rising politician, the post of Secretary for War, in wartime, was clearly full of pitfalls. When Parliament met on January 21, 1808, it was widely rumoured that the ministry was to be invigorated by restoring Melville to the Admiralty and replacing Castlereagh by Lord Wellesley, who since his return from India had been playing hard to get but was believed to be aiming at nothing less than the premiership. Castlereagh was to be given a Cabinet post of 'secondary importance', and was to be banished to the Lords.[1] No changes materialised, and it seems unlikely that Castlereagh's demotion was really being seriously considered. But the fact that it was a subject of speculation suggests that the almost unbroken series of military setbacks and his shortcomings as a speaker were already having a baneful effect on Castlereagh's reputation.

Early in February, however, Perceval, in his amiable way, praised his contribution towards fending off one of the Opposition's attacks on the Copenhagen expedition. 'Lord Castlereagh', he told the King, 'showed that he was well recovered, as he took a very useful part in the debate at a very late hour, and was fully equal to the exertion.'[2] From a military point of view there was little to attack in the Copenhagen expedition; it had been prepared with unusual speed and efficiency and had been completely successful. But the Whigs vigorously attacked the government on moral grounds for its bullying of poor little Denmark, and on political for failing to demonstrate that it had really been necessary to turn the neutral Danes into bitterly hostile enemies. Canning was the real target, and, unfortunately for Castlereagh, what was under scrutiny was not how the Secretary for War had set the expedition up, but how the Foreign Secretary had treated the Danes. And when, after several attacks on Canning's diplomacy, an Opposition motion directly censuring the Copenhagen expedition was overwhelmingly rejected, it was Canning who distinguished himself and was hailed by the Tories as the hero of the hour.

The government was more vulnerable on the economic front for the lengths to which it was carrying its trade war with Napoleon. In November 1807, after much discussion, the Cabinet had issued a new Order-in-Council designed to close the loopholes in the Talents' original Order. Based, in effect, on the principle that anyone who wanted to trade with Europe must do so only through the British, it declared that all ports from which the British flag was excluded were in a state of blockade and that, with certain exceptions designed to placate the neutrals, any ship which wished to visit them must first call at a British port and pay a duty on the re-shipment of its cargo.

The Order was certainly high-handed, and not all the members of Portland's Cabinet were happy about it. They were worried, not so much about the hardship that the economic war was causing at home, as because they realised they were making themselves extremely unpopular abroad, especially in the United States, and doubted whether they were really justified in making such ruthless use of their naval power.

Castlereagh had no doubt at all that they were. He was perhaps the most urgent and vehement advocate of the new Order-in-Council, although he was anxious to spare the neutrals where possible. The war, he told Perceval, 'is no longer a struggle for territory or point of honour, but whether the existence of Great Britain as a naval power is compatible with that of France'. Britain could not survive unless it used its sea power to defeat Napoleon's attempt to destroy its commerce, and no peace terms could be contemplated which did not end the economic as well as the military conflict. 'The contest may be a long one, but if we succeed in successfully sustaining it, we may hope for a real instead of a nominal peace.'[3]

Napoleon was reported to be 'very angry and very sore' at the new Order-in-Council.[4] His riposte, announced from Milan in December, was to authorise the seizure of any neutral vessel which had submitted to a British search or called at a British port. In the same month, the Americans, exasperated by the effects on their own trade of the Europeans' quarrels, proceeded to make them worse by slapping an embargo on all trade with France or Britain. By the beginning of 1808 international trade had been practically brought to a standstill, while industrial England was suffering all the worst effects of a serious slump: warehouses were stuffed with unsold goods, unemployment was rising, wages were falling and workers in the northern towns were simmering with discontent. Their feelings – and their employers' – were summed up in the petitions for peace from Bolton, Oldham and Manchester laid on the table of the House of Commons at the beginning of the session.

But the government was thinking not of peace but of how to break out of the tantalising military stalemate in Europe. It was a fair guess that Spain, like Portugal, would soon be placed under French occupation, and at the end of December 1807, just before some 80,000 French troops did begin to cross into Spain, Castlereagh asked General Dalrymple, the Governor of Gibraltar, to keep a close watch for any signs of popular revolt in southern Spain. The following March a series of risings by the Spaniards against the French occupation forced King Charles IV to abdicate in favour of his son Ferdinand. In April 1808 Napoleon bullied both Charles and Ferdinand into surrendering all claim to the Spanish crown and transferred his brother Joseph from the Neapolitan to the Spanish throne. From London it looked as if Spain had succumbed completely to French domination, and that Napoleon had taken a long stride towards controlling its overseas empire as well. Once more Castlereagh began to plan a South American expedition with the eager assistance of a plausible Venezuelan adventurer, General Miranda.

The military expedition that was actually launched that spring had little more to recommend it than any South American excursion except that, being sent no further than Sweden, it was easier to recall. King Gustavus, loyal as ever, had ignored the Tsar's warnings that he would lose Finland if he did not agree to help keep the British out of the Baltic. In February 1808 Russian troops duly invaded Finland and shortly afterwards the Danes also declared war on Sweden.

The Cabinet found it impossible to refuse the Swedish king's urgent appeal for help, especially as his predicament was largely due to his refusal to change sides. On April 17 General Moore was informed that he was to lead an expedition of 10,000 men to Gothenburg. What he was to do when he got there, beyond vaguely helping the King of Sweden, was not indicated, and the reason, Moore felt, was because the ministers had no specific plan to suggest.[5] Castlereagh confessed as much in his instructions to Moore. But, he added, anxiety to send prompt help to Sweden, the slowness of communications and the pressing appeals of the Swedish envoy in London, had 'prevailed over all other considerations . . .'[6] The ministers did their best to limit the risks of this leap in the dark. They reserved the right to withdraw the British force if it were needed elsewhere; the troops were to be used only in defensive operations along the coast, where they could keep in touch with the fleet; above all, they were to remain under Moore's command, although he was to pay the utmost respect to the Swedish king's wishes unless these were inconsistent with the principles of his orders. What Castlereagh did not know was that Gustavus was determined not to use British troops in the defence of Sweden, but only to help him capture Zealand from the Danes. Count Adlerberg, the Swedish envoy in London, knew this, but he kept it to himself for fear it might sap the British government's resolution to send the expedition at all.

Three days after arriving off Gothenburg on May 17, Moore confided to his diary that he saw no useful way of employing his small force in coastal operations. He could not in fact see any useful way of employing them at all. Finland had by now been swallowed up by the Russians; a Swedish invasion of Norway was making no progress; and Zealand was so strongly defended that it would be hopeless to try to take it. Moreover, in his opinion, the Swedes were not making nearly enough effort to help themselves.[7]

To make matters worse, Gustavus, contrary to previous assurances, refused the troops permission to land. He was furious at the limitations placed on their use, and in a letter to Moore expressed himself so forcibly, and at the same time so reasonably, that Moore sent the letter back to London with a request for further instructions. Castlereagh did his best, but his attempt to spell out the relationship between Moore and Gustavus in a way that would pacify the king without depriving the general of his freedom of action, only obfuscated the matter further. It was, commented Moore, 'upon the whole sufficiently inexplicit and contradictory'.[8] Castlereagh did, however, clearly instruct Moore to bring his troops home if he could not get permission for them to land.

Before obeying this order, Moore decided to go to Stockholm himself and try to come to terms with Gustavus. But a series of interviews with the king generated more heat than light and eventually Moore declared that he had better carry out his orders to take the troops home. This provoked the king to put him under arrest. Moore escaped, disguised as a peasant, returned to the fleet at Gothenburg and on July 3 sailed for home.

Fortunately, the expedition got home safely; it was only a fiasco, not a disaster. It should, of course, never have been sent in the first place. But the pressure on ministers from Gustavus was undoubtedly very heavy, and they were understandably anxious to get back into Europe – in April 1808 they were only hoping for, not counting on, a rising in Spain. They could not have foreseen that Adlerberg would withhold vital information about his king's intentions, and the dearth of military intelligence was an accepted hazard of military operations. Castlereagh tried to circumvent it by appointing a thoroughly trustworthy general and then more or less leaving it to him. He had been assured by Arthur Wellesley that he could safely confide in Moore's discretion.[9]

Wellesley was quite right. Moore carried out his impossible brief with realistic good sense. Unfortunately, although he was emphatically not a man to be overwhelmed by difficulties, he was not one to make light of them either. It was not his way to put on rose-tinted spectacles for the benefit of his political masters. But inevitably his honesty generated an aura of defeatism and left the ministers with a vague feeling that Moore had let them down. By far the worst consequence of the Swedish fiasco was that it soured the Cabinet's relations with their most experienced general, just when popular risings throughout Spain gave them their first real opportunity to break Napoleon's grip on Europe.

'This', pronounced Cobbett in his *Political Register*, 'is the *only* fair opportunity that has been offered for checking the progress of Napoleon.' And for once the ministers agreed with him. The King might urge that nothing should be done hastily, but to Castlereagh and Canning the greatest danger was that they might miss this golden opportunity through hesitation or delay. To the disgust and fury of General Miranda, Castlereagh finally abandoned his improbable South American plans and switched the destination of the 9000-strong expedition being assembled at Cork from South America to the Iberian Peninsula. No one could have been more delighted with the change than Sir Arthur Wellesley, who had already been appointed to command the Cork expedition. At last the 'sepoy' general had a chance to show what he could do in Europe – the only battle-front that really mattered.

He set out from Cork on July 12, not, as had been originally planned, for Spain, where the Spaniards insisted they could manage without foreign troops, but for Portugal, where by the end of June the whole country was up in arms. General Brent Spencer was instructed to join him from Gibraltar with his 5000 men, and somewhere down the Portuguese coast they were to make a landing.

Two days after Wellesley's departure the Cabinet decided on a radical revision of plan. A dispatch from General Spencer estimated that General Junot had 20,500 French troops under him in the Peninsula – four times as many as the estimate sent by Admiral Cotton from the mouth of the Tagus, on which Castlereagh's plans for Wellesley had been based. At the same time came news of the imminent return of Moore from Sweden. The obvious course seemed to be to reinforce Wellesley immediately with 5000 men who were being prepared in England for a raid on Boulogne, and to send Moore and his 10,000 men after them as soon as their transports could be reprovisioned.

'PRESERVE ME FROM MY FRIENDS' 1808–09

This would mean employing a total of 30,000 men on operations in Portugal – far too many, in the opinion of the Horse Guards, to be entrusted to the youngest lieutenant-general in the army. Castlereagh did not share this opinion, but he had to defer to it. The obvious choice as Wellesley's replacement was Sir John Moore, at 47 eight years Wellesley's senior, very popular with the army, and with a record of active service far longer and more distinguished than all but a very few of his seniors could boast. But Moore's outspokenness had made him so disliked by some ministers, particularly, it seems, by Canning, that the Cabinet flatly refused to let him have the command in Portugal. The choice eventually fell on Sir Hew Dalrymple, who was 58 and whose career had included only one year of active service some fifteen years earlier. On the other hand, as Governor of Gibraltar, Dalrymple had made himself well-liked by the Spaniards and probably knew as much about conditions in Spain as anyone. As his second-in-command he was given Sir Harry Burrard, an amiable but not very bright general, who appears to have owed his appointment principally to the government's determination that the command should not pass to Moore if he should happen to get to Wellesley before Dalrymple.

None of these arrangements was personally congenial to Castlereagh. If he could not have Wellesley, he would have settled for Moore. He realised (as we have seen) that Moore's outspokenness had its drawbacks, but he appreciated his qualities as a soldier and had stood up for him in the Cabinet. Not surprisingly, therefore, when he found himself obliged to tell the commander-in-chief of the Swedish expedition that he was not even to be the second-in-command in Portugal, Castlereagh's customary smoothness and *savoir faire* completely deserted him. It was evident, wrote Moore afterwards, that Lord Castlereagh was ashamed of himself – so much so that he could not bring himself to tell Moore plainly that he had been passed over. He even failed to offer him the courtesy of an explanation, so that to Moore's disappointment at being superseded was added furious anger at the way it had been done. He told Castlereagh that he had been 'unworthily' treated – 'Had I been an ensign it would hardly have been possible to treat me with less ceremony' – and having unburdened himself at some length, he got up abruptly and walked out of Castlereagh's office.[10]

A few days later, while waiting at Portsmouth to follow Arthur Wellesley to Portugal, Moore received a letter from Castlereagh informing him that the Cabinet considered his complaint unfounded, and if the expedition on which he was going had not been so far advanced, 'there would have been every disposition on their part . . . to relieve you from a situation in which you appeared to consider yourself to have been placed without a due attention to your feelings as an officer'. Moore believed that the letter was designed to goad him into an intemperate reply which would give the ministers an excuse to recall him. He refused to oblige, returning a civil but crushing reply in which he expressed his pleasure that the affair had been reported to his Majesty on whose justice he had 'the most perfect reliance'.[11]

Moore was, it is true, too touchy. But he was still smarting from having been sent on what he believed to be a fool's errand to Sweden, and to find on his return to London that the ministers had dealt him this further blow – and moreover dealt it so shabbily – was more than he could take. Far more difficult to understand or excuse is Castlereagh's letter. To threaten to dismiss – or to try to provoke into resigning – one of the country's most distinguished generals, at a most crucial point in the war, merely because he spoke his mind too freely was both irresponsible and petty. Whether Castlereagh wrote the letter willingly or under pressure from his colleagues, we do not know; either way, the responsibility, and therefore the blame, was his.

His handling of Dalrymple, if not nearly as bad, was uncharacteristically tactless. In his official letter Castlereagh managed to create the impression in Dalrymple's mind that his appointment was only temporary; and in a private letter he praised Sir Arthur Wellesley to the skies, and recommended that he should be used as prominently as possible.[12] Dalrymple immediately suspected a plan to replace him by Wellesley and the dislike which this suspicion generated was enough to destroy any chance of a harmonious working relationship between the two men. In fact, the phrasing of Castlereagh's official letter may well have been prompted by nothing worse than the Duke of York's well-known longing to take the field again, while the glowing recommendation of Wellesley was almost certainly only a rather clumsy attempt to do a good turn to a friend, who he knew would be deeply disappointed at having to step down.

Wellesley received the news of his supersession on August 1 at Mondego Bay, about a hundred miles north of Lisbon, where he had decided to land his troops. He was certainly disappointed. But he knew the ways of the army all too well, and his private letter from Castlereagh was as soothing as Dalrymple found his disturbing. Moreover, until Dalrymple, or Burrard, or Moore, or any other more senior general turned up he was his own master. 'I hope', he wrote to a friend, 'that I shall have beaten Junot before any of them shall arrive, and then they will do as they please with me.'[13] By great good fortune – and Junot's precipitancy – his hope was fulfilled.

'PRESERVE ME FROM MY FRIENDS' 1808−09

Wellesley set off down the coast road to Lisbon, carefully rejecting – as he had promised Castlereagh – any temptation to rush things in order to get the credit for defeating Junot. After a sharp engagement with the French at Rolica, he got to Vimeiro, and there, on the evening of August 20, was joined by Sir Harry Burrard, who decided not to come ashore until next day. Early the following morning Junot suddenly attacked Wellesley's army. By noon the French had been put to flight. It was Wellesley's victory, but Burrard, who had come ashore during the battle, refused to let him pursue the French and turn their defeat into a rout.

'There was something whimsically providential', wrote Castlereagh to Wellesley afterwards, 'in the enemy forcing upon you, at the very moment the command was passing – indeed, had formally passed into other hands – the glory of an achievement which your personal moderation and sense of duty had induced you not to invite by any extraordinary acceleration of your exertions.'[14] Wellesley, more briefly, described himself as 'the most fortunate man in the world'.[15] But his luck had run out. On the 22nd, the army's third commander-in-chief in twenty-four hours, Sir Hew Dalrymple, turned up. He too spurned Wellesley's proposals for an immediate advance, but agreed to a French request for an armistice. Since Sir Harry had thrown away the chance to chase the French ignominiously out of Portugal, there was much to be said for negotiating their departure without further bloodshed. But the terms which Dalrymple accepted for a French evacuation of Portugal were quite unnecessarily generous. The French troops were to be transported back to France in British ships with all their arms, baggage and 'personal property' intact. There was nothing in the agreement to stop them from taking all their Portuguese loot with them. Nor was there anything to prevent them from returning to fight in the Peninsula – as indeed most of them did.

'It was', as Wellesley said when he signed it, 'a very extraordinary paper.'[16] Next day he begged Castlereagh not to believe 'that I negotiated it, that I approve of it, or that I had any hand in wording it'.[17] Why, then, did he put his name to it? Partly, it seems, because in principle he was in favour of an armistice, and partly because his commanding officer had asked him to sign it.*

---

*Dalrymple would have signed himself, but General Kellerman, the French negotiator, suggested that Wellesley, being of corresponding rank to himself, was the appropriate signatory. This armistice agreement was then transformed into a convention which became known as the Convention of Cintra, because Sir Hew's dispatch announcing it was dated from that place.

The news of Vimeiro arrived in London on September 1. A British victory was all that was needed to cap an unaccustomed series of cheerful bulletins from the continent, including the news that Joseph Bonaparte had retreated from Madrid only eleven days after entering his new capital. Now, with Vimeiro, the expulsion of the French from the whole Peninsula seemed imminent – even, according to *The Times*, the final overthrow of 'the Tyrant' himself – and the government which had helped to bring about this happy consummation of everyone's hopes enjoyed, for once, praise and popularity.

The press and public were still in a state of euphoria when the Cabinet – shocked and furious by what they had to reveal – published the terms of the armistice. The reaction was violent. Church bells were tolled and some newspapers appeared with black borders round their reports of the convention. After Vimeiro, Cobbett had lavished praise on the 'foresight, promptitude and vigour' of the ministers. Now, like the rest of the press, he roundly attacked them, especially the Secretary for War, for their choice of generals. With withering scorn, he remarked that he had never heard any good or any harm of Sir Hew, for until the Portuguese expedition he had never heard his 'uncouth name' pronounced. But it was against Arthur Wellesley that the public's wrath was concentrated. Wellesley had actually signed the hated armistice; he belonged to a well-known – and not much liked – political family; he was himself a politician, a member even of the government – which, it was assumed, was why he had been pushed into an important command in front of his seniors.

That Arthur Wellesley's career was not broken there and then upon the rock of Cintra was largely due to Castlereagh and Spencer Perceval, who agreed that he was far too good a general to be sacrificed to popular clamour. Canning, quite unhinged by disappointment and indignation, declared that he would rather break the whole agreement than let the French carry off their plunder.[18] And he could see no reason at all why the generals responsible for it should not feel the full weight of the government's public disapproval.

The debate in the Cabinet raged for more than a week. Eventually a majority (not including Canning) agreed that only Dalrymple should be held responsible for the convention, and that if it came to a public inquiry Wellesley must be protected. 'My first object', wrote Castlereagh to Wellesley afterwards, 'is your reputation; my second is, that the country should not be deprived of your services at the present critical conjuncture.' But his conscience pricked him about Dalrymple, whose excellent judgment he had once praised. 'I hope', he continued to

'PRESERVE ME FROM MY FRIENDS' 1808–09

Wellesley, 'the anxious solicitude which I feel for your fame and interest is not incompatible with what in justice I owe others. Dalrymple's misfortune I cannot but feel, as having been the person to bring him from a situation in which he was respected and happy, to plunge him in his present embarrassment.'[19]

There was worse embarrassment to come. The public was no more appeased by Dalrymple's recall than was the Foreign Secretary, and by the end of October the Cabinet had decided that an official inquiry could not be avoided. William Wellesley-Pole feared that Castlereagh would think more of shielding his own reputation than saving Arthur's. But after a visit from Castlereagh to discuss the inquiry, Wellesley-Pole was ashamed of his suspicions. 'Castlereagh', he wrote to his brother, 'desired me particularly to say to you that he begs of you to arrange for entering into every particular of your proceedings ... so as to place your own merits most prominently forward, and not upon any account to consider his character or that of the government in anything you may have to state.' In short, concluded William, 'Castlereagh's whole conduct to me quite charmed me ...'[20] Unfortunately it was only in private, and under the spur of strong feeling, that Castlereagh's charm could break through the cold reserve with which he protected himself from the world.

At the court of inquiry Arthur Wellesley turned out to be quite capable of looking after himself. His cool defence was completely convincing, in spite of Dalrymple's efforts to shift the blame on to him. The court's report, in effect, praised Wellesley and excused Dalrymple and Burrard. It concluded that no further proceedings were necessary against any of the generals. But neither Dalrymple nor Burrard was ever employed again.

Writing to Charles Stewart a year later, Edward Cooke remembered 'the battles your brother encountered to get Sir Arthur received at Court, to counteract the Horse Guards, and to prevail on the Cabinet to defend Sir Arthur and the Convention'.[21] His efforts were appreciated as well as successful. After Castlereagh's resignation the following year, Wellesley wrote to him: 'if I had been your brother, you could not have been more careful of my interests than you have been in the late instances, and on every occasion it has always appeared to me that you sought for opportunities to oblige me and to mark your friendship for me.'[22]

To the Cabinet, in mid-September 1808, speed seemed of the essence.

The French, abandoning three-quarters of Spain, had been pushed back behind the Ebro. They had to be expelled from the country altogether before Napoleon sent massive reinforcements – as he surely would. The Spaniards had failed to agree on a commander-in-chief but they had agreed on a plan of campaign. It was not a very sound one, but it stimulated the various generals to work together and it made them abandon their hostility to British military help. From London, the situation seemed more promising than it really was and the ministers convinced themselves that they had at last found an opening in Spain.*

On September 26 Castlereagh wrote to Moore appointing him commander-in-chief of the British army in Spain and instructing him to co-operate with the Spanish armies in expelling the French.[23] It would have been difficult for the Cabinet to appoint anyone else, but at least they did it handsomely. Moore was given a free hand and nearly 40,000 men – the largest British army to operate on the continent since Marlborough's wars a century earlier. He was to take 20,000 infantry and two cavalry regiments from the British force in Portugal, and about 12,000 men under Sir David Baird would join him from England, disembarking at Corunna. It was left to Moore to decide where he would rendezvous with Baird and exactly how he would then help the Spaniards. There was none of the 'plausible verbose nonsense' which was Moore's contemptuous description of Castlereagh's long-winded attempt to give guidance to Dalrymple on possible operations in Spain.[24]

The news of his assignment reached Moore at Lisbon on October 6. He was greatly surprised. 'How they came to pitch upon me', he commented, 'I cannot say, for they have given sufficient proof of not being partial to me.'[25] By a great effort, he managed to get his whole force equipped and on its way before the end of October, and by November 13 he had reached Salamanca. Two days later he heard that the French had advanced to Valladolid, only three to four days' march away. By now he realised that the situation in Spain was very different from what Castlereagh, buoyed up by misleading reports, optimistically believed it to be. The massive reinforcements summoned from Germany, Italy and France were overrunning northern Spain, Napoleon

*Castlereagh also intended that Sir John Stuart, the British commander-in-chief in Sicily, should send a British force to help the Catalonians, hoping, as he told Stuart, that 'the Court of Palermo will feel that ... the completion of the great work in Spain is of more consequence than an imperfect attempt in Italy ...' But Stuart apparently never felt that he could detach enough troops from the defence of Sicily to make the attempt feasible. (C.C.VII, p.1. Nov. 8, 1808)

himself had arrived to take command, and the Spanish armies, weak in numbers and quality and with commanders as disunited as ever, were being destroyed piecemeal. The authorities in Madrid lacked energy and ability and the ordinary people seemed to have lapsed into hopeless passivity. With the French so far advanced, Moore's chances of linking up with Baird, whom he had ordered to make for Astorga, were doubtful.* His whole situation in fact was far more precarious than he had anticipated.

It is not hard to imagine the acute disappointment with which Moore's dispatches were read by ministers in London. It did not help that he already had a reputation for making the worst of everything. But Castlereagh accepted his analysis and thanked him for 'the plain and candid' manner in which he had presented it. He was confident, he added, 'however delicate the decision on certain occasions may be, that you will fulfil the task imposed on you with ability and judgment'.[26]

During the weeks that ended at Corunna Moore had more than his fair share of delicate decisions to make. His aim was to seek a victory that might rouse and rally the Spaniards without risking the useless sacrifice of his own army. Hence the long wait at Salamanca; the decision to retreat after learning that the last Spanish army had been defeated; the countermanding of the retreat after hearing that Madrid had risen (unsuccessfully) against the French; the advance on Marshal Soult's isolated corps near Sahagun; finally, the retreat on Corunna, after learning that Napoleon was in pursuit with an overwhelmingly superior force.

Moore believed that he had 'risked infinitely too much; but something, I thought, was to be risked for the honour of the service and to make it apparent that we stuck to the Spaniards long after they themselves had given up their cause as lost'.[27] But in London the long wait, the apparent indecisiveness, the precipitate retreat, all made a lamentable impression. It was not of course immediately apparent that Moore's campaign had thoroughly disrupted Napoleon's ambitious plans to sweep Portugal and southern Spain into his net before advancing through Gibraltar into North Africa. Even the British victory at Corunna and Moore's gallant death were blotted out in the popular mind by the ignominious evacuation which followed and the shocking state of the emaciated, wounded soldiers who were disem-

*Baird and his infantry arrived at Corunna on October 13, but it was nearly a fortnight before he could persuade the local junta to let his troops disembark. His cavalry did not arrive until November 13. The whole of Baird's force was eventually united with Moore's on December 20 at Mayorga.

barked at ports all along the south coast. There was an outburst of public indignation against the Spaniards who – by the soldiers' accounts – had treated their allies so badly, against the general who had led them to disaster and against the government which was ultimately to blame for it all.

Not all the Cabinet were prepared to accept the blame. Moore's candour, for which Castlereagh had been grateful, infuriated Canning, who for several weeks before the general's death had been agitating for his recall on the grounds that he was far too defeatist to achieve anything in Spain. When his criticism seemed to be vindicated, Canning apparently urged the Cabinet to shift the blame for what had happened on to the dead general. But Castlereagh would no more make a scapegoat of Moore, who could contribute nothing more to Napoleon's defeat, than he would of Arthur Wellesley, of whom he hoped so much. On January 25, 1809 he gave the House of Commons a moving account of Moore's death and categorically acquitted him of any blame for the failure of the expedition.[28]

If the general was not to blame, then the ministers surely must be, and a month later George Ponsonby, the leader of the Opposition, moved for an inquiry into the Corunna campaign. He was answered by Castlereagh who, in his plodding way, gave what Perceval described as 'a very full and able exposure of the whole of the proceedings in Spain'. But the star turn that evening was Canning. In spite of a stunning counter-attraction provided by 'the immense blaze of light' from Drury Lane Theatre, which had caught on fire, the Foreign Secretary's 'commanding' speech, reported Perceval, 'had a very great effect on the House'.[29] Even without spectacular distractions, the same could only very rarely be said of Castlereagh's speeches.

Even the most eloquent of War Secretaries would not have found it easy to put a brave face on a campaigning season marked by Moore's Swedish fiasco, the Cintra convention and the Corunna evacuation. Ponsonby, whose own grasp of strategy was minimal, described the government's war effort as 'a sort of pantomimical movement of fleets and armies from one end of Europe to the other without effecting anything'.[30] It was unfair but cruelly plausible, especially against a background of persistent rumours that the ministry was at sixes and sevens and likely soon to fall apart altogether.

On the domestic front too the government was under constant attack. Early in the session, a certain Gwyllym Wardle MP alleged that the

'PRESERVE ME FROM MY FRIENDS' 1808 – 09

Duke of York's mistress, Mary Ann Clarke, had been selling army commissions, and for nearly two months parliamentary business was either totally monopolised or heavily overshadowed by an inquiry into Wardle's allegations. The duke himself was acquitted of any personal involvement, but hostile debates in the Commons and public clamour without eventually forced him to resign as commander-in-chief. It was a sharp rebuff for the government which had been drawn (very ill-advisedly, in Canning's opinion) into wholeheartedly espousing his cause.

The success of the York inquiry, and the public acclaim it brought its instigators, encouraged the more radical members of the Opposition to pursue their spring-cleaning activities. In particular they renewed their efforts to promote parliamentary reform by attacking the traditional and well-accepted (not least by Whig grandees like Grey and Grenville) practices by which governments were in the habit of managing Parliament. If this involved throwing mud at eminent members of the Treasury bench, so much the better. Castlereagh was an obvious target because of the reputation he had acquired in Ireland and because – as Lord Bathurst commented – of 'his general unpopularity (I know not why)'.[31] A radical member, William Madocks, tried to put both Perceval and Castlereagh in the dock for corrupt electoral practices, but his charges were so vague and his motion so obviously focused on parliamentary reform, that the House, as Castlereagh cheerfully reported, 'disposed of the question with a high hand'.[32]*

But while only a few really wanted to turn the whole political system upside down, many more were ready to attack an unpopular minister in an increasingly discredited ministry. A Commons committee inquiring into the East India Company's patronage unearthed the fact that when Castlereagh was President of the Board of Control, he offered Lord Clancarty the disposal of a writership (clerkship) to help him obtain a seat in Parliament. It was a common enough practice of which no notice would normally be taken. But it was undoubtedly a technical offence, and the Opposition, sensing the mood of the House, decided that they might force Castlereagh to resign. On April 25, he made a personal statement, admitting the offence but denying any corrupt motive, and then withdrew from the Chamber. In the subsequent censure debate,

*Madocks's most specific allegation was that Mr Quintin Dick, who had purchased the seat for Cashel, an Irish borough, through the good offices of the Treasury, had been told to resign after voting against the government on the York inquiry. In fact, Dick seems to have resigned voluntarily in accordance with the customary practice of members who voted against the known wishes of their patron, in this case the Treasury.

several speakers brought up his Irish past, but Grattan, his bitterest opponent in Dublin, praised his 'frank and well-judged' statement and thought it unfair to bring up his Irish conduct when he was accused of something quite different.[33] (He was, Castlereagh thought, 'particularly gentlemanlike'.[34]) Although many speakers felt the censure motion to be unnecessarily harsh, the temper of the House was such that Perceval thought it wiser to settle for a conciliatory amendment which passed by the not very impressive majority of forty-nine.

Castlereagh, however, professed himself perfectly satisfied with the outcome. 'Having got into the scrape', he wrote to his brother Charles, 'I cannot regret that the whole has been sifted to the bottom.'[35] The prime minister was relieved; it was, he felt, impossible to attribute any bad motive to Castlereagh, and his enforced resignation would have 'the most injurious consequences to the interests of the public'.[36] But Canning, although he had played his part in defending Castlereagh, complained privately that he ought to have resigned before the debate.

In the weeks following the Corunna disaster it was not immediately obvious that the government ought to persevere with hostilities in the Peninsula. In the spring of 1809 other parts of the continent looked more promising. Stimulated by the Spanish example, nationalists in northern and central Europe were reported to be on the verge of revolt. In April, the Austrian government, encouraged by the unrest, declared war on France, forcing Napoleon to hurry across Europe from Paris to repel an Austrian advance into Bavaria. In the Peninsula, on the other hand, the Spanish armies were in disarray, French troops were poised to overrun Spain, the Spaniards – suspecting the British of plotting a second Gibraltar – refused to let British troops establish a base at Cadiz and Soult was advancing southwards through Portugal.

The Cabinet's doubts were reflected in the confused instructions sent to General Cradock, Moore's successor in Portugal. But by the end of February 1809, the ministers had made up their minds not, if they could help it, to be ejected from Lisbon. 'Maintain yourself as long as possible in Portugal', was Castlereagh's unusually terse instruction to Cradock.[37] Shortly afterwards the Peninsular option was clinched by Arthur Wellesley with a memorandum arguing that, with 20,000 British troops and a reconstituted Portuguese army, Portugal could and should be held whatever happened in Spain.[38] Castlereagh's faith in Wellesley was unlimited. Before the end of the month he had persuaded his colleagues not only to accept Wellesley's plan but to give its author a second chance in the Peninsula.

Sir Arthur Wellesley arrived at Lisbon on April 22, and found the city *en fête* to welcome him. He went through the uncomfortable business of taking over from his old friend Cradock,* and then made a quick decision to march north and rescue Oporto which the French had captured and sacked a few weeks earlier. On May 12 Soult and his men were bundled out of Oporto and five days later they were chased over the frontier into Spain. With the minimum of casualties to the British, Portugal was once more freed of the French.

It was a notable achievement, even though Wellesley failed to bring Soult to bay and destroy his army completely. In England there was some grumbling that he had not. Wellesley felt let down and complained that the government was too weak to give a lead to public opinion.[39] But perhaps the ministers simply had too much else to worry about. For Castlereagh the damaging effects on the army of the Corunna retreat and evacuation greatly increased all the usual difficulties of organising an expeditionary force. But he was delighted and exhilarated by Wellesley's success, adding to his congratulations 'my best wishes for your future success and personal glory. I am doing what I can to promote it by strengthening you from hence, and shall press everything forward as much as possible.'[40]

Wellesley was promised 5000 more men and authorised to extend operations into Spain on his own initiative. Maybe with Napoleon busy fighting the Austrians, a breakthrough in Spain was really possible, and in the hope of propelling the Spaniards into more effective co-operation, the government appointed Arthur's eldest brother, Lord Wellesley, as ambassador to Seville. 'So', commented Castlereagh cheerfully to his brother Charles, who was serving with Arthur Wellesley, 'if you don't kick up a dust in the Peninsula during the summer, it's not our fault.'[41]

Wellesley had every intention of kicking up a dust in the Peninsula. He planned to advance eastwards up the Tagus, link up with his Spanish allies and make for Madrid. But he could not move from his headquarters at Abrantes without supplies, reinforcements and, above all, money. In London Castlereagh toiled away to meet all Wellesley's demands – bread, flour, forage and 50,000 pairs of shoes, 20,000 more than had been requested, so as not to run short of 'so important an article'.[42] The 3000-strong Light Brigade, which Castlereagh had had

---

*In a letter of monumental tactfulness, Castlereagh offered Cradock a transfer to Gibraltar, but Cradock was not to be consoled and preferred to come home. (C.C.VII, pp. 44/5)

the greatest difficulty in assembling, eventually sailed from the Downs on May 24, only to be driven by gales into Portsmouth where it still was on June 11. Breaking the news to Wellesley, Castlereagh was reduced to a portentous statement of the obvious: 'It is', he wrote, 'a lamentable proof of the uncertainty of all military combinations, which depend on maritime movements, to state that Craufurd's Brigade is still in port, having been ready since the 24th of last month.'[43]*

Contrary winds held up most of the reinforcements which Castlereagh had intended for the advance into Spain. But it was lack of money, not men, that really held Wellesley up. 'We are terribly distressed for money ...', he wrote to the British minister in Portugal. 'I suspect the Ministers in England are very indifferent to our operations in this country.'[44] Nothing could be more unfair. The ministers were at their wits' end to find him money. By early June the Treasury had managed to scrape together £230,000 in Spanish and Portuguese currency, but Castlereagh warned Wellesley that, until fresh supplies arrived from South America, he would have to try to raise more money by bills.[45]

The specie reached Abrantes on June 25, and two days later Wellesley set out for Spain. A month later, on July 28, he defeated the French at Talavera. The victory earned him a peerage but got him nowhere. The dearth of supplies, the shortcomings of his Spanish allies, and half a dozen encircling French marshals – all these forced him to turn round and embark on the long, dreary retreat back to Lisbon and, eventually, to the protection of the lines of Torres Vedras.

'We are getting troops ready', wrote Edward Cooke on June 6, 'but [are] not resolved how to use them.'[46] The news that the Austrians had beaten Napoleon at Aspern made the urge to use them all the stronger. But where and how? A bigger build-up in the Peninsula was ruled out by the dire shortage of specie. So was north Germany for the same reason, and also because without Russian and Prussian support the operation would be too risky. There remained the Scheldt, which had often been thought of but never attempted. Twenty new French warships were lying in the river below Antwerp and there were said to be many fewer enemy troops than usual in the surrounding region. Why not send an amphibious force to seize the island of Walcheren, demolish the naval

*Craufurd's Brigade eventually caught up with Wellesley early on the day after the battle of Talavera.

installations at Flushing and Antwerp, destroy all enemy shipping, perhaps make the river unnavigable and, last but not least, make a powerful diversion which would draw troops back from the Austrian front? Such an operation, Castlereagh argued, would 'bring the greatest possible amount of force naval and military to tell against the enemy'. With their 'very limited command of money' there was, he felt, really no other option. 'We could only look, at the present moment, to a coup de main, and in no [other] quarter could such an effort be made to comprehend so many objects.'[47]

But the military were heavily discouraging. When asked for his professional opinion, Sir David Dundas, the new commander-in-chief, produced five memoranda, one written by himself and the others by four different senior officers, all agreeing that the enterprise was extremely hazardous and had little, if any, chance of success. Much essential intelligence – about enemy strength round Antwerp, navigable channels in the river, landing places, fortifications, roads – was either meagre, non-existent, or precariously based on the recollections of someone who had fought there fifteen years earlier. The objectives of the operation were bold and clear, but how to reach them was shrouded in obscurity.

Castlereagh, however, had set his heart on a Scheldt expedition. On his own initiative (but with Portland's approval) he had already offered the command of the expedition to Lord Chatham eleven days before he inquired at the Horse Guards whether it was feasible.[48] He seems to have determined to discount the forebodings of the military, and most of his colleagues gradually came, if not to share his optimism, at least to agree that the risks were worth taking. On June 21 the Cabinet finally made up their mind, 'not disguising from themselves', Castlereagh told the King, 'the difficulties of the enterprise but deeply impressed with its importance ...'[49] By that time the French, whose intelligence was invariably far superior to that of the British, had a pretty shrewd idea of what was afoot and were busy repairing defences and bringing in reinforcements. The operation which Castlereagh had meant to be a swift surprise attack was neither swift nor a surprise.

It had been hoped to get the troops equipped, the transport collected and the expedition away well before the middle of July. But it was the 28th before it finally sailed – an impressive armada of thirty-five ships of the line, twenty-three frigates and nearly 200 smaller vessels, carrying between them nearly 40,000 troops. Castlereagh, Canning and Perceval all went down to Deal to see them go. For Castlereagh it was 'a busy and anxious week, worried with the east wind and the other inevitable impediments'.[50] There was also bad news from Austria. A report of Napoleon's victory at Wagram on July 6 reached England on the 21st, and only the day before the expedition sailed it was learnt that the Austrians had been granted an armistice.

There was still a chance that the armistice would not be converted into a peace, but Castlereagh's optimism had been sharply dented. He still confidently anticipated the capture of Walcheren, but further operations against Antwerp were, he told Charles Stewart, 'much more questionable',[51] and the value of the operation as a diversion had been ended by the Austrian armistice. Presumably it was too late, even if it was ever considered, to put the whole thing into reverse.

The Austrian collapse would also allow the release of more French troops for Spain. 'We have a *devil of a task* before us in the Peninsula', wrote Castlereagh to Charles on August 5, 'now that Austria is disposed of – If any man alive can carry us through it Wellesley will, and whatever may be the issue, I am confident he will *personally* rise with his difficulties.'[52]*

The news of Talavera, which arrived nine days later, confirmed Castlereagh's faith in his favourite general. A few days later he heard that Flushing had been captured on August 16. It was well behind schedule, but at least it was a success, and the heady mixture of jubilation and apprehension made his composition even more convoluted than usual – 'so hazardous and critical an operation (danger of navigation included) as our expedition to Antwerp is, I believe never was before attempted – so God send us a good deliverance'.[53]

By then, August 21, only divine intervention could have saved the expedition. From the beginning very little had gone right for it. The weather had been consistently dreadful, with 'very severe blowing weather'[54] and the heaviest rain Lord Chatham had ever seen.[55] The French had opened the dykes so that the troops were often up to their knees in water. The navigational difficulties had proved unexpectedly baffling. The tight co-operation between army and navy, indispensable to success, was conspicuously lacking, and soon after the fall of

---

*A few days earlier Castlereagh had found time to write a long letter to Charles Stewart about his jealousy of Arthur Wellesley. Stewart had complained that Wellesley held him back, and criticised him for being insufficiently bold in war. Wellesley had in fact had to halt a foolhardy and unauthorised attack, led by Stewart, during the pursuit of Soult. On August 31, Castlereagh again admonished his brother on this subject. 'You have a taste rather for a quarrel', he wrote, 'this may do better with your mistress than with your wife, but it will not do at all with your General – so for God's sake put an end to it...'. (Castlereagh Mss (Belfast) D3030.Q/2)

Flushing, Chatham was openly at odds with his naval commander, Sir Richard Strachan. Lastly, the troops began to succumb at an alarming rate to the malignant fever which was endemic in Walcheren and the surrounding country at that time of year.

Meanwhile the French had moved their warships under the guns of the citadel at Antwerp and had had plenty of time to repair the town's fortifications and to pour troops into Antwerp and the neighbouring towns. By the end of August it was clear to Chatham that the odds had turned too heavily against him and he decided to order a withdrawal, leaving behind a sufficient force to hold the island of Walcheren.[56]

In the circumstances, Chatham really had no choice, but this did not prevent him from being savagely criticised, both privately and in the press, for his allegedly slothful and ineffective conduct of the expedition. His indolence was notorious, but his reputation as a soldier was by no means negligible, and it is unlikely that anyone else could have done much better. The operation could only have succeeded in ideal conditions and with plenty of luck. It had neither.

The Walcheren fever was the last straw. When Chatham decided to withdraw, there were about 3000 men on the sick list. Thereafter the number rose steeply; by September 6 it was over 8000 and by the 11th nearly 11,000. Castlereagh, who had laboured so strenuously to equip the expedition, did not warn the medical authorities to expect a high sickness rate. He knew that Walcheren was 'exceedingly unwholesome' late in the year[57] (in fact July to October was the worst period) but had never intended or envisaged that the army should be locked up there so long.[58] In any case, neither he nor the medical authorities could have foreseen the calamitous effect of incessant rain, permanently wet feet and unsuitable food or the men's lack of resistance to disease. And in any case, in the state of medical knowledge at that time, more doctors and quinine could have done little to improve matters.

When the government did realise the scale of the disaster, Castlereagh and Perceval made every effort to send medical supplies and doctors and to arrange for the sick to be brought back to England. They were only moderately successful, because civilian doctors were unwilling to go, and the army medical authorities, with some honourable exceptions, were either cocooned in red tape, absorbed in internal feuds or downright incompetent. Throughout September and October the disease continued to attack the garrison of about 16,000 men left on Walcheren. In the middle of September half the men were in hospital. In the last week of October nearly 1300 fresh cases were reported and nearly a hundred deaths. As many as possible of the sick were sent home to give them a better chance of recovery, and by the beginning of November the army was so depleted that the island was virtually defenceless.[59]

At long last, on November 4, the government ordered the evacuation of Walcheren. The decision should have been taken many weeks earlier. But for nearly two months the government had been almost totally preoccupied with its own internal dissensions.

On September 7 Castlereagh began to discover that for the past five months an axe had been suspended over his head. Over dinner, Lord Camden reluctantly revealed that the Duke of Portland had resigned as prime minister the previous day because of ill-health, and the rest of the Cabinet had decided to strengthen the government by a reshuffle which would include the removal of Castlereagh himself from the War department. According to Camden, it was a 'very long and painful conversation', but Castlereagh received the astonishing news 'firmly and reasonably'.[60] Next day, after an interview with Portland, he sent in his resignation. For the time being he continued to transact the official business of his department, especially whatever concerned the needs of the Walcheren sick, but refused to take any part in decisions on policy.

Camden, anxious to spare his nephew's feelings, had not told him the full story. But a few days later, Perceval, not realising how much Castlereagh still had to learn, showed him some correspondence which had passed between himself and Canning. From this Castlereagh learned that his removal from the War department, far from being – as Camden had suggested – a direct consequence of Portland's resignation, had been discussed by his colleagues for months past and, moreover, had been firmly settled before the Cabinet decided to go ahead with the Walcheren expedition.[61] As long ago as the previous April Canning had made it clear to Portland that he was thoroughly dissatisfied with the conduct of the war, and unless Castlereagh was removed from the War department, would resign himself.[62]

Canning's ultimatum gradually became known to the King and most of the Cabinet, who all set themselves to find a way of pacifying Canning, who was considered indispensable, without mortally offending Castlereagh. But the weeks passed and nothing was settled. Nor, to the acute embarrassment of his colleagues, including Canning, was anything said to Castlereagh – partly because the King wished to find a solution first, partly because it was considered unkind to tell Castlereagh when he was working so hard on the Walcheren expedition, and partly because Camden, when definitely deputed to break the news, shirked the task. In the end Portland reluctantly decided he must undertake it himself. But before he could do so, he was seized by a serious paralytic stroke.

By this time it was the middle of August. The duke recovered surprisingly quickly, but it was clear he could not go on as premier. The choice of a successor promised to be difficult largely because Canning's colleagues were unwilling to gratify his barely concealed pretensions. But at least the leadership crisis offered a solution to the intractable problem of the Secretary for War: in the general reshuffle that would naturally follow the appointment of a new prime minister, Castlereagh could be shunted from the War department to another post with the minimum of unpleasantness.

At the beginning of September there was bad news from both war fronts: Chatham had decided to retire from the Scheldt, and Wellesley had begun to retreat into Portugal. Canning renewed his pressure for Castlereagh's immediate replacement by Lord Wellesley. But Perceval, Liverpool and Bathurst, determined not to risk losing Castlereagh altogether, refused to move him except as part of a general reshuffle. They tactfully urged Portland to resign without delay. He did so on September 6, and on the same day told Canning that Castlereagh could not be summarily dismissed without destroying the ministry.[63] The Foreign Secretary's response was to hint at his own resignation and refuse to attend the Cabinet meeting next day. It was Castlereagh's persistent questioning, over the dinner table next day, about the reasons for Canning's absence, that finally forced his uncle to begin to reveal what had been going on for so long.

The full story of the summer's political manoeuvrings, of which this account is a very brief summary, can only have become gradually known to Castlereagh – if indeed it ever was fully known. But by the middle of September he had learned enough to be very angry indeed. 'I consider', he wrote to Cooke on the 16th, 'that I have been sacrificed to a colleague, both unjustly and ungenerously, and under circumstances of concealment the most unjustifiable. It is impossible for me to disguise from Mr Perceval or myself the extent to which my confidence in my colleagues has been shaken by what has passed.' If, he went on, the campaigns in Spain and Holland have been disappointing, 'I cannot submit to charge myself with any excessive portion of the blame (if blame at all exists) which may be thrown upon those failures. If my colleagues (whose support and confidence I had no reason to doubt accompanied me throughout my late anxious and laborious duties) are either *unable* or *unwilling* to sustain me in that situation [i.e. the War department] I desire in that case only the privilege of being allowed to defend out of office my own public character and conduct.'[64]

As for his private honour, there was, he felt, only one way to defend it from the injury it had received from the long concealment of the intention to remove him. On the 19th Castlereagh sent Canning a very stiffly worded challenge. He accepted Canning's right to demand his removal, but not 'at the expense of my honour and reputation'.[65] In fact Canning, far from being responsible for the concealment, had frequently protested against it. His second, Charles Ellis, tried to explain this to Lord Yarmouth, Castlereagh's second, and Perceval sent some of Canning's letters, which clearly showed he had been opposed to secrecy. But Castlereagh would not withdraw.

The duel took place on Putney Heath at six o'clock on the morning of September 21. On the way there, Castlereagh and Yarmouth discussed Catalani, a fashionable opera singer, and Castlereagh hummed snatches from her songs. The two opponents emerged untouched from the first round. Castlereagh insisted on a second and hit his opponent through the fleshy part of the thigh. Only then was he satisfied and went forward to take Canning's arm and, together with Ellis, help him to a neighbouring house. Mr Canning's conduct on the field, he conceded afterwards, had been 'very proper'.

On the same day Castlereagh poured out his furious indignation in a long letter to his father that was obviously meant to justify the extreme lengths to which he had just gone. 'I was', he wrote, 'by the infatuation and folly of those who called themselves my friends, allowed to remain in total ignorance of my situation – to plunge into ever heavier responsibility after my death warrant was signed, and further, I was to be kept in profound ignorance of this until the moment should arise, namely, the close of the expedition, when I was to be equally dismissed in the event of failure, or success, unless Mr Canning in his mercy should be disposed to spare his victim, being made absolute master of my fate. I hope my public and private character will survive the perils to which it has been exposed, but you may imagine what would have been the impression had I submitted to be so duped and practised upon, and how small a portion of the world would have believed that I was not *privy to my own disgrace*, it being more generally credible that a public man should be guilty of a shabby act to keep himself in office, than that his colleagues, his friends, his private connection Lord Camden should presume without any authority from him, and *without even his knowledge*, to place him in a situation so full of danger and so full of dishonour. I must give them credit for good intentions but I can only say in that case preserve me from my friends and I shall not fear my enemies.'[66]

Poor Lord Camden, the friend and connection most bitterly blamed by Castlereagh, was shattered by his nephew's wrath. Shortly after the duel, he rushed out to Castlereagh's country home at Stanmore, just outside London, broke into his nephew's room, burst into tears and wholeheartedly condemned his own conduct. Castlereagh gave him his hand and disclaimed any personal resentment. But he added that he could never forget the political injury done him, and a few days later turned down a suggestion from Camden that he should pay him another visit.[67]* By this time Canning had definitely resigned, the Portland ministry had finally disintegrated and the survivors were striving to patch together an alternative. But Castlereagh refused even to be told what they were about, 'having', he told his brother, 'quite enough to do to save my own reputation from being buried in the ruins of intrigue, shabbiness and incapacity'.[68]

Like most extremely reserved men, when he did lose his temper, Castlereagh did it thoroughly. And the fact that he had apparently waited so long before issuing his challenge gave it an unfortunate and unfair appearance of being a deliberate and cold-blooded act of revenge. Most people felt he was not justified in challenging Canning on the grounds he gave, and that he had in any case directed his wrath at the wrong target. (Wellington, however, admitted that 'your feelings could not have been otherwise satisfied'.[69]) It was the King's well-meaning prohibition, the poor old duke's misguided kindness and Camden's weakness and moral cowardice that were really responsible for leaving Castlereagh in ignorance for so long.

Yet basically his instinct was correct. It was Canning and no one else who had started the political crisis by criticising Castlereagh behind his back, and protracted it for five months by keeping up the pressure to move the Secretary for War. It was not attractive behaviour and Canning's published attempt to put it in a favourable light did not impress even his friends. After all, he could have ended the concealment at any time by writing to Castlereagh himself. When the dust had settled, Castlereagh was found to be enjoying a good deal of public sympathy for the underhand way he had been treated, and the revelation that he had a

---

*Relations remained severed until December 1810, when Camden sent Castlereagh a note about some discussion in a Lords' Committee. Castlereagh called next day to thank him for it, 'thinking it better to put an end to that total interruption of intercourse which makes other[s] uncomfortable'. (Castlereagh Mss (Belfast) D3030. Q2. to Charles Stewart, Dec. 21, 1810)

spirited Irish temper under his cold reserve helped to raise him in popular estimation.

The lengthy post-mortem on the causes of the crisis, by politicians, press and society in general, centred almost entirely on the way Castlereagh had been moved, not whether he deserved to be moved in the first place. Canning had originally complained of the government's 'spirit of compromise' and desire to get round difficulties rather than confront them boldly. His chief specific complaint was that the government had lost 'character' and popularity by accepting responsibility for the Cintra convention and the failure of Moore's campaign in Spain.[70] Castlereagh felt that it would have been thoroughly discreditable to do anything else. In the apologia he sent the King after the duel (written in the formal third person), he wrote: 'If an earnest desire to protect the fame and characters of officers, exposing their reputations as well as their lives in your Majesty's service ... can be denominated *compromise*, Lord Castlereagh cannot wish to exculpate himself from the imputation. He can never cease to reflect with satisfaction ... that he never yet has abandoned one of them in a manner, of the justice of which, they felt themselves entitled to complain – he cannot persuade himself that it would either have been consistent with justice or for the advantage of your Majesty's service that Sir J. Moore (had his life been happily spared to your Majesty) or that Lord Wellington should have been disgraced by your Majesty's Government.'[71]

The Opposition were constantly complaining about the mismanagement of the war. But, as we have seen, the difficulties of organising military operations through a number of separate antiquated bureaucracies were formidably daunting. Castlereagh was not daunted, and his colleagues seem to have agreed that he was an able, conscientious and immensely hard-working departmental minister. It was only Canning's restless prodding that pushed them into agreeing to move him. Several of them offered to give up their own posts if that would help to keep him in the Cabinet. And Perceval was distressed that although Castlereagh's resignation was 'entirely independent' of the Scheldt expedition, in the public mind the two would almost inevitably be connected.[72]

Castlereagh's faults as a war minister arose more from trying to do too much than from not trying hard enough. They were faults of judgment. Moore, Wellington and Chatham all complained at one time or another that his dispatches were unrealistically based on inaccurate or over-optimistic assessments. He hated to feel he was not making use of all the available troops all the time. He always sought and valued military

'PRESERVE ME FROM MY FRIENDS' 1808–09

advice, but he was capable of ignoring warnings about the military risks of an operation when he was convinced of its political importance. The proposal to invade southern Italy in 1807 (which the generals ignored), the abortive expedition to Sweden, Moore's campaign in Spain, and the Walcheren operation were all responses to military or political developments on the continent made against the professional advice of the military.

In retrospect Castlereagh realised that Moore's assessment of the support to be expected from the Spaniards was more accurate than the optimistic reports from diplomats on the spot or the 'sanguine conceptions' of ministers at a distance.[73] But at the time it was very hard to strike the correct balance between the military risks and the undeniable political advantages of further intervention in Spain. The Walcheren expedition was his biggest gamble, and perhaps had the least political or military justification, although the French were at first greatly perturbed. At the time critics complained that the troops should have gone to Spain. But Wellington himself said he did not want them while his supply difficulties were so great.[74] The real criticism is that the risks were too great, the timing was wrong, and the troops should have been kept in reserve until a more promising means of using them could be found. But Castlereagh had a weakness for 'coups de main' and a strong reluctance to husband his resources.

In the early nineteenth century, to plan and direct a global war successfully from Downing Street was an almost impossible operation, and not only because of the appalling deficiencies of the administrative machine. If the minister waited for adequate information, he would, as Castlereagh once told the Commons, be accused of the 'most culpable tardiness'.[75] But operations planned on the basis of incomplete, inaccurate and conflicting information were unlikely to go smoothly or according to plan, even if they escaped being disrupted by the unpredictable vagaries of the weather. Once an operation was launched, however, there was little the minister could do to influence its course. By the time his dispatches reached the commanding general they were usually hopelessly outdated. Inevitably, the attempt to respond to events gave an impression of confused fumbling, especially when the theatre was as distant as the Mediterranean. In theory, the sensible course was to choose a good general and then more or less give him a free hand. In practice, this was not always possible, either because no good general was available or because of opposition from the Horse Guards.

If a military operation was, against all the odds, successful, the general got the credit. If it failed the minister got the blame – or did if he was Castlereagh, who scorned to try to shift it elsewhere. But he was too unpopular to win much sympathy when he denied that any blame was justified. 'I know', commented the Duke of Richmond from Dublin, 'Castlereagh is so unpopular that most things he does will be disapproved of.'[76] Even his colleagues, who appreciated his merits and liked him personally, were ready to spare his feelings but not give him unqualified backing. Unpopularity is a damning liability for a politician.*

As for Castlereagh, in the weeks after the duel he seems to have become increasingly convinced that he was well quit of his former colleagues. The King was sympathetic although he strongly disapproved of duels. He assured Castlereagh that the only reason for his removal had been Canning's threat of resignation which it was feared might break up the government.[77] So long as he could believe that his misfortunes were not the result of his own failure, Castlereagh could bear them with equanimity. 'I have every reason', he wrote to Charles on October 16, 'to be satisfied with the course I have pursued ... and as it has pleased Providence that I should begin the world again, I need not fret my heart at losing so shabby a set of friends as mine have proved themselves.'[78]

*About this time Perceval commented to Plumer Ward on the importance of reputation, whether well or ill founded. 'He illustrated this by the instance of Lord Castlereagh, who had very considerable talents, added even to great conciliation of manners, but yet whose great want of popularity made it impossible in some people's minds to derive advantage from a junction with him. He laid a stress on *some people's minds*, as if it was not a sentiment of his own, but one to which he had been obliged to defer.' (R. Plumer Ward. *Memoirs*, I, pp.290/1)

CHAPTER X

'I am not playing a game for office'
1809–12

Castlereagh's new life began with nearly two and a half years of freedom from the responsibilities of a departmental minister and the nightly strain of defending government policy in the Commons. Unlike Canning, for whom a day out of office was a day wasted, he thoroughly enjoyed his new independence. Far from being inhibited by painful recollections, he positively blossomed on the back benches, speaking with a vivacity and assurance that surprised his listeners.

His former colleagues may well have envied him, since their own situation was far from happy. Once Canning had eliminated himself, Portland's mantle descended without much further argument on to Perceval's shoulders. Mild and unassuming, Perceval possessed the advantages of an excellent brain, an outstanding reputation for personal integrity, and the wholehearted support of the King. But with Canning and Castlereagh as well as Sidmouth now on the sidelines, the old party of Mr Pitt's Friends seemed to be fast falling apart. It took Perceval two months of laborious negotiations to fill all the posts in his government, although nearly half the members of the old Cabinet (the worst half) remained where they were. Lord Wellesley graciously agreed to return from his Spanish mission and take over the Foreign Office. Lord Liverpool (as Hawkesbury had now become) moved to the War department, and was succeeded at the Home Office by Richard Ryder, an old friend of Perceval's, much given to headaches, who felt his health would not stand up to the work and worry of the War department. Perceval would have liked to give up the Chancellorship of the Exchequer, but after six people had refused the post, he had to keep it himself. The second-rank and junior posts were equally hard to fill. Nobody wanted to join a government whose chances of survival seemed so poor.

With the failure of the Walcheren expedition and Wellington's retreat into Portugal, the war gave the Opposition plenty of ammunition. Their problem was to agree at which target to aim, some letting fly at the generals in the field, especially Wellington, and some at the government at home. Their amendment to the Address deplored the Walcheren expedition in such imtemperate terms that it was handsomely defeated by 264 votes to 167. Speaking from his new place under the Gallery, Castlereagh stoutly defended the expedition and the Talavera campaign.[1] For once his speech was warmly cheered. The Whig diarist Creevey – not usually a friendly witness – reported that on everything that concerned himself personally, Castlereagh spoke 'with a conscious sense of being right, and a degree of lively animation I never saw in him before'. 'Well Creevey, how do we look?' he called, 'with the gayest face possible', as he went out into the lobby with the ayes'.[2]

Castlereagh's freedom was of course restricted by the fact that he shared responsibility for most of the policies under attack. But he differed from his ex-colleagues in not shirking inquiry into their outcome. To the government's consternation, an Opposition motion for an inquiry into the Walcheren expedition was carried by nine votes. Castlereagh and four of his friends voted for the inquiry.* If they had voted the other way, the motion would have been lost by one vote.† For the rest of the session Castlereagh continued cheerfully on his independent way. But he could hardly fail to support the government when the Opposition introduced a string of very hostile amendments at the end of the Walcheren inquiry. The government, rather to its surprise, defeated them all, although only by small majorities. The Opposition overplayed their hand by the severity of their censure.

When Parliament rose on June 21, 1810, Castlereagh's reputation at Westminster was probably higher than it had ever been before. People felt he had had a raw deal at the hands of Canning; they were impressed by the robust way he stood up for himself; and, last but not least, he was making much better speeches. 'Being turned out', commented Canning ruefully, 'has certainly done him [Castlereagh] a world of good – both given him speech and obtained him a hearing.'[3] One at least of the Opposition was pleased at his success, for, wrote J. W. Ward, 'though an abominable minister, he is an excellent man and a perfect gentleman'.[4]

---

*It was an inquiry of the whole House, lasting from February 2 to March 15. Castlereagh was examined twice, largely on whether the expedition had been justified on the basis of the available intelligence.

†Castlereagh never seems to have had more than six supporters in the Commons, including Charles Stewart, who was often away on active service. Canning had as many as sixteen.

'I AM NOT PLAYING A GAME FOR OFFICE' 1809–12

'Idleness', Castlereagh told his brother Charles on June 28, 1810, 'agrees with me marvellously.' By 'idleness' he meant freedom from Parliament and office. In other directions he was busy enough. He had just leased 'a little place in Kent', in beautiful country fourteen miles from Westminster Bridge. The house was small but secluded, and 'new and fresh'.[5] The 40-acre farm was surrounded by a trout stream, the land provided excellent grazing, and Castlereagh was soon, according to Edward Cooke, 'Merino-mad'.[6]

Like other out-of-office politicians, he had decided to go in for sheep farming. The fashion had been started by the King with his imports (and gifts) of Merino sheep from Spain and his experiments in scientific breeding. Castlereagh also aspired to be scientific. 'I have not thought of anything of late but of sheep farming', he wrote on July 6, 'I have been studying under Sebright and other learned breeders in Hertfordshire, and mean to have the best Merino flock in England ... Emily says I shall soon bleat and be covered with wool.'[7]

Emily's taste in animals was more exotic. She was already planning the zoo which later was to be displayed to somewhat astonished visitors, and had organised her brother-in-law in Spain to contribute. 'Lady C.', wrote Castlereagh to Charles, 'is very much obliged to you for executing her commission about the ass, which will be an excellent cross for the zebra.'[8]

But even Merinos – '50 of the very best' – had to take second place to a visit to Mount Stewart. 'I am quite satisfied with my present pursuits', wrote Castlereagh to Charles on July 18, 'and look forward with great pleasure to passing my summer at Mount Stewart without any political worry.'[9] For once there was time for both business and sightseeing on the way north. They began by going to Holbeach to inspect an estate belonging to Emily and to plan how to make it more profitable. Then they explored the wonders of Lincolnshire. 'I passed yesterday', wrote Castlereagh from Hull, 'through what is called a fen of 40,000 acres, which is nevertheless covered with the most luxuriant crops, over the whole surface of which 4 years since boats used to navigate.' And he added a comment typical of men of his background and upbringing: 'To observe the wealth, the industry, the comfort of the country which I have passed through since I left London, and to know that there are people ready to hazard all these blessings does astonish, if we did not know what human nature always has been and will be.'[10]

The tour continued by way of Harrogate and the Lakes (where Castlereagh pursued his investigations into sheep farming), and eventually they landed in Ireland on September 3 'after a pleasant tour and a rough, long passage...'.[11] For the past eight years, Castlereagh had been able to find very little time for his parents and his tribe of siblings, most of them a good deal younger than himself. They were probably all the dearer to him since he had no children of his own, and no elder brother could have felt, either at this time or later, a closer or more affectionate interest in their welfare.* They were a closely-knit family, and in the autumn of 1810 the links were tightened by the death of the youngest boy, Thomas, while serving in the Peninsula. Castlereagh heard the news first in a letter from Wellington. It arrived a day before a messenger from Charles, thus, as Castlereagh told Wellington, enabling him 'to break the fatal event gradually to my sisters...' There were three of them at home and Thomas had been their companion and their favourite. 'Their sufferings cannot be expected shortly to terminate, but I trust we shall carry them safely through them. My father and mother support themselves better than I could have hoped.'[12]

Thanks to the Castlereaghs' efforts, all the family were in 'tolerable spirits' a few weeks later. Robert had managed to interest his father again in the farm and estate, while Emily had enlisted the girls in her gardening projects and in establishing a school for two hundred children.

During this holiday in Ireland, Castlereagh received a proposal from Perceval that he and Canning should both rejoin the Cabinet.† He promptly turned the offer down on the grounds that no one would believe that the ministry 'was really united within itself'. He added the hope that he had not been influenced by 'any unbecoming feelings of a personal nature'.[13] But it would have been surprising if he had not been. It was, after all, barely a year since the duel. No doubt he felt much better after winging Canning, but some resentment must have remained, especially as his further probings into 'the whole intrigue in all its complicated refinement' had only confirmed his feeling that Canning was the most to blame.[14]

In any case, he enjoyed his independence. In January 1811, when the

*Sometimes tinged with slight exasperation. In a letter to Charles in the autumn of 1812, he lamented that two of their sisters who had been visiting London, had failed to get themselves married. 'It is vexatious with so many opportunities, these girls should have done so little either for themselves or for each other.' (Castlereagh Mss (Belfast) D3030. Q/2, Nov. 5, 1812)

†All the Cabinet wanted to bring Castlereagh back. They also wanted Canning, but not by himself. They eventually thought up the extraordinary plan of offering the Admiralty and the Home Office jointly to them, and asking them to decide between themselves who should have which post. As Castlereagh refused to play, the plan fell to the ground.

'I AM NOT PLAYING A GAME FOR OFFICE' 1809-12

Regency crisis* greatly accentuated party divisions, Castlereagh assured his brother Charles that he was 'the freest man alive to take any line in public life (as far as individuals are concerned), my own judgment dictated. I have no wish but rather the reverse to return soon to office, my health and spirits, I may add my personal enjoyments, have all been improved since I was free, in a degree that you will hardly believe, and I am sure it will neither be for my fame or happiness to be precipitately again embarked in business . . .' He was still a little sore and spoke rather bitterly about again exposing himself to the troubles of political life. 'The fact is that I am not playing a game for office, I really do not abstractedly wish it . . . my object is to take the necessary part in Parliament which I think becomes me, and I shall leave it to events hereafter to decide my fate . . .'[15]

Meanwhile, he was still absorbed by his sheep farming, and early in 1811 was able to announce that the West of England prize for the best cloth had just gone to some made from '*my wool*'. He had received 'all sorts of congratulations, and shall probably go down to posterity as the greatest shepherd of the time in which I lived'.[16] He was, however, destined to go down to posterity with a very different reputation, and early in the following year, 1812, he took the first step towards acquiring it.

By the end of 1811 it had become clear that the King was not going to recover his sanity. The restrictions on the Regent were due to end on February 18, 1812, and it was widely assumed that he would celebrate his freedom by changing his ministers. Presumably he would send for the Whig leaders, Lords Grey and Grenville. But Lord Wellesley considered that he ought to be Perceval's successor. In mid-January 1811, he told the Regent that he would like to resign, whenever convenient, because he could no longer serve under such a second-rate premier as Perceval. This was apparently intended as a signal that he was willing to move from the Foreign Office to the Treasury. But his exasperated colleagues, who had always found Wellesley thoroughly tiresome, decided to insist that the Regent should accept his resignation at once. When Perceval suggested that the Foreign Office should be offered to Castlereagh, the

*The crisis was over the terms of the Regency Bill which became necessary when the old King again lapsed into insanity in November 1810. The Opposition violently opposed Perceval's proposal that for a limited time the Regent's powers should be restricted. But by the beginning of February 1811, his bill had become law. Greatly to everyone's surprise, the Prince Regent decided not to bring in the Whigs, but to keep Perceval.

Regent said he had no personal objection to Castlereagh whom he hardly knew; he believed him to be 'a man of honour and of talents', although he was the worst war minister the country had ever had. To Perceval's further request that he might also open negotiations with Lord Sidmouth, the Regent's reply was a violent negative. Anyone but 'that d---d scoundrel'.[17]

Perceval offered Castlereagh the Foreign Office on January 23, and after sleeping on the proposal, Castlereagh turned it down. Like most people he assumed that the Perceval ministry was doomed and he did not believe that he alone could save it. He did not, he told Perceval, wish to come in without Sidmouth, whom he felt 'could not be properly excluded from any arrangement'. Nor did he wish to act merely as a stop-gap until the Regency restrictions ended a few weeks later.[18]

In the event, the Regent was obliged to fall back on Perceval after all. He had drifted too far away from his old friends the Whigs to be willing to put himself entirely in their hands, and they rejected his suggestion that they should form part of a broadly-based coalition. On February 18, Perceval was confirmed in office, and on the same day he again offered Castlereagh the Foreign Office. This time his offer was not refused. He had apparently thought of restoring Castlereagh to the war ministry, but Liverpool felt, very reasonably, that he could not leave his post at such a critical stage of the war.[19]* So, rather fortuitously, instead of being given a chance to retrieve his reputation as a war minister, Castlereagh was given an opportunity to make a far greater one as a peace-maker.

But in February 1812 no one was thinking much about peace. Wellington had embarked on another gallant attempt to expel the French from Spain. Napoleon was about to launch half a million men across Europe against Russia. And the British government, doggedly pursuing its economic war against France, was slipping into a shooting war with the United States.

So beleaguered was Britain that there was barely a handful of foreign envoys in London to take up the time of the new Foreign Secretary. But his predecessor, who had attended to business only when the spirit

---

*Canning reluctantly followed his ally, Lord Wellesley, into the political wilderness. Early in April 1811, Perceval at last overcame the Regent's opposition to bringing Sidmouth into the government. Sidmouth himself was made Lord President of the Council, and two of his supporters – his brother-in-law Charles Bragge-Bathurst and Lord Buckinghamshire – were also brought into the Cabinet.

Napoleon's farewell to his Guard at Fontainebleau,
20 April 1814

Encampment of the British Army in the Bois de Boulogne, 1815

Two portraits of Tsar Alexander I, on the left by Monnier painted in 1806, and on the right by Lawrence in 1815

Peace celebrations in Hyde Park, 1814

moved him (which was seldom), had left behind a disorganised office and a mass of paper-work. Six weeks after taking over, Castlereagh was still struggling to get up to date. 'I have been very hard worked since I came in', he told Charles. 'A heavy job in every quarter. I don't ever recollect to have had so tough a task.' Perhaps that accounts for his modified enthusiasm for his new post. 'When I have worked up the arrears, the business will not be more than I should like, and it is of a nature both to interest and improve.'[20]

His most urgent priority — whether or not he realised it — was to avert war with the United States. The Americans' trade had suffered badly from the European economic war (together with their own retaliatory measures) and they were much more inclined to blame the British, their old enemies, than the French, who had helped them to achieve independence. The British always claimed that their Orders-in-Council were not restrictions on commerce, but retaliatory measures against Napoleon's Berlin and Milan decrees. However that might be, the British were in fact controlling the trade of the whole commercial world in their own interests. Napoleon tried to do the same, but he lacked the necessary control of the seas. The British could prevent American ships from trading with Europe while allowing their own ships to do so under licence. They were also able to enforce their own interpretation of neutral rights at sea. In spite of American protests, the Royal Navy regularly boarded neutral ships to search for contraband and — much worse — for English deserters, whether or not they had already become naturalised American citizens. To economic damage, 'impressment' added a sense of national humiliation all the more galling for being inflicted by the British.

Early in 1811, both the Americans and the French stepped up their counterattacks on the Orders-in-Council. The effect on the British economy was calamitous. In 1811 the country endured a worse slump than even in 1808. During the winter of 1811-12, rioting and machine-breaking spread throughout the Midlands and the northern industrial districts. The government sent troop reinforcements and encouraged severity at the assizes. But the Whigs were convinced that the situation at home would never improve so long as the government persisted with its economic warfare against the French. Moreover, warning signs from Washington suggested that the Americans would go to war rather than put up with the Orders-in-Council any longer.

On March 3, therefore, Henry Brougham moved for a committee of inquiry into the Orders, and when he was defeated, he turned from

Parliament to the country and appealed for petitions against the Orders. The response was so overwhelming that on April 28 the government gave way. Castlereagh, one of the staunchest supporters of the Orders as a weapon against Napoleon, voted for the inquiry. He did not, he said, admit the merits of the question, but he wished to make a concession to the feeling of the country.

On May 11, as he was on his way to attend the inquiry into the Orders, Spencer Perceval was shot through the heart in the lobby of the Commons by a bankrupt commercial agent called Bellingham, who had a crazy grievance against the government. Outside Parliament there was plenty of savage rejoicing among those for whom Perceval symbolised uncaring, repressive authority. But in the House of Commons next day there was universal grief. The Home Secretary, Richard Ryder, who should have read a Message from the Regent, was too overcome even to try; and Castlereagh, who took his place, broke down when he had to mention Perceval's widow, and was obliged to sit down 'amidst the loud cheers and strong sympathy of the House'.[21]

For the Regent, Perceval's death meant a return to the trials and tribulations of Cabinet-making from which he had escaped only three months earlier. Perceval's colleagues were prepared to carry on, with Lord Liverpool as their new leader, but they had little hope of surviving without substantial reinforcements. The obvious sources of strength were Wellesley and Canning, and it was presumably in order to remove a possible obstacle to securing them that Castlereagh offered his own resignation four days after Perceval's death.[22] But his colleagues refused to accept the sacrifice, and when Liverpool made his overtures to Wellesley and Canning on May 17, he made it clear that Castlereagh was to continue as Foreign Secretary and also take Perceval's place as leader of the House of Commons. Thomas Grenville thought that Liverpool must be as mad as Bellingham to expect that Canning would accept such pre-eminence in the Commons for his rival.[23] However that may be, Liverpool's overture was rejected, ostensibly because of disagreements over policy. And so, with Nicholas Vansittart (one of Lord Sidmouth's friends) as the new Chancellor of the Exchequer, the ministry decided they could manage as they were.

The House of Commons, however, thought differently. On May 21, Mr Stuart Wortley, who usually supported the government, introduced a motion praying the Regent to take steps 'to form a strong and efficient administration'. The motion was carried by four votes, Liverpool resigned next day, and the Regent found himself back at square one. For more than a fortnight, with increasing exasperation, he tried in vain to construct a new government, until eventually he gave up and turned back to the old team. On June 8, Lord Liverpool – rather bumbling and awkward, but sensible and decent – entered on his fifteen-year tenancy of 10 Downing Street.

It never occurred to Wellington, surveying the political battleground from the Peninsula, that the new ministry might enjoy such remarkable longevity. 'You have undertaken a most gigantic task', he told Liverpool, 'and I don't know how you will get through it.' Remembering, without pleasure, his own parliamentary experience, he pointed out that it had been difficult enough to carry on in the Commons when Perceval, Canning and Castlereagh all sat on the Treasury bench. Now only one of them was left. 'However', he concluded encouragingly, 'there is nothing like trying.'[24]

Wellington slightly misjudged the situation. So, with less excuse, did Castlereagh when he deplored in the Commons the publicity that had surrounded the recent negotiations. 'For his part', he was reported as saying, 'he could never augur well of any negotiation in which two men could not approach each other in a private room, although on public principles, without coming armed with pen and ink, and prepared to allow everything they might utter to go forth immediately for the judgment of the public.'[25] That was not going to be his way as a diplomat. But in politics publicity has its uses. On this occasion the clear demonstration that there was no alternative team gave Liverpool's ministry the parliamentary backing it had previously lacked. On June 11 a motion almost identical with Stuart Wortley's was defeated by 125 votes.*

But over the Orders-in-Council the government was forced to give way. On June 16 Brougham moved for the repeal of the Orders. The House was clearly on his side, and Castlereagh, unsure of himself and at his least lucid, eventually conceded that the Orders would be unconditionally suspended at once. The government, as Wilberforce noted in his diary with astonishment, had given way completely, 'yet most awkwardly'.[26]

The awkwardness was not surprising since the government almost certainly had not intended to give way so far and so fast. Even so, the repeal was too late to avert the hostilities with the United States, which

*Sidmouth took over the Home Office, and Lord Bathurst took over from Liverpool as Secretary for War and the Colonies. He also kept his former post of President of the Board of Trade.

as late as June 8 Castlereagh had denied were imminent. Two days after the government's climb-down, President Madison declared war on Britain. Somewhere in mid-Atlantic, the ship carrying the American declaration of war passed the ship carrying the repeal of the Orders-in-Council.

Nobody in England, and only a small party of 'war hawks' in the United States who aimed at expelling the British from Canada, wanted an Anglo-American war. The American war preparations had begun partly as bluff, but as the weeks passed they gathered momentum, spurred on by the apparent intransigence of the British. For Castlereagh, as for his colleagues, the American problem had lacked urgency. It was early April 1812 before he turned his attention from the administrative confusion bequeathed by Wellesley to compose a dispatch for Augustus Foster, the British minister in Washington. He wrote very reasonably, without hostility or threats, and he offered to modify the British licensing system so as to make it more acceptable to the Americans. It was an important concession, as the Americans would at one time have acknowledged. But when it reached the White House some six weeks later, it fell on deaf ears. By that time, economic grievance had been powerfully reinforced by feelings of wounded pride and national honour, and Castlereagh, mild and courteous though he was, showed no sign of appreciating that more than matters of trade and commerce were at stake. He left Madison and his Secretary of State, James Monroe, with the conviction that they had no alternative to war but national degradation.[27]

Nor were they mollified when they learnt that the Orders-in-Council had been revoked. On the contrary, they were affronted by the British government's threat to reimpose them the following year. Castlereagh, who almost seems to have made up policy towards America as he went along, withdrew the threat a few days after it had been made and substituted an offer to negotiate on any further trade restrictions that might be thought necessary. But it was too late. His second, more conciliatory, dispatch reached Washington after Foster had left, and Madison never learnt its contents.[28]

Perhaps this did not matter very much. By this time the Americans were insisting that impressment as well as the Orders must be abolished, and in the peace-making efforts which Castlereagh continued through the British naval commander off the North American coast, he had nothing to offer on impressment or neutral rights. Nor did he need to have. On this issue, in contrast to the Orders-in-Council, the British government enjoyed strong public backing. Even the Whig *Edinburgh*

Review, which blamed the ministry for the war, supported the principle of impressment. Any threat to Britain's unfettered exercise of its maritime supremacy was not to be tolerated.

The war which ended in stalemate two years later failed to settle the Anglo-American quarrel over impressment and neutral rights. The quarrel over trade restrictions, on the other hand, was virtually settled before the shooting started. The French economy was no better able than the British to withstand the strains of the long commercial war, and Napoleon was forced to allow trading licences to be granted on an increasingly liberal scale. By the end of 1812 his Continental System had largely collapsed. English merchants (and smugglers) pushed hard at the slowly-opening doors into European markets and during 1812 trade revived swiftly.

The upsurge in trade stimulated a revival of industry which, together with an adequate harvest, gradually removed, for the time being, the worst causes of social distress and unrest. But in the middle of 1812, alarming reports of outrages, plots and secret meetings were still streaming into the Home Office. Was the unrest due to distress or had it a political origin? Secret parliamentary committees were set up to examine the evidence of subversion. They concluded that an extensive secret organisation did exist and was plotting to overthrow the government. The Cabinet reacted with commendable calm. A bill was introduced to strengthen the powers of justices of the peace, but not in an excessively draconian way. In the Commons, Castlereagh firmly took the line that the troubles were largely due to unemployment, aggravated by the high price of food.[29] His moderation did not prevent his record in Ireland from being repeatedly attacked during the debates on the magistrates' bill. The Opposition produced specific cases of torture and ill-treatment during the 1798 rebellion in order – so they said – to warn members before they committed the country's liberties to the discretion or mercy of the leader of the House. Such attacks were standard Opposition practice. But they all helped to support the picture of Castlereagh as painted by Byron and Shelley.

The Commons – and the newspaper-reading public in general – were also regularly reminded of Castlereagh's allegedly broken promises to the Irish Catholics. In fact he had never wavered in his support of the principle of emancipation, although he had argued that it should be postponed to a more propitious time. Canning, whose loyalty to the Catholic cause was never questioned, had done the same. But in the spring of 1812 the outlook for the Catholics looked more promising. The old King was no longer capable of conscientious scruples; the Regent's conscience towards the Protestant establishment was less troublesome; opinion in Parliament and among the educated public beyond Westminster seemed increasingly friendly towards the Catholics' claims; in Ireland, the attempt by the moderate Catholics to force the pace of change had been checked; and the Irish had settled back into as much tranquillity as they ever enjoyed.

In June 1812, Castlereagh announced that Lord Liverpool's new government would allow its members a free vote on the Catholic issue, a concession which he had always privately insisted on for himself. In the same month a pro-Catholic motion introduced by Canning passed easily in the Commons, and a similar vote in the Lords was lost by only one vote. It was confidently hoped that next year, with one more heave, the Catholic cause would be won. But these hopes were dashed the following April when the supporters of the Catholic relief bill introduced by Grattan found they had underestimated the tenacity of those Protestants who believed that Ireland could be either Catholic or Protestant, but not both.*

Castlereagh emerged from the Catholic debates of 1812 and 1813 with his reputation as a committed supporter of the Catholic claims firmly established. Shortly afterwards, Robert Peel, then Chief Secretary in Dublin, attended an Irish dinner in London. He noticed how conspicuous was Protestant feeling among the assembled company, but although 'the Protestant Ascendancy' was put down among the printed toasts, it was not actually given – 'on account, I presume, of Castlereagh being present'.[30] Astonishingly, the man who had made his name as one of the most dedicated – and most hated – defenders of the Protestant Ascendancy, now had to be spared the embarrassment of toasting it.

Before Parliament rose for the summer recess in 1812, Liverpool made one more effort to strengthen his team in the Commons. Apart from the Chancellor of the Exchequer, Vansittart, the only other senior minister sitting with Castlereagh on the Treasury front bench was Charles Bragge-Bathurst, the Chancellor of the Duchy of Lancaster; he owed his position entirely to his brother-in-law Lord Sidmouth, and in general debate was even more of a broken reed than Vansittart. As always, the

*No further attempt to carry Catholic emancipation was made until 1821, when Plunket's bill, powerfully supported by Canning and Castlereagh, passed successfully through all its stages in the Commons. It was then thrown out by the Lords.

most useful recruit would be Canning, and the Regent was anxious to get him. So too, with varying enthusiasm, were the members of the Cabinet, but no longer at the expense of Castlereagh. To deal him such a swingeing blow twice would have been inconceivable. In any case, his merits, and Canning's defects, were more apparent than three years earlier. The best solution, of course, would be an end to their feud, so that they could both serve, and some time in June the Regent set himself to promote a reconciliation. He sent for Charles Stewart and began by warmly assuring him that he liked his brother far better than Mr Canning. According to Stewart's account of the interview, the Regent went on to avow that 'in his judgment the solid and useful abilities of the one [Castlereagh] added to his mild and gentlemanlike manner had an irresistible influence for HRH far superior to anything he felt or could ever feel for the other [Canning]'. But the fact remained that Canning's powers of debate, 'especially of retort', made it vital to have him in the government. And the Regent went on to suggest that as Castlereagh had emerged triumphant from his differences with Canning, it was up to him to be magnanimous and take the first step towards a reconciliation. He added, with real good sense and some exasperation, that he could not for the life of him conceive what could have passed between two individuals 'which the weighty, enormous and difficult crisis of the country ought not to soften down and bury in oblivion ...'[31]

Castlereagh was not the man to ignore this appeal. So a few weeks later, with the help of a little quiet diplomacy from the prime minister, the two rivals met, and with handshakes and mutual professions of goodwill agreed to let bygones be bygones.

No doubt they meant it, but they still could not fit themselves into the same Cabinet. Castlereagh immediately offered to let Canning have the Foreign Office, while he himself took over the Chancellorship of the Exchequer, an unpopular and not, as it later became, major post, for which, on rather slender grounds, he seems to have felt himself equipped. It was, as Canning afterwards recognised, an astonishingly generous offer.[32] But Castlereagh insisted on keeping the leadership of the House which, in Canning's view, meant that he himself would be serving under, not with, Castlereagh. This he would not accept, and on this rock, compounded of false pride, ambition and jealousy, the whole arrangement foundered.

Canning spent much pen, ink, paper and ingenuity on devising arrangements for managing the Commons' business so that he and Castlereagh could enjoy equality without superiority. Castlereagh maintained, no doubt sincerely, that he was not making any invidious claim to superiority. He simply meant that there must be some *one* person in charge of Commons' business if it was to be managed efficiently. (Or, as Thomas Grenville put it, 'when two men ride a horse, one must ride behind'.[33]) Castlereagh also felt that he personally would lose 'character' if he gave up the leadership of the Commons as well as one of the most important posts in the Cabinet.[34] Altogether, it was a perfectly reasonable approach. Unfortunately, it was expressed with Castlereagh's chronic verbal clumsiness, and this, together with Liverpool's well-meaning efforts to smooth things over, added misunderstanding and irritation to a situation already sufficiently confused by almost metaphysical efforts to define equality, superiority and leadership in House of Commons terms.

Not much sympathy was bestowed on Canning, except by his particular friends who had unwisely egged him on. The Regent was thoroughly exasperated with him for failing to make allowance for 'the blundering expressions of so puzzled a writer as Lord Castlereagh'. He told Lady Bessborough that Castlereagh had been 'ridiculously obstinate and absurd at first', but had become 'quite reasonable, only wishing for a *perfect equality*' with Canning. And, the Regent pointed out, that in fact meant giving Canning 'the lead without the plague of the situation, for that with his powers poor Lord Castlereagh would stand but a poor chance of being listened to'.[35]

It was four years before Canning returned to the Treasury front bench and got a chance to upstage his rival. By that time it was too late. Castlereagh had made his mark on the European stage, and even his bumbling oratory could not shake his supremacy at Westminster.

PART III
European Statesman
(1812–22)

CHAPTER XI

Closing the net round Napoleon
1812–13

In June 1812, Napoleon led more than 400,000 men across the Niemen into Russia. Six months later, only some 40,000 dragged themselves back across the river. It was an appalling disaster, but at the time few would have predicted that it was the beginning of the end of Napoleon's empire. The Russian army had suffered almost as much as the French, and very few of the Tsar's advisers wanted to pursue the invader beyond their own frontier. The Emperor Francis of Austria was Napoleon's father-in-law as well as his ally and the Austrian Chancellor, Clement Metternich, feared the largely unknown Russian colossus more than Napoleon's France. The King of Prussia, weak and vacillating, still seemed unable to throw off his uncongenial alliance with Napoleon, while Bernadotte, formerly one of Napoleon's marshals and now Prince Royal of Sweden, was more concerned with consolidating his own position than with fighting his old master.* The British had just taken on a new military commitment in North America. They were also heavily involved in the Peninsula where Wellington, having entered Madrid in August 1812, was forced in November to retreat once again into Portugal. Whether or not it was, as Napoleon claimed, only the Russian winter that had defeated him, there seemed little likelihood that his enemies could now finish him off.

In England, the news of Napoleon's discomfiture was received with amazement and wild rejoicing. For the government, however, exhilaration was mingled with perplexity. The itch to open a second front in northern Europe – in Hanover or Holland – was strong. But fortunately the ministers accepted Wellington's emphatic advice to concentrate Britain's military effort where it could have most effect – in the Peninsula. In any case, what the European powers needed most from Britain was not men, but money and munitions. Consignments of muskets and other arms and equipment were sent to the Baltic, as it were, like bread upon the waters. But money was in far too short supply

*In March 1809, Gustavus IV of Sweden was deposed by an army coup and succeeded by his uncle, Charles XIII, who was old and childless. Bernadotte was appointed heir apparent to the Swedish throne in August 1810.

to be promised, let alone sent, without a carefully spelled out quid pro quo. The difficulty was to reach satisfactory agreements. 'The crisis is of that magnitude', wrote Castlereagh in January 1813, 'that *we must not starve the cause* by suffering any great object to fail, which can by an effort be brought within our grasp.'[1] In practice, however, these generous sentiments were severely tried by the difficulty of reconciling the Europeans' exorbitant demands with Britain's ability to meet them. It was not easy to make the Russians, Austrians or Prussians believe that Britain, envied and disliked for its commercial wealth and maritime supremacy, and for long the paymaster of Napoleon's enemies, might also have its economic problems.

At first Castlereagh had little real understanding of the intricacies of European politics, or of the aims, prejudices and idiosyncracies of the rulers and ministers with whom he was dealing. He tended naively to assume that they would behave with the same decency and moderation that he would hope to show himself. He did not suppose, he wrote, that there would be any great reluctance on the part of Prussia 'to gratify the Prince Regent' by surrendering some small enclaves of Prussian territory obtruding into Hanover.[2] Nothing could have been more mistaken; the Prussians objected most strongly. Castlereagh had to learn as he went along.

Britain's isolation did not make this easy. The Foreign Office's main source of information came from Hanoverian diplomats in Vienna and Berlin (there were none in St Petersburg) by way of Count Munster, the Hanoverian minister in London. There were also a few British agents on the continent, but their reports tended to be highly suspect, and the French press contained only what Napoleon wanted his enemies to believe. Nor was Castlereagh's education greatly helped by Britain's diplomatic representatives in Europe. By far the ablest British diplomat was young Stratford Canning, George Canning's cousin, who returned from Constantinople in the summer of 1812 after persuading the Turks to make peace with the Russians. His success earned Canning a diamond-studded snuffbox from the Tsar and a pension from his own government, but, as Castlereagh told him later, he was unfortunately 'both too high and too low' for another active diplomatic post in the immediate future.[3]* Only two diplomatic missions were established in northern and central Europe at the beginning of 1813 – Edward Thornton's in Stockholm and Lord Cathcart's with the Tsar. Thornton, described by an acquaintance as 'mild, amiable and good-natured',[4] was

---

*In April 1814, Stratford Canning was made minister plenipotentiary to Switzerland, in which capacity he played a useful role at the Congress of Vienns.

CLOSING THE NET ROUND NAPOLEON 1812-13

a hardworking and concientious diplomat, but his relations with the Foreign Office were strained by his uncritical admiration for Bernadotte. Lord Cathcart had been sent to the Tsar, with £500,000 in his baggage, the previous July, as soon as Castlereagh learnt of the invasion of Russia. He was elderly, ponderous and slow-thinking, but he was completely reliable, and as a high-ranking general he had the great advantage over a civilian diplomat of being able to remain at the Tsar's side – within reach of his ear – during a campaign.

By the middle of January 1813, Alexander had made up his mind to continue his campaign; he would liberate Europe as well as Russia. As his troops began to move westwards into Prussia, Castlereagh, in London, confessed to Cathcart that he was too ignorant of what was actually happening in Europe to send him more than the most general instructions. 'Whatever scheme of policy', he wrote, 'can most immediately combine the greatest number of powers and the greatest military force against France ... before she can recruit her armies and recover her ascendancy is that which we must naturally desire most to promote.'[5]

If, as Castlereagh desperately hoped, the Russians did continue the struggle, the Swedes, on the flank of the advancing Russian armies, would be in the best position to help them. A year earlier, after Napoleon had seized Swedish Pomerania, Bernadotte had allied himself with Russia and sent an overture to London. But at first his terms were considered too high, and by the end of 1812 nothing had been settled. In the new year, however, no price seemed too high to secure Sweden's help, and it was eventually agreed that in return for taking 30,000 men immediately into north Germany, Bernadotte should receive a huge subsidy and a promise of British naval help, if necessary, to seize Norway which, he claimed, he must have to ingratiate himself with his Swedish subjects.

Castlereagh greatly regretted the Norwegian promise. 'We never have disguised from ourselves the embarrassments of the Norwegian point', he confessed to Cathcart; 'but it was an engagement made in the day of adversity, for the preservation of Russia.'[6] Ironically, by the time the treaty with Bernadotte was actually signed, on March 3, 1813, Prussia's entry into the war had already made his help much less indispensable. That did not, in Castlereagh's view, allow the treaty to be repudiated, but it made it all the more difficult to justify. Nor did Bernadotte's tardiness in fulfilling his side of the engagement make it any more popular in England; 11,000 Swedish troops had arrived in Stralsund by the end of April, but Bernadotte showed no signs of taking them any further. In the House of Commons, where even government supporters were hostile, Castlereagh made the best of a poor case, arguing that Sweden had to have security on the side of Norway if it was to help Russia. But in spite of his dexterous arguments and the Opposition's divided counsels, he had to threaten the government's resignation in order to get the treaty approved.[7]

The King of Prussia's chronic indecisiveness was finally, and rather unexpectedly, overcome by pressure from his own people, whose seething nationalism finally boiled over after General Yorck, commanding the Prussian contingent serving with the French, had defected to the Russians. In terms of military manpower, Prussia could make little immediate contribution beyond Yorck's men. But at least, by a treaty signed on February 27, it was firmly committed to the Allied camp. Castlereagh had been taught by Pitt that a strong Prussia was essential to keep France in order. He had not yet given much thought to the place of Germany as a whole in Europe after the war. But he sent Cathcart, for the Tsar's enlightenment, a copy of the 'interesting document' on the reconstruction of Europe produced by Pitt in 1805 – '... (interesting it is to my recollection, as I well remember having more than one conversation with Mr Pitt on its details, *before he wrote it*) ...' Some of the paper's suggestions were now inapplicable, but the outline of postwar Europe was 'masterly'.[8] It was to be Castlereagh's bible for the next two years.

But before Napoleon could be decisively defeated, Austria had to be prised out of its ambivalent position, still nominally allied to France, but in reality on the sidelines. Metternich's devious policies were governed by various fears: that either France or Russia would gain an overwhelming predominance in Europe; that Russia and France would make peace at Prussia's expense, leaving Austria isolated; that a nationalist rising in Germany would release uncontrollable forces. His aim was a negotiated peace with France, including all the powers, which would curb Napoleon's ambitions but leave him on the throne of France.

In England, Metternich's peace feelers were dismissed with uncompromising contempt. In November 1812 he sent the British government an urgent appeal for peace talks through Count Munster. It was received with all the more indignation because it happened to arrive just after the arrival of the news of Napoleon's disastrous retreat from Moscow; 'nothing can be more abject', wrote the prime minister to Wellington, 'than the councils of Vienna at this time, and I fear that neutrality is all that can be expected from them'.[9] In the new year, Metternich tried again. But his emissary, Count Wessenberg, who brought an offer of mediation, received a very chilly reception. He also arrived in London at an unpropitious moment, when government and country were rejoicing over Prussia's entry into the war, and Napoleon had just made a particularly truculent speech. The press abused Wessenberg, society ostracised him and the Regent treated him to a heated discourse on the iniquities of Napoleon. Castlereagh received the unfortunate Wessenberg with distant civility and flatly rejected any kind of peace negotiations. At this juncture he believed in waging war, not talking peace, and while Wessenberg was unhappily trying to fulfil his mission, Cathcart was told to negotiate a subsidy agreement with the Tsar, and Charles Stewart was accredited to Frederick William with similiar instructions.

Castlereagh's choice of Stewart reflected more credit on his brotherly affection than on his judgment. Charles was in need of employment. His military career had just been blocked by Wellington, who refused to give him the cavalry command which he believed was his due because his sight and hearing had both been impaired by a wound. There were of course advantages in sending a high-ranking officer to a monarch actively engaged in a military campaign, and Stewart had liaison duties with the Prussian and Swedish armies. He found these much more congenial than his diplomatic role. For the latter it was clear to most people, except his brother, that he was not well suited. According to Wellington as reported by John Croker, 'Castlereagh had a real respect for Charles's understanding, and a high opinion of his good sense and discretion.' He added that this might seem incomprehensible to those who knew the two men, but it was so.[10] Wellington may have been a little hard on Stewart, who was in many ways an able man. He was also energetic, hospitable, and popular with fellow soldiers. But he was impatient and indiscreet and many people could not take him seriously because of his overweening vanity and an impulsive tendency to show off which sometimes made him seem a little mad. He was hardly the man to promote respect for British views in the councils of the Allies.

Vain though he was, Stewart was somewhat overawed by his new responsibilities. He felt, he confided to Edward Cooke, 'devilish nervous about it all'.[11] He took with him George Jackson, a budding young diplomat, and they were sped on their way by the Foreign Secretary who, according to Jackson, 'when we parted wished us success two or three times over, and on each occasion shook hands upon it'.[12]

Stewart and Jackson joined Cathcart at the Allied headquarters at

Dresden towards the end of April 1813. On the 29th they were received by Frederick William 'in the most private manner possible, as if His Majesty still had the fear of Boney before his eyes and was terrified at his own boldness in the step he was taking'.[13] Only the day before, in fact, Boney had arrived at the French headquarters near Leipzig. On May 2 he inflicted a partial defeat on the Allies at Lutzen, forcing them to retreat eastwards. On the 20th he defeated them again at Bautzen, and pushed them back into Silesia. Cathcart and Stewart were never far from the fighting, and at Bautzen Stewart distinguished himself by gallantly rallying some of the Russian infantry. It was not a very suitable milieu for complicated diplomatic negotiations, but by the middle of June agreements with Russia and Prussia had been signed, and all that financial inducement could do to make them fight had been done.

It was only at this point that Stewart and Cathcart learned, to their surprise and indignation, that on June 4 Russia, Prussia and France had agreed to a six-weeks' armistice. It was a product of Metternich's ceaseless efforts to end the conflict in a way that would leave no single power, or combination of powers, capable of dominating the rest. In the secret treaty of Reichenbach he agreed with Russia and Prussia on the minimum terms to be offered Napoleon and pledged Austria to go to war if they were rejected. The terms were very moderate, but Napoleon was not tempted – perhaps because he realised that there would certainly be further demands. But after a long and tense interview with Metternich at Prague, he agreed to extend the armistice to August 10, and to send a representative to a peace congress with Russia and Prussia at Prague. Neither Metternich nor Napoleon regarded the congress as more than a convenient façade behind which they could each complete their preparations for war.

From all these portentous developments Cathcart and Stewart were rigidly excluded. Metternich had no intention of jeopardising the chances of a continental peace by making an issue of special British interests like Spain or Holland. Cathcart accepted the situation with his usual calm. Stewart was alarmed and protested to the Prussians. But he did not let his anxiety deprive him of the congenial task of inspecting the Swedish forces away in north Germany. George Jackson was inclined to think that Britain would have been treated better if it had been better represented at Allied headquarters. Between them, he felt, Cathcart and Stewart had 'contrived rather to retard and confuse than to advance and explain matters', and he suspected that the Prussian Chancellor, Prince von Hardenberg's ill-humour and reluctance to talk was largely due to his lack of confidence in the British representatives 'and their unusual mode of transacting business'. Sir Charles, he added, was the greater sinner.[14] But although abler diplomats might have extracted more information, they could hardly have deflected the Russians and Prussians from their course.

In London, information was in very short supply. 'We are in great anxiety to hear from you upon the armistice', wrote Castlereagh to his brother, after hearing the news from the French press.[15] But neither Charles's dispatch, when it arrived, nor any other source could throw much light on what was afoot. Castlereagh betrayed his ignorance of the continental scene by blithely assuming that British aims and views were sufficiently well known to the Allies 'to have their due influence in any decision to be taken'. All the same, he urged Cathcart to try to get a 'private explanation' of Metternich's views and to offer immediate subsidies if Austria would declare war. Conscious perhaps that the paymaster's role is not a very glorious one, he pointed out that the rapid progress of the British army in Spain proved 'that it is not by pecuniary efforts alone that we are ready to contend for a better order of things'.[16] He did not yet know that nine days earlier, on June 21, Wellington had won a great and decisive victory at Vitoria. Joseph Bonaparte had been bundled out of Spain, only isolated garrisons of French troops remained behind, and the British were poised on the Pyrenees ready to sweep forward into France.

The news of Vitoria threw Napoleon into a violent rage against his brother, and moved the Tsar to order a *Te Deum* – the first ever sung by the Russians in thanksgiving for a foreign victory. Throughout Europe it made a great impression. It did not, as Stewart and Jackson in their exuberance claimed, settle the issue of peace or war at Prague – Napoleon's intransigence did that. But it helped to rescue the British army from its dismal reputation of bungling and retreat, and gave a lift to British influence and prestige just when this was most needed.

It was nearly the end of August before Castlereagh, to his relief, heard that Austria had at last declared war on the 11th. They had all been, he told Cathcart, 'deeply anxious'.[17] But how far could Britain really trust the continental powers? By this time Castlereagh had learned of the Treaty of Reichenbach, signed secretly by Russia and Prussia shortly after they had accepted large British subsidies and promised to hide no political secrets from Britain. It made him wonder what else they might be hiding from him. He had the greatest confidence in the Tsar, he told Cathcart, somewhat disingenuously, 'but I do not like his concealing anything that is in progress from your Lordship ... Engagements of secrecy against us are of bad precedent, and must not be.'[18] Charles, thoroughly shaken by the armistice, had already warned his brother to be on his guard. If he was thinking of sending anyone to Vienna, he would need to be 'a devilish clever fellow'.[19]

That description hardly fitted the young Earl of Aberdeen, the Cabinet's choice for the Vienna mission. Not quite thirty, he had already refused several diplomatic posts, and only accepted this one after considerable persuasion and on the understanding that he would be on a footing of 'perfect equality' with any other British envoy and could come home at any moment he thought fit.[20] For Castlereagh he must have had the great attraction of having been Pitt's ward and a frequent member of Pitt's household, and by contemporary standards he was not ill-fitted for an important diplomatic mission.[21] But he was both very diffident and extremely conceited, and these two qualities, combined with his inexperience, made him vulnerable to all the arts of flattery which the Austrian Chancellor could use with such lethal effect. To Metternich, Aberdeen was soon 'that dear simpleton of diplomacy'.[22]

Aberdeen caught up with the Allied sovereigns at Prague early in September. His aloofness and ignorance of French made a poor first impression, and he was openly laughed at when he complained about the hardships of his journey. But the flattering warmth of his reception by the Emperor Francis and Metternich more than made up for any lack of appreciation by lesser mortals. Within a week he was uncritically swallowing Metternich's fulsome assurances that he had never lost sight of the value of a close connection with Britain. Now that Austria was committed to fight Napoleon, Metternich's cordiality was genuine enough; he needed British money and munitions. To get them he was prepared to pay lip service to Britain's war aims, although the objectives on which Austria, Russia and Prussia had just privately agreed (in the Treaty of Toeplitz) were limited to central Europe. At one point the thought did cross Aberdeen's mind that the Austrian Chancellor was 'only the most consummate actor'.[23] But such a disagreeable idea quickly withered in the genial glow of Metternich's flattery, and a few days after an Anglo-Austrian treaty had been signed, Aberdeen was assuring Castlereagh that the Austrian government was the most zealous of the Allies in prosecuting the war.[24]

Although they now outnumbered Napoleon's forces, the Allies at first had mixed fortunes after the fighting was resumed in the middle of August. But two months later, Napoleon found himself being steadily encircled. He decided to stand and fight at Leipzig, and after a four-day battle was decisively defeated. By the beginning of November,

Napoleon and the remnants of his army had retreated across the Rhine. While Charles Stewart was having the time of his life on the battlefields of Europe (except when temporarily laid up by a shell splinter above the knee), his brother was fretting himself into a state of near collapse over the possibility that peace might come too soon. He was not convinced that the powers of Europe, now united in an unprecedented collective effort to cut Napoleon down to size, would stick together long enough to make sure that an overmighty France never again troubled the tranquillity of Europe. If a peace settlement was to be durable, it must be collectively negotiated, and the Allies might well be tempted, Castlereagh feared, to settle separately on the basis of their particular interests. He also suspected that they were still unwilling to concede Britain's right to a place in their inner councils. He did his best to accept Aberdeen's estimate of Metternich, but doubts kept breaking in. His remedy was a new treaty of alliance. In addition to being bound, as they already were, in a series of bilateral and trilateral treaties, the Allies would commit themselves jointly to a set of common peace objectives with the general aim of delivering Europe from French control and restoring the status quo. They would also – and this was the only novel suggestion – sign a 'perpetual defensive alliance' to preserve the peace.[25] Britain's particular war aims were the independence of the Peninsula, and the establishment of an independent Holland separated from France by an 'adequate barrier'. It also had treaty obligations to restore Naples (or a 'suitable equivalent') to the King of Sicily, and to ensure that Norway went to Bernadotte.

Castlereagh sent Cathcart the draft of his treaty in the middle of September, with copies for Aberdeen, Stewart and Thornton, in the sanguine hope that he would be able to present the completed treaty to Parliament when it met on November 4. But as he recuperated at Dover Castle from the strain and overwork of the past summer, his confidence in his allies, especially Austria, ebbed away. The shortage of news from the continent – delayed by exceptionally bad autumn gales – increased his anxiety. So did the Russian ambassador, Count Lieven, with his account of the tripartite Treaty of Toeplitz just signed by Austria, Russia and Prussia. On October 14, two days before the first guns boomed out at Leipzig, Castlereagh told Cathcart he felt sure they were faced with a long conflict, and Metternich ought to make up his mind that it could only be sustained 'by calling the mass of the people into action', as Russia and Prussia had already done. 'It is become a contest of nations to all intents and purposes and not a game of statesmen, and he [Metternich] will play into Bonaparte's hands if he deals with it upon any other principle.'²⁶ To Aberdeen, he was even more vehement, insisting that Austria had not an hour to lose before harnessing the nationalist ferment in Germany and the Tyrol to the common cause. 'The people are now the only barrier.'²⁷ Of course, Castlereagh mistook his man completely. Nothing could be more calculated to make Metternich search feverishly for a compromise peace with Napoleon than the argument that only a people's war could overthrow him. To the man who ruled the multinational Austrian empire, nationalist aspirations were anathema.

The new treaty project, admiringly described by Charles Stewart as 'this sheet anchor alliance',²⁸ did not reach Allied headquarters until two days after the end of the battle of Leipzig. Cathcart, in his easy-going way, foresaw little difficulty or delay in getting it signed. But the Tsar was absorbed, naturally enough, in military matters, and when he was eventually persuaded to study Castlereagh's draft treaty he was far from enthusiastic. He complained that it failed to mention subsidies, maritime rights or Britain's colonial conquests. None of these omissions was accidental. Subsidies depended on whether the Allies went on fighting. Maritime rights were the sacred cow of British diplomacy. They had never before been discussed at a peace conference, and Castlereagh had no intention of letting them be now. As for colonial conquests, he had already let it be known that Britain would be prepared to surrender some of these in the interests of securing a general peace.²⁹ But he did not intend to surrender this important bargaining counter, with all the weight it gave to British views, by naming in advance which colonies Britain was prepared to give up.

Metternich's reception of the draft was much blander than the Tsar's. So far as Austria was concerned, he assured Aberdeen, the treaty was a 'work of supererogation', but he was willing to do what the British government wanted, and would try to overcome the Tsar's objections.³⁰ The Prussians made no difficulties, and the Swedes, at the Tsar's request, were dropped from the discussions. Throughout November, talks dragged on at Frankfurt, where the Allied sovereigns had established themselves. Aberdeen confidently predicted that the treaty would soon be signed, and condescendingly reproved Castlereagh for his doubts about Metternich.³¹ He completely failed to realise that the Austrian was making a fool of him.

Metternich was not interested in making closer combinations to continue the war. By now virtually all the German states had deserted Napoleon's sinking ship. His viceroy, Eugène de Beauharnais, still had to be expelled (or negotiated) out of Austria's former possessions in

Italy, but Metternich's main preoccupation was to come to terms with Napoleon before Russia and Prussia tried to extend themselves in central Europe and before the German nationalists could gain the upper hand. He feared his allies and the turbulent forces of grassroots nationalism more than Napoleon.

In his determination to secure a swift peace, Metternich had an eager ally in Aberdeen, who had been profoundly shocked by his close contact with the sufferings and horrors of war. He entered enthusiastically into Metternich's plan to send secret peace proposals to Napoleon through Baron St Aignan, a French diplomat on his way home from Germany. The proposals were based on France's 'natural' frontiers (the Rhine, Alps and Pyrenees), which excluded Holland but not Belgium, and contained a reference to Britain's maritime rights which Aberdeen at first opposed and then accepted. He sent a cautious and placatory account of these transactions to Castlereagh on November 9,[32] but left his colleagues, Cathcart and Stewart, to find out for themselves. Stewart extracted the text of the proposals from Hardenberg, after a furious scene, and with Jackson's help, composed an extremely caustic commentary on them for Castlereagh's enlightenment.[33] Jackson felt the whole episode showed the importance of having one British representative of weight and consequence at Allied headquarters. 'Of the two ambassadors we now have, one is cajoled and bamboozled [Aberdeen], the other laughed at and neglected [Cathcart]. Sir Charles Stewart has not sufficient weight to counteract this, and *faire valoir* his good sense and judgment. He is not, as he says, "an adept in difficult diplomacy".'[34] But at least Stewart, unlike Aberdeen, realised his limitations in this field.

Meanwhile, in London, Castlereagh and his colleagues were beginning to feel soberly confident that Napoleon would soon be safely corralled. There was, it is true, no new grand alliance to flourish before Parliament, but the reports of the battle of Leipzig, followed soon after by the news that Wellington had resumed his advance across the Pyrenees, threw the country into a state of happy expectancy. For once in their lives the ministers basked in popular approval. In Parliament criticism was transformed into commendation; even that scourge of the Tories, Samuel Whitbread, declared that he did not wish to replace a single member of the Cabinet.

In the middle of November the Dutch, encouraged by the appearance of some Cossack cavalry, rose in revolt. By the end of the month the Prince of Orange (with £100,000 in cash) had landed in Holland from a British warship, and an improvised force of 10,000

British troops was only prevented by contrary winds from following him immediately. 'The popular spirit', wrote Castlereagh, 'which has shown itself there [in Holland] I look upon as one of the most fortunate events of the war.'[35] The whole question of guaranteeing Dutch independence suddenly became much more urgent, and with it the issue of protecting England from the threat that Antwerp in hostile hands was always felt to be. Castlereagh begged Cathcart and Aberdeen to impress upon the Allies the vital importance of Antwerp to Britain. 'To leave it in the hands of France is little short of imposing upon Great Britain the charge of a perpetual war establishment.'[36]

But the arrival of the St Aignan peace proposals revived all Castlereagh's worries' about the Allies' intentions. He complained strongly to Aberdeen about the 'very loose and equivocal description' of the British government's stand on maritime rights, and told him to insist in writing that this subject was not open to discussion. 'You know ... that at all times a maritime question touches us to the quick.'[37] There was worse to come from Frankfurt. Towards the middle of December the Tsar's Corsican adviser, Pozzo di Borgo, arrived in London and revealed that the Allies would not sign Castlereagh's new treaty of alliance unless it was enlarged to include a British commitment on subsidies and on the colonial conquests Britain was willing to surrender. They also strongly suspected the motives behind Castlereagh's proposal for a permanent defensive alliance. He was profoundly disheartened, perplexed and exasperated. Surely it must be obvious that Britain, which had least to fear from a resurgent France, had no motive beyond the common good in proposing a permanent alliance. If Napoleon were to be replaced on the throne of France by a more pacific government, it would not be necessary. But since they could not assume this, 'nothing ... but a defensive league is likely to deter France from returning to the old system of progressive encroachment'.[38]

The remedy for Castlereagh's frustration came from an unlikely source – the Allies themselves. They had had enough of exploiting the divisions, weaknesses and vanity of the three British representatives, and asked that a single authoritative British negotiator should be sent to Frankfurt. The suggestion once made, nothing could seem more sensible. But it did not at first occur to Castlereagh that he might go to the continent himself. He asked Lord Harrowby to go and seemed surprised when Harrowby suggested it would be much better if he went himself. How could the Secretary of State desert his post in Downing Street? His colleagues did not see why not. Liverpool would stand in for him at the Foreign Office and he could be spared until Parliament reassembled in March. In a few days it was all settled, and Castlereagh was writing friendly letters to his envoys in Frankfurt, praising their efforts, ignoring their disputes and omissions and blaming himself for not having instructed them to negotiate collectively.[39] 'I feel confident', he told Charles, 'that when we all get together at headquarters *we shall give the whole the ensemble it requires.*'[40]

He was to go with full powers to take decisions, and the Cabinet held several meetings over Christmas to work out his instructions. They produced a rather rough and ready document,[41] but his colleagues trusted Castlereagh's good sense and discretion and he himself was in a hurry to get away. He felt he was being overtaken by events. Napoleon had accepted the St Aignan proposals as a basis for peace talks, and the Allies were simultaneously invading France (they began to cross the Rhine on December 2) and preparing to negotiate with Napoleon's representative, Caulaincourt. Moreover, the situation in the Low Countries was causing acute concern in London. Although William of Orange was installed in The Hague, the British expeditionary force under General Graham was making no headway in expelling the French from the Scheldt, and Bernadotte, absorbed in his private war against Denmark, refused to send the help he had repeatedly promised. An 'adequate' barrier for Holland and the expulsion of France from the Scheldt were both *sine qua non* for Britain. To secure the first the Cabinet authorised Castlereagh to give up both French and Dutch colonial conquests; to gain the second, he could threaten to keep the lot. Once satisfied that Holland, the Peninsula and Italy would be independent and secure from French penetration, he could use Britain's colonial conquests, with certain exceptions, 'to promote the general interests'. Exactly how, the Cabinet's instructions left vague. For northern and central Italy some tentative suggestions were made, but German internal arrangements were left a blank. So was the future of France, although by this time there was a good deal of speculation in the English press about a Bourbon restoration, and ministers were being besieged by Bourbon princes who wanted to join Wellington's army and raise the south of France against Napoleon.

But perhaps the most difficult part of Castlereagh's mission concerned the Allies, not the enemy. He was to try to persuade them to negotiate with Napoleon 'in perfect concert, and together maintain one common interest'. The Allies were certainly prone to disagree, and Britain stood outside most continental differences. But could a British representative inspire enough confidence to promote harmony? Castlereagh and his colleagues genuinely believed that they were good

Europeans. They were now financing and arming the continental powers on a far more generous scale than even Pitt had attempted. For five years they had managed (in spite of the war with America) to keep Wellington supplied with fresh troops. The effort and strain had been unprecedented. But it all counted for very little against the Europeans' ingrained dislike and distrust of the arrogant island power who ruled the seas and grew rich – so they firmly believed – at their expense. The Cabinet's dawning awareness of this hostility was reflected in Castlereagh's instructions: he was 'to avoid everything that might countenance a suspicion that Great Britain was inclined to push them [the Allies] forward in the war for our purposes'. No man could act as a conciliator if his motives were suspect.

Castlereagh could at any rate be sure of a warm welcome. The news that he was coming was greeted with unfeigned pleasure by the Allies and unabashed relief by the British envoys. Even Aberdeen had been moved to tell Metternich that the Allies seemed almost as anxious to make common cause against the British as against France.[42] 'Everything which has been so long smothered is now bursting forth', he told Castlereagh in one of several welcoming letters. 'Your presence is absolutely providential. If you come without partiality or prejudice, as I make no doubt you do ... you will be able to perform everything; and no words are sufficient to express the service you will render. I am most anxious that you should come.'[43]

CHAPTER XII

Mission to Allied headquarters 1813–14

Castlereagh set out on his mission to the Allies late on Boxing Day 1813, accompanied by his wife and her niece, Lady Emma Edgcumbe. He took with him as his principal aide Frederick Robinson, vice-President of the Board of Trade, and the rest of his modest staff consisted of his private secretary at the Foreign Office, Joseph Planta, and two clerks. They were to cross from Harwich to Holland in HMS *Erebus*, but for three days they were held up by contrary winds. While they waited in the local inn, Castlereagh occupied himself by writing letters and reading dispatches – 'which he does', William Montagu, one of the clerks, noted with amazement, 'in the room with us all and never seems in the least disturbed by the noise or impeded in his progress'.[1]

Their journey across the North Sea was reasonably swift, but too rough for most of the passengers. Castlereagh, however, 'seemed to thrive most amazingly, devoured broiled bones, and rather laughed at the sick ones'. But among the shoals and narrow inlets of the Dutch coast, the voyage nearly ended in disaster. Neither the captain nor the crew had any idea where they were, and when a Dutch pilot eventually came out to guide them, they were immobilised by contrary winds. After a second night rocking at anchor in a 'tremendous swell', even Castlereagh was obliged to keep to his cabin.[2]

It was January 5, 1814 before they at last arrived at Helvoetsluys. They were received with a salute of guns from the fort and the cheers of the local inhabitants as they stepped ashore. Two days later, they were welcomed at The Hague by the British envoy, Castlereagh's friend, Lord Clancarty, who had accompanied the Prince of Orange on his return. The Dutch were in a state of euphoria after their recent liberation, and seemed to have accepted their new ruler with enthusiasm. Emily and her niece, who were to remain with Clancarty for the time being, created much pleasure by appearing at a dinner party in dazzling orange gowns. Castlereagh only stayed long enough for discussions on the country's final frontiers – he persuaded the Dutch to leave him to do the best he could for them – and a private audience with the Prince about the proposed marriage between his son and Princess Charlotte. Late on the evening of January 8, he and Robinson resumed their journey, leaving the rest of the mission to follow at a less breakneck speed.

Spending only one night in bed, they managed to reach Frankfurt in six days. It was the worst winter in living memory, and they travelled through country that had been much fought over. The roads, cut up by artillery and then frozen solid, were worse, Castlereagh thought, than a frozen ploughed field. The windows of their coach were permanently covered with thick frost, so that 'we were in fact imprisoned in an Ice House for days and nights, from which we were occasionally removed into a dirty room with a black stove smelling of tobacco smoke or something worse'.[3]

At Frankfurt Castlereagh received, through Cathcart, a message from the Tsar asking that he should be the first to talk to him. This suggested increased Allied discord, and Castlereagh hurried on to the Allied headquarters at Freiburg, reaching it late on the 17th. But the Allies had just moved on to Basle, and Castlereagh learned that the Tsar, after waiting several days for him, was about to join his army in France. So after stopping a few hours for a midnight briefing from the German publicist, Friedrich Gentz (whom Castlereagh impressed by his earnest desire to learn about Europe as well as by his bright scarlet breeches,[4]) they pressed on to Basle, which they reached late on the 18th. The Tsar, however, had departed the day before, reluctantly leaving the Austrians and Prussians to get their word in first with the British Foreign Secretary.

It was the first time Castlereagh and Metternich had met, and first impressions on both sides were favourable. Castlereagh had feared that the Austrian Chancellor would settle for a compromise peace. But now that Napoleon really seemed to be cornered, Metternich was prepared to stiffen the terms he had offered through St Aignan. At that moment, however, he was more preoccupied with Russia than with France. He had heard alarming reports that Alexander wanted to replace Napoleon by Bernadotte. Castlereagh had also heard the reports and was more than ready to share the Austrian's perturbation at the prospect of a Russian puppet on the throne of France. Metternich was sufficiently alarmed to assure Castlereagh that Austria would not – as had been hinted – try a similar ploy by proposing a regency for Napoleon's half-Austrian son. He would prefer a Bourbon restoration to Napoleon, but not against the wishes of the French people. This was the position to which the British Cabinet, after much careful and anxious thought, had moved. They could not give official backing to the Bourbon princes living in England, who were determined to try their fortunes in France, but they

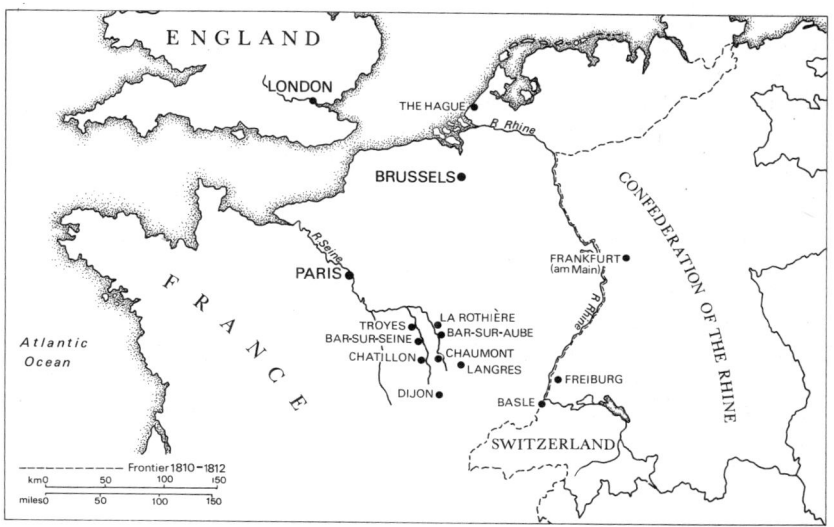

FRANCE. SPRING 1814

would not try to stop them either; 'we cannot conceal from ourselves', wrote Liverpool, 'that if we were in their situation, we should act as they are acting ...'[5]

Thus at their first encounter, circumstances – or the Tsar's vagaries – brought Castlereagh and Metternich together. A genuine understanding on an issue which at that moment was at the forefront of both their minds was a good basis for a relationship. Moreover, they got on well together. Metternich was delighted by Castlereagh's energy, pleasant manners, good sense and moderation. 'I get on with him', he wrote, 'as if we had spent all our lives together.'[6]

In a few days Castlereagh was ready to set out through the snow for the Allied headquarters at Langres, north of Dijon. Before starting he found time to buy some presents for Emily. 'I send by the messenger', he told her, 'a little box with some of the products of this town. The lady is very pretty and a little like your ladyship, therefore you will keep this for me. The two gentlemen I send to comfort you, which is being more generous than you were to me in giving me your last instructions. If you are satisfied with one beau, keep the handsomest, and give Emma the old fellow with a beard with my love to hang about her beautiful neck.'[7]

He was bombarded by appeals from Emily to let her join him. It was obviously impracticable, both because of the weather and because of the uncertainty of his movements. In war-ravaged eastern France he could find no more pretty presents for her, but he placated her as best he could with chatty letters, assuring her that he was well, working hard and never saw a 'single princess'.[8] His arguments that she must stay put were not helped by the wife of Lord Burghersh, the British representative with the Austrian army. This enterprising lady, who was Wellington's niece, turned up at Basle and firmly attached herself to the Allied diplomats. She was evidently good company, which perhaps consoled Castlereagh for the additional force her presence gave to the appeals from The Hague. 'I quite delight in "Cas"', she wrote, 'I had no idea he had so much fun in him, though he is impenetrably cold . . .'[9]

From Langres he told Emily that he had now met 'all the great wigs here. The Emperor Alexander would be your favourite. He has 30,000 Guards here that are the finest soldiers I ever beheld.'[10] Lady Burghersh reported that 'Lord Castlereagh has pleased very much here. They say he has *une fort belle physiognomie*, and seem to like him extremely. His placidity of course never ruffles.'[11] After several days at Langres, and two lengthy interviews with the Tsar, who was not in the best of tempers, Castlereagh needed all the unassailable composure for which he was soon famous at Allied headquarters.

He found the military very much at odds, neither the Tsar nor the Prussian generals having any confidence in the judgment of the Austrian commander-in-chief, Prince Schwarzenberg. There was also much political intrigue among the Austrians and Russians, and much mutual mistrust, especially over Poland and Saxony.* The Tsar was suspicious by temperament, and 'Metternich's character furnishes constant food for the *intriguants* to work upon'. It was a perceptive comment, but Castlereagh's claim that he had 'got some way with both the parties' on Poland and Saxony showed how much he still had to learn about the complexities of central European politics.[12]

On the immediate problem of how to deal with France there was also discord. Alexander seemed disposed to give way about Bernadotte, but he had not a good word to say for the Bourbons, claiming that not one of

---

*By three successive partitions, in 1772, 1773 and 1795, Poland had been entirely divided between Austria, Russia and Prussia. Napoleon had formed the Grand Duchy of Warsaw out of the parts of Poland seized by Prussia and Austria. The Tsar wished to reunite Poland under his own sovereignty. He proposed to compensate Prussia with Saxony, and Austria with territory in Italy and Dalmatia. The Austrians were opposed to Russia and Prussia obtaining such large accessions of territory.

them was competent to rule France. Worse still, he seemed determined to press on to Paris, leaving the peace talks to take care of themselves, although Caulaincourt had already been asked to meet the Allies at Chatillon. Alexander, wrote Castlereagh, 'has a *personal* feeling about Paris ... He seems to seek for the occasion of entering with his magnificent guards the enemy's capital, probably to display, in his clemency and forebearance, a contrast to that desolation to which his own was devoted.'[13] The possibility that a quick and successful negotiation with Caulaincourt might rob him of this triumph increased Alexander's anxiety to push on. There was a real danger that the exasperated Austrians might refuse to accompany the Tsar on what they called his crusade to Paris, and that he might go on without them.

Castlereagh sat the Allies down round one table and after three days of hard talking, the Russians, finding themselves in a minority of one, agreed to begin peace talks at Chatillon, while Schwarzenberg continued the campaign 'with due regard for military prudence'.[14] The three continental Allies agreed that Britain's maritime rights should be excluded from the talks. They also agreed that their military position now entitled them to negotiate with France on the basis, not of its 'natural' frontiers, but of its more restricted pre-1792 frontiers. Since the Austrians did not want to take back the former Austrian Netherlands (or Belgium), Castlereagh could now plan to strengthen Holland by the addition of this territory.

All this was satisfactory, so far as it went. But the Allies, claiming, on rather tenuous grounds, to represent the whole of Europe except Turkey, had assumed the right to dispose of Napoleon's conquests throughout the continent, although they were deeply divided on how this should be done. Realising that Poland, Saxony and other bones of contention would be exploited by the French after a peace, Castlereagh tried to avert this threat to European stability by persuading the Allies to agree on the outlines of a blueprint for a reconstructed Europe in time to present it to Caulaincourt. This was far too optimistic. The Allies insisted on leaving all the contentious issues to be settled later at a congress in Vienna. Since Castlereagh's arrival they might have learned to disagree more civilly, but they still disagreed.

The peace talks opened at Chatillon on February 5. Since none of the Allied sovereigns or senior ministers attended, Castlereagh felt he could not either, at least not officially. Instead, he hit upon the curious expedient of appointing that well-assorted trio, Aberdeen, Cathcart and Stewart, as a joint British delegation. None of the three was at all pleased, Cathcart and Stewart because they infinitely preferred their military duties and Aberdeen because he had confidently assumed he would be in sole charge. He was consoled by being made *primus inter pares*, while the two generals were gently rapped over the knuckles and told they had had 'fighting enough to satisfy reasonable appetites'.[15] Charles, however, found Chatillon extremely tedious. His part, he confidentially informed Edward Cooke, 'puts me in mind of some play, where three conspirators stalk in, muffled up in cloaks, and sit down, and two remain very quietly on the bench, while the one who is to perform [i.e. Aberdeen] gets up and makes his speech and stabs the King'.[16]

The Chatillon conference was, in fact, doomed to become a long-drawn-out farce, and a poor one at that, its proceedings entirely dominated by the fortunes of the war which raged to and fro over the surrounding countryside, sometimes within earshot of the little town. A few days before the talks began, Schwarzenberg and the Prussian general, Blucher, inflicted a severe reverse on the French at La Rothière, near Brienne. Napoleon was forced to retreat, first to Troyes and then to Nogent. At Nogent he learned that Murat, the friend whom he had made king of Naples, had deserted to the Allies. Blucher was marching swiftly on Paris, and from Chatillon came Caulaincourt's report that the Allies were insisting that France should be restricted to its 'ancient' frontiers. On February 8, after much agonising, Napoleon instructed Caulaincourt to get the best terms he could.

The next day, without consulting his allies, the Tsar abruptly suspended the Chatillon talks. Now that the way to Paris was open, he saw no point in further negotiations. He would march on the French capital and there summon an assembly to decide who should rule France. Metternich was appalled and urged Castlereagh, who had gone over to Chatillon, to rejoin the Allied headquarters which by now had advanced as far westwards as Troyes. Castlereagh was equally appalled. Napoleon was in great difficulties militarily, but he was still ruler of France, and there was as yet no sign that the French people were ready to reject him in favour of anyone else. He was now apparently willing to accept the Allied terms. It would, Castlereagh felt, be folly to let slip this chance of peace, and risk getting embroiled in a civil war between Bonapartists and Bourbons. But in two long and sometimes heated interviews with Alexander at Troyes his arguments failed to make any impression. The Tsar did not apparently want to act the king-maker; he would accept the French people's choice – even a Bourbon prince, even Napoleon himself. But he would not be deprived of the triumphant Parisian scenario he had worked out for himself.

The disagreement was resolved by Napoleon himself. Hearing that

Blucher and Schwarzenberg had separated and were marching on Paris by different routes, he snapped out of his despair and resolved to defeat them piecemeal. In nine days he won five victories, ignored Schwarzenberg's request for an armistice, and advanced on Troyes. At Chatillon the roles were reversed. The Tsar, alarmed by the Allied defeats, was now willing to resume negotiations, and on February 17 a draft peace treaty, brought to Chatillon by Castlereagh, was presented to the French. But Napoleon was now demanding France's 'natural' frontiers, and Caulaincourt was no longer interested in settling quickly on the Allied terms. The negotiations ground to a halt while both sides waited for the outcome of the fighting. 'The negotiators at Chatillon', reported Castlereagh, 'are spitting over the bridge, which Charles says is very bad fun.'[17] The Austrian guard and the town commandant left on the 25th, and small parties of French cavalry began to pass through the town. A National Guard was formed to keep order and protect the diplomats – 'a ragged-looking fellow is this moment parading before the door', wrote Montagu – and the mayor published 'a most flaming handbill' appealing to the inhabitants to respect the peace-makers.[18]*

At Allied headquarters the collapse in morale was swift and startling. Instead of trying to restrain the Tsar's bellicosity, Castlereagh found himself striving to sustain his Allies' will to fight. Before setting out from Chatillon to return to Troyes, he sent Metternich an eloquent appeal not to let a few military reverses panic him into relaxing the peace terms on which they had agreed. 'If we act with *military* and *political* prudence, how can France resist a just peace demanded by 600,000 warriors?'[19] He arrived at Troyes to find the Allies all gone, except for an outpost, and the enemy approaching the town. He rejoined the Allied sovereigns and their ministers at Bar-sur-Aube, and there on February 25, in the Prussian king's quarters, a gloomy council of war was held. Of the two Allied armies, the larger, commanded by Schwarzenberg, had been severely mauled, and he insisted on seeking an armistice and retiring until he had established contact with his reserves. Castlereagh therefore proposed that two corps, one Russian and the other Prussian, which were on their way to join Bernadotte, should be diverted to reinforce Blucher's army. The plan had been canvassed before, but dropped for fear of Bernadotte's reactions. Castlereagh, however, undertook to square him, and Blucher got the reinforcements which helped him to fend off Napoleon's desperate attempts to knock him out of the war.

---

*Chatillon had been declared neutral territory for the duration of the conference.

Next day the Allies continued their retreat to Chaumont, taking their fears and discords with them. 'I cannot conceal from you', wrote Castlereagh to Liverpool, 'that the internal temper here is very embarrassing, if not alarming. The criminations and recriminations between the Austrians and Russians are at their height, and my patience is worn out combating both.' The Tsar, 'not quite satisfied with himself', was full of complaints about Schwarzenberg's caution, while the arrival of the Polish leader, Prince Czartoryski, had thrown Metternich into alarm about Alexander's plans for Poland. Castlereagh had been labouring to achieve an understanding between them, but Alexander was 'with fine qualities both suspicious and undecided' and Metternich was 'constitutionally temporising'. Alarmed though he was by the Allies' quarrelling, and even more by the pall of defeat that hung over their headquarters, Castlereagh did not despair; 'when things are at their worst, they mend'.[20]

He was right. By early March 1814 Allied morale had begun to recover and the military situation had been stabilised. The intrepid Blucher resumed his advance on Paris, drawing Napoleon after him, while Schwarzenberg recovered his nerve sufficiently to break off his armistice negotiations. The retreat of the Allied sovereigns stopped at Chaumont – 'a dull and dirty town', according to Castlereagh. It was also extremely crowded. The one small room in which Castlereagh worked and slept was also used as a dining room by the whole British mission – when there was anything to eat. The armies had devoured everything in the neighbourhood, but a foraging expedition to Dijon yielded three dozen fowl and six dozen bottles of wine.[21] Public morale was sustained by the Tsar's band, which Montagu thought played 'most delightfully'. But a week later he reported that Castlereagh gave them so much work that he had no time to go and see the sights.

Montagu was working overtime because his chief had just pulled off a diplomatic coup: he had successfully negotiated the four-power treaty of alliance which he had first suggested in London six months earlier. Practical experience of his Allies had made Castlereagh even more anxious to bind them more closely: 'we must not go to sea in search of adventures with such a bark as we sail in'.[22] At Chaumont he found the Tsar in a much more friendly mood. 'I see him almost every day', reported Castlereagh, 'and he receives me with great kindness, and converses with me freely on all subjects.'[23] He was also able to trade on the Allies' perennial shortage of cash. At first he had refused to link subsidies with the treaty of alliance, but by now he realised that he could not afford to dispense with these carrots. The treaty, however, still fell

Metternich
by Lawrence

The Congress of
Vienna, 1815,
after a painting
by Isabey

1	The Duke of Wellington	England	12	Duc de Dalberg	France
2	Count Lobo da Silveyra	Portugal	13	Baron von Wessenberg	Austria
3	Duke de Saldanha de Gama	Portugal	14	Prince Rasoumoffsky	Russia
4	Count of Lowenheim	Sweden	15	General Lord Stewart	England
5	The Prince of Hardenberg	Prussia	16	Don Pierre-Gomez Labrador	Spain
6	Count Alexis de Noailles	France	17	Lord Clancarty	England
7	Prince Metternich	Austria	18	M. Wacken	England
8	Count de Latour du Pin	France	19	M. Gentz	England
9	Count Nesselrode	Russia	20	Baron Wilhelm von Humbolt	Prussia
10	de Sousa-Holstein, Count of Palmella	Portugal	21	General Lord Cathcart	England
			22	Prince de Talleyrand-Perigord	France
11	Viscount Castlereagh	England	23	Count Stackelberg	Russia

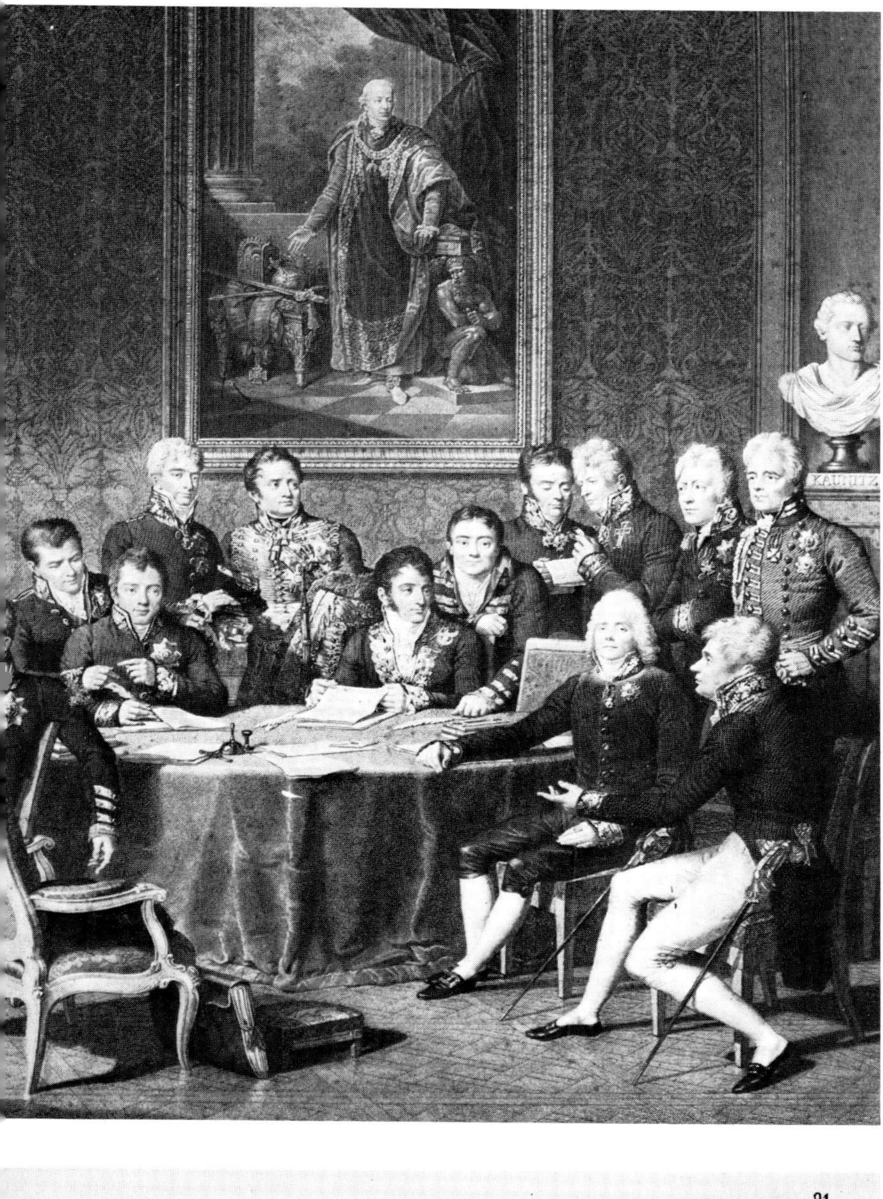

3
4
5
6
7
8
9
10
11
12
13
14
15
16
17
19
20
21
22
23

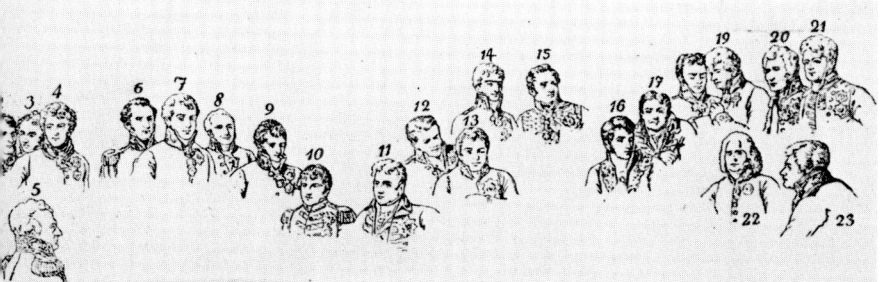

Castlereagh
by Lawrence, painted c. 1815

MISSION TO ALLIED HEADQUARTERS 1813-14

short of Castlereagh's maximum aims, even after a promise of five million pounds to be divided between the three continental powers. The four signatories agreed to continue the war against Napoleon with armies of at least 150,000 men; not to make peace except by mutual consent; and to maintain the peace settlement for twenty years with armies of at least 60,000 men. For twenty years Europe was to be guaranteed against French aggression. But measures to prevent aggression by anyone else – that is, a falling-out among the Allies – were confined to a vague resolve to consult together on how best to guarantee the continuance of the peace.[24]*

All the same, Castlereagh was jubilant. He reckoned that Britain's contribution would equal those of all the rest put together. 'What an extraordinary display of power. This, I trust, will put an end to any doubts as to the claim we have to an opinion on continental matters.'[25] When the treaty was signed at Chaumont on March 9, the four signatories, observing that they happened to be sitting round a whist table, agreed – according to Castlereagh – 'that never were stakes so high at any former party'.[26] For him, it was certainly an exhilarating moment. The others probably took it all much more calmly. By now Napoleon's downfall seemed virtually assured, and they could not share Castlereagh's optimistic hope that four signatures on a piece of paper would really bring them much closer together. (A week later, the Austrians and Russians were sparring as energetically as ever.[27]) But the treaty was a foundation, however fragile, for the edifice of European cooperation on which Castlereagh believed Britain's security depended.

Meanwhile, at Chatillon, Caulaincourt was stalling desperately in the hope of getting fresh instructions from Napoleon. They never came. He begged Aberdeen to send for Castlereagh with whom he felt sure he could soon settle everything: 'For the love of God, engage him to return.'[28] But Castlereagh, with his Chaumont treaty in the bag, felt that Napoleon was now determined to fight to a finish and the peace talks only sapped the resolve of the Allied armies to fight vigorously. The Tsar was of the same mind, and although Metternich, typically, tried to spin things out, the conference was formally ended on March 19.

Two days later, Napoleon, who had been fighting against increasing odds with a skill and determination that evoked Charles Stewart's

---

*Britain reserved the right to supply the equivalent of 60,000 men in subsidies. It was also agreed that Spain, Portugal, Sweden and Holland should be invited to 'accede' to the treaty. This would not involve them in the obligations assumed by the four great powers, but it would, Castlereagh hoped, protect them from French bullying after the peace.

reluctant admiration, came upon Schwarzenberg's whole army and only escaped from complete disaster with heavy losses. He now decided on his last throw. He would retire eastwards, collecting reinforcements from his frontier garrisons, and force the Allies to abandon their advance on Paris by relentlessly attacking their lines of communication.

Napoleon's lunge eastwards put the Allied diplomats to flight. While the Tsar and the King of Prussia went off to goad the ever-cautious Schwarzenberg into making more haste for Paris, the Emperor Francis, Metternich, Hardenberg and Castlereagh were chased from pillar to post, 'beating about', as George Jackson cheerfully put it, between Troyes, Bar-sur-Aube, Bar-sur-Seine and Chatillon. All the time the French were hard on their heels. At Troyes Napoleon stayed in the house Castlereagh had just left, and a few days later, at Bar-sur-Aube, the French emperor slept in the same bed that the Austrian emperor had got out of that morning. After this close shave, the Allied missions had to abandon any hope of rejoining their armies. They made their way southwards and finally came to rest at Dijon.

For Castlereagh, the constant journeying through the still snow-bound countryside was a sobering experience. He was shocked by the desolation wrought by war on the hapless civilians in its path, just as the previous year Aberdeen had been appalled by the sufferings of the soldiers as he rode across the battlefield of Leipzig. 'I am sorry to say', he wrote from Bar-sur-Aube, 'this country is in a most deplorable state ... It is a most distressing sight, to traverse repeatedly as we have now done, this wasted district in which for a space of thirty miles, from hence to Troyes, when I last rode it, I saw more human bodies dead than alive.'[29]

By contrast, he found Dijon 'a delightful town'. It was, he told Emily, the only one he had seen 'where the people looked clean and good-humoured'. The intrepid Lady Burghersh had also turned up there, after various vicissitudes which Castlereagh reported to his restless wife with obvious satisfaction. She was 'obliged to fly from Chaumont and live in a bivouac with all the heavy baggage of the army, without the possibility of changing her chemise unperceived, except the ceremony was performed in the dark of the night'.[30] Lady Burghersh unwittingly turned the other cheek to this ungallant revelation by enthusiastically rhapsodising about Castlereagh. 'You never saw such a *beauty* as Lord Castlereagh has become. He is as brown as a berry, with a fine bronzed colour, and wears a fur cap with gold, and is really quite *charming*. There never was anybody so looked up to as he is here.'[31]

Whether or not Lady Burghersh was a little carried away, the Allied ministers did not want to lose Castlereagh, who was proposing to return to England to take his place in Parliament. He himself was reluctant to go, but felt he should. 'We have got so much into the habit of acting together', he told Liverpool, 'and the ministers of the three courts press my remaining with a degree of earnestness which would make me anxious, if possible, to comply with their wishes.'[32] But it was the swift and tumultuous rush of events which really decided him to wait and then go home by way of Paris.

Napoleon's last desperate plan to save his throne foundered on two miscalculations: the Allied armies did not turn aside to fight him, and Paris did not bar its gates and defy the invaders. On March 30 the final battle was fought at Montmartre, and that night Marshal Marmont signed the capitulation of the city. A few hours later, Napoleon, racing back to try to save the situation, arrived at Fontainebleau and learned that he was too late. Next day, March 31, the Tsar realised his long-cherished dream and rode in triumph into Paris.

Alexander, an idealist as well as a conqueror, went straight from reviewing his troops in the Champs Élysées to Napoleon's former foreign minister, Prince Talleyrand, whom he believed best able to tell him the wishes of the French people. Talleyrand, convinced by now that France could choose only between the Bourbons and chaos, assured the Tsar that the French wanted their legitimate sovereign, Louis XVIII. Within two days, a provisional government had been appointed, with Talleyrand at its head, and the French Senate, after formally deposing Napoleon, had invited Louis XVIII to return.

Fortunately for the unity of the Allies, the Austrian, Prussian and English ministers marooned at Dijon had also decided to plump for a Bourbon restoration. Castlereagh's colleagues in London had left him in no doubt about the popular frenzy in Britain against making peace with Napoleon; and the news that Bordeaux had declared for the Bourbons after its capture by Wellington swept away Metternich's remaining doubts. On March 28, at a party given by Castlereagh to celebrate Wellington's latest successes, Louis XVIII was enthusiastically toasted by the whole company. 'The Allies support the King', reported Castlereagh, 'in the mode of doing so making it as much as possible the act of the nation.'[33]

The news of the Allied entry into Paris did not reach Dijon until April 4. Castlereagh immediately wrote to Emily, hoping 'that we may meet without further delay in Paris' and sending her advice and instructions for the journey. He had laid in a stock of silks and old Sèvres china, but he would give it to some belle in Paris if she did not come to fetch it herself. 'God bless you dearest friend', he ended, 'I am a bad boy but you will forgive me when we meet which I trust will be in the fewest days possible.'[34]

He waited another five days before he himself set out for Paris. Like Metternich, he preferred to leave Alexander to enjoy his triumph without competition. Lord Clancarty in The Hague deplored the absence in Paris of 'something more possessing weight and intelligence than the Emperor of Russia and Nesselrode [his foreign minister] during the fabrication of a constitution by Talleyrand and his colleagues'.[35] But Castlereagh was almost obsessively determined that Britain should not seem to be interfering in the arrangements for the future government of France. It was only after he reached Paris that he realised the risks of leaving the chivalrous Russian emperor to come to terms with the man he had once so greatly admired.

CHAPTER XIII

The search for peace: Paris, London, Vienna 1814–15

By the time Castlereagh and Metternich reached Paris on April 10, 1814, Napoleon's future had been settled and a treaty with him was about to be signed. He was to keep his imperial title and receive the sovereignty of Elba with an annual revenue of two million francs; the Empress Marie-Louise was to have the duchy of Parma with reversion to her son; and pensions were to be provided for the Bonaparte family. Although the Treaty of Fontainebleau drove Napoleon to attempt suicide, it clearly reflected the Tsar's magnanimous notions on how to treat a fallen foe, and by providing Napoleon with what Talleyrand called a *pont d'or* to exile, it also represented a prudent precaution against the not inconsiderable risk of civil war.

Castlereagh, however, found the treaty hard to swallow. Like most of his fellow countrymen, he felt a passionate dislike for the man who was always known officially in England as General Bonaparte, and he was outraged that the treaty allowed Napoleon to keep his imperial title. For that reason he refused to sign it – although he 'acceded' to the territorial provisions – and he persuaded the Allies not to make Napoleon's title hereditary. But the main objection to the treaty was that it established Napoleon on an island close to France, and even closer to Italy, where Murat was still half-loyal to his brother-in-law. Castlereagh's opposition was strongly supported by Metternich, who maintained that Napoleon on Elba would mean war within two years.[1] Perhaps – but only perhaps – if they had arrived earlier they might have been able to argue Alexander out of his airy insistence that they could trust the word of a soldier and a sovereign. It was certainly too late now, and in any case every other place suggested seemed to have some drawback.* Everyone was anxious to get rid of the looming presence of

---

*Castlereagh did not respond to Napoleon's repeated wish to go to England, although on May 5 he wrote to Liverpool: 'If [Bonaparte's] taste for an asylum in England should continue, would you allow him to reside in some distant province? It would obviate much alarm on the continent.' It would also probably have caused a riot in the 'distant province'. (C.C.X, p.10)

the former French emperor only forty miles away at Fontainebleau and still surrounded by his army, so that they could safely turn to making peace with the Bourbons.

Unfortunately, the heir to the Bourbons was still in England, prostrated by an attack of gout. So it was Louis's brother, the Comte d'Artois, on whom the Parisians had to expend their newly-discovered enthusiasm for the old regime. D'Artois made his triumphal entry into Paris on April 12, and among the cavalcade which set out to welcome him were Castlereagh and Frederick Robinson. They drew up by the roadside to await the count's arrival. 'He was on horseback', reported Robinson, 'surrounded by officers of the National Guard, and some of his personal attendants. As soon as he saw Castlereagh he called him up and we proceeded with the procession close to him ... No words can describe the joy and enthusiasm of the innumerable crowds who literally *paved* the street.'[2]

'If you hurry the King off', wrote Castlereagh to Liverpool next day, 'I may be with you this day month. It may appear presumptuous in me to say so, but my remaining till this new scene takes a shape is beyond all comparison more important than my original mission.'[3] His conscience no longer pricked him about deserting his post in Parliament. His colleagues in London, he felt, could manage better without him than his allies in Paris. But he himself could manage better with the backing of Wellington. 'His military name', explained Castlereagh to Liverpool, 'would give him and us the greatest ascendancy.'[4] So Charles Stewart posted off immediately to Wellington's headquarters at Toulouse to explain his brother's 'strong wish' to see him. He also carried an offer of the Paris embassy after peace was signed, 'if you have no other object immediately in view, repose after such exertions being in itself a very natural one'[5]. Not feeling the need for repose, Wellington accepted the embassy by return. He reached Paris on May 4 in time to watch the parade of Russian and Prussian guards before the newly-arrived king, Louis XVIII. That evening he appeared at a ball given by Charles Stewart, where, reported Castlereagh proudly, 'he was the great object of admiration'.[6]

Balls, receptions, parades, gala performances – life in the French capital was one long celebration, and droves of English people flocked over to share in the gaieties. Among the glittering crowd of royalties, generals and ministers, Castlereagh was almost the only person of note without any decorations. But when someone remarked on this, another replied: '*Ma foi, il a l'air bien distingué.*' 'And he had', wrote Emily's niece, who recorded this incident, 'with his tall figure, his handsome countenance, and his simple, unaffected, yet dignified manner, which made one feel very proud of him.'[7] After Emily's arrival the Castlereaghs entertained frequently and lavishly. French and Allied ministers met at their formal dinners, and each evening Emily gave informal suppers to which everyone she knew could come without invitation and bring their friends as well. Mme de Staël came frequently, and one evening Talleyrand's mistress, the Duchess of Courland, appeared with her daughter, Mme de Périgord, the wife of Talleyrand's nephew. Mme de Périgord was highly rouged and flamboyantly dressed in a pink gown with roses in her hair. Afterwards, Emily, who had decided views on the ladies she was obliged to entertain, remarked to her niece: 'Emma, I am afraid we live in very bad company.'[8]

Whether good or bad, the company took up a great deal of time. 'Paris is a bad place for business', wrote Castlereagh to Lord Bathurst, when apologising for being such a bad correspondent.[9] He did most of the business himself. That discordant trio – Aberdeen, Cathcart and Stewart – were kept in attendance, but largely, it seems, for decorative purposes. Castlereagh kept Frederick Robinson as his right-hand man until he felt he could no longer ignore Liverpool's urgent pleas to send Robinson home because the Opposition were asking awkward questions (especially on Norway) and no one else on the government front bench knew anything about foreign affairs.* 'I can hardly conceive', wrote Castlereagh, 'that the Opposition will persevere in pressing discussion.'[10] The House of Commons had receded to the back of his mind.

At least, however, Castlereagh's concentrated exposure to European diplomacy at the highest level gave him a new assurance. When Louis, influenced by some of his generals, insisted that France must have a large slice of Belgium, Castlereagh opposed the demand so 'peremptorily' that Talleyrand persuaded the king to give way. There was also trouble over France's colonies. Wishing to be generous to the restored Bourbon king, Castlereagh decided that Malta, the Cape, Mauritius and Tobago werethe only colonies which Britain must insist on keeping, and only

---

*By the Treaty of Kiel (January 1814) Denmark agreed to cede Norway to Sweden. But the Norwegians, refusing to be handed over to the Swedes, declared their independence and elected Prince Christian Frederick, the heir to the Danish throne, as their ruler. The British government was reluctantly obliged to honour its commitments to Bernadotte; it turned down the Norwegians' appeals for help and continued a naval blockade of Norway. Eventually, in November 1814, the King of Sweden succeeded to the throne of Norway, but the Norwegians were allowed to keep their own constitution, instead of being incorporated in Sweden.

the last two of these were originally French. When his colleagues in London insisted that the Royal Navy must have a good harbour in the West Indies, he added St Lucia to the list. But the French were reluctant to lose even three islands, and Castlereagh again had to recall Talleyrand very firmly 'to a sense of our claims, to the forbearance shown, and to the true relations of the parties'.[11]

Far more difficult to solve was the question of the slave trade. The British public were fanatically determined that the French should be made to give up the trade before receiving back their colonies, while the French were convinced that the hypocritical English were moved solely by a wish to cripple France's economic recovery. Neither Louis nor Talleyrand was hostile to abolition, but they convinced Castlereagh that it would be unwise to try 'to tie France too tight on this question'. His colleagues in London, more exposed to pressure from Wilberforce and other abolitionists, were not convinced, but in the end reluctantly agreed to accept a French undertaking to abolish the trade in five years and to support the principle of abolition at the forthcoming congress at Vienna. Making the best of this compromise, Castlereagh argued that it would be of 'immense value' to have French support when trying to persuade Spain and Portugal to agree to abolition.[12]

Castlereagh did not have to make his colleagues swallow any other disagreeable compromises. He asked Liverpool for discretion 'to act for the best',[13] and although he did not entirely omit to inform and consult the Cabinet – especially on issues affecting Britain – he was too busy to send home frequent and detailed reports. His colleagues accepted the situation with remarkable docility. 'We have heard nothing from you since the 5th', wrote Liverpool on May 16, 'but I conclude you are too hard at work to have much time to write.' And he added, rather tentatively: 'As your treaty is to be definitive, there would be some advantage if it were possible that we could see it (to guard against *minor errors*) before it was actually agreed.'[14]

The draft treaty that arrived for the Cabinet's inspection about a week later was based on the Allies' belief – strongest in the British and Russians, weakest in the Prussians – that it was in all their interests to underpin the new Bourbon regime as much as possible. It was therefore an astonishingly generous settlement for a country which for so long had caused such upheaval throughout Europe. France had to surrender Napoleon's conquests, but it received some not insignificant additions to its 1792 frontiers and regained most of its colonial empire. It did not have to disarm, nor suffer the cost and indignity of an army of occupation, nor pay any reparations apart from indemnity for private

THE SEARCH FOR PEACE: PARIS, LONDON, VIENNA 1814–15

individuals. It did not even have to hand back the looted art treasures adorning the Louvre.

The first Peace of Paris was signed on May 30, 1814, and later on the same day Castlereagh set out on the journey home. By coincidence, the captain of the frigate waiting for them at Boulogne had been responsible for sending the Dutch pilot to rescue Castlereagh and his party during their adventurous crossing of the North Sea five months earlier. 'Our voyage this time', wrote Emma Edgcumbe, 'was most delightful, and in the afternoon of June 3rd we landed at Dover, where Lord Castlereagh was received with cheers by the crowds assembled on the beach, who followed him as he walked through the town.'[15] For once he enjoyed a little popular approval.

In Paris, the Allies successfully made their peace with France, but on the more controversial aspects of the disposal of Napoleon's forfeited empire they made no progress, except to agree that no one else – and of course they had France particularly in mind – should be allowed to interfere in the solution of these problems. All the states involved in the war would be entitled to attend the Congress at Vienna, but their role would be simply to ratify decisions already taken by the four major Allies.

Castlereagh was not greatly dismayed that so much remained to be settled because he had managed to use the Tsar's determination to visit England – he had virtually invited himself – to get the Allied consultations transferred to London. In Paris Alexander, the benevolent conqueror, had been fêted, flattered and applauded wherever he went, and he could expect a similar reception in England, where he had been a popular hero ever since Napoleon's retreat from Moscow. The Regent and his Cabinet shared the general admiration for Alexander. But Castlereagh, who alone had met him, described him as 'full of ambition under the garb of moderation',[16] and suggested that the other two Allied monarchs should be invited as well. 'The [Russian] Emperor', he explained to Liverpool, 'has the greatest merit, and must be held high, but he ought to be grouped, and not made the sole feature for admiration.'[17] The Emperor Francis, after much dithering, declined to be 'grouped', but he sent his Chancellor instead – which from a practical point of view was much more satisfactory. With Metternich, Hardenberg and the Russian foreign minister, Count Nesselrode, all in London, they would be able, Castlereagh hoped, 'to decide finally on several important points previously to the congress at Vienna'.[18] He blithely overlooked his parliamentary duties, the backlog of work waiting him at the Foreign Office, and, above all, the peace celebrations.

For the British people, especially Londoners, the Allied visit was one long celebration. 'The peace and the sovereigns', wrote Emma Edgcumbe, 'and the princes, and Wellington, and Blucher, and Platoff [the Cossack commander] all coming at once, upset the sober mind of John Bull. Night and day everybody was rushing everywhere.'[19] There were fireworks and illuminations, a fair in Hyde Park, frigates firing on the Serpentine, as well, of course, as innumerable dinners, balls, receptions and state visits to the theatre and opera. In the Commons, Whitbread suggested that in view of 'the very extraordinary state of dissipation of the metropolis' and the consequent poor attendance of members, it might be better to postpone important business.[20]

By the end of the visit many people had had more than enough, and none more so than the Regent, who after little more than a week was reported to be 'worn out with fuss, fatigue and *rage*'.[21] The rage was caused by the Tsar and his extraordinary sister, the Grand Duchess Catherine. For some reason both of them chose to treat the Regent with the grossest discourtesy and seize every opportunity to upset and insult him. Even the Whig lords, whom Alexander assiduously courted, were repelled by his behaviour; he was, said Lord Grey, 'a vain, silly fellow'.[22]

At least, however, the Tsar's uncouth behaviour removed a possible disagreement between Castlereagh and his colleagues. Alexander had wiped the shine off his own halo far more effectively than anyone else could have done. By contrast, Metternich, who was widely disliked in Britain as the man responsible for marrying off his emperor's daughter to the Corsican ogre, behaved with impeccable tact and discretion. He flattered the Regent shamelessly, never went near the Opposition and altogether vindicated Castlereagh's approving reports of him. The growing understanding between the two men was given a firmer backing, but any chance of putting it to immediate use was ruled out by the scale of the celebratory entertaining and the tension created by the Tsar's behaviour. Some discussions there were and some matters were settled, but when the sovereigns at last embarked at Dover on June 27, the future of the two largest apples of discord – Poland and Saxony – was as unsettled as ever.

On one issue to which Castlereagh attached particular importance – the future of the Netherlands – important progress was made in London. France had been committed in the peace treaty to an enlarged Dutch state, but the final frontiers of the new Netherlands could not be settled because they depended on arrangements yet to be concluded for the reconstruction of Germany. In the meantime, to his intense annoyance, William of Orange, the Sovereign Prince, was excluded from his new territories which remained provisionally under Austrian administration. From this frustrating situation he was fortuitously rescued by the breakdown of the proposed marriage between his son William (the Hereditary Prince) and Princess Charlotte. Anxious to demonstrate that Charlotte's decision in no way diminished Britain's interest in the Netherlands, Castlereagh persuaded the Allied ministers in London to agree at once to a protocol formally recognising the union of Holland and Belgium and to hand over the provisional administration of Belgium to the Sovereign Prince without delay. The Belgians were guaranteed equality of rights and freedom of religion. The fact that they heartily disliked the Dutch and had vociferously opposed a union with them did not, in Castlereagh's mind, outweigh his conviction that 'to make Holland and Belgium capable of sustaining a real independence, upon the confines of France, they must form one state'.[23] Now that the war was over, national aspirations counted for little compared with the stability of Europe as a whole.

A few weeks later the future of the Dutch colonies was settled. Castlereagh had always intended that Holland should get most of them back, once it was strong enough to defend its possessions. The exception was the Cape, the vital staging post on the route to India, and in response to strong commercial pressure in England, Castlereagh also decided to keep the three small Dutch settlements on the coast of South America (British Guiana) where considerable British investments had already been made. Holland's extensive possessions in the East Indies were handed back intact. Even if their potential wealth had been better appreciated, it is unlikely that Castlereagh would have agreed to keep them. He had a strong distaste for the indiscriminate acquisition of colonial possessions which he did not believe necessary for Britain's commercial greatness. He was firmly convinced that Britain's reputation in Europe, and therefore its influence, would be diminished if it tried too greedily to hang on to its colonial conquests.[24]

The opening of the peace congress in Vienna was postponed from mid-August to the beginning of October to allow the Tsar to pay a quick visit to St Petersburg, but the principal Allied ministers agreed to meet in Vienna about mid-September for preliminary talks. It was a tight schedule. But Europe would remain a tinder-box so long as frontiers remained undefined, rulers were uncertain of their titles and the extent of their possessions, and the armies of the victorious powers remained sprawled across Europe. 'It unfortunately happens', wrote Castlereagh at one of the bleakest moments of the congress, 'that never at any former period was so much spoil thrown loose for the world to scramble for.'[25] He went to Vienna determined to see that the spoil was distributed so as to establish 'a just equilibrium in Europe'.

Castlereagh set out for Vienna on August 16, travelling by way of Ghent, Brussels and Paris. At Ghent peace talks between American and British commissioners had been stumbling along for a fortnight. During his brief visit of barely two days, Castlereagh, who did not even meet the Americans, showed no wish to intervene in the negotiations himself. But he insisted that Henry Goulburn, the chief British negotiator, should adopt a milder, more conciliatory, attitude and obtain the Cabinet's approval before making any important move. With so much else to worry about, he was presumably thankful to leave the American negotiations in the hands of his colleagues in London.

The visit to Paris was at the invitation of Talleyrand, who was determined to recover France's seat at the top table of European powers without delay, and had decided that the British were most likely to help him. Castlereagh had five hours of talks with Talleyrand as well as a two-hour private audience with Louis. He found that the French were just as opposed as he was to the Tsar's designs on Poland, and he managed to reconcile Talleyrand to his exclusion from the preliminary talks at Vienna – which, after all, the French foreign minister had no real claim to attend. Castlereagh resumed his journey to Vienna with the comfortable, if erroneous, impression that his chief task with the French was to curb the 'exuberance' of their cordiality.[26]

There were no formal invitations to the Congress of Vienna, simply a public announcement that it would open on October 1, 1814. Everybody who was, or considered themselves to be, somebody took advantage of this open invitation, with the heads of five reigning dynasties and more than two hundred princely families leading the descent upon the city. At that time the Habsburg was the most brilliant of all the courts of Europe, and the Emperor Francis decided (although his Treasury was nearly empty) that no expense should be spared. A Festivals Committee was set up and week after week it organised balls, concerts, reviews and entertainments of all kinds. In addition, an unceasing round of private hospitality was provided by the aristocracy of Austria and Hungary, and indeed all of Europe, as well as by the delegates to the congress. It was in the salons and ballrooms of Vienna, where everybody from the Russian emperor down mingled informally and on more or less equal terms, that much of the business of the congress was transacted. Castlereagh sometimes felt that the fêtes and balls 'waste a great deal of valuable time, and prevent P[rince] Metternich from giving his mind to the subjects that ought to engross him'. He was not the only one to be exasperated by Metternich's sometimes apparently total immersion in the lighter side of the congress.[27]

Against this glittering and sophisticated background the English delegation cannot be said to have shone. According to William Montagu, the Viennese 'quiz very much the English dresses', and he felt bound to agree that English fashions were not well represented; two of Castlereagh's sisters, who were staying in Vienna, were both 'abominable dressers'.[28] Neither the Castlereaghs' strict sabbatarian principles, nor their marital devotion, were likely to recommend them to Viennese society,[29] and Emily caused some umbrage by failing to hide her reluctance to visit a certain famous hostess of whose morals she disapproved.[30] But Emily carried out her duties as a hostess with energy and some success. Her nightly suppers were, according to Montagu, 'sometimes very pleasant', and according to Cooke, 'curious medleys'.[31] The papal nuncio and the Turkish minister came frequently, and so did the gallant and glamorous Eugène de Beauharnais with whom Emily enjoyed a mild and decorous flirtation. She also gave some gay and well-attended dances, at which, reported Montagu, her husband was a 'constant waltzer'. Emily's only serious gaffe was to appear at a ball wearing her husband's Garter (presented by the Regent in June) as a decoration in her hair. Castlereagh was let down much more seriously by his brother Charles, now Lord Stewart and ambassador to Vienna, whose uninhibited behaviour – he once threw a cab driver into the Danube – got him so talked about that the Viennese came to consider him unworthy of his post.[32] The other members of the British delegation did not make much mark either for good or ill. Lord Cathcart, quiet and elderly, made little contribution at all, either to work or play. Lord Clancarty, ambassador to The Hague and Castlereagh's faithful friend, took his duties very seriously and worked tremendously hard. So did Edward Cooke, until ill-health forced him to leave Vienna just when he could least be spared.

When the ministers of the four Allied powers met in the middle of September, their first task was to decide how the congress should be organised. None had given the matter much, if any, thought, but all were determined to have, jointly, the first and last word on any territorial issues. After some reflection they decided they would also run the congress, perhaps with help from France and Spain. There were, however, differences of approach to the presentation of these somewhat arbitrary decisions. Castlereagh found the other three much less conciliatory towards France and Spain than he himself was inclined to be after his visit to Paris. He had a brisk exchange of memoranda with Humboldt, the Prussian minister, but he was in a minority, and did not press his case beyond formally recording his opinion that France and Spain should be treated as friendly and not hostile powers.[33] Eventually, on September 23, the Four signed a protocol agreeing to reserve to themselves all territorial decisions, which would be communicated to France and Spain before being sent to the congress as a whole for ratification. A Committee of Six (the Four plus France and Spain) would discuss the arrangements for the congress and a committee of the five principal German states would draft a plan for a German federation.

When these decisions were revealed to Talleyrand a week later, he promptly treated the Allied ministers to a lecture on the iniquity of excluding Bourbon France from their inner councils and demanded that the full congress should be immediately summoned. Discomfited, the ministers meekly withdrew their protocol. But in practical terms Talleyrand's victory was a hollow one. The Allies adamantly refused to summon the congress to meet until they had agreed on its procedure – after all, as Humboldt pointed out, they must first find some way of preventing the princes of Leiden and Liechtenstein from interfering in the general arrangements of Europe.[34] And unless he could appeal to the congress, Talleyrand had no lever with which to prise his way into the Allies' private councils. Disappointed in his expectations of Castlereagh's support, he – unfairly – blamed him most for his exclusion, and henceforward persistently ran him down, both in the salons of Vienna and in his reports to Paris.

As the weeks passed, the Four became increasingly involved in their own dissensions and less interested in the congress. Eventually, it was postponed *sine die*, but it acquired a kind of reality through the committees which materialised to deal with specific questions – Italy, Switzerland, the slave trade and so on. When Castlereagh described these practical arrangements to Lord Liverpool, he claimed that the plenipotentiaries of the lesser powers had got over their 'extreme susceptibility' about the role allotted to them.[35]

By then he was smarting from his failure to shift the Tsar from his stand on Poland. Alexander was determined to set up an autonomous Polish kingdom under his own sovereignty. Castlereagh strongly opposed the plan. Ideally, he would have liked to see a completely

THE SEARCH FOR PEACE: PARIS, LONDON, VIENNA 1814–15

independent Poland, but since that was obviously impracticable, he was prepared to settle for a repartition of Poland between the three central powers. What he was not prepared to accept was the westward extension of Russian power implicit in the Tsar's plan. But with half a million troops occupying every town and village in the Grand Duchy, Alexander saw no reason why he should budge. He remained, however, friendly, assuring Castlereagh that he respected his *'franchise'*, although he differed from him in opinion.[36] They pursued their argument in a series of wide-ranging memoranda in which Castlereagh's frankness sometimes bordered on bluntness. If Russia has sought – with Britain's help – security against Persians and Turks, can it complain if Austria and Prussia now seek security against Russian troops? Russia should recollect that the European powers 'avowedly fought for their own liberties and for those of the rest of Europe, and not for the extension of their dominion'.[37]

While these exchanges were still going on, Castlereagh began to work for an Austro-Prussian understanding that could increase the pressure on the Tsar. Metternich himself believed in collaboration with Berlin, but Prussia had been guaranteed territories as extensive as those it held in 1805, and this raised all sorts of sensitive issues for the Austrians. The most important was Saxony. Unlike most of the other German rulers, the unfortunate King Frederick Augustus of Saxony had failed to desert Napoleon in good time. The victorious Allies had therefore made him prisoner after the battle of Leipzig and declared his kingdom forfeit. In October 1814, his only notable champion was Talleyrand, who vehemently upheld the principles of legitimacy and opposed the extinction of the kingdom of Saxony, but he was still too much of an outsider to have much influence on the Four. The Tsar was willing to let Frederick William have Saxony to compensate him for the formerly Prussian-held provinces of Poland which Napoleon had seized and included in the Grand Duchy. Castlereagh was prepared to let the Prussian king have Saxony, not as compensation for his Polish provinces, but because he was anxious to make Prussia strong. Metternich had no wish to bring Prussia so much closer to Austria's frontiers, but that was a lesser evil than allowing Russia to make such a giant stride westward. So after much hesitation – which, according to Cooke, made Castlereagh 'rather fidgety'[38] – Metternich eventually agreed that Prussia could have Saxony if the Tsar abandoned his Polish plan. Castlereagh then prepared a joint démarche to be made by Austria, Prussia and Britain to the Tsar, and so carried away was he that he even proposed to appeal to the as yet non-existent congress 'to declare to the

Emperor of Russia, to what extent and upon what conditions, Europe in Congress can or cannot admit his Imperial Majesty's pretensions to an aggrandisement in Poland'.[39]

Whether Alexander would have been impressed by such an appeal was never known, because he angrily stamped on the whole project before it ever got off the ground, and persuaded Frederick William to forbid Hardenberg to have any further dealings with his Austrian and English colleagues over Poland. It was a major setback for Castlereagh. Taught by Pitt to distrust Russia and support Prussia, he had set his sights on a strong Germanic bloc which would form a barrier to both French and Russian expansionism. He ignored the possibility that such a bloc might be a threat to anyone else, and although he clearly felt uncomfortable about Saxony's fate, he justified himself with the argument that the Saxon king deserved to become 'a sacrifice to the future security of Europe'.[40] But with Hardenberg forbidden to keep his side of the bargain, Metternich angrily withdrew from his, and the two German powers were left further apart than they had been when Castlereagh began his attempt to bring them together. Moreover, the Tsar had eventually become irritated by Castlereagh's persistence and begun to complain that Britain was his principal enemy. Meeting Stewart at a ball, Alexander shook hands with him, and then expressed surprise that Stewart would speak to him since they differed so much.[41]

Castlereagh's failure gave a sharp knock to his prestige at Vienna, and it sank still lower when reports began to seep through from London that his own Cabinet did not support him. The reports were largely true. His colleagues had become increasingly alarmed by his involvement in matters which they thought were not really Britain's concern. In the middle of October Liverpool told Castlereagh he thought the less they had to do with Poland the better. The peace talks with the Americans at Ghent had been going badly, and if, as seemed likely, the American war continued, it would entail 'prodigious expense, much more than we had any idea of'. Lastly, France seemed to be in a very 'combustible' state, and if an explosion there led to renewed war, 'there is no saying where it might end'.[42]

To add to Liverpool's agitation, when Parliament met early in November, the Opposition refused to preserve a tactful silence about the proceedings at Vienna; it was, reported Liverpool on November 18, being 'particularly rancorous'. Reports of the prospective extinction of Saxony led to two angry debates in the Commons, and Liverpool warned Castlereagh that there was strong feeling on the subject throughout the country.[43] Castlereagh admitted that he had taken a more prominent part in the Polish discussions than he had originally intended; 'when I saw the service suffering from inaction, I found it difficult to be passive ... England is still the only power that either can, or dares, raise her voice against the powerful and the oppressor'.[44] He warned Liverpool that it might be necessary to resist Alexander as if he were another Bonaparte; 'and if I were to speculate upon the course most likely to save your money, and to give you the longest interval of peace with such a character, I should say that it would lie in never suffering him for a moment to doubt your readiness to support the continental powers against his ambitious encroachments'.[45]

The unpalatable fact remained that Castlereagh had failed to get the Tsar to change his mind. He withdrew from any further attempt to mediate on the Polish issue, and for several weeks there was some truth in Talleyrand's gibe that Castlereagh was like a man who had lost his way,[46] although – contrary to reports circulating in Vienna – he had no intention of going home till he had found it again.

Meanwhile there was growing tension between Austria and Prussia, and in the Austrian camp there began to be talk of war being preferable to having Russia in Cracovy and Prussia in Dresden. Alarmed by the warlike reports from Vienna, the Cabinet in London forbad Castlereagh to involve Britain in hostilities for any of the objects so far discussed at Vienna.[47] While this instruction – the only important one he received at Vienna – was on its way, Castlereagh wrote to Liverpool on December 5 to warn him that in the present 'extremely entangled' state of affairs, a sudden outbreak of war was possible, and he did not think Britain could keep out of it.[48]

By the middle of the month, however, Castlereagh had realised that Poland would have to be written off and Saxony saved. In Vienna, it was assumed that his change of attitude towards Saxony was due to pressure from government and parliament at home. But he needed to look no further than the pressures building up in Vienna to be convinced that Saxony must be preserved if Europe was to remain at peace. The problem was to find compensation for Prussia. The search for a solution brought Castlereagh back into the centre of the stage at Vienna. Austria and Prussia asked for his mediation, and Russia supported their request. (Alexander was now demonstrating rather spurious goodwill towards Castlereagh by dancing polonaises with his wife and country dances with his sister, while trying to undermine his position in London through the Russian ambassador.[49])

At the same time, Talleyrand began to make determined efforts to use the Saxon crisis to insinuate himself into the inner councils of the four great powers. Metternich encouraged him, but Castlereagh advised caution, fearing that open co-operation with such a fervent champion of King Frederick Augustus would do more harm than good. By the end of the year, however, the Prussian attitude had become so menacing that he decided to risk playing the French card. At a four-power meeting on December 31, Castlereagh and Metternich pressed for France's admission to the negotiations on Saxony. Russia and Prussia refused, Hardenberg so vehemently that he let slip a threat of war if Prussia's right to Saxony was not acknowledged. Castlereagh reacted very sharply, and refused to be mollified by Hardenberg's explanations.[50]

Next day Castlereagh presented Metternich and Talleyrand with the draft of a tripartite defensive treaty, which provided for mutual aid in case of attack. By a fortunate coincidence the news that an Anglo-American peace treaty had at last been signed arrived in Vienna on the same day. Whether or not the news produced 'the greatest possible sensation', as Castlereagh claimed, it certainly strengthened his hand at a crucial moment.[51] On January 5, two days after the signature of the tripartite treaty, Castlereagh reported to Liverpool that Hardenberg had given way over French participation in the Saxony negotiations, and he had every reason to hope that the alarm of war was over.[52]*

How real was the crisis? Perhaps not quite as real as Castlereagh feared. Prussia was becoming isolated, and the behaviour of its occupying troops was making it unpopular throughout Europe. Metternich was successfully rallying the minor German states, while Alexander, with his own position in Poland now secure, was anxious to find a solution for the Saxon crisis that would suitably acknowledge the claims of legitimacy. But Castlereagh may well have been right to fear that Prussia at bay might suddenly attempt 'some bold and dangerous coup'.[53] At any rate, he was sufficiently impressed by the danger to flout his instructions from London, and he clearly felt reasonably confident that if boldly confronted the danger would recede. If, however, Prussia did go to war over Saxony, it was – he assured Liverpool – 'quite out of the question that we should remain quiet spectators'.[54]

Liverpool accepted the treaty with remarkable equanimity. At that moment he was less worried about the possibility of war in Europe than by the certainty of war in the Commons when Parliament reassembled on February 9, 1815, and his main preoccupation was to get Castlereagh back on the government's lamentably weak front bench by then. Castlereagh had written to Wellington in Paris on December 17, asking

*From henceforward Talleyrand was accepted in the Allied councils and the Council of Four became the Council of Five.

him to take his place in time for him to be back in London by mid-February.⁵⁵ But by the end of the year he had become so involved in the negotiations that he could not bear to leave unfinished what he had begun and not even Wellington, he felt, could do it so well. He reckoned he could complete the important business in four to five weeks and he assumed that the American peace would make Parliament 'comparatively quiet'.⁵⁶ Quite wrong, Liverpool hastened to assure him. Party strife had burst out with redoubled vigour, and few were interested in what happened at Vienna unless it involved expense. Unfortunately, all the controversial financial debates had to be held before the end of March, and 'if the government in the House of Commons should lose credit and be considered beat in debate before you return, it will be no easy matter to recover the ground which has been lost'.⁵⁷

Agitated letters flowed from Liverpool's pen to Castlereagh and Wellington, who found himself commanded by one to go and by the other to wait. He waited, but with friendly tact urged Castlereagh to go home. His brother, Wellesley-Pole, wrote Wellington, seemed to think it would be impossible to meet Parliament without Castlereagh – but, he added, 'his feelings are like those of all others at a weak advanced post'.⁵⁸ Castlereagh, however, was determined not to be driven precipitately from his post, not even when a definite recall arrived on January 30. His negotiations on the Prussian-Saxon problem had reached a crucial point, and 'you might as well', he assured Lord Bathurst, 'expect me to have run away from Leipzig (if I had been there) last year to fight Creev(e)y and Whitbread, as to withdraw from hence till the existing contest is brought to a point; and I think you do both injustice to your own supporters, and too much honour to me, in supposing my presence so necessary'.⁵⁹

It took several weeks to argue the Prussians out of their stubborn demand for the whole of Saxony. But by the second week of February a compromise had been reached. Austria and Prussia each received back part of their Polish territories, and the rest of the Grand Duchy was made into a kingdom under the Tsar.* The King of Saxony got back three-fifths of his territories and more than half his subjects. Prussia got the rest of Saxony and a solid block of territory in the Rhineland to add to the Hohenzollerns' Westphalian possessions.

Abandoned by the Tsar, the Prussians would have had to give way in the end. But Castlereagh, by his firmness, patience, persistence and sheer hard work, did more than anyone else to break the log-jam and secure a

*'Congress Poland' was endowed with a constitution by Alexander, but after an unsuccessful revolt in 1830–31 it was absorbed into Russia.

settlement. Even Friedrich Gentz, one of his sharpest critics, acknowledged that Castlereagh had worked day and night to reach a compromise on Saxony.[60] He failed in one important respect – to prevent Russia's westward expansion through Poland – but he had succeeded in strengthening Prussia, not, as he had originally intended, in central Europe, but further west. Thus, almost fortuitously, and without any great inclination on the part of the Prussians themselves, Prussian ambitions were given a westward orientation.

There was still a good deal of tiresome bargaining to be done among the south German states, and the Dutch frontiers still had to be drawn in detail (by the admirable Clancarty), but on the whole the territorial arrangements north of the Alps were largely settled by the time Castlereagh handed over to Wellington in the middle of February.

Europe south of the Alps, Castlereagh regarded as largely Austria's concern. The popular nationalism which he had been so keen to encourage as a weapon against Napoleon, was now a force to be curbed, lest it get out of control. 'It is not', he had written a year earlier, 'insurrections we now want in Italy, or elsewhere – we want disciplined force under sovereigns we can trust.'[61] He saw no reason why Austria should not be placed firmly in control in northern Italy, both for the sake of its own prestige and security and as a barrier to French infiltration. On the same grounds of security against France, he justified the forcible incorporation of Genoa into Piedmont. The future of Joachim Murat in Naples caused more soul-searching. All the great powers wanted to get rid of Napoleon's brother-in-law, but Austria had guaranteed Murat his throne in return for help against Napoleon, and although he was strongly suspected of treachery, documentary proof was lacking. Castlereagh, who seems to have been genuinely convinced of Murat's treachery,[62] was indignantly attacked by the Opposition for supporting Austria's plans to overthrow him by force. More important, the Cabinet had serious doubts whether support for Austria in Italy need go so far. Fortunately, perhaps, for Castlereagh, after Napoleon's escape from Elba, King Joachim contrived his own downfall.*

Throughout all his complicated and sometimes stormy negotiations on the reconstitution of Europe, Castlereagh hammered away at the very different issue of the slave trade. His failure to get immediate abolition written into the peace treaty with France had sparked off a new abolition

*After an unsuccessful attempt to rouse Italy against Austria, he had to flee the country in May 1815. The following October he tried to invade the kingdom of Naples, was captured and executed.

campaign throughout Britain. 'The nation is bent upon this object', wrote Castlereagh; '... and the ministers must make it the basis of their policy.'[63] Characteristically, he deplored the popular fervour; it was, he believed, more a hindrance than a help since foreigners were convinced that it could only spring from selfish and mercenary motives.[64] He preferred the ordinary means of influence and persuasion, backed up by generous offers of monetary compensation and an educational campaign. (He circulated translations of the voluminous evidence on the slave trade presented to the House of Commons.) He was warmly supported by the three non-colonial powers (which had nothing to lose), especially Russia, but in face of the strong public opposition in the slave-trading countries, he did not get very far. Even near-bankrupt Spain was completely recalcitrant. But Castlereagh's proposal for committees of ambassadors in London and Paris to monitor the enforcement of abolition was accepted, and he was able to get a declaration condemning the slave trade inserted in the Final Act of the Congress.* Even Wilberforce agreed that 'all done that could be done'.[65]†

From his dignified, if sometimes heated, diplomatic negotiations at the highest level, Castlereagh returned to find the London mob demonstrating with uninhibited abandon against the government's bill to restrict the import of corn. On March 6, the day he reappeared in the Commons, the military had to be called in to deal with the huge crowd which was swarming round the House of Commons, attacking members and trying to force them to vote against the bill. Croker was dragged out of his coach by his collar, and another member complained that he had been 'buffeted about like a battledore between two shuttlecocks'.[66] Four days later, the news of Napoleon's escape from Elba reached London, and so

*The Final Act of the Congress, comprising 121 articles, was signed on June 9, 1815 by Austria, Britain, France, Portugal, Prussia, Russia and Sweden. Almost all the smaller powers later added their signatures.

†After his return from Elba, Napoleon abolished the slave trade in France, in an attempt to curry favour with the British. The restored Bourbon government did not bring it back. The Netherlands abolished the slave trade completely in June 1814. By the end of 1817, Portugal and Spain had been persuaded to agree to the gradual abolition of slave trading by their nationals in return for commercial and financial inducements by Britain. Both countries, as well as the Netherlands, also agreed to allow the Royal Navy to enforce abolition through a limited right of search of their ships. But Castlereagh failed in his persistent efforts to get France and the United States to allow their ships to be inspected.

far as Castlereagh was concerned the intractable problems of building what he called the country's 'peace system' had to wait until peace had been re-established.

In March 1815 it was not at all obvious that Napoleon's dash for freedom was going to end so soon at Waterloo and St Helena. Nor was it obvious that Louis XVIII would be replaced on the throne of France, even if Napoleon could be turned off it again. On March 19, the day before Napoleon returned in triumph to the Tuileries, Louis, once more a despised refugee, fled secretly from Paris to seek asylum in Belgium. 'The great question', wrote Castlereagh a week later to Wellington in Vienna, 'is, can the Bourbons get Frenchmen to fight *for them* against Frenchmen? If they can, Europe may soon turn the tide in their favour; and the process of fermentation once begun, they may create real partisans instead of criers of "Vive le Roi" and doers of nothing. If we are to undertake the job, we must leave nothing to chance. It must be done upon the grandest scale ... you must inundate France with force in all directions.'[67]

The 'job' was to get rid of Napoleon, not to impose anyone particular in his place. But privately Castlereagh was convinced that Louis was still the best horse to back, if only he would entrust his government to intelligent and competent men like Talleyrand and Fouché. He knew the first was unreliable and the second a regicide, but they were better than the feeble and corrupt émigré courtiers surrounding the king. Castlereagh converted Wellington, who had been inclined to favour the Duke of Orleans, to his views, and together, by letter and by interview (after Wellington had arrived in Belgium), they strove to turn Louis into a better constitutional monarch ruling through a more efficient government.

Whatever doubts might be felt about the Bourbons – the Tsar had many – Wellington had no difficulty in reaching agreement with Russia, Prussia and Austria for a campaign against Napoleon 'on the grandest scale' – at least 150,000 men from each of the four. The British as usual were expected to foot the bill, and as usual were accused of parsimony. Castlereagh was indignant: 'the powers of Europe must not expect us to subsidise all the world ...'[68] But unlike Liverpool and other colleagues, he never suffered serious qualms about distributing the taxpayers' money on a lordly scale in a good cause. By the time the Waterloo campaign began, the five million pounds originally set aside for the war had swelled to nine million, and it was intended to finance nearly one million Allied troops.

Only about a fifth of this huge force – mostly British, Dutch and

THE SEARCH FOR PEACE: PARIS, LONDON, VIENNA 1814-15

Prussians – took part in the battle of Waterloo, and the march across France to, and through, the gates of Paris. When the battle was fought, the Tsar's 200,000 men had not even begun to cross the Rhine, and the subsequent collapse of Napoleonic resistance was so swift that Wellington was left with a free hand (Blucher not being interested) to strike a bargain with Fouché, who had put himself at the head of a provisional government. So Castlereagh's plans duly materialised, and by the time the Allied sovereigns again rode into Paris, Louis had been quietly placed back on his throne, with Talleyrand, somewhat reluctantly, heading a government of which Fouché was a prominent member. The inclusion of a regicide was extremely repugnant to the king and much criticised in England. But only Fouché could have brought the king back so quickly and easily. The danger of civil war, much greater than the year before, had been averted; Napoleon's partisans had been immobilised; and France had a moderate government competent to negotiate with the Allies and likely to attract wider support than any other.*

The Castlereaghs were back in Paris by July 6, installed in state on the first floor of the imposing Hôtel Borghese, which had just been acquired for the British embassy. Instead of Cossacks encamped in the Champs Élysées, there were British troops bivouacking in the Bois de Boulogne – according to one English observer, there were very few red coats to be seen, and the camp looked more like a fair. But in other respects it seemed very like a re-run of the previous year's peace conference. In a few days most of the well-known faces were back, and the familiar round of dinners, receptions, balls and Lady Castlereagh's post-theatre parties began again. Emily's niece thought that the Castlereaghs' parties were much bigger and more brilliant than the previous year as regards the rank of the guests. But probably for Castlereagh the most important difference was that instead of having Wellington for only a brief visit, he now had him all the time as a fellow plenipotentiary. 'Nothing could go on better than Wellington and I did to the last', wrote Castlereagh afterwards. 'I do not recall a single divergence of opinion between us throughout the whole.'[69]

The Allies did not enjoy such unanimity, and consequently the peace-making, which had been polished off in five weeks the year before, now dragged on for nearly five months, with some 900,000 foreign

---

*Neither Talleyrand nor Fouché lasted long after the election of an unexpectedly right-wing Chamber of Deputies in August. The Duc de Richelieu, who succeeded Talleyrand at the end of September, was inexperienced, but moderate, intelligent and disinterested; he was also much more realistic than his predecessor in negotiating the peace treaty.

troops occupying the country.* Little time or controversy was wasted over Napoleon's future, but the fate of the country which had accepted him back was far harder to settle. Prussia, supported by Holland and the smaller German states, was all for harsh, punitive measures, going as far as partial dismemberment. The Prussian counsels were dominated by the generals, who were as unwilling to moderate their demands as to control the excesses of their troops. (Hardenberg confided to Clancarty that he felt surrounded by Praetorian bands.[70]) Castlereagh and Wellington, on the other hand, wanted a temporary occupation until France's peaceful intentions had been adequately demonstrated, combined with a moderate settlement that would not humiliate the country but allow it to settle down into 'a useful rather than a dangerous member of the European system'. France, Castlereagh suggested, should be made to withdraw to its 1790 frontiers, which would involve only small territorial losses (principally the Saar valley). He also strongly supported Wellington's opinion that it would be much better to occupy some fortresses temporarily than insist on actual cessions which would give the French a permanent grievance. No doubt, he told Liverpool, it would be much more popular to extort one or two great fortresses. 'But it is not our business to collect trophies, but to try if we can to bring the world back to peaceful habits.'[71]

The Tsar strongly supported the moderate British views. So too, on the whole and in a more muted way, did Metternich. Apart from the German states, the main opposition came from the British government in London and an ill-informed and hysterical campaign in the British press. In the end, Castlereagh decided he had had enough of the stream of letters from London urging him to be tough with the French. He sent his brother over with a detailed defence of British policy, and this, combined with Charles's eloquent advocacy, silenced the dissidents in Downing Street – and in Carlton House, where the Regent had been fed a stream of criticism by his Hanoverian minister, Count Munster.

The treaty, which was finally settled early in October, was too moderate to satisfy the hard-liners in Berlin, The Hague, Munich and London, but – inevitably – not moderate enough for the French. France had to retire behind its 1790 frontiers; temporarily hand over fourteen fortresses; pay an indemnity of 700 million francs; support an army of occupation of 150,000 men under Wellington for five (perhaps three)

*Wellington went on signing subsidy treaties with minor German states for some weeks after Waterloo, since it was not immediately obvious that the war was over. He was criticised by the Cabinet for this, but Castlereagh strongly supported him. All the subsidy treaties expired when the peace treaty was signed.

years; and restore all the art treasures looted by Napoleon.

This last provision caused much ill-feeling among the Parisians. They vented their ire on Wellington, hissing him at the opera and cutting him at parties. (They must have forgotten how he had stopped Blucher from blowing up the Pont d'Iéna.) But nothing could have stopped the Prussians, Dutch and others from forcibly removing what had, after all, been taken from them by force. Canova, the Pope's representative, who had no force at his command, used to haunt Lady Castlereagh's parties, earnestly buttonholing anyone who he thought might help him to remove the papal treasures. Partly for this reason, perhaps, Castlereagh arranged for some British, Austrian and Prussian troops to move the treasures. He also gave Canova £5000 to cover the cost of 'packing and sending off the gods and goddesses, so that for heretics we behaved handsomely ...'[72]

The Tsar left Paris before the detailed negotiations were completed. Castlereagh had never known him 'in a more cordial, contented, and at the same time reasonable disposition'.[73] He even tried to make amends for his rudeness to the Regent during his London visit. Alexander, in fact, was embarking on his religious phase. Every evening in Paris he visited a certain Mme de Krüdener, irreverently described by Castlereagh as 'an old fanatic, who has a considerable reputation amongst the few high-flyers in religion that are to be found in Paris'.[74] When Alexander tried to bring his mystical Christianity to bear upon international politics through his proposal for a Holy Alliance, Castlereagh and Wellington found it difficult to listen with 'becoming gravity'. In Castlereagh's opinion, the Holy Alliance was 'a piece of sublime mysticism and nonsense'. Metternich and Hardenberg agreed, but their masters signed all the same, and Alexander was very anxious to add the Prince Regent's signature. This put Castlereagh into 'what may be called a scrape', since the only thing wrong with the alliance was its 'excessive excellence', and it would not do to antagonise the Tsar. 'The fact is', wrote Castlereagh tolerantly, 'that the Emperor's mind is not completely sound.'[75] Fortunately, constitutional objections could be found to the Regent signing. Instead he sent a letter – 'very properly drawn', Castlereagh thought – which Alexander apparently found a perfectly satisfactory substitute.

The Tsar also drafted a second treaty, pledging the four Allies to uphold the settlement imposed on France. This was much more to the taste of the pragmatic British, although Castlereagh thought the Tsar's text committed the Allies too strongly to uphold the existing regime in France.[76] Such blatant interference in a country's internal affairs would never get through Parliament. (A clause banning any member of the Bonaparte family from the French throne was another matter.) Castlereagh produced a draft – very largely the one signed – which he liked much better; 'these gentlemen who have no Parliament to watch them, never hit the tone upon such matters . . . I rather flatter myself that I have got the whole on right grounds'.[77] According to the sixth article of the Tsar's draft of the Quadruple Alliance, the signatories were to meet at fixed intervals to confirm that the treaty was being carried out. Castlereagh widened the purpose of these periodical meetings to consult upon their 'common interests'. It was the genesis of the so-called congress system. But neither in his dispatch to Liverpool, nor in his private letter to his brother, did Castlereagh comment on his rewriting of the sixth article. Was this, one would like to know, because he thought it too important, or not important enough?

The complicated financial provisions of the peace settlement, and the detailed arrangements for the Allied occupation, took weeks to negotiate, and it was November 20 before the treaty with France was signed. The Quadruple Alliance was signed on the same day. Castlereagh left Paris well pleased with all he had done, and he arrived in London to find that Prince and people now seemed satisfied too. 'I do not find any cavil or critique', he told Charles, 'except the general nonsense of the *Morning Chronicle*, afraid that our Treaty of Alliance will enslave mankind.' London seemed very dull, and he did not stay there long. 'I am going Thursday to Cray and the Merinos, thank God that I am once more *unsaddled* and may roll on the grass.'[78]

CHAPTER XIV

Parliamentary battleground
1816–18

'Economy is more the order of the day than war ever was', wrote Castlereagh on March 16, 1816; '... you have no conception of anything more intractable than the House of Commons now is.'[1] In recent years the Opposition had had a thin time. To attack a government that was at last getting the better of Bonaparte was unpopular and unpatriotic; and disagreements over how far hostilities to him should be pushed made the Whigs still more ineffective. But with the coming of peace they could all unite behind a policy of retrenchment and strict economy, which would have the additional advantage of exploiting to the full the instinctive belief of most MPs that all governments were incorrigibly extravagant. So far as the Liverpool government was concerned, this was certainly not true. Although writing from a Foreign Secretary's standpoint, Castlereagh represented all his colleagues when he wrote: 'I am so thoroughly satisfied that a sound state of finance is the true lever of our power, and that our credit is the real basis of our influence abroad and means of doing good, that nothing shall be wanting on my part to bring our expenditure within our income...'[2] But the difficult transition from war to peace took time, and with distress and discontent growing throughout the country, domestic politics provided the Opposition with what Brougham called 'the richest mine in the world'.[3]

In the prevailing mood of economy, the independent members would not vote for expenditure unless a really excellent case was made for it. They might not vote for the Whigs either. But if enough of them simply abstained, the government was in serious trouble. Even those usually numbered among its 'friends' could not always be kept steady. Castlereagh reckoned that at least twenty-five of them voted with the Opposition over the army estimates. Whereas the navy was the country's bulwark, a standing army in time of peace was, by hoary tradition, a threat to every Englishman's liberties. The ministers pared the estimates down far below what the Duke of York thought was needed, but the government still had to fight for them 'inch by inch', as Castlereagh feelingly wrote, through ten nights of debate. He himself had to rise from a sick bed to stop the rot (after Vansittart, according to

Peel, had 'made himself ridiculous'[4]), and as usual when really hard pressed, he did it very well.

One of his most effective arguments that night was that the government was only asking for a temporary, intermediate, army establishment to cover the transition from war to peace. To him and his colleagues it seemed obvious that since wartime expenditure could not be suddenly cut off completely, no more could wartime taxation either. The case for temporarily renewing the property (income) tax at a lower rate appeared to be so unanswerable that it never seems to have occurred to the Cabinet to back down before the popular outcry against a tax whose 'inquisitorial' aspects were passionately resented. More than 400 petitions against the tax piled up in the Commons. Castlereagh was attacked for dismissing them as 'clamour' when, according to the Opposition, they were a decisive expression of the 'sense of the people'. He denied this, pointing out that a third of the petitions came from Devon and Middlesex and a quarter of the counties had not petitioned at all. In any case, he said (like Burke), the House should not be ruled by opinions expressed outside its walls.[5]

On this occasion, opinion inside and outside the House coincided (as it had not done the previous year over the Corn Law). On March 18, the Commons rejected the property tax by a majority of 37 – 'in opposition', wrote Castlereagh sadly, 'to our utmost exertions'.[6] It was not a resigning matter, but it was a nasty jolt – the Treasury (against all the evidence) had reckoned on a majority of forty. Writing to the Regent immediately after the vote, Castlereagh hoped that 'in the present rage for taking off taxes', the war malt tax would be spared.[7] But two days later the Cabinet voluntarily scrapped it, arguing that since there was so little chance of carrying it, it would be better not to make 'perhaps an ineffectual attempt to force this tax upon the poor, when the rich had delivered themselves from the property tax'.[8]

Liverpool, always prone to panic, thought the government was certainly hanging by a thread.[9] But in the following weeks the thread did not snap, in spite of unremitting Opposition onslaughts. Castlereagh, out of touch with the domestic scene, was reported to be in very low spirits.[10] At the beginning of the session, he had expected to have to do battle only on his foreign policy, and the vigour and venom of the Opposition's attacks on domestic issues was an unpleasant surprise. 'Whatever I may have done for Europe as to peace', he wrote rather bitterly to Charles, 'it is pretty plain I have not succeeded for myself at least in a parliamentary sense – there never was more of malice, violence and persevering obstruction known in Parliament...' He simply could not understand how those who the year before would have given millions to save the continent were now making such a fuss over petty salary increases. 'I never', he wrote despairingly, 'found the House of Commons so dead to my voice.'[11] Sheer fatigue must have added to his depression. In addition to the daily, or nightly, debates in the Chamber, each averaging about eight hours, he made a point of attending the Finance and Poor Law Committees, one or other of which met every morning; and on top of his parliamentary labours he had all his work at the Foreign Office.

It was, Castlereagh told Wellington, one of the most disagreeable sessions he had ever known.[12] At least, however, he could look forward to being better supported in the Commons when Parliament reassembled. In February 1816, Lord Buckinghamshire, the President of the Board of Control, had died, and Liverpool had offered his post to Canning, who was just about to complete a two-year exile in Lisbon as British ambassador. By now, Canning had been sufficiently chastened by some six years in the political wilderness not to turn up his nose at a comparatively lowly Cabinet seat. Presumably, Castlereagh offered no objection. He had told Mrs Arbuthnot in Paris the year before that having gained and maintained his point with Canning, he saw no reason to object to his return to office.[13] However, a phrase in a letter to his brother in June suggests some uneasiness that Canning's return might lead to 'cabals'.[14] He need not have worried. Canning had lost the urge to cabal.

The 1816 session of Parliament taught Castlereagh, if he did not realise it already, that with Napoleon safely locked away in St Helena the great majority of English people were completely indifferent to what went on in Europe. Or if not indifferent, they were hostile. Brougham and the Whigs strongly criticised Britain's involvement with the autocratic continental rulers and resented British troops being used to help keep a Bourbon on the throne of France. For the time being at least, Britain lacked the will, the means and the manpower to intervene in Europe or elsewhere, either as paymaster or military power. Apart from a commitment to help keep France in check, its contribution to maintaining the peace would have to be conciliation and mediation, not threats of armed intervention.

It was a role that suited Castlereagh's temperament. He preferred gentle persuasion to thumping the table, 'management' to mobilisation. Austria, he told his brother in Vienna, must 'for some years to come rely more upon our influence than on our army'.[15] That it would have to be largely his own personal influence did not trouble him. After negotiating at such close quarters with the rulers and statesmen of Europe, he felt, without arrogance, that he knew better than most, and certainly better than Parliament, how best to conduct the country's foreign affairs. Unfortunately, this not unjustified belief led him to regard Parliament, not as an aid to more effective diplomacy, but as a potential or actual handicap which had to be circumvented, occasionally by deviousness little short of deception.

In 1816, peace seemed a fragile plant which might not survive more than a few years. France, where Louis was perched precariously on his throne, was still felt to be the greatest hazard – and would have been an even greater one if Wellington, with his incomparable prestige and authority, had not, in effect, been controlling its destiny. But throughout Europe, from Prussia to Sicily, revolutionary ideas – sometimes confused with merely liberalising aspirations – were smouldering. To Castlereagh they were a threat to the stability of the whole continent, and hence to Britain itself. The best defence against them, he felt, was 'the great machine of European safety', the alliance of the four great powers that had overthrown Napoleon. To the 'secondary' powers, like Spain, Sweden and the Netherlands, which might resent their exclusion, he made protestations of goodwill and pointed out that to have too many round the council table 'would be utterly incompatible with the march of business'.[16]

Although Castlereagh treated the Tsar's 'Sacred Treaty' (Holy Alliance) with amused tolerance, his own concept of international cooperation was highly idealistic and required a degree of mutual trust and shared interests between the Four which in fact did not exist. His idealism found its most extreme – or naive – expression in a dispatch sent to all British missions abroad at the beginning of 1816. Its aim was 'to discourage that spirit of petty intrigue and perpetual propagation of alarm, upon slight evidence and ancient jealousies, which too frequently disgrace the diplomatic profession . . .' He loftily pointed out that 'there is no longer any object which the Prince Regent can desire to acquire for the British Empire, either of possession or fame . . . his only desire is, and must be, to employ all his influence to preserve the peace, which in concert with his Allies he has won'. Without becoming 'the dupe of designing men', British diplomats were therefore to try 'to inspire as far as possible a temper of morality and confidence amongst those who are accredited to the same Court'.[17]

The chief disrupters of Allied concord were Russian diplomats and agents whose activities, real or imagined, at Madrid, Paris, Naples and elsewhere provoked the suspicion and hostility of their British colleagues. Russia's recent intervention on such an impressive scale in the affairs of Europe was a new phenomenon. Combined with the puzzling enigma of Alexander's personality, it aroused lively fears, especially in Vienna, about the great eastern power's long-term intentions. Suspicion was inflamed by the Tsar's failure to disband his huge armies – or even remove them behind his own frontiers – and by the numerous reports and rumours of Russian intrigues. In spite of his high-minded professions of devotion to peace, the Tsar seemed unsettled and dissatisfied, and it was feared that his secret aim was to establish a dominating position in Western Europe and the Mediterranean by alliance with the three Bourbon powers and by encroaching heavily on the decrepit Ottoman Empire.

Castlereagh, however, refused to treat Alexander as the new bogyman of Europe. He believed that the reports of Russian activities were greatly exaggerated, and that to treat the Tsar with suspicion and scarcely-veiled hostility was the worst possible way of handling him. His own attitude was friendly but guarded. The Tsar, he felt, would not disturb the peace if he was allowed to occupy his proper place in European affairs. Alexander saw himself as the 'Grand Pacificator' of Europe, and Castlereagh did not despair of confirming him in that role; 'if', he wrote with cheerful cynicism to Charles, 'we can bind him down in the trammels of his own Christian maxims, it is a very cheap protection...'[18] He defended the Tsar stoutly in the Commons, and was rewarded with a private letter of thanks from Alexander. The letter contained a proposal for simultaneous disarmament by all the powers. Castlereagh sent a carefully reasoned reply, pointing out the practical complications, and suggesting instead that each power should disarm as far as it considered expedient.[19] It was typical of Castlereagh's way of 'managing' the Tsar that he persuaded the Regent ('although the Regent does not *love* the Emperor'[20]) to provide a cordial private letter to accompany his own rather discouraging reply.*

No more was heard from St Petersburg about general disarmament. Nor did Alexander seem in any hurry to demobilise his own armies. But

---

*Castlereagh realised that the Russian military machine, once allowed to run down, was very difficult to reassemble quickly, and also that demobilisation was complicated by the fact that the peasant-soldier lost his master and his home when he enlisted. (Alexander tried to solve these problems by founding military colonies.) But a year later, in 1817, he was feeling less tolerant of the Tsar's failure to demobilise, pointing out to Cathcart that for a power to keep 300,000 men under arms in time of peace was a novel state of things and was bound to cause alarm. (FO. 65/117. May 16, 1817)

Castlereagh refused to let this alone throw doubt on the Tsar's pacific intentions – 'as the Emperor likes an army, as he likes an influence in Europe and is under an impression of some alarm with respect to the political effervescence of the times, I do not expect him very rapidly to part with the troops he has formed...'[21]

Castlereagh realised that Metternich disliked his 'coquetry' with the Tsar, but pointed out that if it kept Alexander on the right path, it would be 'everything' to Austria; it would also prevent Russia and France from getting too close, 'which is bad for us both, but much more formidable for Austria'.[22] The interests of Britain and Austria largely coincided, and by now Castlereagh and Metternich had formed a close working relationship based on mutual personal esteem. But since one country was a continental power and the other enjoyed the protection of the Channel moat, their ministers inevitably had a somewhat different approach to political issues. While Castlereagh could rely on 'management' and mediation, Metternich might feel obliged to take a more active line. Castlereagh understood this, but still found plenty to criticise. Metternich's timidity, his continual sounding of the alarm against Russia, exasperated him. So did the Austrian Chancellor's addiction to espionage. Castlereagh's comment on a report from the Netherlands, passed on to him by Metternich through Charles Stewart, was typical: it 'is, I suspect, one of the *mystifications in which* he [Metternich] is so often involved by his inordinate taste for spies and police, and which as far as my experience enables me to judge put their employer much oftener on the *wrong*, than the *right* scent'.[23] He deplored Metternich's tactics in continually raising a number of comparatively minor but contentious issues in Germany and Italy, thus allowing Russia to pose as the protector of weaker states against a domineering Austria.[24] He greatly disapproved of Metternich's deviousness, which sometimes involved him in contradictions and even double-dealing, and his readiness to contrive expedients rather than stick to principles. His friendly but rather schoolmasterish attitude to Metternich is summed up in a letter written to his brother in August 1816: 'Say everything from me to Prince Metternich, he knows I have no object nearer at heart than what I consider to be the true interest of Austria, and if I now and then counteract him *in his expedients*, it is because my conviction is to make solid work. We must act upon broad principles, and our influence will be more useful to Austria in proportion as other powers see we are not subservient to all her projects.'[25]

It was in Italy, in particular Sicily, that Castlereagh was most 'subservient' to Austria's 'projects', but only because he believed in them himself. He genuinely, and rightly, felt that the constitution bequeathed to Sicily by the British ambassador, Lord William Bentinck, was unworkable, but he knew there would be a great fuss at Westminster if he supported any attempt to revise it, even if a parliamentary façade were preserved. The dubious disingenuousness with which he covered up his private approval in his public dispatches showed how far he was prepared to go in support of Austria.[26]* On the other hand, he was equally determined not to give way to Metternich against his own judgment. In the spring of 1817 Castlereagh received an overture from him for a secret pact against Russia. He roundly rejected what would have been a damaging blow to the Quadruple Alliance, and in effect told Metternich to pull himself together and not give way to his alarms about Russia.[27]

Nor would he allow the machinery of the Alliance to be used for purposes for which it was not intended. He strongly condemned Metternich's plan to use the four-power ambassadors' conference set up in Paris to oversee the implementation of the French peace treaty as a clearing-house for police reports on subversive activities throughout Europe. The Allied ministers at Paris must not, he told the British ambassador in Paris, try 'to present themselves as an European Council for the management of the affairs of the world'.[28] It was the first sign of a serious rift between Castlereagh and the other members of the Quadruple Alliance.

Distress and disaffection were the government's chief preoccupations at home during 1816–17, as economic recession led to bankruptcies, cuts in wages, and unemployment both in industrial towns and on the land. Rapid demobilisation increased the numbers out of work and added to the distress. In May 1816 an epidemic of rioting spread throughout East Anglia. Farm machinery was smashed, barns burned and food shops looted. In some parts of the north and midlands sporadic disturbances flared up during the summer, while in others there were orderly protest marches by the unemployed. It was one of the coldest and wettest summers in living memory, and when the harvest failed, the price of bread rose sharply, distress grew more severe and the reports of unrest became more alarming.

*Metternich wanted to suppress the Sicilian constitution altogether, but Castlereagh insisted privately that he would have to intervene if a parliamentary framework was not left, and if there was any harshness to individuals. But in December 1816, Sicily and Naples were, by decree, united in the Kingdom of the Two Sicilies, and Sicily then in effect lost its separate institutions. Castlereagh had advised against the union.

The economic distress greatly stimulated the movement for political reform and helped to give what had been an essentially middle-class movement a more popular base. Workers who had gained nothing by rioting and violence were more willing to listen to the argument that only through a reformed, truly representative Parliament could they hope to get economic and social justice. Most of the leaders of the movement were entirely peaceful in their methods and moderate in their demands. But when the flashy demagogue, 'Orator' Hunt, harangued a huge meeting at Spa Fields in London on November 15, 1816, his escorts carried a tricolour flag and a cap of liberty on top of a pike. A second meeting at Spa Fields a fortnight later developed into a crazy attempt by part of the crowd to terrorise the City. On January 17, 1817, as the Regent was driving home after opening Parliament, an object – bullet or stone – pierced the window of his coach.

After this apparent attempt on the Regent's life, secret committees of both Houses of Parliament were appointed and given a mass of evidence of seditious activities throughout the country, including a plot to seize the Bank and the Tower and incite the army to mutiny. The information was based largely on the reports of government informers, most of whom were neither reliable, efficient, nor very scrupulous; much of the evidence was exaggerated or absurd, some was probably pure invention. But even making allowances for 'questionable' evidence, as the committees tried to do, their reports were alarming enough, and in the prevailing climate of opinion, the government could not take them lightly. Revolutionary Jacobinism was still a very lively memory, and even if there was not, as the ministers alleged, a nation-wide conspiracy to overthrow the government, they firmly believed that there was. Even the mild and moderate Wilberforce fully accepted the need for measures against 'the danger of bloodshed and conflagration'.[29]

A temporary suspension of habeas corpus was rushed through Parliament within a week, and it was quickly followed by a ban on seditious meetings for a limited period. (A year earlier the Cabinet had turned down Sidmouth's plea for a general ban on meetings.) If the danger was as great as the ministers (and others) feared, these weapons were not excessive, nor do they seem to have been used recklessly or immoderately. In March six to seven hundred hungry weavers set out to march from Manchester to London. They were entirely non-violent and were quickly and easily dispersed, but the 'March of the Blanketeers' seemed to confirm all the government's worst fears. The unrest rumbled on into the summer, culminating in an attempted rising by a band of Derbyshire labourers. It was a pathetic fiasco. But before Parliament rose for the summer recess, the ministers thought it prudent to arm themselves with a further suspension of habeas corpus.

With the Home Secretary in the House of Lords, it fell to Castlereagh to introduce and defend the government's repressive legislation in the House of Commons. Perhaps inevitably, he did not escape fresh attacks on his record in Ireland, including the atrocities he was alleged to have condoned. On the last day of the session, an unexpected personal attack by Brougham, in a debate supposedly about the state of the nation, shook Castlereagh out of his customary calm and provoked a passionately bitter reply. He knew, he said, he would never be forgiven for having prevented Ireland from being separated by traitors from the rest of the British Empire. But those who knew him would do him the justice to believe that he never had 'a cruel or an unkind heart', or had gone further in prosecuting even the guilty in Ireland than necessity required.[30]* How much these attacks now mattered, it is hard to say. In popular estimation, Castlereagh was already the most hated member of the government (with Sidmouth coming a close second), partly because he was the best known, partly because of his coldly aloof manner, and partly because the popular mythology about his role in 1798 had followed him across the Irish Sea. He never shook it off.

No one believed that the government could prevent or remedy the vagaries of the economy, any more than it could alter the weather; economic slumps and drought were both part of a natural process which no man could change. But there was a widespread feeling that 'extravagant' government spending made a bad situation worse, and in the 1817 session the Cabinet redoubled its efforts to cut spending to the bone. Castlereagh assiduously attended both the Finance and the Poor Law Committees of the Commons. The two were not unconnected. Castlereagh was convinced that 'unless we can do something to check the growing abuses of the *Poor Laws*, our utmost attempts at reduction of public expenditure will be ineffectual towards settling the mind and giving free scope to the industry of the nation'. Not only, he pointed out, was an overwhelming proportion of the profits of the soil being absorbed by the parish rates, and unproductively consumed, but the

*In 1839 Henry Brougham wrote that the complaints made of Castlereagh's Irish administration 'were entirely unfounded as regarded the cruelties practised during and after the Rebellion. Far from partaking in these atrocities, he uniformly and strenuously set his face against them. He was of a cold temperament and determined character, but not of a cruel disposition; and to him, more than perhaps to anyone else, was owing the termination of the system stained with blood.' (*Statesmen of the Times of George III.* Vol 2, pp.125/6)

system was thoroughly demoralising to those it was meant to help.³¹*
He found time to work out a plan of his own, designed to prevent abuses
while safeguarding those who really needed help, but whether he did
more than circulate it privately we do not know.

In any case, the Poor Laws had grown into an almost sacrosanct
institution, and the labours of the three select committees of the
Commons gave birth only to some minor amendments. But, contrary to
its reputation for single-minded repression, the Liverpool government
did tentatively accept a duty to try to provide work for the unemployed
– and by some more fruitful method than digging a hole one day and
filling it up the next, which was Castlereagh's unfortunate way of
expressing concern at the demoralising effects of idleness.³² The Poor
Employment Act, which made loans available to create work for the
unemployed, was essentially Vansittart's idea. It was not, as it happened,
very successful, and although Castlereagh rushed it through Parliament
as quickly as possible, by the time it became law in midsummer 1817, the
need for it was rapidly diminishing.³³

In the autumn of 1817 an excellent harvest coincided with the end of
the trade recession. The price of bread dropped, demand for British
manufactures soared, jobs became plentiful and political agitation died
away. As soon as Parliament reassembled in January 1818, the
suspension of habeas corpus was repealed. (Sidmouth had already
quietly released most of those held under it.) The session saw a
comparative lull in the storms of the postwar years, and although the
government tarnished its well-deserved reputation for financial sobriety
by trying to get Parliament to vote allowances for the greatly despised
royal dukes, the ministers optimistically decided to consolidate their
position by going to the country a year earlier than they need have
done.†

It was an unfortunate decision. Many more seats than usual were
contested, and when all the returns were in, the government was found
to have suffered a net loss of between 10 and 25 seats. Clearly, it had lost
the popularity accruing from victory over Bonaparte and its peacetime

*He was thinking of the Speenhamland system of poor relief, first introduced in
Berkshire in 1795. It was a well-meaning attempt to relieve poverty by guaranteeing a
minimum wage out of the poor rate, adjusted according to the price of bread. It spread
widely throughout the country, and led to a huge increase in the poor rate as well as
keeping wages down and demoralising the farm workers.

†Princess Charlotte, who had married Prince Leopold of Saxe-Coburg in 1816, died in
November 1817, and the government was anxious to encourage the Regent's bachelor
brothers to marry and produce an heir.

record had been found wanting. After a 'pretty fatiguing fortnight' in Liverpool, Canning wondered whether the public mind might not have been more tranquillised if they had waited a year.[34] But in County Down, Castlereagh seemed at last to have sailed into calm waters. His election, he reported, 'was disposed of in an hour's time, with more good humour amongst all ranks than I have witnessed upon any former occasion'.[35]

In London, where he cast his own vote, he got off less lightly. He was recognised at the polling station at Covent Garden by a ferociously yelling mob, who hustled him away through the streets. His only companion was his private secretary, Lord Clanwilliam. They took refuge in a shop in St Martin's Lane, which unfortunately had no back exit. So the resourceful Clanwilliam crawled out on all fours through the legs of the crowd and fetched a band of twenty constables. Accompanied now by constables as well as mob, Castlereagh decided to make for the Admiralty, rather than lead the crowd to his own house. Arriving at the Admiralty gate, he turned, took off his hat, bowed and thanked the crowd for their escort, adding that he would not trouble them to accompany him any further. This earned him a few cheers.[36]

One of those who saw the Foreign Secretary being chased from Covent Garden was the American minister, Richard Rush, who had been talking with him in St James's Square earlier in the day. There was a good deal of Anglo-American consultation that summer because Castlereagh was anxious to settle outstanding issues with the United States before departing for the European congress due to meet at Aix-la-Chapelle in September. In the post-Napoleon period, he set great store on putting Anglo-American relations on a better footing. There were no two countries, he firmly told the House of Commons in 1816, 'whose interests were more naturally and closely connected'.[37] Few on either side of the Atlantic would have agreed – at least not in their hearts. The War of 1812 had created much bad feeling on both sides, and the peace treaty signed at Ghent had left many potentially explosive issues unsettled. Moreover, among the Americans there was a bitter legacy of suspicion and soreness at real or imagined British high-handedness and arrogance. Characteristically, Castlereagh tried first to create better personal relationships. With the implacably anti-British John Quincy Adams, who was American minister in London in 1815 and 1816, he did not get very far (although he earned Adams's respect), but Richard Rush, who arrived in December 1817, was won over at their first meeting by the 'simplicity' of Castlereagh's manner and his 'very conciliatory' welcome.[38]

Castlereagh had already secured an important agreement to end an incipient naval armaments race on the Great Lakes.* Various commercial, boundary, fisheries and other questions remained, and in August 1818 Albert Gallatin, the American minister in Paris, came over to join Rush in an attempt to settle them. Castlereagh had to leave the British side of the negotiations in the hands of Frederick Robinson and Henry Goulburn, but, typically, he did his best to create a propitious atmosphere. All four negotiators were invited down to Cray for the night, and after the forthcoming negotiations had been gone over in a very friendly manner, Rush found himself swept into the Castlereaghs' domestic circle, where everything was talked of except the negotiations, 'conversation games' were played, and the hospitality was altogether 'as easy as delightful'.[39]

On one issue, Castlereagh made a special effort to get agreement before leaving London. In return for a suspension of impressment, the Americans had offered to ban the employment of British sailors on their ships. The Cabinet were divided on an issue that aroused the most jingoistic instincts of the British public. But Castlereagh, who realised much more clearly than in 1812 what an emotive issue impressment was for the Americans, was in principle anxious to accept the offer. Just before setting out for Aix, he summoned Rush to his house and told him, with obvious pleasure, that the Cabinet had been persuaded to drop their most difficult condition for agreement and were prepared to outface any public clamour. Unfortunately, the negotiations then got hopelessly bogged down in technical details – which, Rush was convinced, would never have been allowed to happen if Castlereagh had been there.[40]

Before leaving for Aix, Castlereagh proposed a ten-year renewal of the Anglo-American commercial convention signed in 1815, which in practice was very favourable to the Americans. But to their demand to participate in trade with the West Indies he had nothing to say. The British were still prisoners of their traditional colonial mercantilist system which restricted trade to ships of the mother country. Castlereagh once confessed to Adams that he did not know whether it was a wise system, but as it had been established so long, the Cabinet thought it best to stick to it.[41] Castlereagh was one of the members of the government who favoured a freer commercial policy. But in 1818 they still lacked enough assurance and parliamentary support to make the

*Negotiated in Washington by Charles Bagot, the British minister, it limited to four the number of warships each country could keep on the Great Lakes, and restricted their activities to revenue and police work.

concessions needed to prevent a minor but irritating trade war in the Caribbean.

On other issues the negotiators were more successful. The northwest frontier was drawn along the 49th Parallel as far west as the Rockies, and an agreement on the Newfoundland fisheries was reached. The latter, which was favourable to the Americans, was strongly criticised in the British press. But Castlereagh was unmoved, thinking – as he told Rush later – that it was 'of less moment which of the parties gained a little more or lost a little more by the compact, than that so difficult a point should be adjusted, and the harmony of the two countries, so far, be made secure'.[42]

The congress of Aix-la-Chapelle, which opened on September 29, 1818, was for Castlereagh 'two months of mere labour... there being no sort of amusement'.[43] This, although an exaggeration, was true by comparison with the endless round of festivities at Vienna and Paris. At Aix the delegates sometimes had to pass the evening playing whist. Castlereagh also complained of the dearth of female society – Mme Lieven, the wife of the Russian ambassador in London, 'reigned with absolute sway'.[44] This was rather hard on Emily who, as usual, held her salons, which Metternich, also as usual, failed to find attractive. Charles Stewart, whom Castlereagh had summoned from Vienna to keep Metternich '*steady*'[45], thought there was much less to interest and amuse him at Aix than at Vienna or Paris, because everything was kept much more secret and everyone was 'most profoundly in the dark'.[46]*

If the gathering at Aix had been anything like as large as the Vienna congress, it would no doubt have been much more lively and much less discreet. Since it was the first such conference to be summoned in time of peace – or not immediately after a war – there had been much argument about who should be invited and what should be discussed. Eventually, it was agreed to limit the formal agenda to the ending of France's period of probation, and restrict the participants to the four wartime Allies plus France. The Russian foreign minister, Count Capodistria, repeatedly pressed for some of the lesser powers, in particular Spain, to be invited, but without success. Castlereagh did not want the meeting 'to assume the character of a congress' at all.[47]† He saw it as the first of the

*A number of champions of worthy causes, like Robert Owen, came, as well as Sir Thomas Lawrence, who hoped to be able to get on with his commission from the Regent to paint the celebrities of Europe.

†Contemporaries were vague and inconsistent about the difference between a congress and a conference. Castlereagh seems to have felt that if a meeting was not declared to be a congress, the secondary powers should not take offence at being excluded.

periodical reunions provided for in the sixth article of the Quadruple Alliance: an opportunity for the great powers to hold intimate discussions and try to work out a common approach to a variety of European problems, from inter-German disagreements and the future of the Spanish colonies to the slave trade and the Barbary pirates. Their aim – as Castlereagh apparently saw it – was not to impose solutions, but to facilitate agreements.

Extensive discussions of these and other issues were held throughout the conference, but with meagre practical results. The exception was the future of the Spanish colonies, on which Castlereagh achieved an important negative success by persuading the Russians and French not to try to intervene on behalf of the King of Spain, with either military aid or economic sanctions against the South Americans. His aim was to hold the ring and leave Spain and its colonies to work out their relationship without interference.

The only formal item on the conference's agenda – France – was expeditiously dealt with. On October 9 a convention was signed with the French prime minister, the Duc de Richelieu, providing for the ending of the Allied military occupation of France by November 30 and payment of the rest of the French war indemnity. But the Allies were still doubtful about France's long-term stability, and instead of responding to Richelieu's urgent pleas to negotiate a quintuple alliance, they secretly reaffirmed their Quadruple Alliance against France. On the other hand, to involve France somehow in the councils of Europe would clearly be safer than to leave it an umbraged and restless outsider. The device adopted was to invite France to participate in the periodic summit meetings, of which the Aix meeting was the first. 'The expedient then', wrote Castlereagh triumphantly, 'is to give France her concert, but to keep our security.'[48]

Delighted by this neat solution, he waxed lyrical on the advantages of direct contacts, pointing out – rather teasingly – to Liverpool 'how little embarrassment and how much solid good grow out of these reunions, which sound so terrible at a distance. It really appears to me to be a new discovery in the European Government, at once extinguishing the cobwebs with which diplomacy obscures the horizon ... and giving to the counsels of the great powers the efficiency and almost the simplicity of a single State.'[49]

Even before receiving this rhapsody, Liverpool had begun to be thoroughly alarmed by the general trend of Castlereagh's dispatches, especially his references to new summit meetings. Canning had made a great fuss in Cabinet, and the new Parliament – which was 'of a doubtful character'[50] – was likely to make an even greater one when it met in the new year. In spite of Wellington's reassuring presence at Aix, a steady stream of warnings and admonitions descended on Castlereagh from London.

For the remaining weeks of the congress, he was trying to keep his balance between the efforts of his colleagues to pull him back from the very discreet step he wished to take into Europe, and the Tsar's attempts to pull him in much further than he intended to go. Alexander had arrived at Aix in a notably friendly and pacific mood, but showing 'a degree of exaltation of mind' which Castlereagh could only hope would gradually subside.[51] Instead, it eventually expressed itself in a proposal, carefully prepared by the Tsar and Capodistria, that all the European powers should guarantee each other against foreign attack and internal change. This 'attempt to do everything for everybody', wrote Castlereagh graphically, was in 'so crude and impracticable a shape, as to remain stagnant in its own impracticability ...'.[52] He immediately sat down and wrote a crushing critique which effectively brought the Russians down to earth, and incidentally gave the lie to Castlereagh's enemies in England who alleged that he was a hidebound reactionary totally opposed to all change.[53] (Unfortunately, this memorandum would not have come their way.) Although Metternich did not share Castlereagh's aversion to meddling in other countries' affairs, he certainly did not want Russian armies tramping all over Europe. So the Russian plan was quietly dropped. So too was a plan put up by the Prussian generals (always neurotically afraid of France) for a European army to be commanded by Wellington. 'A more ingenious device', wrote Castlereagh indignantly, 'for keeping us in hot water could not have been invented.'[54]

On the whole, he was well satisfied with his labours at Aix. 'We have done more business', he told Arbuthnot, 'than in double the time at any of our former reunions, and all are gone home in good humour and vowing eternal peace and friendship ...'[55] He himself went home by way of Paris for a week's amusement, which he thought he deserved. He was destined never again to attend one of the reunions by which he set such store.

CHAPTER XV

Unrest at home and abroad
1819–21

On January 1, 1819 Castlereagh entered his fiftieth year. His European reputation had never been higher, his popular reputation in England never lower. In the Cabinet, his influence was second only to Wellington's. In the House of Commons, he still lacked skill as a speaker, but he was always listened to with attention; and his good sense, quiet courtesy and dogged courage, together with his occasional impromptu outbursts (when he always spoke best), had given him a personal popularity that would have seemed inconceivable when he first became leader of the House.

He once said that he would never go to the House of Lords because it was too quiet and sleepy for him; he needed the violence and goading of the Commons to rouse him.[1] By temperament, he was a placid and good-humoured man, who faced the world with an outward serenity which only those who did not know him mistook for unfeeling coldness. To his guests he was a charming and easy host, and to his family and friends he revealed a warm and affectionate nature. With the ladies he was a great favourite. 'It was impossible', wrote Mrs Arbuthnot, 'to look at him and see the benevolent and amiable expression of his countenance without a disposition to like him ...'[2] The sophisticated and worldly-wise Countess Lieven, wife of the Russian ambassador, was pleased and flattered by his friendship, even though she did privately make fun of his peculiar French, his taste in furnishings, and his style of waltzing. 'You cannot imagine', she told Metternich, after an absence from London, 'how pleased Lord Castlereagh was to see me again. He came in with open arms; I simply had to open mine half-way, so that we gave each other a kind of semi-tender embrace.'[3]

In London the Castlereaghs entertained lavishly in their house in St James's Square, where the reception rooms were strewn with massive porcelain objects and other splendid gifts from the crowned heads of Europe. At North Cray the entertaining was usually more informal, although the diplomatic corps were invited there too, and in the summer the Castlereaghs gave large 'fêtes', with dancing in the ballroom and sitting-out in the garden.*

Castlereagh escaped to Cray whenever he could. He loved the country and country pursuits, riding or driving in the neighbourhood, walking in his beautifully laid out gardens – he was extremely fond of flowers – or supervising his farm. He enlarged and improved the house, and liked to fill it with young people. He had his own study, but usually sat and wrote in the drawing room, undisturbed by the talk and laughter around him. 'If', wrote Emily's niece many years later, 'an air were played that pleased him, he would go to the pianoforte and sing it; if a waltz, he would say, "Emma let us take a turn", and after waltzing for a few minutes, he would resume his writing.'[4]

In the postwar period he managed to make only one long holiday visit to Mount Stewart, in the autumn of 1816. 'I went little from home', he told Charles afterwards, 'and passed seven weeks there in great domestic comfort. We often longed for you to complete the family group.'[5] He was always closely involved in family affairs, and watched over his father's welfare and peace of mind with sensitive and affectionate sympathy. Late in 1820, Lord Londonderry became worried about Charles's financial extravagance which he thought was upsetting a family settlement made two years earlier. It was a time of particularly acute crisis at home and abroad, but Castlereagh found time to go into the matter and then write to his father, carefully explaining away Charles's extravagance. To the culprit he sent a gentle reproof which included the percipient comment: 'I know the serenity of my Father's mind depends in a considerable degree upon the impression that his affairs are in good order.' No financial worries must be allowed to cloud the 'repose of an old age [the] most amiable and respectable that I ever witnessed'.[6] His father died a few months later.

In the autumn of 1819 Castlereagh had to cancel a visit to Mount Stewart because of serious unrest in England. He managed to go shooting in Norfolk and Suffolk instead and felt all the better for it. 'I was in a fright lest the gout was preparing to pay me a visit, but it has taken itself off.'[7] Gout and shooting parties were a regular refrain in his life, the latter being partly an attempt to ward off the former. After a visit to Suffolk one October, he wrote that the party 'answered every purpose of air and exercise, but was not so brilliant as heretofore in point of

---

*Richard Rush and his wife once arrived very late to dinner at Cray because of a carriage accident. Castlereagh said: 'Never mind – it is all as it should be – America being farthest off, you had a right to more time in coming.' Rush was much impressed by the good breeding of his host in producing this ingenious excuse for him. (Rush. 2nd Series, I, pp.173/4)

sport'.[8] As a bodily affliction gout seems to have been in a class of its own – more an occupational hazard than a regular illness. Gout, wrote Castlereagh once, 'still torments me a little, though it does not materially affect my health'.[9] Its chief drawback was that it prevented him from attending Parliament, which he found 'very mortifying'.

A severe attack of gout forced Castlereagh to miss the first ten days of the new Parliament which met on January 21, 1819. Early in March he was again away for a week after the death of one of his sisters. Charles Arbuthnot, a Joint Secretary at the Treasury, who helped him with parliamentary business, greatly lamented his absence, especially as a new House of Commons always tended to be unstable and unpredictable. To make matters worse, government office-holders were not bothering to attend. And why, said the independent MPs, should we bother to support a government whose members would not take the trouble to support it themselves?[10] Moreover, the Treasury front bench inspired even less confidence than usual. Peel had resigned the previous summer, after six exhausting years as Irish Chief Secretary; Canning was preoccupied with his personal frustrations; and Vansittart's stewardship of the Exchequer was being criticised even by his close supporters.

According to Arbuthnot, Castlereagh himself stood as well as a man could do, and when he was able to play an active part all was well.[11] But even when Castlereagh was in his place, it was still difficult to persuade government supporters to stick out the debates, and the government suffered several humiliating defeats and near-defeats. In the middle of May Lord Liverpool said it would be far better for the ministry to resign if it could not carry three million pounds of new indirect taxation which was essential to put the country's finances on a more stable footing.[12]

The government's poor performance was presumably partly due to Castlereagh's failure to find enough time and energy for parliamentary management. At any rate, a bolder approach and a willingness to face resignation soon brought better results. The government's danger was in fact more apparent than real, since the Whigs, divided and poorly led, were not really an acceptable alternative. When Tierney, the Whig leader, rather unwisely proposed an inquiry into the state of the nation, his motion, which both sides took to be a vote of confidence, attracted the largest attendance since the debates on the union, and was overwhelmingly defeated by a two to one majority, after Canning had wound up for the government with a very powerful speech. Before the tax measures were introduced, Castlereagh circularised all government supporters and also invited them to a private meeting with him. The taxes were then carried without difficulty, after Castlereagh had made a stirring and much-applauded debating speech in reply to Tierney. Lastly, a bill providing for the gradual resumption of cash payments passed easily into law.* As Sidmouth remarked, the session ended far more satisfactorily than it had begun.[13]

Lord Sidmouth, the Home Secretary, was not, however, destined to enjoy a tranquil summer holiday. After a bad harvest in 1818 and renewed economic difficulties, manufacturing districts were again simmering with unrest. Cuts in wages led to strikes and sporadic outbreaks of violence, and since early in the year radical agitators had been busy trying to harness the unrest to political ends. A series of huge mass meetings was organised with the perfectly legal aim of petitioning for a reform of the parliamentary franchise and the repeal of the Corn Law. They began in Lancashire and by July had spread up into Scotland as well as through the northern and midland counties of England. On August 16, 1819, a vast but orderly crowd assembled in St Peter's Fields in Manchester to listen to Orator Hunt and petition for parliamentary reform. The watching magistrates allowed Hunt to get up on to the platform, and then belatedly decided to send in the local yeomanry to arrest him. When the yeomanry got into difficulties, some hussars were sent in to rescue them, and in the ensuing mêlée, eleven people were killed and several hundred wounded.

The 'massacre of Peterloo' was greeted with shock and alarm throughout the country. And the promptness with which Sidmouth conveyed the Regent's warm thanks to the magistrates and yeomanry increased the sense of outrage at the brutal cutting-down of helpless men, women and children. (Henceforth, whatever their private view of the magistrates' conduct, ministers had no choice but to defend them in public.) The magistrates were condemned in private conversation, in the press, in pamphlets and at protest meetings. At the same time, Sidmouth was inundated with alarming tales of plots and secret drillings, and magistrates all over the country appealed to him for more rigorous powers to deal with disaffection.

Deeply impressed by all he read, Sidmouth was anxious to oblige

*Cash payments had been suspended in 1797 as a wartime measure, but the government had kept on deferring their resumption on the advice of the Bank of England. In 1819 it announced a further year's postponement, but was forced by the House of Commons and public pressure to change its mind. A Committee of Inquiry was set up with Peel as chairman (and Castlereagh as a member). The bill providing for a gradual return to cash payments was based on the committee's report.

them. But to his great exasperation the handful of ministers who had not dispersed on holiday (Liverpool, Wellington, Castlereagh, Eldon and Vansittart) took a cooler view. Wellington, it is true, feared that a full-scale insurrection was imminent,[14] and there was general agreement that the traditional virtually unlimited right of assembly would have to be curbed. But Liverpool, anxious not to seem provocative, wanted to let the situation calm down first. What Castlereagh said is not known, but presumably he belonged to the anti-alarmist school, since on September 24 he cheerfully told Charles that he had feared 'the Radicals would chain me to the oar, but I have made my escape . . .' He was, he wrote, setting out next day for Ireland by way of Suffolk, and the Cabinet was determined not to meet Parliament until after Christmas unless matters got much worse.[15] But early in October, further mass meetings in manufacturing towns, and a series of county meetings organised by the 'respectable' Whigs, led the prime minister to change his mind. Parliament was summoned for November 23, and Sidmouth and the Law Officers were left with barely six weeks to devise new legal remedies for the crisis.

Drawn up by men who genuinely believed that the country was on the verge of armed revolt, the notorious 'Six Acts' were surprisingly restrained. The main aim was to prevent radical agitators from making use of social distress to 'delude' poor people and lead them astray, either at meetings or through the printed word. The first bill restricted the size of public meetings and carefully defined their 'legality'. The second imposed heavy penalties on the publishers of seditious libels. The third extended the fourpenny tax on newspapers to pamphlets (thus, it was hoped, limiting their sales by raising their price). The fourth bill prohibited unauthorised military drilling. The fifth empowered magistrates, for a limited period, to search private property for arms, and the sixth speeded up the administration of justice. No attempt was made to renew the suspension of habeas corpus, introduce censorship, or stop the trial of libels by juries. County meetings regularly convened, and meetings called by grand juries or corporate bodies were exempted from restrictions.

Castlereagh was said to be in gay spirits at the usual eve-of-session dinner which he gave in St James's Square. To one of his guests, who said they would have a warm struggle, he replied that it was always better to have a great object to fight for than to be lingering on mere general business.[16] But the struggle turned out to be neither so warm nor so protracted as the ministers had feared. The great majority of the Commons agreed that something must be done, and many even of the

UNREST AT HOME AND ABROAD 1819—21

Whigs found it hard to oppose the government's measures with real conviction. Castlereagh, for his part, was ready to meet criticism and accept amendments, thereby earning the furious criticism of one of Lord Grenville's supporters for letting himself be 'bullied by the country gentlemen'.[17] His most substantial concessions were to limit the seditious meetings bill to five years and exempt indoor meetings from its restrictions. Contrary to the government's expectations, four of the bills had become law by Christmas and the other two by the end of the year.

Towards the end of February 1820 the political unrest reached a bizarre climax with the discovery of a plot to assassinate the whole Cabinet while they were dining at Lord Harrowby's. The government had been warned what was afoot, and the pathetic band of misguided and incompetent conspirators, led by a prominent agitator called Arthur Thistlewood, were arrested at their hideout in Cato Street before they could do any damage. Castlereagh had wanted the ministers to meet as planned, suitably armed to repel their would-be assassins. But the cooler counsels of Wellington prevailed: 'we thought it better', reported Castlereagh, 'to stay away from the festive board and not to suffer it to go to single combat between Thistlewood and Marshal Liverpool'.[18]* According to Wellington, he himself was to have been Thistlewood's intended victim, and there had been a long argument among the conspirators over who should have the honour of cutting Castlereagh's throat.[19] Sidmouth was convinced that the plot was part of a nation-wide conspiracy. But no firm evidence to support his belief was ever unearthed.[20] On the contrary, with the Six Acts safely on the statute book, the need to use them seemed largely to die away. Whether because of the government's show of strength, or because of an improved economic situation, the disturbed districts (except, temporarily, in Scotland) were much quieter than for months past. During 1820 the government's chief troubles came from quite a different source.

Some ten days before Thistlewood's abortive attempt to murder the whole Cabinet, the ministers' political lives also seemed in great

---

*A few days later, when Mme Lieven dined at the Castlereaghs', she found constables in the house and her host, whom she sat next to, made her extremely nervous by showing her the two loaded pistols in his breeches pockets. 'I was nervous every time he made a movement to offer me anything; I sat sideways on my chair; I edged away from the left and got so near to my right-hand neighbour that he could put nothing in his mouth without elbowing me... Gradually, hunger reasserted itself at the expense of terror, and I ended by eating as usual.' (*Private Letters*, pp.17/18.)

jeopardy. On January 29 the old King died. The new King immediately told his ministers to get him a divorce. Since 1814 the Princess of Wales had been travelling abroad, and a steady stream of reports about her scandalous conduct had percolated back to England. In 1818 the Regent sent a commission to Milan to investigate the reports, in particular the Princess's alleged adultery with her Italian courier, Bartolommeo Pergami. The evidence produced by the commission seemed completely damning, and George IV was determined to use it to get rid of the woman he loathed. His ministers, however, realised that any proceedings against the Queen would not only be fraught with legal and technical difficulties, but might also rock the throne. The King was already tremendously unpopular, and his own irregular private life, for long the subject of disapproving private comment, might well become exposed to censure or ribaldry in every newspaper and tavern in the kingdom.

After meeting daily for more than a week, the Cabinet finally decided to advise the King not to seek a divorce, but to offer his wife a generous financial provision if she would agree to a permanent separation and renounce her royal title. To make the compromise more palatable to the King, they also agreed to his demand that the Queen's name should be omitted from the Liturgy – thus implying that she was not fit to be prayed for. But the King was determined on a divorce and threatened to dismiss his ministers if he did not get one. The ministers took the threat seriously. For three days they believed themselves out, and Castlereagh began to clear his desk at the Foreign Office.[21] There had been talk of a visit to London by Metternich, and on February 13 Castlereagh wrote to his brother in Vienna regretting 'the pleasure I should have had in officially talking over in this country with Prince Metternich all our future plans for settling and keeping the world at peace...' But he hoped that 'as a *Kentish farmer*' he might still have the gratification of talking over old times with him.[22]

Four days later the King gave way. 'We have had the devil of a brush on the divorce', wrote Castlereagh.[23] He himself was largely responsible for the outcome. In a long audience of more than five hours on the 14th, and in a subsequent interview, he managed to persuade the King not to risk the scandal of a public inquiry. He could hardly have been successful without some pretty plain speaking.

Meanwhile, whatever the King's domestic difficulties, the government had to go on. With the new reign, there must be a new Parliament, and as soon as the Cabinet had dealt with the aftermath of the Cato Street conspiracy, Castlereagh set off to get himself re-elected for County

UNREST AT HOME AND ABROAD 1819-21

Down. He hoped, he told the King, to be back by April 1, and 'as my journey must necessarily be a forced march, Lady Castlereagh ... will remain in charge of the farm, menagerie, etc, till my return'.[24]

It was his last election, and it turned out to be a very jolly one. 'I never saw so much cordiality amongst all ranks, even to the lowest of the mob. Not a voice raised against our return, and Mr Lawless, the Belfast demagogue, who evidently came there to make a speech, thought better of it, and carried his oration back with him.' Afterwards a hundred gentlemen sat down to a celebratory dinner – 'we were very noisy, loyal and loving till past two in the morning'. Two of the company were reported 'unfit for service' the next day, but the only effects Castlereagh experienced were 'profound sleep and an increase of appetite'.[25]

Elsewhere in Europe, the demagogues were less retiring. During 1820 there were revolutionary disturbances throughout the continent. They began on New Year's Day with an army revolt in Cadiz. On February 13, the duc de Berry, the French king's nephew, was assassinated in Paris. In March, the Spanish unrest spread to the capital, and the reactionary and incompetent king, Ferdinand VII, precipitately agreed to restore the ultra-democratic and quite impracticable constitution of 1812. The upheaval in Madrid was received with jubilation by liberals and nationalists and with dismay by governments. The French, because of the Bourbon connection and France's geographical proximity to Spain, wanted to intervene. So, even more, did the Tsar, who had never really abandoned the plans for policing Europe which he had put forward at Aix. Metternich, faced with a choice of two evils in Madrid – democracy or Russian intervention – hesitated, hoping for a lead from London.

There could be little doubt what that lead would be. Throughout the previous year, 1819, Castlereagh had firmly turned down the Tsar's pressing requests for a resumption of Allied surveillance of France through meetings of the four Allied ambassadors.[26] Alexander was alarmed by the French government's liberal leanings, but Castlereagh believed that France simply needed time to purge itself of the lingering effects of the Revolution and to accustom itself to representative institutions. However unstable France seemed, meddling foreign interference could only make matters worse. Moreover, non-interference in other countries' internal affairs was a cardinal maxim of British foreign policy. For that reason Castlereagh had refused to give any approval to the Carlsbad decrees, issued in December 1819, by which Metternich tightened control over Germany's restless universities and too-outspoken press. Privately, he warmly welcomed Metternich's action against revolutionary 'germs', but it was an internal German affair, which did not call for official British comment.[27]

Castlereagh was not opposed to 'just and necessary' revolutions as opposed to the 'system of universal subversion' which he believed existed throughout Europe.[28] He realised that constitutional reforms were needed in some countries and would contribute to European stability. In Spain, the king's misrule justified revolt, but the liberals had gone too far. So long, however, as their constitutional experiment did not pose a threat to other states, they should be left alone to work out their own salvation. To interfere for any other reason would stretch the Alliance beyond its original object of safeguarding the settlement with France. It was never 'intended as a Union for the government of the world, or for the superintendence of the internal affairs of other states'.[29]

Castlereagh did not rule out joint action on issues outside the original scope of the Alliance, but it must be agreed by all. And unanimity, it was clear, was increasingly hard to achieve. The Allies, as Castlereagh pointed out, were 'essentially different' – in their institutions, ways of thinking, popular prejudices and in many other ways. Whereas the Tsar of Russia could do virtually what he liked, the British government had to conform to the nature of the British constitution.[30] It could do nothing without the backing of public opinion (which, in the case of Spain, was violently hostile to King Ferdinand). 'This is our compass, and by this we must steer ... They [the Allies] must not, therefore, press us to place ourselves on any ground that John Bull will not maintain ...'[31]

The government's attitude to the Alliance in general, and to the Spanish revolution in particular, were set out in a long state paper, drafted by Castlereagh and then exhaustively gone over by the whole Cabinet. The final product, dated May 5, 1820, remained substantially Castlereagh's, but since it satisfied all his colleagues, including Canning, its tone and phrasing were probably made more downright.[32] Copies were sent to the Allies, and whatever Metternich may have thought of the paper's attitude to the Alliance, it at least supported him in resisting the Tsar's pressure for active intervention in Spain.

The state paper made the point that in a period of serious domestic unrest the British government could not afford to have 'the public mind soured by a meddlesome policy in Spain'. But it was not internal unrest that weakened the government that summer; it was, once again, the

King's domestic difficulties. Queen Caroline, furious at the insulting implications of her omission from the Prayer Book, insisted on returning to England. On June 6 she drove in triumph into London in an open carriage, welcomed by cheering crowds all the way. 'The Ministers are in a most dangerous position', wrote Mme Lieven the same day: '... they have triumphed over the greatest difficulties, foreign and domestic, that have ever confronted a government; and now they are going to be defeated by a woman.'[33]

The outcome was more a draw than a defeat. After the failure of last-minute efforts to find a compromise, the Cabinet decided to proceed against the Queen by way of a Bill of Pains and Penalties (a parliamentary device for punishing someone without a legal trial). The bill, introduced by Liverpool in the House of Lords, was based upon evidence which, according to a committee of the Lords, attributed to the Queen 'conduct ... of the most licentious character'. Castlereagh felt that the public trial of the Queen – since that was what the bill amounted to – was a calamity, but he and his colleagues had done all they could to prevent it and must now brazen it out. 'The public mind is still much poisoned', he loftily informed Metternich: 'but truth never fails in this country finally to triumph.'[34]

In the meantime the coronation was postponed, since it was felt unwise to crown a king and divorce a queen at the same time. Castlereagh reluctantly agreed that this was a sensible decision, 'but it has sadly stuck in my stomach from the indecency of her Majesty's conduct'. He was also considerably pained by the conduct of the King, who insisted on having his new favourite, Lady Conyngham, and her husband to stay at the Cottage in Windsor Park, and walked out publicly with the lady every day. 'Never', lamented Castlereagh, 'was such an unfortunate infatuation at his age and in his position.'[35]

The Queen's 'trial' in the House of Lords began in mid-August, and it was the end of October before the prosecution and defence had finished arguing over the sordid and intimate details of her life abroad.* By that time, few doubts about her guilt remained, but many peers had doubts about the morality and expediency of the bill. The majority for the second reading on November 6 was only twenty-eight, much less than the Cabinet had hoped, but enough, they felt, to establish the

---

*During the 'trial' the Queen elected to move into a house in St James's Square. Castlereagh told Mme Lieven 'that it would not disturb him in the least, except that the mob might begin to pull down his house'. But he was persuaded to move out in order to avoid rioting for which he might be held responsible. He sent Emily down to Cray and moved a bed for himself into the Foreign Office. (Lieven. *Private Letters* pp.59, 62).

Queen's guilt. By this time, most of the ministers, not least Castlereagh, realised that the bill would have an extremely rough passage in the Commons, and when the majority in the Lords for the third reading of the bill fell to nine, the Cabinet decided to drop it.

Castlereagh was greatly relieved. The Queen now stood degraded, but not punished, he told Charles; and upon the whole 'my conviction is that in going further we should have fared worse'.[36] Most of his colleagues felt the same. The Queen, however, chose to consider herself vindicated and the country agreed with her. Bonfires were lighted, church bells were rung, and a few weeks later Caroline drove to St Paul's through a jubilant crowd to give thanks for her deliverance. The King, on the other hand, had been deprived of his deliverance, and for this disappointment he, of course, blamed his ministers. For weeks he brooded on the possibility of sacking them, at one point even setting down, in his own hand, the pros and cons of a change of government. Among the 'evils', he included a change in the foreign policy which had 'brought back everything to the country, and established a power and friendships with the sovereigns and gov[ernmen]ts of Europe, that England never before possessed'.[37] On the other hand, his ministers, he felt, had sacrificed both his feelings and his happiness, and he went so far as to sound out both the Whigs and Lord Grenville as possible replacements. Neither, however, was forthcoming; they needed, after all, Parliament's approval as well as the King's.

The ministers, for their part, might well have greeted their dismissal by such a hostile master with philosophic relief. And to add to what Liverpool called their 'sea of troubles', in the middle of December, Canning resigned. His former friendship with the Queen would not, he felt, allow him to remain a member of a government which still insisted on treating her as guilty. (The ministers were determined not to include the Queen in the Liturgy, or grant her a royal residence.) After Peel had refused to come back, Bragge-Bathurst was persuaded, much against his will, to take temporary charge of the India Board. Castlereagh and Arbuthnot would have liked to make a cautious approach to Lord Grenville (who had at last parted company with the Whigs), but the prime minister thought it a mistake to advertise their weakness by knocking on too many doors.[38]

To the diplomats in London, the government's weakness was already strikingly apparent, and the reports they sent back to their own governments did not strengthen the Foreign Secretary's prestige and authority during a particularly troubled summer, autumn and winter of European diplomacy. Early in July, 1820, Naples followed Madrid's example, and with very little difficulty the army and local Carbonari forced King Ferdinand IV to accept the ultra-liberal Spanish constitution. In August a military revolt broke out in Oporto and by October the Regency ruling in Lisbon on behalf of King John (still in self-imposed exile in Brazil) had been supplanted by a revolutionary junta. For Castlereagh the Portuguese revolt was among the least of his worries. The predominance of British influence in Portugal was so much taken for granted by the other powers that when Castlereagh warned both the Allies and the Spanish liberals against any intervention in Lisbon, his warning was heeded. His aim was to persuade King John IV, for whom he had small respect, to return at once and settle as best he could with the Portuguese liberals. To push the king towards compromise, he told the British minister in Lisbon to assure him that he could expect no outside intervention, either by the European powers, or by Britain, whose long-standing guarantee of Portugal covered invasion from outside but not internal revolution.[39]*

In Castlereagh's view, the rising in Naples had less justification on grounds of misrule than those in Spain and Portugal. It was also more dangerous, because sparks fanned by the Carbonari and other secret societies might start conflagrations throughout the Italian peninsula. Like most of his contemporaries, he did not take Italian nationalism seriously, and believed that Austria would be entirely justified in intervening in Naples, preferably not just to restore the status quo, but to replace the extreme Spanish constitution by a more moderate one. What he wanted above all to avoid was a joint police operation by the Allied powers. Austria's local interests made 'her interference both more natural, more justifiable and less odious than ... interference ... upon abstract and consequently more controversial grounds by powers less directly menaced'.[40]

He was of course thinking particularly of the Tsar. Alexander's liberal leanings, enthusiastically encouraged by his Greek foreign minister, Capodistria, were gradually being replaced by alarm at the spread of revolutionary activity in Europe. Still hankering after intervention in Spain, he proposed an October summit meeting at Troppau in Silesia. It would discuss the revolutionary danger in general

---

*After much dithering, King John at last sailed from Rio in April 1821. On his arrival in Portugal he was obliged to submit to the newly-elected Cortes. A year later, his son, Dom Pedro, whom he had left behind as his regent in Brazil, declared his independence.

as well as joint measures against Naples. Metternich would much rather deal with Naples without outside aid, as Castlereagh was privately urging him to do. But Castlereagh refused to give public support to unilateral Austrian action because that would be tantamount to subscribing to theories of collective intervention in which he did not believe. So Metternich, bereft of open British backing, felt he could not risk a breach with Russia, and eventually agreed to a meeting at Troppau on the Tsar's terms.

This placed Castlereagh in a painful dilemma. It was difficult to participate in a conference when he strongly disapproved of its aims and feared it might lead to commitments which neither he nor Parliament could accept. On the other hand, he was desperately anxious not to advertise a breach in the Alliance. In the end, the Cabinet decided that Stewart should attend, but as an observer only. But even an observer, Castlereagh warned Lieven, could remain at Troppau only if the Tsar and his foreign minister refrained from issuing high-sounding declarations whose only practical effect would be to outrage British opinion. 'The more Russia wishes to transport us to the heights, the further we must descend into the plain.'[41]

At Troppau, Metternich at any rate kept his feet firmly on the plain. The conference was very much an Austro-Russian affair. The Prussians danced to whatever tune Metternich chose to play, and the French had decided to follow the British example and send only a couple of (mutually hostile) observers. Metternich's chief preoccupation at Troppau was not so much Naples as his struggle with Capodistria, whose influence was already on the wane, for control of the Tsar's mind. Capodistria accepted Alexander's enthusiasm for collective intervention, but wanted to use it to install moderate constitutions. To Metternich, on the other hand, all constitutions were anathema, and repression the only remedy for revolution. He had little sympathy for Alexander's yearning for cloudy declarations of moral solidarity and collective intervention, but was ready to pay lip service to them if that was the only way to commit the Tsar firmly to the preservation of the status quo. He might have conceded less, if sure of British backing. But the reports from London early in November (after the Queen's 'trial') spoke of the government's imminent demise.

The upshot of the Troppau conference was that Metternich succeeded in gradually establishing a dominant influence over the Tsar. But on Naples he had to accept a compromise which, however much he made light of it afterwards, widened the gap opening up between Britain and the rest of the Alliance. In a 'preliminary Protocol', the Allied powers affirmed their determination to intervene whenever they deemed that an illegal change in a state threatened its neighbours. With regard to Naples, the Austrian army was authorised to occupy the country, but it was to be accompanied by Allied representatives, and the King of Naples was to be invited to meet the Allied sovereigns at Laibach to discuss the future of his kingdom.

From most of the crucial discussions at Troppau the English and French observers were excluded. But in London Castlereagh felt which way the wind was blowing much more promptly than his brother on the spot. Before the text of the Protocol arrived on his desk, he was already expostulating with the Russian and Austrian ambassadors and sending critical dispatches to Stewart. To Lieven he flatly denounced the Allies' claim to judge and condemn the actions of other states as 'a precedent dangerous to the liberties of the world'.[42] And after seeing the Protocol he told the ambassador he had never so much regretted not being with the Tsar – so convinced was he that he was right, he felt sure he could get Alexander to agree with him.[43] Castlereagh's strongest card in dealing with foreign statesmen had always been his powers of personal persuasion, and now he could not play it. Instead, he had to rely on diplomatic broadsides sent to Stewart for transmission to Alexander and Metternich. But his arguments had little effect. The Allies dropped the offending Protocol, but soon afterwards produced a diplomatic circular which not only was scarcely less objectionable, but attempted to implicate Britain (and France) in the decisions taken at Troppau. This supposedly confidential document was widely leaked, and when it was summarised in the *Morning Chronicle* and reprinted by the rest of the English press, Castlereagh immediately prepared a counterblast, firmly restating the British position. This celebrated dispatch, dated January 19, 1821, caused Metternich for once to lose his composure. He told Stewart it would have been better if England had kept out of the conference altogether – to which Castlereagh's brother promptly retorted that England was only there because it had been urged so strongly to go.[44] But liberals throughout Europe were delighted by Castlereagh's circular. When it was read out to the Assembly at Naples, it was received with applause and cries of *Viva l'Inghilterra*.

The applause was premature. When King Ferdinand met the rulers of Russia, Austria and Prussia at Laibach in January 1821, he repudiated the oath he had taken in Naples to uphold the constitution, and insisted on replacing it by one which even Metternich felt was too blatantly a sham. But the Austrian Chancellor accepted it, and set in train an invasion of Naples by Austrian troops. The Neapolitan forces were routed at Rieti on March 7, and on the 24th the Austrians entered the city of Naples. In the same month, a military revolt in Piedmont quickly fizzled out after a show of strength by the Austrian army, backed by 90,000 Russian troops. Henceforward, Metternich's sway over Italy (and Germany) was unchallenged.

Castlereagh might possibly have intervened at Troppau and Laibach with more effect if his Allies had believed he meant what he said. But they assumed his disapproval was the result of parliamentary pressure and his government's weakness. He always placed such emphasis on the constraints imposed by domestic opinion that it was easy for wishful-thinking foreign diplomats to assume that he was constrained against his will, especially as he continued to insist on his devotion to the Alliance. His heart bled, he told Lieven, when he had to criticise the Troppau Protocol so strongly.[45] The 'cordiality and harmony of the Alliance' on all other matters must, he instructed British diplomats abroad, be firmly emphasised.[46] In the House of Commons he strongly defended the Austrian intervention in Naples;[47] and when the eastern Allies closed their Laibach conference with a self-justificatory declaration, he managed to combine categoric disapproval of the sentiments expressed in the declaration, with a warm defence of the Allied sovereigns who had issued it.[48] But when he heard that Metternich was assuming that the government would change its foreign policy after it had overcome its domestic difficulties, he assured Stewart that such a misconception could only lead to a separation that they all wanted to avoid.[49]

There is no reason to suppose that if he had had an entirely free hand, Castlereagh would have been any less critical of the Allies for setting themselves up as 'the armed guardians of all thrones'. On the contrary, he believed that an interventionist policy was objectionable in theory and unworkable in practice. Europe in 1821 could not be treated as the Allies had treated France in the special circumstances of November 1815. Castlereagh realised that times had changed, and that the Allies differed in outlook, interests and institutions. But he still yearned to preserve the system of intimate consultation that had served them so well in 1814–15. He found it hard to recognise that this 'concert' had little chance of flourishing without the unity imposed by the struggle against Napoleon.

CHAPTER XVI

The enemy within
1821—22

When Parliament reassembled on January 23, 1821, the first issue to be settled was the future of the Queen. It turned out to be much less difficult than the ministers had feared. Castlereagh's unexpected announcement that the government intended to take no further proceedings against her took the wind out of the Opposition's sails; and when she decided to accept the government's offer of an annuity of £50,000, her Whig adherents rapidly lost all interest in her. So too did the general public. The King, on the other hand, began – rather unaccountably – to rise in popular estimation. Instead of hardly daring to show his face in his capital, he found himself greeted with enthusiastic applause when he visited the theatre.

The King's new-found popularity raised his spirits, but did not remove his discontent with his ministers. They had failed to get him a divorce, his wife was still in London, and it was not immediately apparent how rapidly she was losing her nuisance value. (In March she threatened to appear at a royal Drawing Room to present a petition for her inclusion in the Liturgy.) Moreover, the King found his prime minister's blundering, nervous, rather irritable manner intolerably tiresome. At Brighton towards the end of February, he called Liverpool all kinds of disrespectful names, and wished that either Sidmouth or Wellington could take his place. According to Mrs Arbuthnot, the King was such a blockhead that nobody minded what he said.[1] But it was difficult for Liverpool not to mind, even after hearing only an expurgated account of what had passed. In April he made his relations with the King even worse by flatly (and rightly) refusing to appoint a protégé of Lady Conyngham's to a vacant canonry at Windsor. He was strongly supported by Sidmouth and Castlereagh, and eventually, with a very bad grace, the King gave way.

The royal infatuation with Lady Conyngham was a great trial to the government because she favoured the Whigs and stirred the King up against his ministers. It was a particular trial to Castlereagh because she had quarrelled violently with his wife. This caused a marked coolness between the King and Emily, although Castlereagh assured Mrs

Arbuthnot that the King's manner to him had not changed. But presumably the two women's quarrel must have cast a shade over his relations with the King, if only because it caused him to be excluded, along with his wife, from the King's intimate circle. It certainly did not make his life any easier that summer. Twice at least he told Mrs Arbuthnot he 'wished he could slip his neck out of the collar and have done with the whole thing'.[2]

He was referring particularly to the endless discussions about Cabinet changes. In the Commons the government seemed more secure than for some time past; it had settled the Queen and successfully repelled attacks on Castlereagh's relations with the European powers. The Whigs were divided and demoralised, and Tierney had thrown up the leadership of the party. The King might hobnob with unofficial advisers, and make his ministers' lives miserable in all sorts of ways. But if they stuck together and continued to carry Parliament with them, it would be difficult for him to turn them out. How long, however, could the government maintain itself in the Commons when the Treasury front bench so conspicuously lacked what Croker called the essential ingredient of 'the gift of the gab'? Without Peel or Canning, the front bench was quite incapable of giving Castlereagh effective debating support against the constant guerrilla warfare of the more extreme Whigs. This might not always matter, but it told in the long run. No wonder Castlereagh described his parliamentary labours that session as 'difficult to endure'.[3]

Yet, curiously enough, he rejected the relief offered him. Liverpool proposed that Peel should succeed Vansittart as Chancellor of the Exchequer; Vansittart should take over the Board of Control, temporarily in Bragge-Bathurst's charge; Canning should replace Melville at the Admiralty; and Melville should take over the Home Office from Sidmouth, who said he wanted to retire. These changes had first been proposed in March and were apparently acceptable to all those involved. But Castlereagh took strong exception to Peel becoming Chancellor of the Exchequer, claiming that this would 'make an opposition' to himself in the Commons.[4] Neither this nor any other of Castlereagh's objections was at all convincing, and most were extremely unfair to Peel. But when Liverpool raised the matter again two months later, Castlereagh's objections to Peel as Chancellor were just as strong.* By that time the King's extreme aversion to bringing back Canning had created an even

---

*In April 1821, after the death of his father, Castlereagh became the 2nd Marquess of Londonderry. In this book he will continue to be given the name by which he is usually known.

greater difficulty, and the whole plan was dropped.*

Surprisingly, the session ended on a more cheerful note, with the Opposition exuding good humour and Castlereagh rejoicing that they had receded from the 'political and constitutional Utopia which they had originally set up'.[5] Arbuthnot claimed that Castlereagh had done wonders and that his reputation stood very high indeed.[6] Arbuthnot was an admirer of Castlereagh's; but he was also exceptionally well-informed about parliamentary feeling.

The King's postponed coronation took place on July 19, and early in August he set out on a state visit to Ireland, with Sidmouth and Castlereagh as ministers in attendance. Castlereagh travelled by coach to join the royal yacht at Holyhead. Throughout his journey large crowds gave him a warm welcome. It was the same surprising change in public sentiment as had been shown at the coronation, where Castlereagh's appearance in the procession had been greeted with repeated cheers. After a friendly reception at Shrewsbury, he wrote, rather complacently: 'It is impossible to have a more decisive proof that our friend John [Bull] has recovered his senses.'[7]

So, it seemed, had Paddy in Ireland. The royal visit began in a muted way because the unhappy Queen, who had knocked in vain on the doors of the Abbey while her husband was being crowned, chose this moment to fall dangerously ill. The news of her death reached the King just after Castlereagh had joined him at Holyhead. Neither King nor minister could pretend to be grieved. 'The King', reported Castlereagh from the royal yacht, 'has been very reasonable in lending himself to every proper arrangement on this occasion, and bears his *good fortune* with great propriety.'†[8]

After spending his first five days in Ireland in suitable seclusion, the King made his public entry into Dublin on August 17. He received a warm and enthusiastic welcome – partly perhaps because of a hope that he might bring Catholic emancipation with him. It was a delightful surprise, and the King responded wholeheartedly with the genial charm

---

*In his biography of Peel, Professor Gash suggests that '... perhaps the true explanation of his [Castlereagh's] otherwise not easily comprehensible hostility to Peel is that his mind was already infected with the psychopathic distrust and persecution-mania that was to bring tragedy only a year later'. (*Mr. Secretary Peel*, p.291)

†Poor Sidmouth, who had gone on ahead to Dublin, hurried back to Holyhead when he heard of the Queen's illness. He conferred briefly with Castlereagh and then returned to Dublin.

which in England he too rarely had occasion to display in public. The hatred and mistrust of centuries seemed suddenly to slip away, and throughout the visit George IV and the Irish people made much of each other. The euphoria rubbed off on to Castlereagh, who was warmly cheered in the streets of Dublin. 'What business has he here?', one Dubliner was reported to have remarked. 'He brought about the union.' To which another replied: 'Never mind that, honey, he has brought us the King.'[9] Castlereagh himself found everything 'perfect'. 'I have not seen a drunken man in the streets. I have not heard an unkind word from a single individual, and yet I have mixed unsparingly with the people ...'[10] He professed not to care whether he himself was popular or unpopular. But he did care about his country's reputation, and when he got back to England he told Mrs Arbuthnot that 'he had felt proud of his country when he had witnessed their [the Irish] order and good conduct'.[11] It may have sounded naive, but it came from his heart. He never saw Ireland again.

The King returned from his Irish junketings more incensed than ever with his prime minister. Liverpool had refused to appoint Lady Conyngham's husband to an important post in the royal Household. He continued to insist that Canning ought to be brought back into the Cabinet. And as a last straw, rioting had broken out when the Queen's coffin was being carried through London, and the King blamed Liverpool for mishandling the arrangements. The Cabinet apprehensively awaited a showdown when the King returned. But he had promised to visit his Hanoverian subjects that autumn, and after mercilessly snubbing his prime minister, he decided to let the political crisis simmer until his return. On September 24, he again embarked on his travels, taking his Foreign Secretary, as minister in attendance, with him.

Castlereagh set off on his obligatory journey to Hanover preoccupied by a problem that had been looming all the summer. In March 1821 Alexander Ypsilantis, a former aide-de-camp of the Tsar, led a revolt against Turkish rule in the Danubian province of Moldavia. The largely Romanian population gave him little support and the revolt quickly fizzled out. But a few weeks later, Bishop Germanos, the Metropolitan of Patras, raised the flag of revolt in the Peloponnese. By the end of April, the rising had spread to the Greek islands and parts of northern and central Greece. The Greeks fought with great courage and ferocity, and the Turks retaliated ruthlessly, massacring Greek communities in

Asia Minor and hanging the Greek Patriarch and several of his bishops outside the cathedral in Constantinople. By the summer, what had begun as a national rising had become a holy war as well.

For nearly fifty years, Russia had had treaty rights allowing it to assume a vague protectorate over orthodox Christians in the Ottoman empire, and the Greeks, who had been working underground against Turkish rule, confidently supposed that a national rising would enjoy Russian support. The Tsar, however, was at Laibach when he heard of the Moldavian rising. With his mind full of his anti-revolutionary crusade, and Metternich at his elbow, he promptly condemned Ypsilantis's enterprise, and even undertook not to take any action against the Turks without first consulting his Allies. But throughout the summer at St Petersburg, Alexander's self-denying ordinance came under increasing strain. The Russians already had a long list of grievances against the Porte, and it was soon clear that the Greek revolt, unlike the Moldavian, was not just a flash in the pan. The reports of Turkish reprisals stimulated Alexander's genuine sense of duty towards his fellow Christians, and he again began to listen sympathetically to his Greek minister. Capodistria's pleas for intervention were supported by many of those around the Tsar, as well as by a bellicose public opinion. In July an extremely stiff ultimatum was presented to the Porte, and when it expired, the Russian ambassador, Baron Stroganov, broke off relations, escaping with his life only through the energetic intervention of his British colleague, Lord Strangford.

To Castlereagh, the crisis was a threat both to the European order and to British interests. If the Tsar's armies overran the huge, decrepit Ottoman empire, the European balance would be upset, the Alliance would be in ruins and Britain's control of the eastern Mediterranean would be seriously threatened.* As soon as Parliament rose in July 1821, he composed a personal letter to the Tsar in which an appeal not to endanger the European order by intervening in Turkey was combined with a firm declaration that the Alliance was alive and well, its value and obligations unimpaired by the recent unfortunate divergences over Italian affairs. In other words, having earlier in the year distanced himself from the Alliance in the name of non-intervention, Castlereagh now embraced it, also in the name of non-intervention. He described the Greek revolt as part of the 'organised spirit of insurrection' that was erupting all over Europe wherever governments were too feeble to stop

*At Vienna in 1815, Castlereagh had suggested that the Ottoman empire should be included in a European guarantee, but neither the Turks nor anyone else had shown any enthusiasm for the idea.

it, and which must be put down if the European order was to be preserved.[12] He believed this was the argument most likely to appeal to Alexander, but he did not believe it was the whole truth about the Greeks – 'the descendants of those in admiration of whom we have been educated'. He could not shut his eyes to their sufferings, and he felt the strongest desire that 'the hand of time and of providence' might bring them relief. But he simply did not feel it was his duty, as a statesman, to support any scheme for 'new-modelling' the position of the Greeks 'at the hazard of all the destructive confusion and disunion which such an attempt may lead to, not only within Turkey but in Europe'. He pinned his hopes for the Greeks on 'the spirit of rational improvement which cannot fail to propagate itself in the present state of mankind, and of the world', but in Greece had been arrested by the 'ill-advised' revolt.[13] It was a limited, uninspiring attitude. But Castlereagh was no more a crusader than he was an oppressor.

Metternich was also alarmed at the prospect of a Russo-Turkish war, and had been doing his best to deter the Tsar by sending him innumerable embroideries on the theme of the ubiquitous revolutionary danger. The time had come, he felt, to look to his links with London, slightly frayed by Castlereagh's strictures on the Troppau-Laibach meetings. Castlereagh was equally anxious for a meeting, and urged Metternich to join the royal party at Hanover. Characteristically, he emphasised the importance of 'an unreserved explanation between us of all those nuances of sentiment and position, which necessarily subsist between even the states which agree the best ... and which are seldom intelligible when treated of on paper, but are easily seized when freely discussed in confidential conversation'.[14] Metternich, who also was addicted to confidential conversation, agreed to come, ostensibly – so as not to arouse the Tsar's suspicions – on a complimentary mission from the Austrian Emperor to the King of Hanover.

The King was delighted with his Hanoverian subjects' cordial welcome, but found them heavy going socially. So did Lord Clanwilliam, who, according to Castlereagh, 'rather scouts them in point of manners and *ton*'. Castlereagh himself was more tolerant. There were, he reported, some good-looking ladies, but unfortunately a 'flight of princes' had monopolised them all. 'I have, however, consoled myself with Madame de Decken, who flourished during the Seven Years' War and is now turned of 82, but has still more to say for herself than the youngest of them.'[15]

But his real consolation for the social deficiencies of Hanover was Metternich. It may be doubted whether they really – as Castlereagh envisaged – explored all the 'nuances' of their respective positions, but they re-established their personal rapport, and agreed without difficulty how to tackle the Turkish crisis. They would separate the insurgent Greeks from Russia's legitimate demands (in particular, for the protection of Orthodox Christians and the evacuation of Turkish troops from the Danubian principalities), and they would urge the Tsar to drop the first, and the Porte to grant the second. It all seemed very satisfactory. 'Metternich's visit went off miraculously', reported Castlereagh jubilantly to his brother. 'We never understood each other so well. It was a great treat to me, I am convinced to both...'[16] But it is difficult not to suspect that they gave themselves this treat by carefully ignoring the issues that divided them.

One issue not ignored at Hanover was the future of the British government. The change of scene had entirely failed to rid the King of his obsession with Lord Liverpool's allegedly 'monstrous' conduct and, with astonishing indiscretion, he complained bitterly and repeatedly to Metternich of all his ministers except Castlereagh. He had always liked his Foreign Secretary, and in the absence of Lady Conyngham (and Emily) there was perhaps nothing to restrain the 'feelings of warm affection and friendship' which he said, more than once, he felt for him.[17] The King was probably also impressed by Metternich, who, finding himself obliged to comment on English domestic politics, naturally emphasised the importance of keeping a Tory government in power, as well as his own personal esteem for the Foreign Secretary. According to Metternich, the King suggested that Castlereagh should take Liverpool's place; Castlereagh did not completely reject the idea as a last resort, but insisted that Liverpool (who was always threatening to resign) should really want to go.[18] In the end, the King declared he could not irritate his 'wounded feelings' by discussing the matter any longer. So he dumped it firmly in Castlereagh's lap, and told him to hurry back to England to begin consultations with the prime minister. The King, it seems, was not yet completely reconciled to keeping Liverpool. But he told Castlereagh he would not oppose Canning joining the Cabinet temporarily, if he replaced Lord Hastings as Governor-General of India as soon as possible; and he was prepared to compromise on the all-important (to him) issue of a post for Lord Conyngham in the royal Household.

Thus on both the domestic and the foreign front the Hanover visit seemed a success. Yet shortly before starting home, Castlereagh grumbled to his wife about the '*sad* trade' he followed, and confided that he felt 'very much out of sorts'. Maybe it was merely disappointment that he could no longer make a detour and meet Emily in Paris as they had planned. Maybe it was merely the after-effects of a very bad cold, caught, he supposed, in the chilly, long-empty house in which he and Clanwilliam had been quartered. (In his unassuming way, he added that he really had no right to complain, 'as they are very good to us, and do their best to make us comfortable'.) Whatever the reason, he was afflicted with the 'blue devils' – 'I don't know why, or when I have been so low.'[19] One would like to know how often the blue devils set upon him when Emily was with him – as she almost always was – to hear, rather than read, about them.

By the time the King had got back from Hanover, he had transformed himself from his government's most perverse and petulant critic into its warmest and most genial friend. Prompted by Castlereagh and Wellington, the prime minister responded as he should, the household question was settled and in due course Liverpool was cordially received by the King. Complete harmony has been restored, reported Castlereagh cheerfully to his brother. The King 'says he has *never* felt *so happy*', and 'such is the harmony of the day', he will not refuse any political arrangements thought necessary to strengthen the government. With some wonderment, Castlereagh added, 'Such a changed man as the King you never saw'.[20]

By the end of the year, Peel had agreed to rejoin the government as Home Secretary (no objections from Castlereagh this time), while Sidmouth, at the King's special request, remained in the Cabinet without portfolio. Lord Wellesley had gone as Lord Lieutenant to Ireland, which was in the throes of a new bout of unrest, and the Grenvilles had been enticed back into the Tory fold, the bait including the Board of Control for a cousin, Charles Williams-Wynn. Pitt's party was reunited for the first time since his death. Of its leading members, only Canning was left out in the cold. In the Cabinet no one but Liverpool had felt really strongly about bringing him back; and eventually the prime minister had given way to the King's rooted dislike and his colleagues' indifference. Canning was left with only one alternative to the obscurity of the back benches: a glittering Indian exile. In March 1822, with Hastings's return definitely settled, Canning reluctantly agreed to take his place.

The session of Parliament which began on February 5, 1822 grappled with a variety of well-worn, interlinked economic and financial issues, which MPs loved to worry over, even though they might often have an imperfect grasp of the technicalities they were discussing. Dominating the debates was the subject of agricultural distress. It had been exhaustively discussed in the two previous sessions and by two select committees. But the agriculturalists were a persistent and powerful pressure group. Nicknamed the 'Dolterheads', they included members of both parties, as well as a large group of independent country gentlemen who usually supported the government.

The 1815 Corn Law prohibited the import of wheat until the price rose to 80s a quarter, which was considered a fair return for the farmer. But since 1815, the price of wheat had rarely risen so high, and in December 1820, after an exceptionally bountiful harvest, it dropped to 54s; in January 1822 it was less than 46s a quarter. Cheap bread, a boon to the industrial workers in the towns, was a disaster for all those whose income or wages came from the land. But instead of blaming overproduction for their plight, the agriculturists found fault with the mechanics of the Corn Law (although these had scarcely been brought into operation), criticised the deflationary effect of the recent return to cash payments and, above all, fulminated against the excessive burden of taxation caused by the government's alleged extravagance. That taxation was at the root of the country's ills was the profound belief of many, both inside and outside Parliament.

The ministers, who since the war had pared the government's income and expenditure heroically, denied that the farmers' difficulties were due to taxation, although they were at a loss to know what else to ascribe them to. They would have agreed with Castlereagh when he assured the Commons that the farmers could only hope for relief from 'the hand of Providence, from the due course of nature and from the uncontrollable operation of all those great laws and principles which govern the markets of the world'.[21] But they worked out some modest financial palliatives, managed to find a few more administrative economies and set up yet another committee on agricultural distress (of which Castlereagh was chairman). How much part Castlereagh played in the Cabinet discussions, we do not know. He was of course no specialist in these matters, but he had applied himself to David Ricardo's writings and conscientiously studied the operation of the Corn Law. On February 15, he treated the Commons to a mammoth survey of the government's financial and agricultural policies running to fifty pages of Hansard. The ministers' greatest fear was that a combination of Whigs and country gentlemen would force through tax concessions that would deprive the government of funds earmarked for repayment of the National Debt, thereby disastrously undermining the public credit. To all Pitt's disciples, his Sinking Fund, however open to criticism, was sacrosanct; to defend it, Castlereagh told the House, was a 'sacred cause'.

By the end of April, the government had managed to beat off all attacks, although sometimes only by a narrow margin. The brunt of the defence still fell on Castlereagh's shoulders. Apart from Peel, the new additions to the government turned out to be broken reeds, and the old members of the front bench too often remained either unwilling or unable to exert themselves. Wellington blamed the country gentlemen for the government's difficulties, complaining that they were treating it 'excessively ill'.[22] Castlereagh was more tolerant. After two close votes, he told Mrs Arbuthnot that the country gentlemen 'only give these votes occasionally to make a figure in the columns of the Opposition papers and please their constituents, and they trust to our good luck that their votes will only lessen not overturn our majority'.[23]

Early in May the government's majority was overturned. A Whig motion calculated to appeal to the country gentlemen's passion for retrenchment – it wanted one of the postmaster-generalships to be abolished – was passed by a majority of fifteen. A few days later, Castlereagh was forced to withdraw two resolutions based on the agriculture committee's report. His other resolutions, including one for a sliding scale of duties on corn imports, were accepted, but the debates were extremely acrimonious. 'We are at *daggers drawn* with all the country gentlemen', wrote Mrs Arbuthnot, 'they join the Opposition in the run that is made at offices and taxes.' In her opinion, they ought to be brought to their senses by giving them Lord Grey and the Whigs.[24]

On May 9, the Cabinet decided to threaten the Commons with this dreadful fate. The word went round that two forthcoming Opposition motions, both aimed at cutting down expenses in the diplomatic service, would be treated as a matter of confidence. The Whigs were furious, but the threat worked. Both motions were resoundingly defeated, and no further threat to the government's majority developed. But the Whigs persisted indefatigably with their harassing attacks, and it was August 6 before Parliament at last rose, and Castlereagh was free to prepare for another meeting with his European allies.

After his talks with Metternich at Hanover, Castlereagh had been fairly confident that war between Russia and Turkey could be averted, if he and Metternich exerted enough diplomatic pressure on the Tsar. But in the new year of 1822 he was not so sure. In St Petersburg, Capodistria seemed to be calling the tune, and from Constantinople Lord Strangford sent gloomy reports of the Turks' intransigence. In the middle of February, however, Alexander drew back from a war in which he realised he could not count on his Allies' support. By the end of April he had agreed to Metternich's suggestion that the whole Eastern question should be submitted to an Allied ministerial conference in Vienna. He was helped to this decision by the news that the Porte had at last succumbed to Strangford's pressure and agreed to evacuate the Danubian principalities. Presumably, he was also influenced by Castlereagh's unwavering refusal to be drawn into any joint action against the Turks, expressed sometimes in undiplomatically blunt language. Neither his colleagues nor the public would have supported Castlereagh in any other attitude. British opinion was violently anti-Russian. Only a few people yet felt any great enthusiasm for the Greeks; the London Committee was not formed until the next year, and Byron had scarcely begun to stir up philhellenic sentiment.

War in the east had been averted – at least until next year's campaigning season – but only apparently at the cost of a scarcely more formidable crisis in the west. Alexander, anxious perhaps to cover up his diplomatic retreat over Turkey, suddenly turned his attention to Spain and revived his plan for an Allied military intervention to rescue King Ferdinand from the liberal revolutionaries and the political turmoil which had engulfed the country for the past two years. Metternich's response was non-committal. Privately, he described the plan as utter nonsense, and feared that it might upset his recent rapprochement with Castlereagh. The Allies were due to meet at Verona in the autumn to survey the state of Italy. It was obvious that neither the Greek situation nor Spain would be excluded from the agenda, and Metternich was anxious not to have to face the Tsar alone. He urged Castlereagh at least to come to Vienna to discuss the most important European problems; if he did not wish to discuss Italian questions, they could be left for the Verona meeting, which he need not attend.[25] 'What force Russian policy has lost in the East', wrote Metternich, 'the [Russian] Emperor will attempt . . . to regain by greater activity in the West . . . If you fail, I shall be alone and the battle will become uneven.'[26]

If left to himself, Castlereagh would no doubt have accepted immediately such a tactful and pressing invitation. But it was nearly the end of July before his colleagues at last decided he could go, and he was able to tell Metternich that he would definitely be setting out about August 15, with his wife, and would stop for a few days in Paris on the way. (He was particularly anxious to probe the intention of the ultra-royalist French government whom he suspected of hankering after intervention in Spain.) He would, he assured Metternich, get to Vienna in good time for them to have preliminary private talks on the issues – 'so numerous and so very important' – confronting them.[27]

The Instructions which Castlereagh drew up for his own guidance and which were approved by the Cabinet, show that he intended to raise two matters which Metternich might not have thought so very important.[28] They concerned, not the putting down of rebellions, but the right policy towards rebels who (like the Greeks) might be successful, or (like the Spanish colonists in South America) had undoubtedly achieved success. In both cases, Castlereagh had established his own guidelines, but he wanted if possible to carry his Allies along with him. The outcome of the Greek revolt was still in doubt, but the Greeks were establishing their ascendancy at sea, they were holding their own in the Morea, and at Epidauros they had set up the fragile façade of a government. Britain was officially neutral between Greeks and Turks (which did not stop Castlereagh from sending a stinging protest to the Porte at the Chios massacre by Turkish troops). But by July 1822 he felt the Greeks had made enough progress for the British government to declare its readiness to grant belligerent rights to a *de facto* Greek government, and to offer its good offices in any negotiations with the Turks.

Between Spain and its former colonies, the time for negotiations was clearly past, and in Britain there was increasing pressure for recognition of the colonies, especially by the trading classes. Commercial recognition was in effect granted in May 1822 by the simple device of including the South Americans in legislation liberalising the Navigation Acts. When the question of diplomatic recognition was raised in the Commons towards the end of July, Castlereagh would not go further than to declare that the government was anxious 'to cultivate good understanding and friendly intercourse' with South America.[29] Privately, however, he believed that recognition was now a matter of time, not of principle, and in June he bluntly warned the Madrid government 'of the rapid progress of events, and of the danger of delay' in South America.[30] His attitude towards the new states was coloured by a preference for monarchical regimes, and a desire to co-operate with his European Allies on the manner and timing of recognition, without sacrificing Britain's right to act independently if necessary.

South America had been a familiar problem for years. Castlereagh saw his way on it reasonably clearly, and in the Instructions he wrote for himself, he gave it more space than any other issue. On Spain itself – the issue that was in fact to dominate the conference – he said little beyond reaffirming Britain's refusal to intervene. He must have realised how divisive the Spanish issue was likely to prove. But until he had a better idea of French intentions, and had discovered how seriously the Tsar was to be taken, it was difficult for him to see how to prevent Spain from fracturing the fragile unity of the Alliance as Naples had done the year before.

If Castlereagh had been in his usual good health and spirits, he would no doubt have faced the difficult diplomacy that lay ahead with his customary courage and equanimity. But he was not. Several times in recent months he had complained that he was sick of politics and the parliamentary grind. At the beginning of June he had astonished Mme Lieven by suddenly flying into a rage at some new example of Lady Conyngham's continuing hostility to him and his wife. Shortly afterwards, Mme Lieven reported that he looked 'ghastly' and had aged five years in a week. Moreover, he seemed to have got it into his head that intrigues were going on to replace him by Wellington. 'Why on earth', asked Mme Lieven, 'has Londonderry contracted these suspicions?'[31] He was seized with equally improbable suspicions against various MPs whose slack attendance he attributed to personal hostility to himself.[32] He was absent-minded, and sometimes forgot what he had just been saying. His nephew, Frederick Stewart, said after Castlereagh's death that he had 'certainly thought my poor Uncle unlike himself for a long time; so much was he altered in his way of speaking and doing anything'.[33]

Yet sometimes he was still his old cheerful self. Mme Lieven reported him to be 'radiant' when the prospects for his trip to Vienna had improved.[34] But by the beginning of August pleasure at the thought of seeing Metternich had been replaced by self-doubt and depression. He told Clanwilliam that he dreaded the responsibility of going to Verona, and suspected plots against him.[35] When the Cabinet met on August 7 to approve his Instructions, Castlereagh took no part in the discussions and, according to Wellington, seemed 'very low, out of spirits and unwell'.[36] At Cray, the next day, he wandered alone around the grounds and there was something 'so melancholy and dejected in his manner' that one of his staff joined him in order to try to cheer him up. But when asked whether he was not looking forward to his continental trip, Castlereagh drew his hand across his forehead and said, very slowly: 'At any other time I should like it very much, *but I am quite worn out here.*' And keeping his hand on his forehead, he added: 'Quite worn out – and this fresh load of responsibility is more than I can bear.'[37]

Next day, Castlereagh had a private audience with the King in London during which he broke down completely, wildly accusing himself of homosexual and every other sort of crime, and insisting that he must flee the country immediately. Eventually the King managed to calm him down and send him away, urging him to see his doctor at once.[38] Later that day, Castlereagh poured out a similar tale of woe to Wellington whom he had asked to come to him in St James's Square. He compared himself with the Bishop of Clogher, whose recent arrest on a charge of homosexual activities with a guardsman had caused a great stir in London. He alleged that Wellington had recently been cold to him and must therefore know about his crime. He also claimed that he had just been accosted by a stranger who told him that his horses had been brought up to London that morning from Cray so that he could flee the country at once. The duke assured him that he must be suffering under a delusion. Castlereagh summoned a servant and demanded to know who had ordered his horses to be brought up to town. When the man replied that they were still at Cray, Wellington exclaimed: 'There you see, it's as I said. From what you have said, I am bound to warn you that you cannot be in your right mind.' Castlereagh covered his face with his hands, and said: 'Well, since *you* say so, it must be so.'[39]

Wellington, who was due to set out that evening for the Netherlands, offered to stay behind with his friend. But Castlereagh refused lest it should arouse suspicion that something was wrong. So, after writing a note to Castlereagh's physician, Dr Bankhead, and another to warn the Arbuthnots, the duke set off on his journey. Not even the novelty of a crossing by steam packet could drive the thought of poor Castlereagh's plight from his thoughts, and next day he wrote to Mrs Arbuthnot from Calais: 'I cannot describe the impression it has made on me. To see a man with such a sober mind, who one would think could not be influenced by any illusion, in a state bordering on insanity is not calculated to raise one's opinion of the strength of the human mind.'[40]

The King also found it difficult to forget Castlereagh. Later on that Friday, the 9th, he sent him a note referring with tactful understatement to his 'state of feverishness', and begging him to see Dr Bankhead, or if he were away, his own doctor, Sir William Knighton.[41] Next day the King was due to begin a visit to Scotland, travelling by sea up to Edinburgh. Before embarking on the royal yacht at Woolwich, he summoned Liverpool and warned him that Castlereagh was so mad that he might try to take his own life and must not be left alone for a moment. Liverpool, assuming that the King, as so often, was exaggerating, merely sent a note to Castlereagh asking him to meet him in London after the weekend.[42] It was a sad stroke of fate that the two friends most acutely aware of Castlereagh's state, the King and the duke, who might by their presence or their inquiries, have brought him additional help that weekend, were both out of the country.

Dr Bankhead had treated Castlereagh for thirty years, believed he knew his 'peculiarities' intimately, and was not greatly alarmed by his illness.[43] He went immediately to Castlereagh in St James's Square on the evening of the 9th, had him cupped and then sent him down to Cray with Lady Castlereagh. He followed them himself the next afternoon, intending to remain at Cray for the rest of the weekend. He found his patient in bed, feverish, disturbed, forgetful, incoherent and morbidly suspicious. Bankhead treated him in the customary way with cooling drinks and aperients, while Emily locked away her husband's pistols, razors and any other object with which he might possibly hurt himself. On Sunday he became worse, talking wildly and incessantly of plots and conspiracies and his own crimes. After noticing his wife and his doctor talking together, he even accused them of conspiring against him. Yet no special watch was kept on him that night, apart from his wife, who was still sleeping with him.

About 7.30 next morning, August 12, Castlereagh sent his wife's maid, Mrs Robinson, to ask Bankhead to come to him. Emily went to her dressing room, and in the brief moment he was alone, Castlereagh rushed out of the bedroom into his own separate dressing room and seized a small knife which had been overlooked. When the doctor followed him seconds later, he saw Castlereagh standing with his back to him, his head raised to the ceiling and the knife clutched in his hand. Turning towards the doctor, he said: 'Bankhead, let me fall upon your arm: 'tis all over.' He fell into the doctor's arms, and as he slipped on to the floor, the blood gushed from a wound in his neck. He died instantly.[44]

Next day, the royal yacht, making a storm-tossed voyage up to Scotland, was driven to take shelter in Berwick Bay. From there the King sent Castlereagh a brief note, begging him not to set out on his continental journey until he felt really equal to it. 'Remember what importance your health is to the country, but above all things to me.'[45]

While the King was writing his note in Berwick Bay, an inquest was being held at Cray Farm. The jury went upstairs to inspect the body, left lying where it had fallen, examined Mrs Robinson and Dr Bankhead, and then decided to return their verdict. It did not seem a complicated case. The Marquess of Londonderry, 'being under a state of mental delusion' and not of sound mind, had killed himself by inflicting a mortal wound on his carotid artery.[46]

All Castlereagh's friends and colleagues were convinced that he had been driven insane by overwork and the strain of coping with two arduous jobs. Twice in the past, in 1801 and 1808, he had had very severe and rather mysterious illnesses which were both attributed to strain and overwork. (In neither case was there any suggestion of mental breakdown.) In 1822 he was also overworking, but no more, it would seem, than in many previous years, and in any case, physical and mental exhaustion do not usually on their own make a person kill himself. It was also rumoured at the time that Castlereagh had been driven to suicide not by mental derangement, but by anonymous letters accusing him of homosexual practices. This story was apparently put about by the wretched Dr Bankhead who, finding himself vilified and ostracised for allegedly neglecting his patient, took this way of exculpating himself. The story gained some support from Castlereagh's self-accusations and the blackmailing letters he is supposed to have shown the King. But, as we have seen, Castlereagh's mind was crammed full of delusions at this time. He accused others of plotting against him, and himself of committing various crimes. It would hardly be surprising if the Bishop of Clogher's misdeeds, so much the talk of the town, had sunk into Castlereagh's disordered mind and given rise to a new delusion.*

Castlereagh may, or may not, have been blackmailed, but it is neither the only – or perhaps the most probable – explanation for his suicide. His delusions, his feelings of persecution, his forgetfulness, his depression, his occasional outbursts – all his symptoms suggest, in the light of modern medical knowledge, that he was suffering from a severe psychotic depressive illness. The symptoms which contemporaries put down to overwork might equally well have been signs of the onset of a

---

*On August 3, 1822 the Arbuthnots raised the subject of anonymous letters with Castlereagh in connection with some that Arbuthnot had received. Two days later, Castlereagh told Mrs Arbuthnot, in a very emotional interview, that he had been receiving threatening letters ever since he had been seen going into a brothel some three years earlier. He then showed two letters to Mr Arbuthnot and the Attorney-General, one of which, according to Mrs Arbuthnot, mentioned 'a crime not to be named'. According to Mme Lieven, Castlereagh showed two similar (or the same) letters to the King during his last audience on the 9th. There is no evidence as to what these letters actually said (or even if the King really read them), as opposed to what Castlereagh, in his agitation, claimed that they said. According to an account published about thirty years later, Castlereagh was blackmailed after being tricked into going into a brothel by a 'woman' who turned out to be really a man. (For a full account, see *The Strange Death of Lord Castlereagh* by Montgomery Hyde.)

mental illness to which a man of his age (just 53) and reserved and tightly-controlled temperament would have been particularly vulnerable, especially after the death of his father, to whom he was devoted, the year before. If this was so, Castlereagh's enemy killed him ninety years before the disease could be accurately diagnosed, and another thirty years before it could be treated with any hope of success.*

He was buried in Westminster Abbey, between the graves of Pitt and Fox. The watching crowds were quiet and respectful, except for a few at the door of the Abbey, who raised a fierce cheer. According to the *Annual Register*, they were probably hired, and their behaviour excited disgust among the bystanders. But their shouts have been taken ever since as the final demonstration of Castlereagh's unpopularity. Those who welcomed his death would have rejoiced even more could they have heard Metternich lament it as a 'great misfortune'. 'The man is irreplaceable', he wrote, 'especially for me ... Castlereagh was the only person in his country who had experience in foreign affairs.'[47] Among the tributes from Castlereagh's own countrymen, two in particular stand out. The first came from Henry Brougham, perhaps his most formidable opponent in the Commons. 'Well! this is really a considerable event in point of size. Put all their other men together in one scale, and poor Castlereagh in the other – single he plainly weighed them down ... One can't help feeling a little for him, after being pitted against him for several years, pretty regularly. It is like losing a connection suddenly. Also, he was a *gentleman, and the only one amongst them*.'[48] The second, involuntary, tribute came from one of Castlereagh's servants at Cray, who, when asked if he had noticed any change in his master just before his death, replied: 'Yes, one day he spoke sharply to me.'[49]

*Dr W.D. Henry discusses Castlereagh's psychiatric illness in *The Practitioner*, Feb. 1970, Vol.204. Dr Henry points out that the death of a close relative 'is a well-known precipitating factor in depression'.

Abbreviations

C.C. Castlereagh Correspondence, 12 vols. Ed. 3rd Marquess of Londonderry
Cast. Mss. (Belfast) Castlereagh Manuscripts. Northern Ireland Public Record Office, Belfast
Cast. Mss. (Norwich) Castlereagh Manuscripts. Norfolk County Record Office, Norwich
Cast. Mss. (Durham) Castlereagh Manuscripts. Durham County Record Office, Durham
Hyde (1933) H. Montgomery Hyde, *The Rise of Castlereagh*
Hyde (1959) H. Montgomery Hyde, *The Strange Death of Lord Castlereagh*
Webster. I C. Webster, *The Foreign Policy of Castlereagh 1812–1815*
Webster. II C. Webster, *The Foreign Policy of Castlereagh 1815–1822*
Brit. Dip. C. Webster (ed), *British Diplomacy 1813–1815*
George III *The Later Correspondence of George III*, 5 vols. Ed. A. Aspinall
George IV *The Letters of George IV*, 3 vols. Ed. A. Aspinall
W.S.D. Wellington, *Supplementary Despatches*, 11 vols
W.N.D. Wellington, *Despatches*, new series, Vol. I
B.L. Add. Mss. British Library, Additional Manuscripts
PRO. FO. Public Record Office, Foreign Office
PRO. HO. Public Record Office, Home Office
PRO. WO. Public Record Office, War Office
India O.L. India Office Library

References

CHAPTER I

1. Hyde. *The Rise of Lord Castlereagh*. pp.16/17.
2. *Ibid.* p.37.
3. Young, A. *Tour in Ireland (1776–79)*. I. p.119 (1892 ed.).
4. Hyde (1933). p.38.
5. Young. *Tour in Ireland (1776–79)*. I. p.136.
6. W. Steele Dickson. *Narrative of Confinement and Exile.* p.14.
7. Charlemont. *Correspondence.* I. p.119.
8. Dickson. *Narrative.* p.14.
9. *Castlereagh Correspondence.* I. pp.4/5.
10. Hyde (1933). p.49.
11. Pratt Mss. U840.C.3.
12. *Ibid.* April 18, 1788.
13. *Ibid.*
14. Bolton. *The Passing of the Irish Act of Union.* p.43.
15. Ehrman. *The Younger Pitt.* p.200.
16. Gwynn. *Henry Grattan.* p.228.
17. Lecky. *History of Ireland.* III. p.79.
18. Gwynn. *Grattan.* p.240.
19. *Belfast News-Letter*, May 4/7, 1790.
20. *Ibid.*
21. Burke. *Correspondence.* VI. p.124. June 26, 1790 (Cambridge Univ. Press, 1967).
22. Hyde (1933). pp.64/5. July 21, 1790.
23. Dickson. *Narrative.* pp.20/1.
24. *Belfast News-Letter.* July 27/30, 1790.
25. Hyde (1933). pp.67/8.
26. Lecky. *Ireland.* III. p.6.
27. Hyde (1933). pp.65/6.

CHAPTER II

1. Hyde (1933). p.77. Jan. 23, 1791.
2. Dropmore Papers. II. p.28. Feb. 5, 1791.

REFERENCES

3. *Ibid.* p.36. Feb. 24, 1791. to Lord Grenville.
4. *Ibid.* p.33. Feb. 15, 1791.
5. *Ibid.* p.35. Feb. 22, 1791.
6. Hamwood Papers. p.274. to Lady E. Butler, June 25, 1791.
7. Charlemont. *Corr.* II. p.153. to Camden, Sept. 1, 1791.
8. *Ibid.* pp.166/73. Nov. 11, 1791.
9. Cast. Mss. (Belfast). D.3030.Q2. to Lord Bayham, Jan.10, 1792.
10. *Ibid.*
11. *Ibid.*
12. Hyde (1933). p.94. Feb. 27, 1792.
13. Cast. Mss. (Durham). D/LO/C.34. March (1792).
14. Hyde (1933). pp.92/3. Feb. 27, 1792.
15. Cast. Mss. (Belfast). to Lady E. Pratt (1792).
16. Pratt Mss. U840.C.161.
17. Lecky. *Ireland.* III. p.130. to Dundas, Jan. 9, 1792.
18. Alison. *Castlereagh & Stewart.* I. pp.12/14.
19. Charlemont. *Corr.* II. pp.243/4. to Haliday, June 23, 1794.
20. Pratt Mss. U840.C.161. Sept. 1, 1793.
21. Cast. Mss. (Belfast). D.3030.Q2. April 3, 1793.
22. *Ibid.* n.d.
23. *Ibid.* n.d.
24. *Ibid.* n.d.
25. Alison. *Castlereagh & Stewart.* I. pp.22/3. Sept. 25, 1793.
26. Londonderry. *Robert Stewart Viscount Castlereagh.* p.8.
27. Hyde (1933). p.113. Sept. 17, 1793.
28. *Ibid.* p.114. Sept. 25, 1793.
29. Cast. Mss. (Belfast). D.3030.Q2.
30. *Ibid.*
31. Cast. Mss. (Norwich). MC3/290/467.
32. Charlemont. *Corr.* II. p.264. to Haliday. July 26, 1795.
33. Hyde (1933). p.134. April 6, 1795.

CHAPTER III

1. Pratt Mss. U840.C.98. March 25, 1796.
2. *Ibid.*
3. Charlemont Mss. II. Royal Irish Academy, Dublin. August 13, 1796.
4. Charlemont. *Corr.* II. p.282. August 23, 1796.
5. Hyde (1933). pp.150/1.
6. *Ibid.* pp.154/5.
7. Cast. Mss. (Belfast). n.d.
8. Hyde (1933). p.165.

9. *Ibid.*
10. State Paper Office, Dublin. 620/18. Nov. 4, 1796.
11. Hyde (1933). pp.166/7.
12. Hyde (1933). p.169. & Cast. Mss. (Norwich). MC3/290/467x.
13. Hyde (1933). p.170.
14. *Ibid.* p.171. Dec. 25, 1796.
15. Cast. Mss. (Belfast). D.3030.Q2. to Charles Stewart, Jan. 14, 1797.
16. Cast. Mss. (Norwich). MC3/290/467x. Dec. 30, 1796, Jan. 4, 11, 12, 1797.
17. *Parliamentary Register of Ireland.* XVII. p.402.
18. Charlemont. *Corr.* II. p.300. Rev. E. Hudson, June 5, 1797.
19. *Ibid.* p.303. to Charlemont, July 13, 1797.
20. *Ibid.* p.306. to Charlemont, Oct. 6, 1797.
21. Hyde (1933). p.188. July 15, 1797.
22. *Ibid.* p.198.

CHAPTER IV

1. Lecky. *Ireland.* IV. pp.203/4.
2. Pakenham. *The Year of Liberty.* p.50.
3. *Ibid.* p.50.
4. *Ibid.* p.55.
5. PRO. HO. 100/75.
6. *Ibid.* March 19, 1798.
7. Hyde (1933). pp.208/9. March 23, 1798.
8. Pakenham. *The Year of Liberty.* p.65. (The following account of the rebellion is greatly indebted to this book.)
9. C.C.I. p.189. April 25, 1798.
10. Pakenham. p.76.
11. B.L. Add. Mss. 34,454. to Auckland, May 21, 1798.
12. *Ibid.* to Auckland, May 20, 1798.
13. Pakenham. p.99.
14. *Ibid.* p.123.
15. Lecky. *Ireland.* IV. p.331. May 26, 1798.
16. C.C.I. p.212. to Wickham, May 31, 1798.
17. Pakenham. p.164.
18. B.L. Add. Mss. 33,105.
19. B.L. Add. Mss. 34,454. to Auckland, May 29, 1798.
20. Pakenham. p.328.
21. *Ibid.* pp.334/5.
22. Cornwallis. *Correspondence.* II. p.385. Cornwallis to Ross, August 16, 1798.
23. *Ibid.* p.358. to Portland, July 8, 1798.

REFERENCES

24. *Ibid.* p.357. to Portland, July 8, 1798.
25. *Ibid.* p.356. to Ross, July 1, 1798.
26. Beresford. *Correspondence.* II. p.169. to Auckland, August 9, 1798.
27. B.L. Add. Mss. 34,454. to Auckland, Sept. 15, 1798.
28. C.C.I. p.219. to Wickham, June 12, 1798.
29. *Ibid.*
30. PRO. HO. 100/78. Sept. 17, 1798.
31. Cornwallis. *Corr.* II. p.357.
32. Pratt Mss. U840.C.98.
33. B.L. Add. Mss. 33,105. July 28, 1798.
34. Pakenham. p.290.
35. C.C.I. p.414. to Wickham, Oct. 29, 1798.
36. PRO. HO. 100/85. Castlereagh to Wickham, April 1, 1799.
37. C.C.I. p.446. to Wickham, Nov. 16, 1798.
38. Cast. Mss. (Belfast). n.d. D.3030.Q2.
39. A. Knox. *Remains.* IV. p.32.

CHAPTER V

1. Hyde (1933). pp.272/3.
2. Pratt Mss. U840.C.98. Oct. 4, 1798.
3. Buckingham. *Memoirs, George III.* II. p.399.
4. Cornwallis. *Corr.* II. p.439. to Portland, Nov. 20, 1798.
5. B.L. Add. Mss. 33,106. Sept. 26, 1798.
6. A. Knox. *Remains.* IV. p.32.
7. Cornwallis. *Corr.* III. p.310. to Ross, Dec. 12, 1800.
8. C.C.I. pp.431/2. Nov. 9, 1798.
9. Pratt Mss. U840.C.98.
10. Lecky. *Ireland.* V. p.135.
11. Cornwallis. *Corr.* II. p.365. July 20, 1798.
12. Hyde (1933). p.281. Oct. 4, 1798.
13. Cornwallis. *Corr.* II. p.416. Oct. 8, 1798.
14. PRO. Chatham Mss. 30/8/327. Oct. 22, 1798.
15. C.C.II. p.9. to Wickham, Nov. 19, 1798.
16. PRO. HO. 100/79. to Wickham, Nov. 30, 1798.
17. PRO. HO. 100/82. to Cornwallis, Dec. 17, 1978.
18. Buckingham. *Memoirs, George III.* II. p.441. Nov. 5, 1798 and p.426. Jan. 4, 1799.
19. Hyde (1933). p.287.
20. Cornwallis. *Corr.* III. p.27. to Wickham, Jan. 2, 1799.
21. C.C.II. p.81. to Portland, Jan. 2, 1799.
22. PRO. HO. 100/85. to Portland, Jan. 16, 1799.
23. B.L. Add. Mss. 33,106. to Pelham, Jan. 7, 1799.

CASTLEREAGH

24. C.C.II. p.81. Jan. 2, 1799.
25. Beresford. *Corr.* II, p.209. to Auckland, Feb. 6, 1799.
26. Bolton. *The Passing of the Irish Act of Union.* p.71. Nov. 9, 1798.
27. Cornwallis. *Corr.* III. p.39. to Ross, Jan. 21, 1799.
28. B.L. Add. Mss. 33,106. R. Griffith to Pelham, Jan. 15, 1799.
29. C.C.II. pp.82/3.
30. *Ibid.* p.113. Jan. 15, 1799.
31. *Ibid.* p.115. Jan. 16, 1799.
32. PRO. HO. 100/85. to Portland, Jan. 16, 1799.
33. Cornwallis. *Corr.* III. p.38. Jan. 16, 1799.
34. PRO. HO. 100/85. to Portland, Jan. 21, 1799.
35. Cornwallis. *Corr.* III. p.35. Jan. 11, 1799.
36. C.C.II. p.84. to Portland, Jan. 7, 1799.
37. Cornwallis. *Corr.* III. p.35. Jan. 11, 1799.
38. Bolton. *The Passing of the Irish Act of Union.* p.71.
39. *Ibid.* p.101.
40. C.C.II. p.143. to Portland, Jan. 28, 1799.
41. Beresford. *Corr.* II. p.194. to Auckland, Jan. 24, 1799.
42. Hyde (1933). p.298.
43. Wellesley Papers. I. p.85.
44. Hyde (1933). p.301.
45. Gilbert. *Documents Relating to Ireland, 1795–1804.* p.202. Shee to Pelham, Jan. 25, 1799.
46. C.C.II. pp.142/3. to Portland, Jan. 28, 1799.
47. Gilbert. *Documents.* p.200. Griffith to Pelham, Jan. 24, 1799.
48. PRO. HO. 100/85. Jan. 26, 1799.
49. *Ibid.* Castlereagh to Portland, Feb. 15, 1799.

CHAPTER VI

1. PRO. HO. 100/85. Jan. 23, 1799.
2. Pratt Mss. U840.C.81. to Camden, May 1, 1799.
3. C.C.II. pp.143/4. to Portland, Jan. 28, 1799; and pp.149/53. Castlereagh memorandum, Feb. 1, 1799.
4. Porritt. *The Unreformed House of Commons.* II. p.500.
5. Pratt Mss. U840.C.98. to Camden, July 17, 1799.
6. Bolton. *The Passing of the Irish Act of Union.* p.205/6.
7. Cornwallis. *Corr.* III. pp.100/1. to Ross, May 20, 1799.
8. Bolton. *The Passing of the Irish Act of Union.* p.220.
9. Pratt Mss. U840.C.98. to Camden, July 17, 1799.
10. *Ibid.* U840.C.81. to Camden, July 24, 1799.
11. *Ibid.* U840.C.98. to Camden, July 17, 1799.
12. PRO. HO. 100/87. to Portland, Sept. 4, 1799.

REFERENCES

13. C.C.IV. pp.8–12. Castlereagh to Pitt, Jan. 1, 1801.
14. PRO. HO. 100/89. Nov. 28, 1799.
15. Hyde (1933). pp.343/4.
16. Cornwallis. *Corr.* III. p.182. to Portland, Feb. 7, 1800.
17. PRO. HO. 100/93. to Portland, Jan. 20, 1800.
18. Cornwallis. *Corr.* III. p.177. to Ross, Feb. 4, 1800.
19. Lecky. *Ireland.* V. pp.360/8.
20. Cornwallis. *Corr.* III. p.182. Feb. 7, 1800.
21. *Ibid.* pp.182/3.
22. Grattan. *Speeches.* III. p.412.
23. PRO. HO. 100/93. March 17, 1800.
24. Cornwallis. *Corr.* III. p.211. to Portland, March 11, 1800.
25. Bolton. *The Passing of the Irish Act of Union.* p.195.
26. Cornwallis. *Corr.* III. p.206. to J. King, March 7, 1800.
27. PRO. HO. 100/93.
28. *Ibid.* to J. King, May 17, 1800.
29. *Ibid.* to J. King, May 20, 1800.
30. Cornwallis. *Corr.* III. p.242. Cooke to J. King, May 27, 1800.
31. Hyde (1933). p.358. to Portland, June 9, 1800.
32. Cornwallis. *Corr.* III. p.250. to J. King.
33. Hyde (1933). p.360.
34. C.C.III. p.340. June 25, 1800.
35. Cornwallis. *Corr.* III. pp.339/40. Feb. 19, 1801.
36. Lecky. *Ireland.* V. p.305, n.2.
37. Hyde (1933). p.361.
38. PRO. HO. 100/94. August 2, 1800.
39. Falkiner. *Studies in Irish History.* p.182.
40. Hansard. XXXVI. 404. May 9, 1817.
41. Hansard. XXXIV. 62/3. April 26, 1816.
42. Hyde (1933). p.349.
43. Colchester. *Correspondence.* I. p.406. to Abbot, August 15, 1802.
44. C.C.IV. p.400. n.d.
45. PRO. HO. 100/94. Dec. 1, 1800.
46. C.C.IV. pp.8–12.
47. *Ibid.* p.13. to Castlereagh, Jan. 2, 1801.
48. Holland Rose. *William Pitt and the Great War.* p.436.
49. Cornwallis. *Corr.* III. p.338. to his brother, the Bishop of Lichfield, Feb. 17, 1801.
50. Castlereagh Mss. (Durham). D/LO/C.436. Feb. 29, 1801.
51. C.C.IV. p.40. Feb. 9, 1801.

CASTLEREAGH

CHAPTER VII

1. Cast. Mss. (Belfast). D.3030.Q2. March 18, 1801.
2. Cornwallis. *Corr.* III. p.235. to Ross, May 18, 1800.
3. C.C.III. p.348. July 2, 1800.
4. *Ibid.* p.350. July 2, 1800.
5. Cast. Mss. (Norwich). MC3/291/467x.
6. Hyde (1933). p.386.
7. *Ibid.* pp.437/8.
8. *Ibid.* pp.400/1.
9. *Ibid.* pp.435/6.
10. Cast. Mss. (Belfast).
11. *Ibid.* D.3030.Q2.
12. State Paper Office, Dublin. 620/18/7.
13. C.C.IV. pp.243/4. to Wickham, Nov. 18, 1802.
14. State Paper Office, Dublin. 620/18/7.
15. India Office Library. Home Misc. 504. to Cornwallis, Nov. 19, 1802.
16. Scott. *Correspondence.* II. p.404. to David Scott, Sept. 13, 1802.
17. Wellesley. *Despatches & Correspondence in India.* III. pp.31/3. August 10, 1802.
18. India O.L. Home Misc. 504. Sept. 11, 1802.
19. *Ibid.* to Dundas, Sept. 11, 1802.
20. *Ibid.* to Cornwallis, Sept. 28, 1802.
21. Dropmore Papers. VII. p.177. H. Wellesley to Lord Wellesley, July 28, 1803.
22. Wellesley. *Despatches.* V. pp.302/18.
23. B.L. Add. Mss. 37, 283. May 27, 1804.
24. Wellesley. *Despatches.* III. p.92. Nov. 14, 1802.
25. *Ibid.* IV. pp.222/6. May 21, 1804.
26. Dropmore Papers. VII. p.348. to Lord Grenville.
27. Cornwallis. *Corr.* III. p.544. to Lake, August 30, 1805.
28. India O.L. Home Misc. 505. to Cornwallis, July 7, 1805.
29. *Ibid.* to Cornwallis, Sept. 10, 1805.
30. C.C.VI. p.19. Oct. 16, 1805.
31. R. Glover. *Peninsular Preparations.* p.19.
32. Dropmore Papers. VII. to Windham, Nov. 5, 1805.
33. C.C.VI. pp.43/4. Nov. 19, 1805.
34. *Ibid.* p.58. Nov. 28, 1805.
35. *Ibid.* p.68.
36. Holland Rose. *William Pitt and the Great War.* p.551.
37. C.C.VI. p.92.
38. *Ibid.* p.96.
39. Dropmore Papers. VII. p.320. to Lord Grenville, Dec. 2, 1805.
40. PRO. WO. 6/13. to Cathcart, Jan. 10, 1806.
41. *Ibid.* to Cathcart.

REFERENCES

42. C.C.VI. pp.125/6. Jan. 19, 1806.
43. *The Later Correspondence of George III.* IV. pp.367/9.
44. Mackesy. *The War in the Mediterranean. 1803–1810.* p.86.
45. Reilly. *Pitt the Younger.* p.341.

CHAPTER VIII

1. B.L. Add. Mss. 49,193. to Camden, Feb. 6, 1806.
2. Lonsdale Papers. p.226. to Lord Lowther, Nov. 30, 1806.
3. *Ibid.* pp.203/4. to Lowther, Oct. 8, 1806.
4. Dropmore Papers. IX. p.441. July 27, 1806.
5. *George III.* IV. p.xxxiv.
6. Hansard. VIII. 725/45. Feb. 12, 1807.
7. Wilberforce. *Life.* IV. p.320.
8. Gray. *Spencer Perceval.* p.75.
9. *Ibid.* p.96.
10. C.C.VIII. p.50. Memo. to Cabinet. March 1807.
11. *Ibid.* p.54. Memo. to Cabinet. May 12, 1807.
12. B.L. Add. Mss. 38,242. Dec. 28, 1807.
13. Wellington. *Supplementary Despatches.* V. p.22. April 25, 1807.
14. C.C.VII. pp. 314/24. Memo. to Cabinet. May 1, 1807.
15. Fortescue. *A History of the British Army.* VI. p.39.
16. *Ibid.* pp.53/4.
17. *George III.* IV. p.588. to Castlereagh, June 2, 1807.
18. PRO. WO. 6/56. April 25, 1807.
19. *Ibid.* May 8 & 17, 1807.
20. Moore. *Diary.* II. p.180. July 5, 1807.
21. PRO. WO. 6/56.
22. Moore. *Diary.* II. p.177. July 3, 1807.
23. *George III.* IV. p.583. May 23, 1807.
24. Fortescue. *British Army.* VI. p.35.
25. *George III.* IV. p.590. to Castlereagh, June 11, 1807.
26. *Ibid.* p.604. Mulgrave to the King, July 14, 1807.
27. Fortescue. *British Army.* VI. p.60.
28. *George III.* IV. p.607. to Castlereagh, July 18, 1807.
29. C.C.VI. p.184. Sept. 22, 1807.
30. *Ibid.* p.193. Castlereagh to the King, Oct. 9, 1807.
31. *George III.* IV. p.617. August 14, 1807.
32. C.C.VIII. p.90. to Hawkesbury, Oct. 8, 1807.
33. W.S.D. V. p.177. Nov.12, 1807.
34. Gray. *Spencer Perceval.* p.140.
35. *George III.* IV. p.645, n.1.
36. W.S.D. V. p.279. to Hawkesbury, Dec. 15, 1807.
37. *Ibid.*

CASTLEREAGH

38. C.C.VIII. p.98. Memo. to Cabinet. Dec. 21, 1807.
39. Ibid. p.97.
40. Mackesy. *The War in the Mediterranean.* p.263.
41. C.C.VIII. p.103.
42. *George III.* V. p.13. Castlereagh to the King, Jan. 30, 1808.
43. Fortescue. *British Army.* VI. pp.114/15.

CHAPTER IX

1. Glenbervie. *Diaries.* II. pp.12/13.
2. *George III.* V. p.15. Feb. 4, 1808.
3. Gray. *Spencer Perceval.* p.170.
4. Ibid. p.171.
5. Moore. *Diary.* II. pp.203/4. May 4, 1808.
6. PRO. WO. 6/42. April 20, 1808.
7. Moore. *Diary.* II. pp.205/6. May 20, 1808.
8. Ibid. p.220. June 25, 1808.
9. C.C.VI. p.230. April 29, 1808.
10. Moore. *Diary.* II. pp.242/3. July 23, 1808.
11. Ibid. pp.251/2. July 22 and 23, 1808.
12. Wellington. *Despatches.* IV. pp.30/1. July 15, 1808.
13. W.S.D. VI. p.95. to Duke of Richmond, August 1, 1808.
14. Ibid. p.125. Sept. 4, 1808.
15. Longford. *Wellington: The Years of the Sword.* p.156.
16. M. Glover. *Britannia Sickens.* p.136.
17. C.C.VI. p.410. August 23, 1808.
18. Ibid. p.439. to Castlereagh, Sept. 17, 1808.
19. Ibid. p.454. Sept. 26, 1808.
20. W.S.D. VI. p.175. Oct. 28, 1808.
21. Cast. Mss. (Belfast). D.3030/AA.Sept. 21, 1809.
22. W.S.D. VI. p.402. Oct. 14, 1809.
23. PRO. WO. 6/47.
24. Moore. *Diary.* II. p.261.
25. Ibid. p.272.
26. Hansard. XIII. cccxxx. Jan 3, 1809.
27. Moore. *Diary.* II. p.287.
28. Hansard. XII. 138.
29. *George III.* V. p.210. to the King, Feb. 25, 1809.
30. Hansard. XII. 41.
31. *George III.* V. p.263, n.1. to Duke of Richmond, March 1, 1809.
32. Ibid. p.278, n.2. to Stewart, May 12, 1809.
33. Hansard. XIV. 235/7. April 25, 1809.
34. *George III.* V. p.263, n.1.
35. Ibid. p.264n.

REFERENCES

36. *Ibid.* p.264n. to Duke of Rutland, April 20, 1809.
37. C.C.VII. pp.38/9. Feb. 27, 1809.
38. Wellington. *Despatches.* VII. pp.39/41. March 7, 1809.
39. W.S.D. VI. p.292. to J.C. Villiers, June 21, 1809.
40. C.C.VII. p.71. May 26, 1809.
41. Cast. Mss. (Belfast). D.3030.Q2. May 27, 1809.
42. C.C.VII. p.84. June 13, 1809.
43. *Ibid.* p.82.
44. Longford. *Wellington.* I. p.185. May 30, 1809.
45. C.C.VII. p.95. July 11, 1809.
46. Cast. Mss. (Belfast). D.3030.AA/2.
47. *Ibid.* D.3030.Q2. to Stewart, July 31, 1809.
48. PRO. Chatham Mss. 30/8/366. May 18, 1809.
49. *George III.* V. p.302.
50. Cast. Mss. (Belfast). D.3030.Q2. July 31, 1809.
51. *Ibid.*
52. *Ibid.*
53. *Ibid.* August 21, 1809.
54. PRO. WO. 1/191. August 7, 1809.
55. C.C.VI. p.302. to Castlereagh, August 11, 1809.
56. Hansard. XV. xli-xliii. to Castlereagh, August 29, 1809.
57. C.C.VI. p.189. to Hawkesbury, Oct. 1, 1807.
58. Hansard. XV. 78.
59. *Ibid.* lxx. Gen. Don to Liverpool, Nov. 3, 1809.
60. Bathurst Papers. p.101. to Bathurst, Sept. 8, 1809.
61. G. Rose. *Diaries.* II. p.422.
62. Walpole. *Spencer Perceval.* I. pp.347/50 (dated March 24, sent April 4).
63. Gray. *Spencer Perceval.* pp.226/7.
64. Cast. Mss. (Belfast) D.3030.Q2. Sept. 16, 1809.
65. *Annual Register.* 1809. pp.562/3.
66. Londonderry. *Robert Stewart.* pp.38/9. Sept. 21, 1809.
67. *Ibid.* pp.40/1. Oct. 3, 1809. to Lord Londonderry.
68. *Ibid.* pp.41/2. Sept. 22, 1809.
69. W.S.D. VI. pp.402/3. Oct. 14, 1809.
70. Walpole. *Spencer Perceval.* I. pp.347/50.
71. *George III.* V. p.380. Oct. 1, 1809.
72. Colchester. *Corr.* II. p.201. to Abbot, Sept. 12, 1809.
73. *George III.* V. p.379. Oct. 1, 1809.
74. W.S.D. V. p.86. to Castlereagh, August 25, 1809.
75. Hansard. XIV. 454. May 9, 1809.
76. Bathurst Papers. p.152. to Bathurst, Sept. 12, 1809.
77. *George III.* V. p.389n.
78. Cast. Mss. (Belfast).

CHAPTER X

1. Hansard. XV. 75/9. Jan. 23, 1810.
2. Creevey Papers. I. pp.122/3.
3. *George III.* V. p.505n.
4. Dudley. *Letters to Ivy.* p.91.
5. Cast. Mss. (Belfast). D.3030.Q2.
6. *Ibid.* D.3030.AA/15. to Stewart, July 11, 1810.
7. *Ibid.* D.3030.Q2.
8. *Ibid.* July 18, 1810.
9. *Ibid.*
10. *Ibid.* to Stewart, August 7, 1810.
11. *Ibid.* to Cooke, Sept. 7, 1810.
12. W.S.D. VI. p.595. Sept. 19, 1810.
13. Walpole. *Spencer Perceval.* II. pp.152/3.
14. Cast. Mss. (Belfast). D.3030.Q2. Nov. 4, 1809.
15. *Ibid.* Jan. 15, 1811.
16. *Ibid.*
17. George, Prince of Wales. *Correspondence.* VIII. pp.306/7.
18. Cast. Mss. (Belfast). D3030.Q2 Castlereagh to Stewart, Jan. 29, 1812.
19. Gray. *Spencer Perceval.* p.448.
20. Cast. Mss. (Belfast). D.3030.Q2. April 8, 1812.
21. Hansard. XXIII. 174. May 12, 1812.
22. B.L. Add. Mss. 38,191. Castlereagh to Regent, May 15, 1812.
23. Dropmore Papers. X. p.261. to Lord Grenville, May 20, 1812.
24. W.S.D. VII. p.343. June 9, 1812.
25. Hansard. XXIII. 461. June 11, 1812.
26. Wilberforce. *Life.* IV. p.35.
27. Perkins. *Prologue to War.* p.401.
28. Perkins. *Castlereagh and Adams.* p.12.
29. Hansard. XXIII. 963. July 10, 1812.
30. Parker. *Sir Robert Peel.* I. pp.86/7.
31. *George IV. Letters 1812–1830.* I. p.130n.
32. Stapleton. *George Canning & his Times.* p.208.
33. Dropmore Papers. X. p.290. to Lord Grenville.
34. Yonge. *Liverpool.* I. p.417. to Liverpool, July 26, 1812.
35. Granville Leveson-Gower. *Private Correspondence.* II. p.443. Lady Bessborough to G. L-G. (London 1916).

CHAPTER XI

1. C.C.VIII. p.313. to Cathcart, Jan. 22, 1813.
2. *Ibid.* pp.355/6. to Cathcart, April 8, 1813.

REFERENCES

3. Lane-Poole. *Stratford Canning*. I. p.212.
4. C.C.IX. p.20. Col. Cooke to Sir C. Stuart, May 22, 1813.
5. C.C.VIII. p.304. Jan. 15, 1813.
6. *Ibid.* p.383. April 28, 1813.
7. Hansard. XXVI. 774. June 18, 1813.
8. C.C.VIII. p.356. April 8, 1813.
9. W.S.D. VII. p.503. Dec. 22, 1812.
10. Croker. *Correspondence & Diaries*. I. p.347.
11. Webster. *The Foreign Policy of Castlereagh 1812–1815*. pp.126/7.
12. Jackson. *The Bath Archives*. II. p.59.
13. *Ibid.* p.82.
14. *Ibid.* pp.163/4.
15. C.C.VIII. p.408. June 22, 1813.
16. *Ibid.* p.411. June 30, 1813.
17. C.C.IX. p.45. Sept. 1, 1813.
18. *Ibid.* p.46. Sept. 1, 1813.
19. *Ibid.* p.23. June 6, 1813.
20. Lady Frances Balfour. *Life of 4th Earl of Aberdeen*. I. p.70. Aberdeen to Abercorn, July 16, 1813.
21. Dudley. *Letters to Ivy*. p.213.
22. Palmer. *Metternich*. p.107.
23. Balfour. *Aberdeen*. I. p.105. to Castlereagh, Sept. 23, 1813.
24. *Ibid.* p.113. Oct. 9, 1813.
25. Webster (Ed.). *British Diplomacy 1813–1815*. pp.24/5.
26. *Ibid.* p.34.
27. *Ibid.* p.105. Oct. 15, 1813.
28. *Ibid.* p.86. to Castlereagh, Oct. 21, 1813.
29. *Ibid.* pp.13/14. to Cathcart, July 13, 1813.
30. Webster. I. p.174.
31. Balfour. *Aberdeen*. I. pp.153/5, and 163. Aberdeen to Castlereagh, Nov. 12 and 25, 1813.
32. *Brit. Dip.* pp.109/11.
33. *Ibid.* pp.88/91. Nov. 28, 1813.
34. Jackson. *Bath Archives*. II. p.368.
35. PRO. FO. 97/343. to Cathcart, Nov. 30, 1813.
36. C.C.IX. p.75. to Aberdeen, Nov. 30, 1813.
37. *Brit. Dip.* pp.116/17. Dec. 7, 1813.
38. *Ibid.* pp.58/9. to Cathcart, Dec. 18, 1813.
39. *Ibid.* pp.62/3. to Cathcart; and p.120. to Aberdeen, Dec. 22, 1813.
40. Webster. I. p.189.
41. *Brit. Dip.* pp.123/8. Dec. 26, 1813.
42. *Ibid.* p.119. Aberdeen to Castlereagh, Dec. 9, 1813.
43. C.C.IX. pp.142/3. Jan. 6, 1813.

CHAPTER XII

1. Goulburn Mss.
2. *Ibid.* and Jones. *Prosperity Robinson.* pp.39/40.
3. Webster. I. p.504.
4. Golo Mann. *Secretary of Europe.* p.197.
5. Webster. I. p.516.
6. Palmer. *Metternich.* p.112.
7. Webster. I. p.504.
8. *Ibid.* p.505.
9. Lady Burghersh. *Letters from Germany & France, 1813–14.* p.185.
10. Webster. I. p.505.
11. Burghersh. *Letters.* pp.144/5.
12. C.C.IX. p.213. to Liverpool, Jan. 30, 1814.
13. *Ibid.* p.212. to Liverpool, Jan. 30, 1814.
14. *Brit. Dip.* p.142. Castlereagh to Liverpool, Jan. 29, 1814.
15. C.C.IX. p.216. to Stewart, Jan. 31, 1814.
16. *Ibid.* p.242. Feb. 6, 1814.
17. Webster. I. p.506. to Emily, Feb. 28, 1814.
18. Goulburn Mss.
19. *Brit. Dip.* p.159. Feb. 18, 1814.
20. *Ibid.* pp.160/1. Feb. 26, 1814.
21. Webster. I. p.507.
22. *Brit. Dip.* p.160. to Liverpool, Feb. 26, 1814.
23. *Ibid.* p.164. to Liverpool, March 5, 1814.
24. Webster. I. pp.225/7.
25. *Brit. Dip.* p.166. to William Hamilton, March 10, 1814.
26. *Ibid.*
27. Palmer. *Metternich.* p.116.
28. C.C.IX. p.335. Aberdeen to Castlereagh, March 10, 1814.
29. B.L. Add. Mss. 38,566. to Liverpool, March 23, 1814.
30. Webster. I. p.508.
31. Burghersh. *Letters.* pp.205/6.
32. B.L. Add. Mss. 38,566. March 23, 1814.
33. W.S.D. VIII. p.708. to Wellington, March 31, 1814.
34. Webster. I. p.509.
35. B.L. Add. Mss. 38,257. to Liverpool, April 15, 1814.

CHAPTER XIII

1. Palmer. *Metternich.* p.119.
2. Jones. *Prosperity Robinson.* pp.44/5.
3. C.C.IX. p.458.

REFERENCES

4. *Ibid.*
5. *Ibid.* p.461. April 13, 1814.
6. C.C.X. p.9 to Liverpool, May 5, 1814.
7. Countess Brownlow. *Slight Reminiscences of a Septuagenarian.* p.110.
8. *Ibid.* pp.93/5.
9. C.C.IX. p.511. April 27, 1814.
10. C.C.X. p.9. to Liverpool, May 5, 1814.
11. *Brit. Dip.* p.183. to Liverpool, May 19, 1814.
12. *Ibid.* pp.184/5. to Liverpool, May 19, 1814.
13. C.C.IX. p.492. April 23, 1814.
14. Webster. I. p.543.
15. Brownlow. *Reminiscences.* p.105.
16. B.L. Add. Mss. 38,191. to Liverpool, May 5, 1814.
17. *Brit. Dip.* p.179. April 20, 1814.
18. W.S.D. IX. p.72. to Wellington, May 15, 1814.
19. Brownlow. *Reminiscences.* p.108.
20. Hansard. XXVIII. 86. June 14, 1814.
21. Creevey Papers. I. p.197.
22. *Ibid.* p.196.
23. C.C.IX. p.356. to Liverpool, March 14, 1814.
24. *Brit. Dip.* p.178. to Liverpool, April 19, 1814.
25. W.S.D. IX. p.465. to Wellington, Dec. 7, 1814.
26. *Brit. Dip.* p.192. to Liverpool, Sept. 3, 1814.
27. *George IV.* I. p.501. to Regent, Oct. 20, 1814.
28. Goulburn Mss.
29. Bathurst Papers. p.297. Lord Apsley to Bathurst, Oct. 4, 1814.
30. Pratt Mss. U840.C.51. Sir H. Hardinge to Camden, Oct. 6, 1814.
31. W.S.D. IX. p.474. Cooke to Liverpool, Dec. 1814.
32. Musulin. *Vienna in the Age of Metternich.* pp.186/7.
33. *Brit. Dip.* p.194. to Liverpool, Sept. 24, 1814.
34. Bernard. *Talleyrand.* p.374.
35. *Brit. Dip.* pp.236/8. Nov. 21, 1814.
36. *Ibid.* p.207. Castlereagh to Liverpool, Oct. 14, 1814.
37. W.S.D. IX. p.415. Memo. Nov. 4, 1814.
38. *Ibid.* p.374. to Liverpool, Oct. 25, 1814.
39. *Brit. Dip.* p.214. Memo. by Castlereagh.
40. W.S.D. IX. p.340. to Hardenberg, Oct. 12, 1814.
41. Pratt Mss. U840.C.51. Sir H. Hardinge to Camden, Nov. 4, 1814.
42. W.S.D. IX. p.342. Oct. 14; pp.401/2. Nov. 2, 1814.
43. *Ibid.* p.438. Nov. 18, 1814.
44. *Brit. Dip.* p.224. to Liverpool, Nov. 5, 1814.
45. Yonge. *Liverpool.* II. p.52. Nov. 5, 1814.
46. Webster. I. p.363.
47. *Brit. Dip.* p.247. Bathurst to Castlereagh, Nov. 27, 1814.
48. *Ibid.* pp.251/2.

CASTLEREAGH

49. W.S.D. IX. p.475. Cooke to Liverpool, Dec. 1814; Webster. I. p.364.
50. *Brit. Dip.* pp.277/8. Castlereagh to Liverpool, Jan. 1, 1815.
51. W.S.D. IX. p.523. Castlereagh to Liverpool, Jan. 2, 1815.
52. *Ibid.* p.527.
53. *Brit. Dip.* p.278. to Liverpool, Jan. 1, 1815.
54. W.S.D. IX. p.524. Jan. 2, 1815.
55. C.C.X. p.218.
56. W.S.D. IX. p.525. Jan. 4, 1815; p.523. Jan. 2. to Liverpool.
57. *Ibid.* p.537. Jan. 15, 1815.
58. C.C.X. p.245. Jan. 17, 1815.
59. W.S.D. IX. p.551. Jan. 30, 1815.
60. Webster. I. p.379.
61. C.C.IX. p.434. to Bentinck, April 3, 1814.
62. Hansard. XXXI. 42/3. May 2, 1815.
63. C.C.X. p.73. to H. Wellesley, August 1, 1814.
64. *Brit. Dip.* p.215. to Liverpool. Oct. 25, 1814.
65. Wilberforce. *Life.* IV. p.244.
66. Hansard. XXX. 30/3. March 6, 1815.
67. W.S.D. IX. p.623. March 26, 1815.
68. C.C.X. p.306. to Clancarty, April 12, 1815.
69. Cast. Mss. (Belfast). D.3030.Q2. to Stewart, Dec. 4, 1815.
70. *Brit. Dip.* p.370. Castlereagh to Liverpool, August 24, 1815.
71. C.C.X. p.490. to Liverpool, August 17, 1815.
72. Pratt Mss. U840.C.98. to Camden, Nov. 5, 1815.
73. *Brit. Dip.* pp.341/2. to Liverpool, July 12, 1815.
74. W.S.D. XI. p.175. to Liverpool, Sept. 28, 1815.
75. *Ibid.* pp.176/7. to Liverpool, Sept. 28, 1815.
76. *Brit. Dip.* p.386. to Liverpool, Oct. 15, 1815.
77. Cast. Mss. (Belfast). D.3030.Q2. to Stewart, Nov. 6, 1815.
78. *Ibid.* Dec. 4, 1815.

CHAPTER XIV

1. Cast. Mss. (Belfast). D.3030.Q2. to Stewart, March 19, [1816].
2. *Ibid.* March 16, [1816].
3. Creevey Papers. I. p.248. Jan. 14, 1816.
4. Cookson. *Lord Liverpool's Administration.* p.49.
5. Hansard. XXXIII. 442/5. March 18, 1816.
6. Cast. Mss. (Belfast). D.3030.Q2. to Stewart, March 19, [1816].
7. *George IV.* II. p.160. [March 18, 1816].
8. *Ibid.* p.161. [March 20, 1816].
9. Yonge. *Liverpool.* II. p.270. to Sir B. Bloomfield, March 21, 1816.
10. Parker. *Sir Robert Peel.* I. p.219. Peel to Whitworth, March 30, 1816.
11. Cast. Mss. (Belfast). D.3030.Q2. to Stewart, [April 15, 1816].

REFERENCES

12. W.S.D. XI. p.401. to Wellington, May 13, 1816.
13. Mrs Arbuthnot. *Journal.* I. p.57.
14. Cast. Mss. (Belfast). D.3030.Q2. June 4, [1816].
15. *Ibid.* June 3, [1816].
16. Webster. *The Foreign Policy of Castlereagh 1815–1822.* p.511. Jan. 1, 1816.
17. *Ibid.* pp.511/12.
18. Cast. Mss. (Belfast). D.3030.Q2. June 3 [1816].
19. Webster. II. pp.97/8.
20. Cast. Mss. (Belfast). D.3030.Q2. to Stewart, June 3 [1816].
21. Webster. II. p.99. to Clancarty, August 6, 1816.
22. Cast. Mss. (Belfast). D.3030.Q2. to Stewart, June 3 [1816].
23. *Ibid.* to Stewart, Sept. 28, [1816].
24. PRO. FO. 7/125. to Stewart, July 9, 1816.
25. Cast. Mss. (Belfast). D.3030.Q2. August 7, [1816].
26. Webster. II. pp.110/11.
27. *Ibid.* pp.105/7.
28. *Ibid.* p.71. July 22, 1817.
29. Wilberforce. *Life.* IV. p.316.
30. Hansard. XXXVI. 1406/8. July 11, 1817.
31. Cast. Mss. (Durham). D/LO/C.440.
32. Hansard. XXXV. 525. Feb. 21, 1817.
33. Cookson. *Lord Liverpool's Administration.* pp.99/101.
34. Hinde. *George Canning.* p.287; Cookson. pp.141/2.
35. B.L. Add. Mss. 40,181. to Peel, June 27, 1818.
36. Rush. *A Residence at the Court of London 1817–1825.* I. pp.264/5; Brownlow. *Reminiscences.* pp.197/8.
37. Hansard. XXXII. 567. Feb. 14, 1816.
38. Rush. *The Court of London 1817–1825.* I. p.27.
39. *Ibid.* pp.306/10.
40. *Ibid.* pp.319/20; 375/6.
41. Adams. *Memoirs.* III. p.422.
42. Rush. *Court of London 1819–1825.* 2nd series. I. p.47.
43. Arbuthnot. *Correspondence.* p.12. Nov. 28, 1818.
44. *Ibid.* p.13.
45. C.C.XII. p.1. Castlereagh to Liverpool, Sept. 2, 1818.
46. Yonge. *Liverpool.* II. p.350. to Liverpool, Oct. 20, 1818.
47. PRO. FO. 27/176. Castlereagh to Sir C. Stuart, June 1, 1818.
48. Webster. II. p.152. to Bathurst, Oct. 20, 1818.
49. C.C.XII. pp.54/5. Oct. 20, 1818.
50. *Ibid.* pp.61/2. Liverpool to Castlereagh, Oct. 23, 1818.
51. PRO. FO. 92/35. Castlereagh to Bathurst, Oct. 3, 1818.
52. PRO. FO. 92/37. Castlereagh to Bathurst, Nov. 10, 1818.
53. Webster. II. pp.150/2.
54. *Ibid.* p.164.
55. Arbuthnot. *Corr.* p.12. Nov. 28, 1818.

CASTLEREAGH

CHAPTER XV

1. Mrs Arbuthnot. I. p.181.
2. *Ibid.* p.181.
3. Princess Lieven. *Private Letters to Prince Metternich.* p.142.
4. Brownlow. *Reminiscences.* pp.191/2.
5. C.C.XI. p.330. Dec. 17, 1816.
6. Cast. Mss. (Belfast). D.3030.Q2. Nov. 15, [1820].
7. *Ibid.* Nov. 9, [1819].
8. *Ibid.* Oct. 6, [1817].
9. *Ibid.* May 20, [1820].
10. Arbuthnot. *Corr.* p.15. Arbuthnot to Castlereagh. March 14, [1819].
11. *Ibid.* p.17.
12. Eldon. *Life.* II. p.329. to Eldon, May 10, 1819.
13. Cookson. *Lord Liverpool's Administration.* p.173.
14. Wellington. *Despatches.* new series. I. pp.80/1. to Gen. Byng, Oct. 21, 1819.
15. Cast. Mss. (Belfast). D.3030.Q2. Sept. 24, 1819.
16. Plumer Ward. *Memoirs.* II. pp.27/30.
17. Buckingham. *Memoirs, Regency.* II. p.382. W.H. Fremantle to Buckingham.
18. Alison. *Castlereagh and Stewart.* III. pp.111/12.
19. Lieven. *Letters.* p.16.
20. Ziegler. *Addington.* p.384.
21. Cast. Mss. (Belfast). D.3030.Q2. Feb. 19, 1820.
22. C.C.XII. pp.213/4.
23. Cast. Mss. (Belfast). D.3030.Q2. Feb. 19, 1820.
24. *George IV.* II. pp.309/10. March 3, 1820.
25. Cast. Mss. (Norwich). MC3/291.467x.
26. W.N.D. I. pp.75/6. Castlereagh to Wellington. Sept. 11, 1819.
27. Webster. II. p.192.
28. Hansard. new series. V. 1257. June 21, 1821.
29. *Cambridge History of Foreign Policy.* II. p.627. Castlereagh's State Paper, May 5, 1820.
30. *Ibid.* pp.627/9.
31. Cast. Mss. (Belfast). to Stewart. D.3030.Q2. Feb. 24, 1820.
32. *Cambridge History of Foreign Policy.* II. pp.623/33.
33. Lieven. *Letters.* pp.39/40.
34. Hyde. *The Strange Death of Lord Castlereagh.* p.117.
35. *Ibid.* p.119. to Stewart, July 15, 1820.
36. *Ibid.* p.128.
37. *George IV.* II. p.390.
38. Bathurst Papers. p.491. Arbuthnot to Bathurst, Dec. 19, [1820].
39. Webster. II. pp.250/1.
40. PRO. FO. 7/160. to Stewart, August 5, 1820.

REFERENCES

41. Webster. II. p.279.
42. Ibid. p.299.
43. Ibid. p.302.
44. PRO. FO. 7/158. Stewart to Castlereagh, Feb. 21, 1821.
45. Webster. II. p.305.
46. Ibid. p.323.
47. Hansard. NS. IV. 865/79. Feb. 21, 1821.
48. Hansard. NS. V. 1256/8. June 21, 1821.
49. Webster. II. p.334. March 13, 1821.

CHAPTER XVI

1. Mrs Arbuthnot. I. p.75.
2. Ibid. p.102.
3. Cast. Mss. (Belfast). D.3030.Q2. to Stewart, March 21, 1821.
4. Mrs Arbuthnot. I. p.90.
5. Hansard. NS. V. 1502. July 3, 1821.
6. Arbuthnot. *Corr.* p.25. to his son, July 4, 1821.
7. Hyde (1959). p.141.
8. Ibid. p.142.
9. Bathurst Papers. p.511. Sidmouth to Bathurst, August 26, 1821.
10. Londonderry. *Robert Stewart.* p.62.
11. Mrs Arbuthnot. I. p.117.
12. C.C.XII. pp.403/8. July 16, 1821.
13. Webster. II. pp.376/7. and PRO. FO. 92/47. to Sir C. Bagot, Oct. 28, 1821.
14. PRO. FO. 92/46. Oct. 1, 1821.
15. Arbuthnot. *Corr.* p.28. to his wife, Oct. 27, 1821.
16. Cast. Mss. (Belfast). D.3030. Q3. Nov. 21, 1821.
17. *George IV.* II. p.466. Oct. 12, 1821.
18. Webster. II. p.369.
19. Cast. Mss. (Norwich). MC3/291/467x.
20. *George IV.* II. p.472n. Nov. 24, 1821.
21. Hansard. NS. VI. 363/4. Feb. 15, 1822.
22. Buckingham. *Memoirs, George IV.* I. p.292. to Buckingham, March 6, 1822.
23. Mrs Arbuthnot. I. p.147.
24. Ibid. p.162.
25. Palmer. *Metternich.* p.212.
26. Webster. II. pp.542/3. June 6, 1822.
27. Ibid. pp.548/9. July 29, 1822.
28. W.N.D. I. pp.284/8.
29. Hansard. NS. VII. 1733/4. July 23, 1822.

30. Webster. II. p.432.
31. Lieven. *Letters*. pp.173/4; 178/9.
32. Cast. Mss. (Belfast). D.3030.Q2. J. Robinson to Stewart, Sept. 7, 1823.
33. *Ibid.* to Stewart, August 13, 1822.
34. Lieven. *Letters*. p.180.
35. Alison. *Castlereagh and Stewart*. III. p.180. to Stewart, August 13, 1822.
36. W.N.D. I. p.255. Memo. August 13, 1822.
37. Alison. *Castlereagh and Stewart*. III. p.181. Hamilton Seymour to Stewart, August 20, 1822.
38. Lieven. *Letters*. pp.189/90.
39. Stanhope. *Conversations with the Duke of Wellington 1831–1851* (London 1888). pp.126, 272/3.
40. *Wellington and his Friends*. ed. The Seventh Duke of Wellington (London 1965). p.25.
41. Londonderry. *Robert Stewart*. pp.63/4.
42. Stanhope. *Conversations with Wellington*. p.272.
43. W.N.D. I. p.251. Bankhead to Wellington, August 9, 1822.
44. *Ibid.* p.254. Bankhead's statement.
45. Londonderry. *Robert Stewart*. p.64.
46. *Annual Register*. 1822.
47. Palmer. *Metternich*. p.213.
48. Creevey Papers. II. p.44.
49. Brownlow. *Reminiscences*. p.198.

Select Bibliography

Manuscript Sources

British Library, Additional Manuscripts. Auckland, Hardwicke, Huskisson, Liverpool, Peel, Pelham, Perceval, Wellesley, Windham Mss.
India Office Library. Home Miscellaneous.
Public Record Office, London. Chatham Mss. Foreign Office, Home Office and War Office Papers.
Public Record Office of Northern Ireland (Belfast). Castlereagh Mss.
Durham County Record Office. Castlereagh Mss.
Norfolk County Record Office (Norwich). Castlereagh Mss.
Kent Archives Office (Maidstone). Pratt (Camden) Mss.
Surrey County Record Office (Kingston-on-Thames). Goulburn Mss.
State Paper Office, Dublin. Rebellion Papers.
Royal Irish Academy, Dublin. Charlemont Mss.

Published Sources

Adams, Henry. *History of the United States (1809–1813).* Vol. 6. New York 1890.
Adams, John Quincy. *Memoirs 1795–1848.* Vols. 3, 4. ed. C.F. Adams. Philadelphia 1875.
Alison, Sir Archibald. *Lives of Lord Castlereagh and Sir Charles Stewart.* 3 Vols. London 1861.
Arbuthnot, Charles. *Correspondence, 1808–1850.* ed. A. Aspinall. Royal Hist. Soc. Camden, 3rd series, Vol. 65. 1941.
Arbuthnot, Harriet. *Journal 1820–1832.* Vol. 1. ed. F. Bamford & the Duke of Wellington. London 1950.
Auckland, Lord (William Eden). *Journal & Correspondence.* Vols. 3, 4. London 1862.
Balfour, Lady Frances. *Life of George, Fourth Earl of Aberdeen.* Vol. 1. London 1923.
Barrington, Jonah. *The Rise and Fall of the Irish Nation.* Paris 1833.
Bartlett, C.J. *Castlereagh.* London 1966.
Bathurst Mss. Historical Manuscripts Commission. London 1923.
Beresford, John. *Correspondence.* Vol. 2. London 1854.
Bernard, J.F. *Talleyrand.* London 1973.

303

CASTLEREAGH

Bolton, G.C. *The Passing of the Irish Act of Union: A Study in Parliamentary Politics.* Oxford 1966.
Bradley, P.B. *Bantry Bay: Ireland in the days of Napoleon and Wolfe Tone.* London 1931.
British and Foreign State Papers, Calendar of, London.
Brownlow, Countess Emma Sophia. *Slight Reminiscences of a Septuagenarian from 1802 to 1815.* London 1867.
Bryant, Arthur. *The Napoleonic Wars.* 3 Vols. London 1942–50.
Buckingham, & Chandos, Duke of. *Memoirs of the Court & Cabinets of George III.* Vols. 2, 3, 4. London 1853–55.
Memoirs of the Court of England during the Regency, 1811–20. 2 Vols, London 1856.
Memoirs of the Court of George IV. Vol. 1. London 1859.
Buckland, C.S.B. *Metternich and the British Government from 1809–1813.* London 1932.
Burghersh, Lady. *The Letters of Lady Burghersh from Germany & France during the Campaign of 1813–14.* ed. Lady Rose Weigall. London 1893.
Butler, Iris. *The Eldest Brother: The Marquess Wellesley, 1760–1842.* London 1973.
Cambridge History of British Foreign Policy 1783–1919. Vols. 1, 2. Cambridge 1922–23.
Castlereagh, Viscount. *Memoirs & Correspondence.* 12 Vols. ed. 3rd Marquess of Londonderry. London 1848–53.
Charlemont, Earl of. *Manuscripts & Correspondence.* 2 Vols. Hist. Mss. Comm. 1891–94.
Colchester, Lord (Charles Abbot). *Diary & Correspondence.* 3 Vols. London 1861.
Cookson, J.E. *Lord Liverpool's Administration 1815–1822.* Edinburgh 1975.
Cornwallis, Marquess. *Correspondence.* Vols. 2, 3. London 1859.
Creevey, Thomas. *The Creevey Papers.* ed. H. Maxwell. 2 Vols. London 1903.
Croker, J.W. *Correspondence & Diaries.* Vol. 1. ed. L.J. Jennings. London 1884.
Coupland, R. *Wilberforce.* London 1923.
Dangerfield, G. *The Era of Good Feelings.* London 1953.
Darvall, F.O. *Popular Disturbances and Public Order in Regency England.* Oxford 1934.
Dickson, W. Steele. *Narrative of Confinement and Exile.* Dublin 1812.
Drennan, W. *The Drennan Letters.* ed. D.A. Chart. HMSO, Belfast 1931.
Dropmore Papers. The Mss. of J.B. Fortescue at Dropmore. 10 Vols. Hist. Mss. Comm. 1892–1927.
Dudley, Earl of (J.W. Ward). *Letters to Ivy.* ed. S.H. Romilly. London 1905.
Dunfermline, Lord. *Lt-Gen Sir Ralph Abercromby KB.* London 1861.
Falkiner, C.L. *Studies in Irish History and Biography, mainly in the Eighteenth Century.* London 1902.
Feiling K. *The Second Tory Party 1714–1832.* London 1938.
Fortescue, J.W. *A History of the British Army.* Vols. 4–10. London 1910–12.
The County Lieutenancies and the Army, 1803–1814. London 1909.

304

BIBLIOGRAPHY

Fulford, R. *The Trial of Queen Caroline.* London 1967.
Furneaux, Robin. *William Wilberforce.* London 1974.
Gash, Norman. *Mr Secretary Peel.* London 1961.
George III. *The Later Correspondence of George III.* ed. A. Aspinall. Vols. 2–5. Cambridge 1963–70.
George, Prince of Wales. *Correspondence 1770–1812.* ed. A. Aspinall. Vol. 8. London 1971.
George IV. *Letters 1812–1830.* ed. A. Aspinall. Vols. 1, 2. Cambridge 1938.
Gilbert, J.T. *Documents Relating to Ireland 1795–1804.* Dublin 1893.
Glenbervie, Lord (Sylvester Douglas). *Diaries.* ed. F. Bickley. 2 Vols. London 1928.
Glover, M. *Britannia Sickens: Sir Arthur Wellesley and the Convention of Cintra.* London 1970.
Glover, R. *Britain at Bay: Defence against Bonaparte 1803–14.* London 1973.
Peninsular Preparation: the Reform of the British Army 1795–1809. Cambridge 1963.
Grattan, Henry. *Memoirs of the Life & Times of Henry Grattan.* By H. Grattan the younger. Vols. 4, 5. London 1842–46.
Gray, Denis. *Spencer Perceval: the Evangelical Prime Minister.* Manchester 1963.
Greville, Charles. *Memoirs.* Vol. I. ed. H. Reeve. London 1874.
Gwynn, S. *Henry Grattan and his Times.* London 1939.
Halévy, Élie. *History of the English People in the Nineteenth Century. The Liberal Awakening 1815–1830.* London 1926.
Hansard. *Parliamentary History* (1794–1803); *Parliamentary Debates* (1803–1820); *Parliamentary Debates,* new series (1820–1822).
Hinde, W. *George Canning.* London 1973.
Hinsley, F.H. *Power and the Pursuit of Peace.* Cambridge 1963.
Hobhouse, Henry. *Diary 1820–27.* ed. A. Aspinall. London 1947.
Horsman, R. *The Causes of the War of 1812.* Philadelphia 1962.
Huskisson, W. *The Huskisson Papers.* ed. L. Melville. London 1931.
Hyde, H. Montgomery. *The Rise of Lord Castlereagh.* London 1933.
The Strange Death of Lord Castlereagh. London 1959.
Iremonger, L. *Lord Aberdeen.* London 1978.
Jackson, George. *The Bath Archives.* Vol. 2. London 1873.
Johnston, E.M. *Great Britain and Ireland 1760 to 1800: A Study in Political Administration.* Edinburgh 1963.
Jones, W.D. *Prosperity Robinson: The Life of Viscount Goderich 1782–1859.* London 1967.
Kissinger, H.A. *A World Restored: Metternich, Castlereagh and the Problems of Peace 1812–22.* London 1957.
Knox, Alexander. *Remains.* ed. J.J. Hornby. Vol. 4. London 1837.
Lane-Poole, S. *The Life of Stratford Canning.* Vol. 1. London 1888.
Leadbeater, Mary. *The Leadbeater Papers: The Annals of Ballitore.* Vol. I. London 1862.
Lecky, W.E.H. *History of Ireland in the Eighteenth Century.* Vols. 3, 4, 5. London 1892.

Lieven, Dorothea. *Private Letters to Prince Metternich 1820–26.* ed. P. Quennell. London 1937.
Londonderry, the Marchioness of. *Robert Stewart Viscount Castlereagh.* London 1904.
Longford, E. *Wellington: The Years of the Sword.* London 1969.
Wellington: Pillar of State. London 1972.
Lonsdale, Earl of. Papers. Hist. Mss. Comm. 1893.
MacDermot, F. *Theobald Wolfe Tone.* London 1939.
Mackesy, P. *The War in the Mediterranean 1803–1810.* London 1957.
Malcomson, A.P.W. *John Foster: The Politics of the Anglo-Irish Ascendancy.* Oxford 1978.
Mann, Golo. *Secretary of Europe: The Life of Friedrich Gentz, Enemy of Napoleon.* Yale 1946.
Markham, F. *Napoleon.* New York 1963.
Marshall, P.J. *Problems of Empire: Britain and India 1757–1813.* London 1968.
Maxwell, C. *Dublin under the Georges 1714–1830.* London 1956.
Mitchell, Austin. *The Whigs in Opposition 1815–1830.* Oxford 1967.
Moore, Sir John. *Diary.* ed. Maj.-Gen. Sir J.F. Maurice. 2 Vols. London 1904.
Musulin, S. *Vienna in the Age of Metternich.* London 1975.
New, Chester W. *Life of Henry Brougham to 1830.* Oxford 1961.
Nicolson, H. *The Congress of Vienna.* London 1948.
O'Connell, M.R. *Irish Politics and Social Conflict in the Age of the American Revolution.* Philadelphia 1965.
Oman, Carola. *Sir John Moore.* London 1953.
Oman, Sir Charles. *A History of the Peninsular War.* 7 Vols. London 1902–30.
Pakenham, T. *The Year of Liberty: The Great Irish Rebellion of 1798.* London 1969.
Palmer, A. *Metternich.* London 1972.
Parker, C.S. *Sir Robert Peel.* Vol. I. London 1891.
Parliamentary Register of Ireland. Vols. 11–17. Dublin 1801.
Perkins, Bradford. *Prologue to War: England and the United States, 1805–1812.* Berkeley, Calif. 1961.
Castlereagh and Adams: England and the United States 1812–1823. Berkeley, Calif. 1964.
Philips, C.H. *The East India Company 1784–1834.* Manchester 1961.
Porritt, E. & A. *The Unreformed House of Commons.* Vol. 2. Cambridge 1903.
Reilly, R. *Pitt the Younger.* London 1978.
Renier, G.J. *Great Britain and the Netherlands 1813–1815.* London 1930.
Roberts, M. *The Whig Party 1807–1812.* London 1939.
Roberts, P.E. *India under Wellesley.* London 1929.
Rolo, P.J.V. *George Canning.* London 1965.
Rose, George. *Diaries & Correspondence.* 2 Vols. London 1860.
Rose, Holland. *William Pitt and the Great War.* London 1911.
Rush, Richard. *A Residence at the Court of London 1817–1825.* Vol. 1. London 1833.
A Residence at the Court of London 1819–1825. Vol. 1. London 1845.

BIBLIOGRAPHY

Rosselli, J. *Lord William Bentinck: The Making of a Liberal Imperialist 1774–1839*. London 1974.
Schenk, H.G. *The Aftermath of the Napoleonic Wars*. London 1947.
Scott, David. *Correspondence*. ed. C.H. Philips. Vol. II. Royal Hist. Soc. Camden, 3rd series, Vol. 76, 1951.
Scherwig, J.M. *Guineas and Gunpowder: British Foreign Aid in the Wars with France 1793–1815*. Harvard 1969.
Smith, E.A. *Whig Principles and Party Politics: Earl Fitzwilliam and the Whig Party 1748–1833*. Manchester 1975.
Stanhope, Earl of. *Life of Pitt*. Vols. 3, 4. London 1862.
Strauss, E. *Irish Nationalism and British Democracy*. London 1951.
Twiss, H. *Life of Lord Eldon*. 3 Vols. London 1844.
Walmsley, R. *Peterloo: The Case Reopened*. Manchester 1969.
Walpole, S. *Life of Spencer Perceval*. 2 Vols. London 1874.
Ward, R. Plumer. *Memoirs*. ed. E. Phipps. 2 Vols. London 1850.
Watson, S. *The Reign of George III 1760–1815*. London 1960.
Webster, C.K. *The Foreign Policy of Castlereagh 1812–1815*. London 1931.
The Foreign Policy of Castlereagh 1815–1822. London 1925.
The Congress of Vienna 1814–1815. Oxford 1919.
British Diplomacy 1813–1815. Select Documents dealing with the Reconstruction of Europe. London 1921.
Wellesley, Marquess. *Despatches & Correspondence in India*. ed. M. Martin. Vols. 3, 4, 5. London 1837.
The Wellesley Papers. by the editor of the Windham Papers. 2 Vols. London 1914.
Wellington, Duke of. *Despatches*. Vols. 4, 5. London 1837, 1838.
Supplementary Despatches, Correspondence & Memoranda. Vols. 5–12. London 1860–65.
Despatches, Correspondence & Memoranda. new series. Vol. 1. London 1867.
White, R.J. *From Waterloo to Peterloo*. London 1957.
Wilberforce, William. *Life of* by his sons, Robert & Samuel Wilberforce. 5 Vols. London 1838.
Woodward, E.L. *The Age of Reform 1815–1870*. Oxford 1938.
Yonge, C.D. *Life of 2nd Earl of Liverpool*. 3 Vols. London 1868.
Ziegler, P. *Addington*. London 1965.

Index

Abbot, Charles, 1st Baron Colchester, 96, 105, 107
Abercorn, John James Hamilton, 1st Marquess of, 78
Abercromby, General Sir Ralph, 53–4, 56, 63, 73
Aberdeen, George Hamilton Gordon, 4th Earl of (1784–1860), 194–200, 205–6, 209, 210, 215
Adams, John Quincy, 245, 246
Addington, Henry, *see* Sidmouth, Viscount
Adlerberg, Count, 146–7
Aix-la-Chapelle, Congress of (1818), 245, 247–9, 257
Alexander I, Emperor of Russia (1777–1825), (1805–7) 119, 132, 135, 137–8, 140; and 1813 campaign, 187–96; and 1814 campaign, 202–12; in Paris (1814), 213, 217; in London (1814), 217–18; at Congress of Vienna, 220, 222–7; after Napoleon's escape, 230; in Paris (1815), 232, 233, 234; and Holy Alliance, 233, 238; and disarmament, 239 and n, 240; at Aix-la-Chapelle, 249; and European unrest, 257, 261–4; and Greek revolt, 268–70, 274–6
Alexander, Henry, 71
Amiens, Treaty of (1802), 67, 107
Antrim, 61–2
Antwerp, 160, 161, 162, 163, 198
Arbuthnot, Charles, 249, 252, 260, 267, 278, 280n
Arbuthnot, Mrs Harriet, 237, 250, 265–6, 268, 274, 278, 280n
Archdall, Richard, 79n
Arklow (Wicklow), 61–2
Armagh, Royal School at, 14
Armed Forces, 67, 117; recruitment and training of, 128–32; King's German (Hanoverian) Legion, 119, 134–5, 138; North German campaign of (1805–6), 119–22; in the Mediterranean, 122–3, 134–43; in South America, 133; in India, 134; and Waterloo campaign, 230–1; army estimates (1816), 235–6;

see also Peninsular War
Artois, Charles Philippe, Comte d' (later King Charles X of France), 214
Aspern, battle of (1809), 160
Assaye, battle of (1803), 113
Auerstadt, battle of (1806), 132
Austerlitz, battle of (1805), 121, 123
Austria, 53, 118–22, 132, 158, 159–61, 162; and 1813 campaign, 187–93; declares war on France, 193; signs treaty of Toeplitz, 194–5; signs treaty with Britain, 194; and 1814 campaign, 202–10; and Congress of Vienna, 221–8, 229n; (1815–16), 237, 240–1; and unrest in Italy, 261–4; *see also* Metternich, Francis I, Emperor of Austria

Bagot, Sir Charles, 246n
Baird, General Sir David, 117, 154–5, 155n
Baltic sea, 134, 138–9, 146, 187
Bandon (Cork), 49
Bankhead, Dr, 278–80
Bantry Bay (Cork), 48–9
Barlow, Sir George, 115
Barrington, Jonah, 79 and n, 80
Barbary pirates, 248
Bassein, treaty of (1802), 112–13
Bathurst, 3rd Earl (1762–1834), 126, 127, 157, 165, 179n, 215, 227
Bautzen, battle of (1813), 192
Beauharnais, Eugène de, 196, 221
Belfast, 13, 17, 22, 27, 28, 44–5, 47, 50, 76, 116
Belfast News-Letter, 18, 22–3, 95
Belgium, 197, 205, 215, 219, 230; *see also* Antwerp
Bellamont, Charles, Earl of, 51
Bellingham, John, 178
Bentinck, Lord William, 241
Berar, Raja of, 113
Beresford, John, 20, 53, 58, 64, 77, 78, 80, 93
Beresford, John Claudius, 78
Beresford, General William Carr, later Viscount Beresford, 133

309

Bernadotte, Jean Baptiste, Prince Royal and later Charles XIV of Sweden, 187 and n, 199, 202, 204, 207; treaty with Britain (1813), 189–90, 195, 215n
Berry, Duc de, 257
Bessborough, Lady, 184
Blackwood, Sir John, 77–8
Blanketeers, March of the, 242
Blucher, General von, 206, 207, 208, 218, 230, 232
Board of Control (India Board), 107–12, 117, 260, 272
Bombay, 111
Bonaparte, Joseph (King of Naples (1806) and Spain (1808)), 132, 143, 146, 152, 193
Bonaparte, Louis (King of Holland), 132
Bond, Oliver, 55–6, 65–6
Bosanquet, Jacob, 109–10, 113
Botany Bay, 66, 67
Boulogne, 118, 148, 217
Bourbon family (French branch), 199, 202–3, 204, 206, 211, 230; *see also* Louis XVIII, Artois, Orléans, Berry
Bragge-Bathurst, Charles, 176n, 260, 266
Brazil, 140, 261 and n
Britain, French invasion threat to, 53 (1798); 114, 118 (1804–5); signs treaty of Amiens, 107; resumes war against France, 114; at war with United States, 176, 179–80, 187, 200; signs peace treaty with United States, 226, 227; signs treaty with Bernadotte, 189–90; signs treaties with Prussia, Russia, 192; and with Austria, 194; peace aims, 192, 194–5, 196; signs treaty of Chaumont, 208–9 and n; signs Final Act of Congress of Vienna, 229n; domestic unrest and economic slump in, 145 (1808), 177, 181 (1811–12), 229, 235 (1815–16), 241–4 (1816–17), 251, 253–5 (1818–19); agricultural distress in, post-1815, 272–4; habeas corpus suspended in (1816–18), 242–4; cash payments resumed in, 253 and n, 273; public opinion on foreign issues, post-1815, 237, 275, 276 *see also* Armed Forces; Corn Law
British Guiana, 219
Brougham, Henry, later Baron Brougham and Vaux, 177, 179, 235, 237, 243 and n, 281
Buckingham, George Nugent Temple Grenville, 1st Marquess of, 71, 75

Buckinghamshire, John Hobart, 2nd Earl of (1723–93), 35
Buckinghamshire, Countess of, née Catherine Conolly, 35
Buckinghamshire, Robert Hobart, Lord Hobart, 4th Earl of (1760–1816), 26, 32, 52, 71, 176n, 237
Buenos Aires, 133, 142
Burghersh, John Fane, Lord, later 11th Earl of Westmorland, 204
Burghersh, Lady, 204, 210
Burke, Edmund, 20, 23, 236
Burrard, General Sir Harry, 149–51, 153
Bushe, Charles Kendal, 96n
Byrne, William, 65
Byron, Lord, 275

Cadiz, 118, 158, 257
Calcutta, 109, 111
Camden, Charles Pratt, 1st Earl (1714–94), 14, 18–19, 22, 24, 25–6, 30, 32, 33–4, 35, 36
Camden, John Jeffreys Pratt, Viscount Bayham, 2nd Earl and 1st Marquess (1759–1840), 28–9, 36, 42, 72, 86, 87, 96, 126; as Lord Lieutenant of Ireland, 39–40, 43, 44, 46, 50, 52; and 1798 Rebellion, 53–68; and Castlereagh's resignation (1809), 164–5, 166 and n
Canada, 142, 180
Canning, George (1770–1827), 36, 188; in opposition (1806–7), 103, 107, 124–6; as Foreign Secretary (1807–9), 127–8, 137, 139, 142, 144–5, 148–9, 152–3, 156, 157–8, 161; and Castlereagh's resignation (1809), 164–8; in opposition (1809–12), 171, 172 and n, 174 and n, 176n; after Perceval's murder, 178–9, 182–4; in Liverpool's Cabinet, 237, 245, 248, 252, 258; resigns, 260; political future of, 266, 268, 271, 272; and Catholic emancipation, 181–2 and n
Canning, Stratford, later Viscount Stratford de Redcliffe, 188 and n
Canova, Antonio, 233
Cape of Good Hope, 117, 215, 219
Capodistria, Count John, 247, 249, 261, 262, 269, 274
Carbonari, the, 260, 261
Carhampton, Henry Luttrell, 2nd Earl of, 47
Caribbean, 117, 247; *see also* West Indies
Carlisle, Frederick Howard, 5th Earl of, 15

310

INDEX

Carlsbad decrees (1819), 257
Carnatic, the, 110, 112
Caroline, Princess of Wales, 255–6, 258–60, 262, 265, 267–8
Carysfort, John Proby, 1st Earl of, 125
Castlebar, 'races of', 62
Castlereagh, Emily, Viscountess, Marchioness of Londonderry, née Lady Amelia Hobart (1772–1829), 104–5 and n, 106 and n, 201, 203, 204, 210, 211, 259n, 272, 275; engagement and marriage, 35–6; character of, 35–6; childlessness of, 36, 80; in Ireland, 44, 46, 47–9, 52, 55n, 95, 97; at Mount Stewart, 36–7, 174; at North Cray, 173, 256; at Congress of Vienna, 221, 225; as a hostess, 215, 221, 231, 233, 247, 250; quarrels with Lady Conyngham, 265–6, 271, 277; and Castlereagh's death, 279
Castlereagh, Robert Stewart, Viscount, 2nd Marquess of Londonderry (1769–1822),
(1769–1793): birth, 13; childhood, 14; schooldays, 14–5; his youth at Mount Stewart, 15; 1st recorded public appearance of, 17; boating accident of, 18; at Cambridge, 18–9; elected to Dublin Parliament, 22–4; enters Dublin Parliament, 25; maiden speech of, 26; visits France, 26–7; supports Catholic Relief bill, 28–9; visits Brussels, 30–1; joins militia, 33;
(1794–7) engagement and marriage, 35–6; enters Westminster Parliament, 36; takes Emily to Mount Stewart, 36; with his militia regiment, 36; summoned by Pitt to Westminster, 37; seconds the Address in Dublin, 39; summoned by Camden to London, 39–40; returns with Camden to Dublin, 40; seconds the Address at Westminster, 40; attends Dublin Parliament, 42; attends Westminster Parliament, 42; decides to opt for a career in Ireland, 42–3; becomes Viscount Castlereagh, 43; and conspirators in Co. Down, 44–5, 46–8; at Bantry Bay, 48–9; attends Dublin Parliament, 49–50; re-elected for Co. Down, 51; appointed Keeper of HM's Signet, 52; made a Lord of the Treasury, 52; joins Irish Privy Council, 52;
(1798–1801): in inner circle at Dublin Castle, 54; appointed temporary Chief Secretary, 55–6; and 1798 Rebellion, 56–68; appointed Chief Secretary, 71; visits London to discuss union, 75; joins English Privy Council, 75; fails to carry union, 74–82; visits London, 84; carries union, 85–95; visits London, 98–9; resigns as Chief Secretary, 99; waives a British peerage, 104;
(1801–07): has serious illness, 106; as President of Board of Control, 107–115; re-elected for Co. Down, 108; joins Addington's Cabinet, 111; as Secretary of State for War and the Colonies (1805–6), 116–23; loses election in Co. Down, 116; in opposition, 124–7;
(1807–9): returns to War Office in Portland's Cabinet, 127; and armed forces, 129–32; and the Mediterranean campaign, 135–7, 139–40, 142–3, 154n; and the Danish expedition, 138–9; has serious illness, 140–1; his demotion rumoured, 144; and expedition to Sweden, 146–7; and Spanish revolt, 148–9; and Convention of Cintra, 151–3; and Peninsular campaign (1808), 154–6; accused of corrupt electoral practices, 157–8; supports Arthur Wellesley's Peninsular plan (1809), 158–9, 162; and Walcheren expedition, 161–3; and resignation, 164; and duel with Canning, 165–8, 174; as Secretary for War, 168–9;
(1809–16): in opposition, 171–2, 174–6; buys a farm at North Cray, Kent, 173, 175; visits Mount Stewart, 173–4; refuses to join Perceval's Cabinet, 174 and n; becomes Foreign Secretary, 176–7; and political crisis after Perceval's death, 178–9, 182–4; and 1813 campaign against Napoleon, 188–98; decides on mission to Allies, 199–200; journeys to The Hague, 201; at Allied headquarters, 202–10; at Dijon, 210–12; in Paris (1816), 213–17; and Allied visit to London, 217–19; visits Ghent peace talks, 220; talks with Talleyrand, 220, 222; at Congress of Vienna, 221–9; disagrees with Tsar over Poland, 222–5; disagrees with Cabinet, 224–5; seeks solution to Polish/Saxon crisis, 225–8;

CASTLEREAGH

signs defensive treaty with Austria and France, 226; reluctant to leave Vienna, 226–7; returns to London, 229; reactions to Napoleon's escape, 230; returns to Paris after Waterloo, 231; and 2nd Peace of Paris, 231–4; his moderate policy attacked by Cabinet and press, 232; (1816–22): and the House of Commons, 235–7; and post-war relations with Europe, 237–41; defends Government's repressive legislation, 243; elected for Co. Down, 245; involved in election riot in London, 245; tries to improve Anglo-American relations, 245–7; attends Congress of Aix-la-Chapelle, 247–9; has difficult parliamentary session, 252–3; and domestic unrest, 254–5; and Cato Street conspiracy, 255; and royal divorce, 256; re-elected for Co. Down, 256–7; and European unrest, 257–8; and the Queen's 'trial', 259–60; and Troppau-Laibach conferences, 261–4; and proposed Cabinet changes, 266–7; visits Ireland with the King, 267–8; visits Hanover with the King, 268, 270–2; and Greek revolt, 269–70; and his last parliamentary session, 273–4; prepares for Allied meetings at Vienna/Verona, 275–7; last illness and death of, 277–81
PERSONAL *Appearance* 204, 210, 214–15; *Characteristics*: love of music, 19, 33–4, 37, 106, 251; love of Mount Stewart, 33–4, 36, 106, 251; love of country pursuits, 33–4, 251; coldness/reserve, 71, 77, 103–4, 153, 167–8, 243 and n, 250; unassuming, 42, 56, 72, 105, 272; good natured/kind/merciful, 64–5, 72, 103–4, 105, 250; hard-working, 168; tactful, 110, 114, 159n, 251n; unpopular, 16, 157, 170 and n, 243, 250, 281; popular, 267–8; as a speaker, 69, 71, 83, 103, 172, 184, 250; as Foreign Secretary, 179, 188, 193, 237–8, 245, 263; *Health*, 19, 106, 140–1, 251–2, 277–81
COMMENTS on, by Camden, 55–6; by Cornwallis, 71, 103; by A. Knox, 69, 71–2; by H. Alexander, 71; by Portland, 75, 158; by Lord Grenville, 75; by Cooke, 83, 104; by H. Dundas, 110; by Wellesley-Pole, 113, 153; by Carysfort, 125; by Perceval, 144, 170n; by Duke of Richmond, 170; by Canning, 158, 172; by Creevey, 172; by Mrs Arbuthnot, 250; by Countess Lieven, 250; by Brougham, 281
RELATIONSHIPS with, his family, 14, 31, 37, 104–5, 173–4 and n, 251; Charles Stewart, 14, 162n, 191; Alexander I, 193–4, 204, 206, 208, 217, 222–4, 239–40, 249, 263; Canning, 125, 164–70, 174, 182–4, 237; Lord Grenville, 125; Metternich, 202–3, 204, 220–1, 240–1, 256, 270–1, 275, 281; Moore, 149–50, 155–6; Peel, 266, 267n, 272; Pitt, 26, 29, 36, 40, 103, 190; Prince Regent/George IV, 176, 183–4, 256, 265–6, 271–2; Talleyrand, 220, 222; Lord Wellesley, 110, 114; Wellington, 150–3, 158–9, 162 and n, 214, 231; House of Commons, 236–7, 238, 252–3, 266, 267, 274; Liverpool Cabinet, 214, 216, 218, 224–5, 226–7, 232, 235, 246, 248–9
VIEWS, on England, 18, 30, 97, 173; Ireland, 27, 29–30, 32, 42–3, 97, 243, 268; Irish Catholics, 28–9, 32, 40, 74, 75, 181–2; the Irish rebellion, 64–8; the Irish union, 73–4, 83; French Revolution, 27, 29, 30, 34–5, 40, 45; patronage (in Ireland), 79, 85, 96; politics, 23–4, 25–6, 27–8, 29, 32, 40, 71, 175; domestic unrest, 40, 181; agricultural distress, 273, 274; Poor Laws, 243–4; public opinion, 264; popularity, 29, 268
FOREIGN POLICY France, 215–16, 232, 240, 248, 257, 275; Bernadotte and Norway, 189–90; Germany, 190, 195–6, 224; Prussia, 190, 223, 224, 228; Greece, 269–70, 275–6; Italy, 240–1 and n, 261, 263–4; Portugal, 261; Russia, 224, 228; Spanish colonists in South America, 133, 142, 146, 276; United States, 179–80, 245–7; Orders-in-Council, 145, 177; subsidies, 119, 187–8, 193, 200, 230, 231n; commercial policy, 246; colonial conquests, 196, 198–9, 219; slave trade, 126–7, 228–9; nationalism, 195–6, 228; post-war revolutionary unrest, 238, 241, 249, 257–8, 261; non-intervention, 249, 257–8, 261–4, 269–70, 275–6; the Allies, 195, 198,

312

INDEX

199–200, 208, 258, 261–4; the Holy Alliance, 233, 238; Congress system, 234, 247 and n; State Paper of May 5, 1822, 258; Circular Dispatch of January 19, 1821, 263; Instructions for Vienna/Verona conference, 275–6, 277; *see also* Alexander I, Metternich, Talleyrand, Belgium, Quadruple Alliance, Vienna, Congress of, Aix-la-Chapelle congress, Maritime Rights
Cathcart, William Schaw, 1st Earl (1755–1843), 121–2, 134, 138–9; as ambassador to Russia, 188–200, 202, 205–6, 215, 239n; at Vienna Congress, 221
Catherine, Grand Duchess of Russia, 218
Catholic emancipation (1792–1801), 31, 37–9, 41, 46, 67, 74, 88–9, 98–100, 107; (1807), 127; (1812–13), 181–2; (1821), 182n, 267
Cato Street conspiracy (1820), 255, 256
Caulaincourt, Armand A.L., Marquis de, 205, 206, 207, 209
Ceuta, 143
Charlemont, James Caulfeild, 4th Viscount, 1st Earl of (1728–99), 17, 23, 29, 33, 39, 40, 43, 45, 51, 90
Charles IV, King of Spain, 146
Charles XIII, King of Sweden, 187n, 215n
Charlotte Augusta, Princess, 201, 219, 244n
Chatham, John Pitt, 2nd Earl of (1756–1835), 117, 119, 121, 127, 142, 168; and Walcheren expedition, 161, 162–3, 165
Chatillon, peace talks at (1814), 205, 206, 207 and n, 209, 210
Chaumont, 208, 210; treaty of (1814), 195–6, 198, 208–9 and n
Christian Frederick, Prince, 215n
Cintra, Convention of (1808), 151 and n, 152, 156, 168
Clancarty, Richard, Viscount Dunlo, 2nd Earl of (1767–1837), 157, 201, 211, 221, 228, 232
Clanwilliam, 3rd Earl of, 245, 270, 272
Clare, John Fitzgibbon, Viscount Fitzgibbon, 1st Earl of (1749–1802), 21, 40, 53, 58, 73–4, 77n, 81
Clarke, Mrs Mary Ann, 157
Cleland, Rev. John, 47
Clive, Robert, Baron Clive of Plassey, 109

Cobbett, William, 148, 152
Collingwood, Cuthbert, Vice-Admiral and 1st Baron, 118
Conolly, Lady Louisa, 55n
Conolly, Thomas, 33, 35, 44, 47, 52, 55n, 99
Constantinople, 135–6, 268, 274
Continental System (blockade), 181; Berlin decree (1806), 132, 138, 177; Milan decree (1807), 145, 177
Conyngham, Henry, 1st Marquess of, 259, 268, 271
Conyngham, Elizabeth, Marchioness of, 35, 259, 265, 271, 277
Cooke, Edward (1755–1820), character and career, 72; at Dublin Castle, 59, 60–1, 74–5, 81, 83, 94, 95, 104, 106; (1809–14), 153, 160, 165, 173, 191, 206, 221, 223
Corfu, 123, 142
Cork, 48, 49, 76, 84 and n, 94n, 148
Corn Law, 229, 236, 253, 273–4
Cornwallis, Charles, 2nd Earl and 1st Marquess (1738–1805), in Ireland, 63, 64, 65, 67n, 68–9, 70–3, 76–9 and n, 82, 85 and n, 86–99, 103–4; returns to India, 114–15; dies, 115
Corry, Isaac, 92
Corunna, 154–6, 158–9
Cotton, Admiral Sir Charles, 148
Courland, Anne Charlotte Dorothea, Duchess of, 215
Cradock, General Sir John, 158–9 and n
Craig, General Sir James, 122–3
Craufurd, Major-General Robert, 160 and n
Creevey, Thomas, 172, 227
Croker, John, 191, 229, 266
Curran, John, 96n
Czartoryski, Prince Adam, 208

Dalrymple, General Sir Hew Whitefoord, 143, 146, 149–53, 154
Dalrymple, General William, 49
Danubian principalities (Moldavia and Wallachia), 135, 268, 269, 271, 275
Dardanelles, 135
Denmark, 138–9, 144, 146, 199, 215n; Danish fleet, 138–9; bombardment of Copenhagen, 138, 144; Zealand, 139, 147
De Quincey, Thomas, 96
Dickson, Rev. William Steele, 17–18, 23
Dijon, 203, 208, 210, 211
Don, General Sir George, 119–20

313

Down, 13, 15, 17, 22–3, 29, 34, 35, 46, 51, 61–2, 108, 116, 245, 256
Downshire, Arthur Hill, Viscount Kilwarlin, Earl of Hillsborough, 2nd Marquess of, 17, 22–3, 46–7, 51, 79, 90–1, 116
Downshire, Marchioness of, 116
Downshire, Wills Hill, Earl of Hillsborough, 1st Marquess of, 15, 17, 22
Drummond, Sir William, 136
Dublin, 13, 20, 24, 25, 31, 38, 39–40, 47, 48, 50, 51, 84, 94n, 116, 158, 267–8; attempted coup in (1798), 55, 58–9, 61; hostile to union, 74, 76, 81, 90–1, 91–2; Phoenix Park, 44, 92, 95; Dublin University, 84, 94n; Dublin county, 58–9
Dublin Castle (or the Irish administration), 16, 20, 24, 25–6, 28, 33, 36, 38, 39, 41, 43, 44, 52, 53–9; and the union, 73–82, 85–96
Dublin (Irish) Parliament, 15, 16, 19, 20, 21, 24, 25–6, 32–3, 37–8, 39, 42, 45–6, 54, 59, 60, 65–6, 68–9; and union, 70–82, 83–96, 103
Duckworth, Admiral Sir John, 135
Duff, General Sir James, 60
Dumouriez, General Charles, 30
Dundas, General Sir David, 161
Dundas, Henry, see Melville, 1st Viscount
Dundas, General Sir Ralph, 60

East India Company, 26, 108–115, 123, 157
Edgcumbe, Lady Emma (later Countess Brownlow), 201, 203, 214–15, 217, 218, 231, 251
Egypt, 135–6, 137, 139
Elba, 213, 228, 229 and n
Eldon, Sir John Scott, 1st Earl of, 126, 127–8, 254
Elliot, William, 56, 65, 72, 77, 79, 104
Ellis, Charles Rose, 166
Ely, Charles Tottenham Loftus, Earl and 1st Marquess of, 79, 85
Emmet, Thomas Addis, 66–7
Enniscorthy (Wexford), 61, 62
Enniskillen, William Willoughby Coke, 1st Earl of, 68
Eylau, battle of (1807), 132

Ferdinand IV, King of Naples, 135, 140, 195, 260, 263

Ferdinand VII, King of Spain, 146, 248, 257–8, 275
Finland, 146–7
Fitzgerald, Lord Edward, 53, 55, 58 and n
Fitzgerald, James, 78
Fitzgibbon, John, see Clare, Earl of
Fitzwilliam, William Wentworth, 2nd Earl, 37–40, 41, 63, 72
Flood, Henry, 16
Flushing, 161, 162, 163
Fontainebleau, 211, 214; treaty of (1814), 213
Fort George, 67
Fort William college (India), 111
Foster, Augustus John, 180
Foster, John, later 1st Baron Oriel, 20, 53, 96n, 103; opposes union, 75, 78–9, 81, 90, 93, 94; accuses Castlereagh of bribery, 87
Fouché, Joseph, 230, 231 and n
Fox, Charles James (1749–1806), 20, 36, 115 and n, 116, 124–5, 135, 281
Fox, General Sir Henry, 135–7
France, 16, 37, 53, 135, 143; French Revolution, 20, 21, 26–7, 84; declares war on Britain, 33, 109; and Irish rebels, 50, 66, 68–9, 83; signs treaty of Amiens, 107, 109, 112; in India, 109, 112; in Italy, 123, 132, 136, 196–7; and Walcheren expedition, 160–3; and its colonies, 199, 215–16; frontiers of, 197, 205, 206, 207, 216, 232; and slave trade, 216, 229n; and Congress of Vienna, 220, 221–2; signs Final Act, 229n; and post-war, 231, 232, 238, 240, 247–8, 257, 264, 275; see also Paris peace treaties, Peninsular War, Napoleon Bonaparte, Talleyrand, Continental System
Francis I, Emperor of Austria, 187, 193, 209, 217, 220, 270
Frankfurt, 196, 198–9, 202
Fraser, Lieut.-General Alexander Mackenzie, 136–7, 140
Frederick, Duke of York (1763–1827), 117, 122, 129, 131, 150, 157, 235
Frederick Augustus, King of Saxony, 223, 224, 226, 227
Frederick William III, King of Prussia, 119–20, 122, 132, 187, 263; and 1813–14 campaigns, 190, 191, 192, 207, 210; at Congress of Vienna, 223, 224; see also Prussia

INDEX

Friedland, battle of (1807), 135

Genoa, 118, 228
Gentz, Friedrich von, 202, 227
George III (1738–1820), 20, 40, 48, 77n, 85, 93, 95, 96, 128, 144, 173; and Castlereagh, 55, 70, 99, 104; and 1809 political crisis, 164, 167, 168, 170; his hostility to Catholic emancipation, 39, 98–9, 107 and n, 127; and the war, 134, 136–7, 138, 139, 148, 150, 161; and C.J. Fox, 115–16, 124; insanity of, 175 and n; death of, 255
George, Prince of Wales, Prince Regent and King George IV (1762–1830), 20, 35; and 1812 political crises, 175–6 and ns, 178, 181, 182–3, 184; (1813–15), 188, 191, 217–18, 221, 232, 233, 234; (1816–20), 236, 238, 239, 242, 244n, 247n, 253; as King, 255–6, 258–60, 265–8, 270–2; and Castlereagh's last illness, 277–80 and n
Germanos, Bishop of Patras, 268
Germany, 118–22, 196–7, 218; and Congress of Vienna, 222, 226, 227, 228, 231n, 232; post-1815, 240, 248, 263; Confederation of the Rhine, 132; see also Saxony
Ghent peace talks see United States
Gibraltar, 139, 140, 142–3, 148, 155, 158, 159n
Goulburn, Henry, 220
Graham, Major-General Thomas, later Baron Lynedoch, 199
Grattan, Henry (1746–1820), 16, 17, 19–20, 21, 25–6, 28, 37, 44, 45, 49, 51, 86; opposes the union, 76, 90, 92–3, 94, 95; and Castlereagh, 97, 158; and Catholic emancipation, 31–2, 38–9, 41, 46, 182
Greece, revolt in (1821), 268–70, 274–6; Chios massacre, 276
Grenville, Thomas, 71, 121, 125, 178, 183
Grenville, William Wyndham, Baron (1759–1834), 26, 71 and n, 120, 157, 175–6, 255; joins Fox, 115 and n, 116; as prime minister, 124–7, 132–3; leaves the Whigs, 260; and Castlereagh, 75
Grey, Charles, Viscount Howick and 2nd Earl Grey, 116, 125, 157, 175–6, 218
Gustavus Adolphus IV, King of Sweden, 119, 134, 139, 146–7, 187n

Haliday, Alexander, 29–30, 43, 51
Hanover, 119–20, 122, 187, 188; George IV's visit to, 268, 270–2, 274
Hardenberg, Prince von, 192, 197, 209, 211, 217, 224, 226, 232, 233
Harrowby, Dudley Ryder, 1st Earl of (1762–1847), 120–2, 198, 255
Hastings, Francis Rawdon-Hastings, 2nd Earl of Moira, 1st Marquess of, 23, 271, 272
Hastings, Warren, 19, 112
Hawkesbury, Lord see Liverpool, Earl of
Hertford, Francis Seymour-Conway, 1st Marquess of (1718–94), 13, 19
Hertford, Francis Seymour-Conway, 2nd Marquess of (1743–1822), 43, 106
Hervey, Frederick William, later 1st Marquess of Bristol, 19, 31, 33–4
Hillsborough, Viscount, see Downshire, 1st Marquess of
Hobart, Robert, see Buckinghamshire, 4th Earl of
Holland, Henry Richard Vassall Fox, 3rd Baron, 125
Holland see Netherlands
Holy Alliance (1815), 233, 238
Humbert, General Joseph, 68–9
Humboldt, Baron Wilhelm von, 222
Hunt, Henry 'Orator', 242, 253
Hutchinson, Major-General Sir John Hely, Baron, 134
Hyderabad, 110

India Act (1784), 108 and n, 109
Ionian Islands, 135, 140
Ireland, 24, 39, 41, 107; trade and commerce of, 26, 93–4; interest in French Revolution of, 20, 41; French invasion threats to, (1778) 16, (1797) 45, 48–9, (1798) 53–6, 61, (1801) 106; armed forces in, 33, 36, 44, 54, 59–68, 106; Volunteers, 16, 17, 31, 33, 44; National Guards, 31, 33; Presbyterians (Dissenters), 14, 16, 23, 27, 28, 41, 62, 76; Presbyterian clergy, stipends for, 98 and n, 100, 107n; Protestants (Church of Ireland), 16, 21, 25–6, 28–9, 32, 38–9, 41, 44, 54, 60–9, 72–82, 182; Orange societies, Orangemen, 41, 50, 61; Roman Catholics, 16, 21, 28–9, 31–2, 38–9, 41, 44, 50, 51, 60–9, 72–82, 88–9; Catholic priests, stipends for, 74, 98, 100, 107 and n; United Irishmen, 17, 28, 38, 41, 44, 47, 50, 55, 57–8, 65–6,

315

83; Irish exiles in Paris, 62, 68;
Amnesty bill, 65 and n; Indemnity
bill, 42; Insurrection Act, 42, 46–7;
Absentee tax proposal, 49–50; George
IV's visit to, 267–8; *see also* Catholic
emancipation, Tithes
Ireland: the 1798 Rebellion, 17, 56–69;
Castlereagh's part in attacked, 181,
243 and n
Ireland: the Union, 72–82, 89–95; Irish
representation at Westminster, 83–5,
94n, 95; allegations of bribery, 79,
86–7, 157; honours controversy, 79,
85, 96
Ireland: the Whigs (parliamentary
opposition), 15–17, 20, 21, 22, 25, 26,
28, 31–2, 37–8, 49–50, 51, 71; oppose
union, 72–82; Dungannon resolutions
of, 16; Whig Club, Dublin, 20;
Northern Whig Club, Belfast, 22, 29;
see also Grattan
Italy, 196–7, 199, 204n, 222, 228 and n;
post-1815, 240, 261, 263, 275

Jackson, George, 191, 192, 193, 197, 210
Jena, battle of (1806), 132
John VI, King of Portugal, 260–1 and
n; as Prince Regent, flees to Brazil,
140
Junot, General, 140, 148, 150, 151

Keith, Admiral Lord, 121
Kellerman, General, 151n
Kiel, treaty of (1814), 215n
Killala (Mayo), 62, 63
Kilwarlin, Viscount, *see* Downshire, 2nd
Marquess of
Knighton, Sir William, 278
Knox, Alexander, 69, 71, 105
Knox, George, 78
Knox, Major-General John, 53
Krudener, Mme de, 233

Laibach, Congress of (1821), 262, 263–4,
269, 270
Lake, General Gerard, 50, 53–4, 57, 59,
62–3, 68, 115
Langrishe, Sir Hercules, 28
Lawrence, Sir Thomas, 247n
Lees, John, 57, 79, 85
Leinster, William Robert Fitzgerald, 2nd
Duke of, 51, 53, 78
Leipzig, battle of (1813), 194–5, 196,
197, 210, 223, 227
Leopold of Saxe-Coburg, Prince, 244n

Lewisham, George Legge, Viscount,
(1801) 3rd Earl of Dartmouth, 108
Lieven, Count (later Prince), 225, 262–4
Lieven, Countess, 247, 250, 255n, 258,
259n, 277
Ligurian Republic, 118
Limerick, 47, 48, 60
Liverpool, Robert Banks Jenkinson, 1st
Baron Hawkesbury, 2nd Earl of
(1770–1828), 107, 123, 124 and n, 126;
as Home Secretary, 127–8, 140–1,
165; as Secretary for War, 171, 176;
forms a government, 178–9, 182–3;
and the 1814 campaign, 190, 198, 203,
208, 211; (1814–15), 213n, 214–17,
222, 224–5, 226–7, 230, 232;
(1816–20), 237, 248, 252, 254–5, 260;
(1820–2), 265, 266, 268, 271, 272, 278
Loftus, General William, 61
Londonderry, Robert Stewart, 1st
Baron, Earl and (1816) Marquess of,
(1739–1821), 13, 15, 17, 22–4, 26, 36,
43, 47–8, 71, 104–5, 166, 175, 251,
266n, 280
Londonderry, Lady, née Lady Sarah
Pratt (1751–1833), 14, 36–7, 43,
104–5, 175
Loughborough, Alexander Wedderburn,
1st Baron, 98
Louis XVIII, King of France, 211, 214,
215, 216, 220, 229–30, 231, 237–8, 257
Low Countries *see* Netherlands
Lutzen, battle of (1813), 192

McCann, John, 65
McNevin, William, 66–7
Madeira, 140
Madison, James, President, 179–80
Madocks, William, 157 and n
Madras, 111, 134
Madrid, 152, 155, 159, 187, 238, 257, 260
Mahrathas, the, 112–13; Mahratha
rulers, (Holkar) 112, 114–15 and
(Sindhia) 112, 115
Malt tax, 236
Malta, 123, 142, 215
Marengo, battle of (1800), 97
Maria Carolina, Queen of Naples, 135–6,
140
Marie-Louise of Austria, wife of
Napoleon, 213, 218
Maritime rights, 177, 180, 196–8, 205,
246
Marmont, Auguste, Marshal, 210
Meade, Colonel John, 116

INDEX

Mediterranean, the, 122, 132–43, 169, 239
Melville, Henry Dundas, 1st Viscount (1742–1811), 99, 108–11, 115–16, 125, 144
Melville, Robert Dundas, 2nd Viscount, 266
Metternich, Clement, Prince, 187, 190–200; meets Castlereagh, 202–3; and 1814 campaign, 204, 206–12; in Paris, 1814, 213; in London, 217–18; at Congress of Vienna, 221, 223–6; in Paris, 1815, 232, 233; post-1815, 240 and n, 250, 256–9, 274–5, 277, 281; at Aix-la-Chapelle, 247, 249; and Troppau meeting, 261–4; visits Hanover, 270–1
Miranda, General, 146, 148
Moira, Lord, *see* Hastings, Marquess of
Monroe, James, 180
Montagu, William, 201, 207, 208, 221
Monte Video, 133, 142
Moore, General Sir John (1761–1809), 59, 62; in Sicily, 136–7, 139, 140–1, 142; his expedition to Sweden, 146–8; and Peninsular War, 148–50, 154–6, 168–9
Mount Stewart, 15, 18–19, 24, 29, 33–4, 36–7, 44, 48, 62, 71, 105–6, 173–4, 251
Mulgrave, Henry Phipps, 3rd Baron, 1st Earl of, 125, 127
Munster, Count, 188, 190, 232
Murat, Joachim (King of Naples), 206, 213, 228 and n
Murphy, Father John, 60–1
Mysore, 110

Naples, 123, 132, 135–6, 143, 196, 228 and n, 238, 241n; revolt in (1820), 260–4; Austrian invasion of, 263, 277
Napoleon Bonaparte, (1797–1806), 53, 61, 109, 114–15, 117–18, 121–3, 125; (1807–9), 132–43, 145–6, 148, 154–6, 158–60, 162; (1812–13), 176, 177, 181, 189–200; (1814–15), 127, 202, 205–13 and n, 216, 217, 223, 225; post-Elba, 228, 229 and n, 230–2, 235, 237, 238, 244; his family, 233, 264
Napoleon Bonaparte, King of Rome (Napoleon's son), 202, 213
Neilson, Samuel, 45
Nelson, Admiral Lord, 68, 118, 120
Nesselrode, Count, 212, 217
Netherlands, the, 38, 119–20, 123, 132, 187, 201, 209n, 229n, 230; post-war settlement of, 192, 195, 197–8, 199, 205, 218–19, 228; colonial empire of, 127, 199, 219; *see also* Belgium, Cape of Good Hope
New Ross (Wexford), 61
Newtownards (Down), 13, 14, 15, 47
Nile, battle of (1798), 68
North Cray cottage/farm, 173, 234, 250–1, 259n, 277–9, 281
North, Frederick, Lord, later 2nd Earl of Guilford, 16
Norway, 147, 189–90, 195, 215 and n
Nugent, Major-General George, 62

O'Connell, Daniel, 86n
O'Connor, Arthur, 66, 67
Orders-in-Council, 138n, 145, 177–8, 179–80
Orford (Suffolk), 43
Orléans, Duc de, later King Louis Philippe of France, 133, 230
Ottoman Empire, *see* Turkey
Oudh, 110, 112

Paget, Sir Arthur, 141
Paine, Thomas, 27
Paris, 27, 30, 62, 205–8, 210–12, 220, 238, 241, 247, 271, 275; Allied entry into (1814), 213–14; Allied entry into (1815), 230–1
Paris, Peace of (1st), 216–17, 218, 230; (2nd), 232–4, 241
Parliamentary reform, 32, 41, 51, 84, 157, 242, 253
Parma, duchy of, 213
Parnell, Sir John, 20, 52, 70, 75, 78, 93
Parsons, Sir Lawrence, 24, 81, 89–90, 94
Pedro, Dom, of Portugal (Emperor of Brazil, 1822–31), 261n
Peel, Sir Robert (1788–1850), 182, 236, 252, 253n, 260, 266, 267n, 272, 274
Pelham, Thomas, Lord Pelham (1801), later 2nd Earl of Chichester, 45, 46, 52, 53–5, 61, 70–1, 73, 77
Peninsular War, (1808–10) 148–52, 154–6, 158–60, 162, 165, 171–2; (1812–13) 176, 187, 193, 197, 200
Perceval, Spencer (1762–1812), 124–6; as Chancellor of the Exchequer, 127–8, 144–5, 152, 156, 157–8, 161, 163, 170n; and Castlereagh's resignation (1809), 164–6, 168; as prime minister, 171, 174, 175–6 and n, 178, 179
Pergami, Bartolommeo, 256

317

Périgord, Comtesse Edmond de, 215
Peterloo, 253
Petty, Lord Henry, later 3rd Marquess of Lansdowne, 126
Piedmont, 228, 263
Pitt, William (1759–1806), 19, 25, 26, 29, 36, 124–6, 127, 129, 190, 194, 200, 224, 273, 281; and Ireland, 20, 28, 31–2, 37–40, 42, 54, 55; and the Union, 73, 75, 84, 87, 94; supports Castlereagh as Chief Secretary, 71; supports Catholic emancipation, 74, 98–9; resigns, 99, 103–4, 107; and India, 108–10; 114–5; forms his 2nd government, 115, 116; and north German campaign, 118–22; death, 123
Pittites, 124–5, 127–8, 171, 272, 273
Planta, Joseph, 201
Plunket, William Conyngham, later 1st Baron, 79–80, 96n, 182n
Poland, 204 and n, 205, 208, 218, 220; and Congress of Vienna, 222–8; Grand Duchy of Warsaw, 204n, 223, 227; 'Congress Poland', 227n
Ponsonby, George, 80–1, 92, 94, 156
Ponsonby, William, 90
Poona, Peishwa of, 112–13
Poor Employment Act (1817), 244
Poor Laws, 243–4; Poor Law Committee, 237
Popham, Sir Home, 133
Porte, the, *see* Turkey
Portland, William Henry Cavendish Bentinck, 3rd Duke of (1738–1809) joins Pitt, 37; as Home Secretary, 38–9, 52, 54, 56, 64, 70, 75, 77, 78, 79, 82, 83, 85 and n, 98; as prime minister, 127, 145, 158, 161, 164, 165, 167, 171
Portugal, 140–1, 146, 195, 199, 209n, 216, 229n; revolt in, 260–1, 261n; Portuguese navy, 141; *see also* Peninsular War
Pozzo di Borgo, Count, 198
Pratt, Lady Elizabeth, 19, 30, 33–4, 35, 36–7, 45, 68, 103, 104
Property (income) tax, 236
Prussia, 119–22, 132, 216; and 1813–14 campaigns, 187–200, 202–12; signs treaty with Britain, 192; at Congress of Vienna, 222–8, 229n; post-1815, 230, 232–3, 238, 249, 262, 263; *see also* Frederick William III

Quadruple Alliance (1815), 233–4,

241, 248, 277; Castlereagh's attitude to, 238, 241, 247–8, 257–8, 261–4, 269

Redesdale, John Mitford, 1st Baron, 97
Regency crises (1788–9), 20–1, 26, 72; (1811–12), 175 and n
Reichenbach, treaty of (1813), 192–3
Reynolds, Thomas, 55
Rhine river, 118, 197, 199, 230
Richelieu, Duc de, 231n, 248
Richmond, Charles Lennox, 3rd Duke of, 170
Robinson, Frederick John, later Viscount Goderich and Earl of Ripon, 201, 202, 214, 215
Robinson, Richard, Primate Archbishop of Armagh, 14
Rockingham, Charles Watson-Wentworth, 2nd Marquess of, 16
Rolica (Portugal), 151
Rose, George, 125
Rush, Richard, 245–7, 251n
Russell, Thomas, 45
Russia (1805–8), 118–22, 123, 132, 135, 147; (1812–14), 176, 187, 188–200, 202–12, 216; signs treaty with Britain, 192; and Congress of Vienna, 221–9 and n; and Waterloo campaign, 230; post-1815, 238–9 and n, 240–1, 248–9; and Greek revolt, 269–71, 274–5; *see also* Alexander I, Tilsit, treaty of
Rutland, Charles Manners, 4th Duke of, 72
Ryder, Richard, 171, 178

St Aignan, Baron, 197, 198, 199, 202
St Helena, 229, 237
St John's College, Cambridge, 18
Salamanca, 154–5
Sardinia, 137
Saurin, William, 91, 93, 96n
Saxony, 204 and n, 205, 218, 223–7
Scheldt river, 120, 160, 161, 165, 199; Scheldt expedition, *see* Walcheren
Schwarzenberg, Prince von, 204, 205, 206, 207, 208, 210
Seville, 159
Sheares, John and Henry, 58, 65
Shee, Sir George, 76
Sicily, 123, 135–7, 139–43, 154n, 238, 240–1 and n
Sidmouth, Henry Addington, 1st Viscount (1757–1844), as prime minister, 99, 105, 107, 108, 111, 114,

INDEX

115 and n; (1806–12), 124, 127, 171, 176 and n, 178, 179n, 182; as Home Secretary, 242–4, 253–5, 265–6, 267 and n; retires as Home Secretary, 272
Sinclair, Rev. William, 48
Six Acts (1819), 254–5
Slave trade, abolition of, 126–7, 216, 222, 228–9 and n, 248
Smith, Sir Sidney, 140–1
Soult, Marshal, 155, 158–9
South America, 132–4, 141–2, 146, 148; Spanish colonists in, 133, 248, 276; *see also* Buenos Aires, Monte Video
Spa Fields riots (1816), 242
Spain, 16, 131, 132, 141, 146; revolt against French, 147, 148; (1813–14), 192, 195, 199, 209n, 216; and Congress of Vienna, 221–2, 229 and n; post-1815, 238, 247–8, 257–8, 261, 275–6
Speenhamland system, 244n
Spencer, General Sir Brent, 140–1, 142–3, 148
Sâel, Mme de, 215
Stewart, Alexander (1700–81), 13, 15
Stewart, Alexander (Alec), (1783–1800), 104–5
Stewart, Sir Charles, Lord Stewart, later 3rd Marquess of Londonderry (1778–1854), 14, 37, 153; (1809–12), 158, 159, 162, 167, 170, 172n, 173, 174 and n, 175, 177, 182–3; and 1813–14 campaigns, 192–200, 205–6, 207, 209; in Paris (1814), 214, 215; at Congress of Vienna, 221; in Paris (1815), 232, 234; (1816–21), 236, 237, 239, 240, 247, 251, 254, 256, 260, 264, 272; at Troppau, 262, 263; character, 162n, 191, 221
Stewart, Lady Elizabeth Mary (Bess) (1779–98), 31, 33
Stewart, Lady Frances, née Lady Frances Seymour-Conway (1747–1770), 13
Stewart, Lady Frances Anne (m. Lord Charles Fitzroy) (1777–1810), 14, 31, 33, 35, 37
Stewart, Frederick, 277
Stewart, Mary, née Cowan (1713–88), 13
Stewart, Robert (1739–1821), *see* Londonderry, 1st Marquess of
Stewart, Robert (1769–1822), *see* Castlereagh, Viscount
Stewart, Thomas (1790–1810), 174
Stewart, William (c.1661–1704), 13
Strachan, Admiral Sir Richard, 163

Stralsund, 119–20, 134, 139, 189
Strangford, 6th Viscount, 269, 274–5
Stroganov, Baron, 269
Stuart, Lieut.-General Sir John, 154n
Stuart-Wortley, James Archibald, 178–9
Sturrock, Rev. William, 15
Sweden, 120, 139, 141, 146–8, 150, 169, 196, 209n, 215n, 229n, 238; *see also* Gustavus Adolphus IV, Bernadotte

Talavera, battle of (1809), 160 and n, 162, 172
Talleyrand-Périgord, Charles-Maurice de, Prince of Benevento, 211, 212, 215–16, 220; at Congress of Vienna, 222, 223, 225, 226 and n; (1815), 230, 231 and n
Tandy, Napper, 68
Teeling, Charles, 45
Thistlewood, Arthur, 255
Thornton, Edward, 188–9, 195
Tierney, George, 141, 252, 253, 266
Tilsit, treaty of (1807), 135, 137–8, 139
Tithes, 41, 67, 74, 88, 98, 100
Toeplitz, treaty of (1813), 194–5
Tone, Wolfe, 27, 28, 41, 53, 66n, 68
Torres Vedras, lines of, 160
Trafalgar, battle of (1805), 120, 138
Tregony (Cornwall), 36, 43
Trench, Frederick, 79n
Troppau, Congress of (1820), 261—4, 270
Troyes, 206, 207, 210
Turkey, 135, 137, 141, 188, 205, 223, 239; and Greek revolt, 268, 269 and n, 270, 274–6

Ulm, battle of (1805), 120
United States of America, 14, 16, 63, 67; and economic war, 138n, 142, 145, 176, 177; declares war on Britain, 179–80, 200; and War of 1812, 245; and peace talks at Ghent, 220, 224; signs peace treaty, 226, 227; and the slave trade, 229n; post-war relations with Britain, 245; and commercial convention with Britain (1815), 246; and agreement with Britain on Great Lakes, 246 and n; and negotiations with Britain (1818), 245–7

Vandeleur, Mr, 50
Vansittart, Nicholas, 1st Baron Bexley (1766–1851), 178, 182, 235, 244, 252, 254, 266

Verona, Congress of (1822), 275, 277
Vienna, 239, 275
Vienna, Congress of, 188n, 205, 216, 217, 219–29, 247, 269n; organisation of, 221–2; Final Act of, 229 and n
Vimeiro, battle of (1808), 151–2
Vinegar Hill, battle of (1798), 62, 63
Vitoria, battle of (1813), 193

Walcheren expedition, 160–4, 165, 168–9, 171–2 and n
Ward, Hon. Edward, 22–3
Ward, John William, 1st Earl of Dudley, 172
Wardle, Gwyllym, 156
Waterford, 61
Waterloo, battle of (1815), 132, 229, 230, 231n
Wellesley, Arthur, *see* Wellington, Duke of
Wellesley, Henry, later 1st Baron Cowley, 111
Wellesley, Richard Colley, 2nd Earl of Mornington, 1st Marquess (1760–1842), 43, 144, 159, 165, 272; in India, 108–15, 117, 123; as Foreign Secretary, 171, 175, 176 and n, 178, 180
Wellesley-Pole, William, 1st Baron Maryborough, later 3rd Earl of Mornington, 56–7, 113, 153, 227
Wellington, Arthur Wellesley, 1st Duke of (1769–1852), 43, 56, 112–13, 131, 132; (1807), 133, 138, 139, 140; (1808–12), 147, 148–53, 158–60, 162, 165, 167, 168, 169, 171–2, 174, 176, 179, 187–90; (1813–14), 191, 193, 197, 199, 200, 204, 211, 214, 218, 226–7; (1815), 228, 230, 231 and n, 232, 233; (1816–21), 237, 238, 249, 250, 254, 255, 265, 272, 274; and Castlereagh's last illness, 277–8

Wessenberg, Count, 190–1
West Indies, 67, 142, 215–16, 246; *see also* Caribbean
Westmorland, John Fane, 10th Earl of (1759–1841), 20, 21, 26, 28, 37–8
Wexford, 61–2, 64, 76
Whig Party, 73; and Regency crises, 20, 175n, 176; and Henry Dundas, 115; in power, 1806–7, 124, 128; and Copenhagen expedition, 138–9, 144; and Walcheren expedition, 174–5; and Orders-in-Council, 177, 179; attacks Castlereagh, 157, 181; and the war, 168, 190; and Norway, 215; and Allied visit, 218; and Murat, 228; and 1816 session, 235–7; and 1819 session, 252, 254–5; and George IV, 260; and 1821 session, 265–6; and 1822 session, 274; the Portland Whigs, 37–8
Whitbread, Samuel, 116, 197, 218, 227
Whitelocke, Lieut.-General John, 133, 141–2
Wickham, William, 64, 67 and n
Wilberforce, William (1759–1833), 126–7, 139, 179, 216, 242
William VI, Sovereign Prince of Orange, (1814) King William I of the Netherlands, 197, 199, 201, 219
William, Hereditary Prince of Orange, later King William II of the Netherlands, 201, 219
Williams-Wynn, Charles, 272
Windham, William, 126, 129–30, 134, 135

Yarmouth, Francis, Earl of, later 3rd Marquess of Hertford, 166
Yorck, General, 190
York, Duke of, *see* Frederick
Young, Arthur, 14, 15
Ypsilantis, Alexander, 268, 269